Educating One & All

Students with Disabilities and Standards-Based Reform

Lorraine M. McDonnell, Margaret J. McLaughlin,
and Patricia Morison, *Editors*

Committee on Goals 2000 and the
Inclusion of Students with Disabilities

Board on Testing and Assessment

Commission on Behavioral and Social Sciences and Education
National Research Council

NATIONAL ACADEMY PRESS
Washington, D.C.   1997

NATIONAL ACADEMY PRESS • 2101 Constitution Avenue, NW • Washington, DC 20418

NOTICE: The project that is the subject of this report was approved by the Governing Board of the National Research Council, whose members are drawn from the councils of the National Academy of Sciences, the National Academy of Engineering, and the Institute of Medicine. The members of the committee responsible for the report were chosen for their special competences and with regard for appropriate balance.

This report has been reviewed by a group other than the authors according to procedures approved by a Report Review Committee consisting of members of the National Academy of Sciences, the National Academy of Engineering, and the Institute of Medicine.

The study was supported by Grant No. H023U40001 between the National Academy of Sciences and the Office of Special and Rehabilitative Services, U.S. Department of Education. Any opinions, findings, conclusions, or recommendations expressed in this publication are those of the author(s) and do not necessarily reflect the view of the organizations or agencies that provided support for this project.

Printed in the United States of America

iii

iv

Acknowledgments

The work of the Committee on Goals 2000 and the Inclusion of Students with Disabilities has benefited immensely from the diverse contributions of many people.

Between May 1995 and November 1996, the committee met seven times. It solicited information from a variety of sources. Jane West wrote an informative background paper and provided the committee with relevant information about the legislative and policy context of the study. Robert Rossi and Fran Stancavage from the American Institutes of Research presented findings from their secondary analyses of the National Educational Longitudinal Study (NELS) and the National Assessment of Educational Progress (NAEP) that helped us think about the challenges associated with including students with disabilities in large-scale national databases. Mary Wagner of the Stanford Research Institute and Marsha Brauen of Westat, Inc., provided a variety of useful data on the status of students with disabilities. Jeff Rodamar at the U.S. Department of Education provided data from the *Prospects* Study that allowed us to compare the elementary school experiences and achievement of students with disabilities with those of their peers. We are especially indebted to Eileen Ordover and Kathleen Boundy from the Center for Law and Education for their comprehensive analysis of the legal entitlements of students with disabilities.

In October 1995, the committee held a workshop with participants from 10 organizations representing general education or disability groups interested in standards-based reform. Through their remarks and written documents, Eileen Ahearn, Joseph Ballard, John Barth, Christopher Button, Speed Davis, Barbara Huff, John MacDonald, Nancy Safer, Jeff Schneider, Shirley Schwartz, and Patricia Sullivan provided valuable perspectives on the complex issues associated with the participation of students with disabilities in standards-based reforms.

Several organizations and individuals provided a variety of research support. The Robert LaFollette Institute of Public Affairs at the University of Wisconsin, Madison, partly supported work on the *Prospects* data, and Troy Sterr skillfully analyzed that data. The National Center for Educational Outcomes at the University of Minnesota helped in collecting state documents and provided the assistance of Kristin Geenen to code selected documents. Lauren Morando-Rhim at the University of Maryland also collected and coded state and local standards and assessment documents, as well as assisting in other research. Margrethe Kamp at the University of California, Santa Barbara, prepared the appendix summarizing the committee's 1995 workshop. We are grateful for all these contributions.

The Office of Special Education and Rehabilitation Services, U.S. Department of Education, sponsored this project, and several individuals from this agency were particularly helpful to the committee. Assistant Secretary Judith Heumann met with the committee and shared her perspective on the issues. We are grateful to Tom Hehir for his support, and also to James Button and Louis Danielson, both of whom met with the committee several times and assisted us in locating needed information. The study's project officer, David Malouf, assisted the committee in understanding the evolving federal policy context for special education and Alexander Vachon, formerly on the staff of Senator Robert Dole, Robert Silverstein, on the staff of the U.S. Senate Subcommittee on Disability Policy, and Michael Cohen, formerly in the U.S. Secretary of Education's office and now at the White House, provided useful insights on the origins of the legislative provision creating the committee.

The Board on Testing and Assessment (BOTA) was instrumental in shaping early discussions about the project and in providing general guidance and support along the way. The chair and vice chair of BOTA, Richard Shavelson and Robert Linn, assisted the committee by reviewing early drafts of the report and by participating in a meeting at which issues related to student assessment were discussed. Their insights and knowledge at a critical point in our work were much appreciated. Two other members of BOTA, Carl Kaestle and Luis Laosa, served as liaisons to the committee, and were extremely helpful. Their apt interpretations and skill at synthesizing various points of view often aided us in moving our discussions forward.

This report would not have been possible without the talents of many individuals at the National Research Council. As executive director of the Commission on Behavioral and Social Sciences and Education, Barbara Torrey helped in the overall administration of the study. Alexandra K. Wigdor, director of the Division of Education, Labor, and Human Performance, provided continuing guidance. Michael J. Feuer, director of the Board on Testing and Assessment, was responsible for overseeing the committee's work and ensuring that we had the resources needed to complete the task. He did all of this and more. Michael contributed to our conversations, always challenging our assumptions and helping us to resolve differences and achieve consensus.

Adrienne Carrington ably assisted the committee by organizing all the logistics for our meetings and producing multiple iterations of the report from the many drafts received from committee members. Each of us appreciates the efficiency with which she managed the technical details associated with this project, but we are also grateful for the gracious hospitality she provided at our meetings. Nancy Kober's skilled editing is evident throughout the report as she was instrumental in turning a weighty technical report into a concise and readable document. Eugenia Grohman skillfully guided us through the intricacies of the NRC review process, and Christine McShane carefully edited the final document. Ella Cleveland was instrumental in getting the project under way and organizing the various committee working groups. Ann Harden and Kathy Guidroz assisted in a number of ways, including conducting literature reviews and analyzing documents.

Above all, the committee acknowledges the ability, patience, and effort of study director Patricia Morison. Patty brought to the deliberations her extensive knowledge of assessment and her own high standards of scholarship. She reminded the committee of its obligation to fulfill its charge with a high level of scientific rigor. Patty's ability to organize and synthesize all the various written drafts provided by committee members was central to the report we have produced. Perhaps her greatest contribution, however, was keeping the committee organized and moving its deliberations forward through the force of her calm grace and respectful attention to everyone's views.

Finally, as cochairs, we would to like thank our fellow committee members, who gave enormous amounts of time and energy to this endeavor and who persevered as we negotiated new and sometimes complex territory. Often members communicated across a chasm created by the historic separation of general and special education. Not only did we have to learn each other's professional language, but we also had to develop an understanding of and respect for perspectives quite different from our own. Inevitably, there were periods of intense disagreement, but there were also times in which fresh understandings produced new ideas and insights. We know we echo the sentiment of all the members when we say that serving on this committee has been a professionally and personally enriching experience.

> LORRAINE M. McDONNELL
> MARGARET J. McLAUGHLIN
> *Cochairs,* Committee on Goals 2000
> and the Inclusion of Students
> with Disabilities

Contents

Educating
One & All

Executive Summary

In recent years, most states have initiated major changes in curriculum, instruction, and testing for elementary and secondary school students. These changes, funded and encouraged by federal and state legislation and implemented by states and school districts, are part of an influential movement known as standards-based reform. This movement seeks to improve educational quality by setting high content standards that define the knowledge and skills that teachers should teach and students should learn, and by holding educators and students accountable for ambitious performance standards that set the expectations for proficiency.

The Committee on Goals 2000 and the Inclusion of Students with Disabilities was established to consider the implications of standards-based reforms for a group of students that is quite heterogeneous—those with disabilities. A significant number of students with disabilities already participate in the general education curriculum, receiving special education for only a part of their day, sometimes in only one or two areas, or to support instruction in the general classroom. Other students are in separate full-day programs, receiving different or modified curricula and instruction designed to meet their individual needs. The enormous variation among students with disabilities makes generalizations nearly impossible, and approaches to their fuller participation in standards-based reforms will need to take this diversity into account.

Most standards-based reforms strive to apply the same high standards to all students, including, in many instances, those with disabilities. For many students with disabilities, this represents a striking change. Whereas the framework of standards-based reform stresses accountability for outcomes and applies uniform standards to all students, the legal framework under which students with disabilities have been educated for two decades stresses the individualization of goals

1

and instruction and emphasizes accountability for procedural compliance rather than outcomes. Moreover, many students with disabilities have been routinely excluded from the large-scale assessments that have now become the backbone of accountability in standards-based reforms.

The committee was established by the Goals 2000 legislation "to conduct a comprehensive study of the inclusion of children with disabilities in school reforms assisted under Goals 2000: Educate America Act" (Public Law 103-227, sec. 1015). Through a systematic comparison of the policies and practices related to standards-based reform and special education, this report assesses the extent to which the goals of common standards and individualized education can be reconciled. Our charge was specific and limited; since the evaluation of these policies themselves was not part of the charge, the committee accepted as given, without necessarily endorsing, the defining elements of the two policy frameworks: the standards-based approach to educational reform and current special education policy.

In conducting its analysis, the committee was constrained by the nature of the policies we were studying and by the available data. There is a scarcity of research evidence directly bearing on the effects of standards-based reforms, much less their impact on students with disabilities. In addition, the research base on instructional practices and achievement contains few studies that include populations of students with and without disabilities, making systematic comparisons difficult. Throughout the report we note where these limitations apply. Furthermore, although the committee's analysis is limited to students with disabilities served by special education, many of the issues we raise also apply to students with disabilities not served under the Individuals with Disabilities Education Act and to other students with unique educational needs who will also be participating in standards-based reforms.

The committee found that in many instances the two policy approaches can be reconciled. Our two guiding principles are that all students should have access to challenging standards and that policy makers and educators should be held publicly accountable for every student's performance. However, we also conclude that adaptations will be required for some students with disabilities, particularly those with significant cognitive disabilities. Moreover, efforts to incorporate students with varying disabilities effectively will be hindered over the short term by a shortage of financial and professional resources, an inadequate research base, and conceptual ambiguities in both policy frameworks. The committee cautions that, even with additional resources, some of the elements needed to integrate all students with disabilities fully into standards-based reform may exceed the limits of current knowledge and technology.

POLICY FRAMEWORKS

Many state education reform laws, the federal Title I law that is concerned with poor, underachieving children, the federal Goals 2000: Educate America

Act, and other federal and state policies intend for students with disabilities to have access to standards-based reforms. But federal and state policies are vague about how to accomplish this goal and offer few incentives to do it well. Furthermore, relevant case law is limited and the precise legal requirements are uncertain.

Standards-based reform is not a single, uniform policy, and it is being implemented in different ways across states and localities. Therefore, for purposes of this report, the committee assumes that two premises define the standards-based approach to educational reform: standards will be high and they will apply to all students. Standards-based reform includes content standards that specify what students should learn, performance standards that set the expectations for what students must know and do to demonstrate proficiency, and assessments that provide the accountability mechanism for monitoring whether these expectations have been met and by whom. In addition, standards-based reforms assume that schools should be held publicly accountable for student performance.

A significant gap exists between policy and practice in the implementation of standards-based reform. For example, technical hurdles have yet to be overcome in many alternative types of assessments, which some states are using in conjunction with or instead of conventional multiple-choice testing. The public strongly supports common standards as a strategy for improving student performance, but the consensus breaks down over such details as the specific content to be taught. States differ widely in how they define critical components of standards-based reform, how they aim to pay for it, and how much flexibility they leave to local districts. Important issues, such as how to translate general standards into specific curricula and classroom practices or how to provide all students with adequate opportunities to learn designated content, have not been resolved. Although the participation of "all students" has been a rhetorical policy goal, its full complexity has yet to be acknowledged.

In the case of students with disabilities, emerging policies for standards-based reform intersect a long-standing special education policy framework, which has evolved over three decades to counteract a history of educational neglect, inequity, and mistreatment. Under the Individuals with Disabilities Education Act (IDEA), other key federal and state laws, and a substantial body of judicial decisions, students with disabilities are accorded the right to a free and appropriate public education. This education must be tailored to individual learning needs; each student must have an individualized education program (IEP) that establishes educational objectives and specifies the kinds of educational and related services to be provided. Education in the least restrictive learning environment is another hallmark of this policy framework.

Although data are not available that tell us how many, a number of students with disabilities already participate in standards-based reform: they are learning in general education classrooms and have full access to the common curriculum and content standards. In addition, most federal and state laws presume that, if standards-based reform is part of a state's general education framework, students with disabilities should have access to the relevant curriculum and assessments. The complicated part is determining how to accommodate individual student needs and provide the special services that some may require, while still affording each student appropriate access to the common curriculum and ensuring accountability for his or her outcomes.

STUDENTS WITH DISABILITIES

More than five million students—about 10 percent of the school-age population—have disabilities and qualify for special education services under the IDEA. These students are extremely heterogeneous in their characteristics and educational experiences. Some students participate fully in the general education classroom and curriculum, while others receive specialized curricula and instruction. Disabilities range from mild to severe and can occur in one or more of a number of dimensions, such as physical, sensory, behavioral, and cognitive. However, more that 90 percent of those who qualify for special education fall into one of just four categories of disability: speech or language impairment, serious emotional disturbance, mental retardation, and specific learning disability; indeed, specific learning disabilities alone account for more than half of all eligible students. As a result, meaningful discussion of the participation of students with disabilities in common standards and assessments cannot occur without attention to the varied characteristics of this large group of students.

Available data on post-school outcomes for students with disabilities suggest that they do not fare as well as youth in the general population with respect to achievement, high school graduation, enrollment in postsecondary education, and employment. However, outcomes vary tremendously, especially among students with different types of disabilities.

Data about students with disabilities are further complicated by the absence of a simple, unambiguous method for defining and identifying which students have disabilities. Although the IDEA and implementing regulations specify 13 categories of disabilities, criteria for defining these categories are not clear-cut, and many states and school districts use modified taxonomies. There are particular problems in distinguishing students with mild cognitive disabilities, such as mild mental retardation and learning disabilities, from some students who are low-achieving. Indeed, identification and classification practices vary so greatly that a student who is identified in one of these categories in one school district may not be so identified in another, and the overall reported prevalence of disability varies across states from approximately 7 to 15 percent of the school-age population.

The diversity among students who are identified as having a disability means that individual students may participate to varying degrees in the common elements of standards-based reform. Because some students with disabilities already participate fully in the general education curriculum, participation in common standards and assessments for them will be compatible with their individualized programs, with or without appropriate accommodation or supports. For a small percentage of students, the goals of the predominantly academic general education curriculum are not relevant to their life goals; these students, many with significant cognitive impairments, often need a completely individualized curriculum. However, alternatives will need to be carefully crafted that still represent challenging expectations for these students. There is another group of students with disabilities who may require some modifications to the common standards and assessments to ensure compatibility of their individualized programs with the standards framework. Decisions will have to be made on an individual basis about whether and what kinds of alterations are appropriate to the common standards, curricula, instruction, and assessments; decisions about participation may differ for any given student as he or she progresses through school.

POST-SCHOOL OUTCOMES, CURRICULUM, AND INSTRUCTION

The goals of standards-based reform to raise expectations, improve educational outcomes, and strengthen curriculum content are as important for students with disabilities as they are for all children. However, our analyses indicate that some features associated with effective curriculum and instruction for some students with disabilities may be at odds with the curriculum and instruction typically embraced by standards-based reform.

Special education has traditionally focused on a broad set of knowledge and skills that go beyond academic goals. To be well prepared for life after school, some students with disabilities require specific instruction in such areas as general workplace readiness, vocational skills, and independent living skills. Indeed, school-to-work transition planning is a mandatory component of special education.

The content standards developed thus far by states focus mainly on academic content in language arts, mathematics, science, and other core academic subjects; to date, vocational and workplace skills have received far less emphasis. Although these academic goals are relevant for many students with disabilities, questions arise about whether the content and performance levels embodied in these academic state standards are useful and realistic learning goals for some students with disabilities, and whether the instructional time required to help these students progress toward standards would take valuable time away from teaching more relevant skills. It is important that broader outcomes and school-to-work transition planning not be neglected in the move toward standards-based reform.

Instructional methodology is another area in which standards-based reform and special education sometimes diverge. Research has identified characteristics of effective instruction for many students with disabilities, including individually referenced decision making that focuses on individual student needs, intensive methods of delivering instruction, and structured teaching of discrete skills in an explicit context. By contrast, the pedagogical methods incorporated into many state standards emphasize active learning, group projects with high cognitive demands, and students "constructing" knowledge from various experiences and information sources. To be effective and maintain student motivation, teachers will need sufficient flexibility to teach students with disabilities in the way they learn best. Furthermore, some students are unlikely to attain certain advanced analytical skills regardless of instructional methods.

Given these considerations, it will be necessary to develop a defensible decision-making procedure to determine the appropriateness of the common content standards for individual students with disabilities. At least three factors should be considered for each individual: the relation of common content standards to desired post-school outcomes, the age of the student, and the extent to which instruction focused on standards takes time away from other instructional goals. A revised IEP system may be necessary to ensure consistency and accountability during this process.

Parent participation is a key element. Research indicates that parental involvement and expectations are positively related to the achievement of students with disabilities, just as they are for other students. In addition, parents of students with disabilities have other unique responsibilities under special education law. They are the primary advocates for their children's rights and crucial participants in educational decision making through the IEP process; this responsibility also means that parents have come to bear the primary burden of enforcement. Evidence indicates that the IEP process has not worked well for all parents, particularly minority and economically disadvantaged ones. Resolving the barriers to parental involvement takes on special importance because standards-based reforms could place new demands on some parents; the IEP process is likely to be the vehicle for making key decisions about how to include students with disabilities in specific aspects of standards-based reform.

ACCOUNTABILITY AND ASSESSMENT

Currently, many students with disabilities are excluded from participation in large-scale assessment programs; reasons for their exclusion vary but include participation in a different curriculum or separate class and a need for accommodations in testing. In most cases, this means they are also excluded from the accountability systems in their states, districts, and schools. As a result, data about the achievement levels of many students with disabilities are absent when judgments about the effectiveness of educational policies and programs are made at the local, state, and national levels. In instances in which large numbers of students with disabilities do not participate in assessment systems, aggregate data are not representative of the entire student population; if they participate at widely different rates, then comparisons among schools and districts are neither valid nor fair. In addition, a just and equitable accountability system cannot be maintained if there are incentives to exempt students with disabilities—especially those who may score low—from large-scale assessments. Public reporting of assessment results for students with disabilities, as well as the percentages of students who participate in different or modified assessments, will be key to ensuring fair and equitable comparisons among schools, districts, and states; in addition, all students should be accounted for in the public reporting of results.

For an unknown number of students with disabilities, participation will mean providing some form of testing accommodation—in other words, providing some students with nonstandard forms of test administration or response. Such accommodations are intended to remove irrelevant barriers to performance. Students with disabilities are entitled by law to assessment accommodations that seek to offset any distortions in scores resulting from their disabilities. But determining which accommodations are appropriate for whom and under which circumstances is difficult. In some situations—for example, for a student with an orthopedic impairment who may not be able to perform such motor tasks as holding a pencil or measuring an object with a ruler—testing accommodations would not obviously affect the underlying construct being measured, such as mathematical reasoning. In other cases—for example, a student with a reading disability who is required to do advanced word problems in mathematics—it is not clear how accommodations, such as an oral reader, may affect the construct being measured. Furthermore, the lack of clear criteria for describing the functional characteristics of disability exacerbates the difficulty of designing valid accommodations. Without such criteria, it is difficult to determine whether or not the disability is directly related to the construct being measured. Almost no empirical data are available to inform guidelines about the effects of accommodations on the meaningfulness of the resulting scores. Currently, decisions about participation in assessments and the use of accommodations are made idiosyncratically by local educators with little or no accountability.

Numerous challenges, including some significant technical ones, will have to be addressed if the dual goals of increased participation of students with disabilities and meaningful test results are to be met. One important issue is to ensure that assessments can accurately measure performance at the low end of the scale, particularly for assessment items that are difficult. Because the performance standard representing the lowest level of achievement is set relatively high in many state assessments, we lack meaningful data about the overall progress of students who fall below that standard. The challenge is to design a scoring and reporting system that signals high expectations for performance but still provides useful information about students who may be scoring at the low end of the distribution but still making significant progress.

Many standards-based accountability systems are premised on new forms of assessment that are still in the developmental phases. Applying these assessments to students with disabilities ratchets up the challenge beyond our existing knowledge of test development. Additional technical problems include providing credible disaggregated scores and accurately measuring the knowledge of students with disabilities using nontraditional testing formats that integrate a variety of knowledge and skill domains. In addition, some students will not be able to participate meaningfully in the common assessments and will require substantially modified or different assessments.

IMPLEMENTATION

Almost no data are available about students with disabilities in large-scale national studies or databases. The collection of data about some of these students and their performance is particularly challenging. Moreover, without good data on such indicators as referral and identification rates and graduation rates and types of diplomas, it will be hard to monitor some of the potential effects of standards-based reforms—both intended and unintended—for students with disabilities.

The number of students with disabilities who may need accommodations or other modifications in standards and assessments is unknown and will depend on a number of factors, including behavioral characteristics and severity of disability, extent of participation in the general education curriculum, and the instructional needs of students. The need for accommodations and modifications will also depend on the nature of a district's or state's particular content standards, performance standards, and assessments—which vary significantly from place to place.

Considerable uncertainty exists about the resource levels that will be needed to support standards-based reforms. These policies are likely to entail additional costs for developing assessments, acquiring technology, implementing new governance models, and increasing through research our understanding of the relationship between curricular strategies and student learning. Because standards-based reform envisions new approaches to instruction, assessment, and classroom organization, considerable investment in professional development will also be needed. Furthermore, we do not know what kinds of programs and resource levels are required to help all students, including those with disabilities, meet high, challenging standards.

RECOMMENDATIONS

The committee was not asked to evaluate the merits of standards-based reform, nor could it do so adequately given the recency of the policy; this report thus neither endorses standards-based reform nor encourages such efforts. Similarly, the committee was not charged with evaluating current special education law, policy, or practice; this report thus should not be considered an endorsement of that policy framework, either. The recommendations that follow represent the committee's advice to states and local communities that have already decided to proceed with standards-based reform and that want to make those reforms consistent with current special education policies and practices. We have sought to develop an approach that is consistent, workable, integrated with the IDEA, and above all takes into account the individual and diverse educational needs of students with disabilities.

Underlying these recommendations are two principles:

- All students should have access to challenging standards.
- Policy makers and educators should be held publicly accountable for every student's performance.

These assumptions are consistent with the goals of both standards-based reform and special education policy, but they are not often met in practice. All of our recommendations flow from these principles, although some apply to policies and decisions about individual students, and others apply to the education system as a whole. Together they form a possible approach for integrating students with disabilities in standards-based reform.

Recommendation 1. States and localities that decide to implement standards-based reforms should design their common content standards, performance standards, and assessments to maximize participation of students with disabilities.

Recommendation 2. The presumption should be that each student with a disability will participate in the state or local standards; however, participation for any given student may require alterations to the common standards and assessments. Decisions to make such alterations must have a compelling educational justification and must be made on an individual basis.

Recommendation 3. The committee recommends strengthening the IEP process as the formal mechanism for deciding how individual students with disabilities will participate in standards-based reforms.

Recommendation 4. States and localities should revise policies that discourage maximum participation of students with disabilities in the common accountability system and provide incentives to encourage widespread participation.

Recommendation 5. When content and performance standards or assessments are altered for a student with a disability:
- the alternate standards should be challenging yet potentially achievable;
- they should reflect the full range of knowledge and skills that the student needs to live a full, productive life; and
- the school system should inform parents and the student of any consequences of these alterations.

Recommendation 6. Even if the individual needs of some students require alterations of the common standards and assessments, the committee strongly recommends that these students should be counted in a universal, public account-ability system.

Recommendation 7.   Assessment accommodations should be provided, but they should be used only to offset the impact of disabilities unrelated to the knowl-edge and skills being measured.   They also should be justified on a case-by-case basis, but individual decisions should be guided by a uniform set of criteria.

Recommendation 8.   States and local districts should provide information to parents of students with disabilities to enable them to make informed choices about their children's participation in standards-based reform and to understand the consequences of those choices.

Recommendation 9.   The committee recommends that, before attaching significant stakes to the performance of individual students, those students should be given an opportunity to learn the skills and knowledge expected of them.

Recommendation 10.   Given the enormous variability in the educational needs of students, the committee recommends that policy makers monitor the unintended consequences of participation in standards-based reform, including consequences for students with disabilities.

Recommendation 11.   The committee recommends that states design stan-dards policies that realistically reflect the time lines and resource levels needed to implement standards-based reforms.

Recommendation 12.   The committee recommends a long-term research agenda to address the substantial gaps in knowledge about the schooling of stu-dents with disabilities and the impact of standards-based reforms.   Areas needing particular attention include research on the school experiences of students with disabilities, the potential of computer-based technologies, how local decisions are made about students' curricular opportunities, alternative student credentials, and the relationship between testing accommodations and validity.

As with any worthwhile undertaking, implementing these recommendations will require effort and a willingness to change.   The logistical and technical chal-lenges are great and rendered more difficult by the need for political and value choices.   But the outcome will be worth that effort if acting on these recommen-dations can begin to build a foundation for blending two very different approaches to improving education for all students with disabilities.

1

Introduction

Few education movements are so clearly identified by a single rallying cry as the standards-based reforms now dominating the nation's education policy agenda. "High standards for all students" has come to represent a set of principles for improving student learning that includes prescriptions for both policy and classroom practice. Standards-based reform is premised on the notion that setting high academic standards and then expecting schools to teach and students to learn to those standards can serve as a potent lever to improve overall educational quality. Although this strategy has taken a variety of forms at the national, state, and local levels, the reforms have four common elements:

- a focus on student achievement as the primary measure of school success;
- an emphasis on challenging academic standards that specify the knowledge and skills students should acquire and the levels at which they should demonstrate mastery;
- a desire to extend the standards to all students, including those for whom expectations have been traditionally low; and
- a heavy reliance on achievement testing to spur the reforms and to monitor their impact.

Standards-based reform poses a host of political and technical questions. For example, is it possible to reach a widespread consensus on what knowledge is most valuable for students to learn? Can the kinds of higher-order, analytical skills expected of students be assessed reliably and validly? Perhaps most challenging of all: Can and should standards be applied to all students? What exactly does "all" mean?

The goal of having all students study similar content is not new. The current rhetoric would sound familiar to the education reformers who issued the 1893 Committee of Ten Report recommending that: "Every subject which is taught at all in a secondary school should be taught in the same way and to the same extent to every pupil as long as he pursues it, no matter what the probable destination of the pupil may be, or at which point his education is to cease" (cited in Cuban, 1990:4). Yet "all students" had quite a different meaning in 1893, when those attending high school represented only a small proportion of all youth, compared with the overwhelming majority of youth who now complete high school (Porter et al., 1991).

Not only does "all students" apply to a different population than it did a century ago, but a variety of social, political, and pedagogical forces have produced diverse educational experiences for students, depending on their abilities, interests, and needs. The "shopping mall" school, with its array of course boutiques offering different learning opportunities, has largely replaced the ideal of the common school (Powell et al., 1985). Some schooling practices that work against common standards, such as tracking, are viewed by many as contributing to greater inequity and harming poor and underachieving students (Oakes, 1985; Kifer, 1993). Other practices that offer differentiated curricula and instructional services, however, are widely accepted as effective strategies for promoting more equitable learning opportunities. These strategies assume that educational expectations and instructional approaches should be tailored to students' individual abilities, needs, and learning styles.

Advocates of standards-based reform acknowledge the importance of attending to the individual needs of students, even as they promote educational strategies that emphasize common standards and "the common needs of society as a whole" (O'Day and Smith, 1993:253):

> Not to accommodate student differences . . . could effectively deny access to large numbers of students. At the same time, such "accommodation," if taken too far, could itself result in substantially different opportunities for different students. For the reform to be successful, the approaches taken by all schools must be based on common curriculum frameworks and all students must be *expected* and *given the opportunity* to perform at the same high standards on a common assessment (p. 265).

Achieving an effective balance between the common purposes of public schooling and the individual needs of students remains an enduring challenge, despite a century of efforts to reconcile the two goals.

Students' individual needs may stem from their differing abilities and interests, their social and ethnic backgrounds, or their prior opportunities. This report focuses on students with disabilities and their diverse needs and abilities. Although federal and state policies may not always detail the specifics of these students' participation in standards-based reform, they assume that students with disabilities are among the "all" who can learn to high standards.

Educating these students also requires attention to their unique needs. For over 20 years, the legal environment and professional norms defining special education have emphasized the right of students with disabilities to an appropriate education, with the outcomes and curriculum articulated through an individualized education program (IEP). Because the term "students with disabilities" encompasses a broad range of physical and cognitive conditions, learning goals and instructional accommodations may vary from student to student. Consequently, a recognition that instructional strategies and assessment techniques need to be tailored to the learning styles and capacities of individual students lies at the core of special education.[1] At the same time, special education policy also requires that students with disabilities be integrated into regular classrooms to the maximum extent possible (i.e., referred to in special education law as placement in the least restrictive environment). Although individualized education has meant specialized services and differentiated outcomes for students with disabilities, the strong presumption in policy and practice has been that these students will share in the collective learning experience that public schooling affords all students. As with most policies, these requirements have been interpreted and implemented differently across the nation's schools and classrooms. Nevertheless, a constant has been the responsibility of the public schools to meet the individual needs of students with disabilities within the common structure that defines the education available to all children.

Recent efforts to implement standards-based reforms come at a time when special education is at a crossroads. The procedural guarantees embodied in federal and state legislation have resulted in significant advances in the access of students with disabilities to schooling. But high dropout rates and low rates of successful transition to postsecondary education, employment, and independent living among students with disabilities suggest that their gains in school access have not been matched by equally successful educational outcomes.

Some advocates of standards-based reform argue that, with its focus on learning outcomes, this strategy will address the perceived shortcomings of current approaches to special education (for one example of such advocacy, see Barrett and Allen, 1996:32-34). At this point, however, it is a promising but as yet unproven alternative for organizing instruction. Before any determination can be

---

[1] Because the population of school-age students with disabilities is so extremely diverse, it is difficult to speak of them as a whole group except in terms of the rights they are guaranteed under one or more existing statutes. Consequently, when we refer to students with disabilities in this report, we are simultaneously acknowledging their diversity and their common entitlements under federal and state law. Although, for a variety of reasons, some students with disabilities do not receive the special education services provided under these statutes, the vast majority do. Since these students are accorded specific educational rights that directly bear on the premises underlying standards-based reform, the committee focused its work most directly on the policies and practices defined through special education legislation and its interpretation by the courts.

made about the effectiveness of a standards-based approach for educating students with disabilities, considerably more information and experience are needed. Melding the principles of standards-based reform and special education and then implementing them in local schools and classrooms require a systematic understanding of the realities of policy and practice as they apply to both approaches. This report is a first step in providing that deeper understanding.

STUDY PURPOSE AND APPROACH

This report assesses the extent to which the goals of common standards and individualized education can be effectively linked. Because the purpose of the report is to analyze the policy and practice issues that must be considered if students with disabilities are to participate in standards-based reforms, we do *not* assess all the various strategies that might be used in educating students with disabilities. Consequently, the report does not consider the broader issue of including students with disabilities in general education classrooms and the larger community. The committee determined that, although many of the issues surrounding standards-based reform relate to where a student with a disability is educated, it made an explicit decision not to consider these placement issues. Therefore, despite the use of the term "inclusion" in the statutory language authorizing the committee, this report does not reflect a particular position either supporting or opposing the inclusion of students with disabilities in general education classrooms. Rather, the analysis presented here examines the educational philosophies, underlying assumptions, and approaches to teaching and learning embodied in standards-based reform and compares them with how special education has treated each of the same dimensions.

Four broad questions frame the report:

• What are the major ideas that standards-based reform and special education prescribe for effective educational standards, curriculum, assessment, and accountability?
• What evidence supports those ideas?
• What are the major points of consistency and difference between standards-based reform and special education?
• What changes in policy and practice will be necessary for the goals of individualized education and common standards to be linked productively for students with disabilities?

The committee's original charge was to "conduct a comprehensive study of the inclusion of children with disabilities in school reform activities assisted under Goals 2000: Educate America Act" (P.L. No. 103-227, sec 1015). The legislation establishing the committee specified that it should evaluate the National Education Goals and other curriculum reforms and standards; review the adequacy of assessments used to gauge progress toward meeting the National Education

Goals and other national and state standards, as well any accommodations necessary to collect data on the progress of students with disabilities and the cost of such accommodations; examine what incentives might be provided to states to develop improvement plans that address the needs of children with disabilities; consider the relationship of Goals 2000 to other federal policies affecting the education of students with disabilities; and investigate any related issues that the National Academy of Sciences considered appropriate.

Although these topics remained a focus of the committee's deliberations, several policy developments required that we modify the scope of our work. During the committee's tenure, the Goals 2000 legislation was substantially altered to reduce the federal direction that states must accept as a condition for funding, giving them greater autonomy in the design of their reforms and increasing the variability among standards policies. These changes meant that, for the committee to fulfill the spirit of its charge, it needed to expand its focus beyond Goals 2000 and to look more generally at standards-based reforms in their various state and local manifestations. Consequently, this report analyzes the Goals 2000 legislation, but it does not explicitly examine the relationship between the National Education Goals and students with disabilities. Rather, it considers how these students are likely to be affected by the content standards, performance standards, and assessments that states and localities are implementing, both within and beyond the Goals 2000 structure.

Our focus on standards-based reform, however, should not be interpreted as an endorsement of it as a strategy for either improving America's schools or enhancing the education of students with disabilities. The committee was not asked to judge the merits of standards-based reforms, nor could it do so, given the recency of these policies and the paucity of data on their effectiveness. Our report provides no advice on whether standards-based reforms are desirable. Rather, we approached our task by asking: "If states and local communities decide to implement standards-based reforms, what conditions will enable students with disabilities to participate in them?" To the extent possible, our analysis takes into account the range of policies being implemented under the standards banner. However, we did assume that at least two premises define the standards approach to education reform: standards will be high, and they will apply to all students.

Just as we did not investigate the effectiveness of the standards framework or its desirability as an educational strategy, we similarly accepted the defining elements of special education policy as a given. We assumed that students with disabilities will continue to be educated according to federal and state laws that mandate that they be provided a free and appropriate public education, through a plan specified in an individualized education program, delivered in the least restrictive environment.

Although some of our analyses suggest that other strategies for educating students with disabilities could potentially be effective, the limitations of our charge and the lack of relevant data did not permit us to investigate these alternatives. Consequently, the recommendations presented in this report are offered as incremental strategies for making the standards-based and special education approaches compatible, improving the likelihood of their successful implementation, and enhancing the knowledge base on which future decisions about policy and practice will be made.

We note, however, that, even though our focus is on students with disabilities, many of the issues we examine and the recommendations we make also apply to other students who share some of the same characteristics and educational needs as those with disabilities. The committee is not in a position to estimate precisely the size of that group or to specify exactly how our recommendations might be applied to them. But we can say that much of what we conclude about the strengths and limitations of the standards movement and about the conditions necessary for full participation in reform curricula and assessments has implications for a broader group of students than just those with disabilities.

Our analysis draws on a variety of sources. The committee examined summary data produced by government agencies and professional associations. We also reviewed a wide body of research literature analyzing the implementation of policy in local communities and the effects of specific educational practices on student outcomes. In addition, the committee commissioned an analysis of the legal history of special education and its implications for standards-based reform. To understand better the perspectives of policy makers, the special education community, and educators more broadly, the committee met several times with congressional and U.S. Department of Education staff to discuss the expectations that they hold for standards-based reform and for the participation of students with disabilities. The committee also sponsored a workshop at which representatives of 10 national organizations outlined what they see as the major unresolved issues with regard to students with disabilities and standards-based reform, as well as the changes in policy and practice they believe will be necessary if these students are to benefit from standards-based instructional strategies. A summary of the workshop is included in Appendix B.

Finally, the committee conducted a new analysis of data from the Prospects study. Funded by the U.S. Department of Education, this study collected data on the first nationally representative sample of elementary school students, allowing a systematic comparison of the school experiences of students with and without disabilities. The results of the analysis are reported in Chapters 3 and 4, and the database is described in Appendix C.

LIMITATIONS OF THE STUDY

In the previous section, we have tried to clearly delimit the scope of the committee's charge. We also acknowledge three significant limitations on our analysis and offer one important caveat. The limitations stem from the nature of the policies we are studying and from the available data. First, in its current incarnation, standards-based reform is less than 10 years old and, in most states, standards policies and new forms of assessment are still in the early stages of implementation. Consequently, although we can describe state policies as they have been enacted and analyze their underlying assumptions, few systematic data are available on the actual implementation of these policies and, in most cases, it is too early to determine their effects.

Second, the committee did not pursue in depth the entire array of issues related to students with disabilities and standards-based reform. One major omission is a discussion of the costs of reform and effective methods for financing it. Because the implementation of standards-based reform is so recent, there are no comprehensive cost studies available, and even the costs of discrete components such as performance assessments can only be estimated at this time. Similarly, no systematic data are yet available on the effects of alternative methods for financing special education. The committee also lacked the time and resources to consider fully the implications of standards-based reform for special and general education teachers. We do identify areas in which teachers will need additional time and resources; however, we could not lay out the specific content and strategies for providing the additional professional development that teachers will need to adapt their instruction to the standards movement and to ensure that the participation of students with disabilities is consistent with their individual needs.

Third, the nature of research on the effects of different instructional practices limits our study. Studies of special and general education have developed largely independently of one another, conducted by different researchers studying different student populations and publishing in separate journals. As a result, valid inferences are difficult to make across students with and without disabilities because so few studies involve both populations and make systematic comparisons between them or even among those with different types of disabilities. Throughout the report, we note when these limitations apply and suggest how the scope and quality of the research base might be strengthened in the future.

Our caveat is straightforward: because standards-based reform and special education tap fundamental values about how equity should be defined, what constitutes valuable knowledge, and who should decide how children are educated, no consideration of these policies will rest solely on the scientific merits of relevant data. Recent controversies over Goals 2000 and the content of state assessments attest to how politicized the issues have become. Public opinion data suggest that parents and the public are considerably less supportive than are education reformers of the curricular content and pedagogical strategies assumed in most standards policies (Johnson and Immerwahr, 1994). Although there is strong public support for the *concept* of higher academic standards, there is little agreement on how to achieve them or even what higher standards means. Furthermore, the public seems willing to accept the possibility of negative consequences from raising standards, such as fewer students graduating from high school. And the public is divided on the appropriateness of including students with disabilities in the general education program (Elam and Rose, 1995).

Although it would be inappropriate for the committee to comment on these value conflicts, we note their intensity because it influences the criteria by which research data are judged by policy makers and the public, and it determines which options for linking standards-based reform and special education will be feasible to implement.

Our hope is that, by presenting a systematic comparison of the two approaches, we can inform national, state, and local deliberations, regardless of which values prevail. One of the major criticisms of education policy making over the past 20 years has been that new policies are typically implemented without regard to prior policies and practices—they are simply layered one atop the other in schools and classrooms (Darling-Hammond, 1990). This report provides an opportunity to stand back and examine how two approaches to improving educational outcomes for students with disabilities might be blended, not as independent and misaligned strata, but as mutually reinforcing foundations.

ORGANIZATION OF THE REPORT

Chapter 2 begins the examination of our four framing questions. Here we compare the policy frameworks supporting standards-based reforms and special education, discuss some of the difficulties of translating policy into practice, and analyze the incentives each framework creates for serving students with disabilities. The vision of standards-based reform is reflected in several federal laws, including Goals 2000 and Title I of the Improving America's Schools Act. Together they provide a variety of incentives to the states to develop more rigorous standards and to implement them through curricula and assessments. It is these state policies that determine how broadly or narrowly standards are defined, what resources are available to implement them locally, and the extent to which students with disabilities are accommodated in instruction and assessment. We therefore examine both federal and state standards policies. In comparing the special education policy framework with standards-based reforms, we examine the Individuals with Disabilities Education Act (IDEA), Section 504 of the Rehabilitation Act of 1973, the Americans with Disabilities Act (ADA), and relevant case law.

In Chapter 3 we describe the enormous heterogeneity that characterizes students with disabilities. We discuss complications in approaches to defining and classifying disability and examine how the population of disabled students varies by social class, ethnicity, and local implementation. The chapter summarizes available data on educational placement, achievement, post-school outcomes, and parental involvement of students with disabilities. It concludes by considering how the variability of this population may affect their participation in standards-based reforms.

Chapter 4 provides an overview of post-school outcomes, curricular and instructional issues for students with disabilities, and their relationship to standards. We examine the content standards and instructional approaches associated with standards-based reform, comparing how consistent they are with what research indicates are the most effective strategies for teaching students with disabilities and the most desirable post-school outcomes. We also consider whether the academic content standards emphasized in standards-based reform are appropriate for the entire range of students with disabilities and examine the curricular, instructional, legal, and resource implications of their participation in the common standards.

Chapter 5 analyzes the use of large-scale assessments for measuring student progress in mastering the knowledge and skills embodied in state standards and for ensuring that the education system is publicly accountable. The chapter describes the approaches to assessment and accountability found in standards-based reforms and how state assessment systems currently address students with disabilities. In keeping with the committee's charge, the chapter focuses particularly on the accommodations, or nonstandard testing conditions, that might be provided some students with disabilities, how accommodations affect the validity of the assessment, and how the performance of students tested under such conditions is reported. The chapter also considers issues in reporting data for public accountability and the implications of increased participation of students with disabilities in assessments, including resource and legal issues.

Chapter 6 presents the committee's recommendations. In these recommendations we sought to develop a set of guidelines that can be used to formulate a consistent strategy for the participation of students with disabilities in standards-based reform.

2

The Policy Frameworks

Twenty years of research on the implementation of federal and state education policies have demonstrated both the limits and the potential of policy as a tool for changing how students are educated. The major limitation is well known: change ultimately depends on the willingness and capacity of local communities. As a result, considerable variation in policy effects is the norm, and policy makers cannot simply mandate the outcomes they desire (McLaughlin, 1987). Yet, despite constraints on its influence, policy does have the potential to shape educational practice in significant ways.

At its most concrete level, policy determines what level of resources will be provided, how those resources will be allocated, who will have authority to deliver educational services, and how policy makers and educators will be held accountable. At a more abstract level, policy also communicates ideas about what constitutes a good education and how that education can best be achieved. It signals what expectations political decision makers and their constituents hold for the education system, and it specifies a set of assumptions about the steps needed to achieve those aspirations. Included in those assumptions are judgments about the incentives most likely to change teaching and learning, the preferred institutional arrangements to promote desired outcomes, and the resources and technical skills most needed.

For 20 years, policies based on individual rights and procedural requirements have been the primary tool for effecting sweeping changes in the education of students with disabilities. Now standards-based reform has introduced a fundamentally different set of policies, based on uniform student learning standards rather than individual rights, and on outcomes rather than process. This new standards-based policy framework has the potential to alter significantly the education of students with disabilities.

In this chapter, we analyze the two sets of federal and state policies that support standards-based reform and special education. We first consider policies enacted by the federal government and the states to promote education reform through the use of student standards, and then we examine policies specifically designed to ensure that students with disabilities receive an appropriate education. We focus on the major ideas and assumptions that characterize each policy framework and then compare their prescriptions for serving students with disabilities.

Our analysis of the two policy frameworks illustrates the wide variation across states in policy choices, the considerable latitude that local school districts have in interpreting and implementing federal and state policies, and the limits of policy in shaping what happens in individual homes, schools, and classrooms. It also demonstrates that these two policy frameworks represent powerful ideas about how to educate children.

Standards-based reform affirms common standards as the catalyst for improved educational outcomes—serving as the basis for what should be taught, measuring what students should be expected to know, and determining whether all students have been given equal learning opportunities. The special education framework defines the rights of students with disabilities to a free and appropriate education and specifies the responsibilities of school systems to accommodate their individual needs. Meeting common standards and accommodating individual needs are the two ideas that animate these frameworks and, as such, they articulate the overarching goal of each policy strategy. Schooling based on common standards and the right of students with disabilities to an individually appropriate education are not inherently inconsistent as policy ideals. Those advocating standards-based reforms assume that students with disabilities will participate in a common schooling experience; special education law assumes that, if states establish outcome standards, they should apply to all students, including those with disabilities.

Nevertheless, despite strong presumptions of compatibility between the two frameworks, they embody very different ideas, policy instruments, and institutional arrangements. One emphasizes the commonality of the educational experience, the other accommodation of individual differences. One promotes its policy goals through an appeal to shared curricular values; the other invests individual students with rights enforced through a set of procedural safeguards. One seeks to ensure accountability through public reporting of aggregate data on student performance; the other relies on an essentially private process—the individualized education program—centered on the individual student.

For both policy frameworks, there is also a wide gap between espousing a desired goal or establishing that a right exists and then implementing it for individual children. Translating a legal or philosophical ideal into practice requires that policy makers, educators, parents, and the public agree on what the ideal means and how it should be applied in classrooms; that resources, technology, and expertise exist to implement the goal; and that variation—a natural part of the federalist system and of professional norms for meeting unique client needs—does not diminish the intent of the original idea.

Our analysis of the two policy frameworks and their implementation thus far suggests that these conditions have not yet been met, and achieving them in the near future is problematic. Public opinion data indicate that those advocating standards-based reform have garnered support for the general idea, but that consensus is thin and does not yet extend to the specifics of curriculum and assessment. Nor is there yet sufficient mastery of the technical requirements of standards-based reform. Similarly, those working within the special education framework assert the right of and the need for students with disabilities to be integrated into the standards reforms, but there is little concrete understanding or consensus within that community of how the goal is to be accomplished for individual students.

This chapter illustrates both the hope and the challenge of standards-based reform by discussing the ideas behind the policy and outlining the conditions that need to be operative if students with disabilities are to be integrated successfully into the standards movement. Subsequent chapters elaborate this theme of promise and pitfalls by analyzing the barriers to be overcome before teaching and testing consistent with standards can be achieved, and by identifying practices that can move the effort in the right direction.

STANDARDS-BASED REFORM

Federal Initiatives

At the federal level, two major pieces of legislation embody the goals of standards-based reform.

Goals 2000

Enacted by Congress in 1994 at the behest of the Clinton administration, the Goals 2000: Educate America Act codifies a set of national education goals and seeks to encourage the states to adopt two types of voluntary standards:

• *Content standards*, defined as "broad descriptions of the knowledge and skills students should acquire in a particular subject area" (P.L. No. 103-227, sec 3, [4]) and

• *Performance standards*, defined as "concrete examples and explicit definitions of what student have to know and be able to do to demonstrate that such students are proficient in the skills and knowledge framed by the content standards" (103-227, sec 3 [9]).

Goals 2000 authorizes modest federal grants to states on the condition that they develop education improvement plans outlining strategies for strengthening teaching and learning and ensuring "students' mastery of basic and advanced skills in core content areas" (103-227, sec 306 b [9]). These strategies must include both a process for developing state content and student performance standards and one for assessing achievement on those standards.

Several provisions of Goals 2000 recognize the relevance of parental involvement and family partnerships to education reform. The last of the eight National Education Goals enumerated in the law directly addresses parent involvement: "By the year 2000, every school will promote partnerships that will increase parental involvement and participation in promoting the social, emotional and academic growth of children." The act also requires states to involve parents in planning, designing, and implementing Goals 2000 programs and provides funding to local education agencies and nonprofit organizations to establish parent assistance centers that will strengthen the relationship between schools and families.

In fiscal 1997, an estimated $491 million will be allocated under Goals 2000 to the states, which in turn will allocate at least 90 percent of those funds to local districts on a competitive basis. As of April 1996, 40 states had received second-year funding and 20 had submitted comprehensive state improvement plans.

Despite its popularity among many state policy makers, Goals 2000 has become controversial at the national level, with most of the differences falling along party lines. From its inception, Goals 2000 was intended to embody an ideal of high-quality, equitable schooling based on voluntary standards and to offer states a small amount of funding to help them implement their own approaches to that vision,[1] but without imposing significant federal mandates on them. Goals 2000, for example, has never had any regulations of the type common to all other federal programs. Nevertheless, opponents have portrayed Goals 2000 as a threat to state and local autonomy, and several parts of the original legislation became focal points for dispute.

A particularly controversial provision of the original law would have encouraged states to develop what were called opportunity-to-learn standards (OTL). These were defined as "the criteria for, and the basis of assessing the sufficiency or quality of the resources, practices, and conditions necessary at each level of the education system (schools, local agencies, and States) to provide all students with an opportunity to learn the material in the voluntary national content standards or State content standards" (103-227, sec 3 [7]). The OTL standards were included in the Goals 2000 legislation at the behest of some Democratic members of Congress who did not want disadvantaged students to be harmed by content standards and testing when they had not been provided the curricular resources to do well

---

[1]In fiscal 1996, all but eight states received less than $10 million in Goals 2000 funding. The largest allocation—to California—was slightly less than $40 million.

on those standards (e.g., appropriate course offerings, rigorous content, and experienced teachers). OTL standards became the most controversial part of the Goals 2000 legislative debate. Opponents argued not only that they would compromise state and local autonomy, but also that they might serve as the basis on which students could sue states to spend more on schooling inputs. As a result, the initial legislation specifically stated that participation in Goals 2000 would be voluntary and that the law should not be construed to mandate either school finance equalization or school-building standards.

The first group of states to submit improvement plans defined their approach to OTL standards in a variety of ways, ranging from general student support programs such as preprimary education and after-school tutoring, to more specific curricular initiatives focusing on teacher professional development, classroom technology, and instructional materials. For the most part, states simply classified existing programs that support and enhance student learning as constituting their OTL strategies, rather than promulgating specific resource or instructional standards as benchmarks for gauging whether local communities have provided students with an adequate opportunity to learn. Despite variation in how states chose to interpret the OTL concept and their intent to apply it in nonbinding ways, all references to opportunity-to-learn standards and strategies have been deleted from the Goals 2000 legislation as a result of recent amendments.

These same amendments, enacted as part of the fiscal 1996 appropriations, also eliminated the requirement that states submit a plan to the U.S. secretary of education as a condition for receiving funding. In lieu of submitting a plan to the federal government, a state may submit assurances from its governor or chief state school officer indicating that it has a plan that meets the Goals 2000 requirements and that information on student performance and implementation benchmarks will be publicly available. States that choose this option also do not need to submit annual reports to the federal government; instead they are required to report publicly on their use of Goals 2000 funds.

The Goals 2000 legislation declares that:

> [A]ll children can learn and achieve to high standards and must realize their potential if the United States is to prosper (103-227, sec 301 [1]).

> [A]ll students are entitled to participate in a broad and challenging curriculum and to have access to resources sufficient to address other education needs (103-227, sec 301 [15]).

The legislation is also clear in stating that "all students" and "all children" include those with disabilities (103-227, sec 3 [1]).

With regard to state assessments, the Goals 2000 legislation specifically declares that state assessments should "provide for the participation in such assessments of all students with diverse learning needs; and the adaptations and accommodations necessary to permit such participation" (103-227, sec 301 [9cBIIIaa-bb]). The legislation is not as specific with regard to how the integration of students with disabilities into state content and performance standards should be accomplished or what expectations are appropriate for them. An analysis of the legal issues surrounding students with disabilities and standards-based reform prepared for the committee argues that the omission may reflect a recognition of the problems inherent in singling out particular groups of students for differential treatment (Ordover et al., 1996:22). They conclude, however, that "the absence of any express exceptions for children with severe cognitive impairments, coupled with Goals 2000's repeated emphasis on 'all children,' suggests that states participating in Title III [the state grants program] should design their content and performance standards in such a way as to reflect outcomes desirable for this population, too."[2]

Improving America's Schools Act

Even though direct federal influence is limited under Goals 2000, the Clinton administration and congressional supporters of standards-based reform have attempted to reinforce that policy direction by making challenging content standards a centerpiece of other federal programs. Nowhere is that more evident than in the Improving America's Schools Act (IASA), the 1994 reauthorization of the Elementary and Secondary Education Act. IASA contains a major new focus and an explicit set of requirements that states and local districts must meet as a condition for obtaining funds under Title I, the largest federal school aid program, which serves poor, underachieving students. The purpose of the new legislation is "to enable schools to provide opportunities for children served to acquire the knowledge and skills contained in challenging State content standards and to meet the challenging State performance standards developed for all children" (P.L. No. 103-328, sec 1001 [d]).

To receive Title I grants, states are required to submit state plans that provide for challenging content and performance standards, state assessments and yearly reports on meeting standards, and provisions for teacher support and learning aligned with the new curriculum standards and assessments. Each section of the Title I law details specific requirements. For example, the assessments and reports must be aligned with the content standards; test at three separate grade levels; be based on "multiple, up-to-date . . . measures that assess higher order thinking skills and understanding"; and "provide individual student interpretive and descriptive reports" as well as aggregated results down to the school level

---

[2]This paper analyzes the implications of federal and state special education statutes, regulations, and judicial decisions for the participation of students with disabilities in standards-based reform. Although the broad parameters of their participation can be clearly inferred from the legal history of special education and related laws, the nature of that participation for any specific student or group of students is less clear because the law has not yet been tested across the full range of issues raised by the standards movement. Where no legal interpretations yet exist, the authors have made a judgment based on their reading of the potentially applicable law.

that are broken down by race, gender, English proficiency, migrant status, disability, and economic status (103-328, sec 1111).

In addition, for local agencies to receive subgrants, they must have on file with the state education agency a local plan "that is coordinated with other programs under this Act, the Goals 2000: Educate America Act, and other Acts, as appropriate." Among other requirements, the local plans must address how students are assessed in accord with the state plan and how well they perform relative to state standards. Title I also requires that parents be involved in local planning, including the preparation of comprehensive school reform plans.

Because Title I provides well over $7 billion a year in federal funding and includes a detailed set of mandates that local districts must meet as a condition for funding, most observers believe that the federal government's influence over the standards and assessment process in individual states will be considerably greater through Title I than through Goals 2000, even though the former is targeted on only a subset of students.

As with Goals 2000, Title I acknowledges students with disabilities and specifies that they are to be included in the teaching and assessment of state content standards. The legislation also indicates that all children are to participate in annual assessments and that reasonable accommodations and adaptations are to be provided students with diverse learning needs.

Because of two changes in the reauthorized Title I program, more students with disabilities are likely to be among the program's beneficiaries. First, the reauthorization relaxed the poverty threshold that schools must meet to operate school-wide programs that allow Title I funds to be used for reform activities throughout the school, rather than just be targeted at the lowest-achieving students. Previously, at least 75 percent of the students in a school were required to be low income before a school-wide program was permitted. Now the threshold has dropped to 50 percent. Second, in schools without school-wide programs, the reauthorization made it easier for students with disabilities to receive Title I services. Previously, these students could be served under Title I only if it were shown that the educational need to be addressed resulted from educational disadvantage and not from a disability. The reauthorization dropped this requirement, stipulating instead that "children with disabilities . . . are eligible for services under this part on the same basis as other children selected to receive services under this part." Eligible students are those identified by school personnel as failing, or most at risk of failing, to meet the state's challenging student performance standards. Schools may not use Title I funds to provide special education and related services required by the Individuals with Disabilities Education Act (IDEA), but they may use Title I funds to coordinate or supplement such services.

State Initiatives

Because the states have primary responsibility for education, the move to set content standards and develop new forms of assessment largely depends on state-level action, particularly the extent to which state governments encourage or mandate local districts, schools, and individual teachers to change their instructional approaches. Although a few states had already begun a standards-setting process prior to the federal initiatives, 48 were engaged in establishing academic standards by 1996 (Gandal, 1996).

Not only are the states at very different stages in that development process,[3] but also the resulting standards vary in their specificity and their use. In some states, content standards are no more than broad, rhetorical goals that local districts are urged to follow. In others, they are considerably more precise, with textbooks and assessments linked directly to the standards and efforts made to train teachers in a pedagogy consistent with the curricular philosophy underlying the standards. (See Chapter 4 for a fuller discussion of the substantive and curricular implications of content standards.) According to a report recently issued by the American Federation of Teachers, only 15 states have developed standards in at least 4 subject areas that are specific enough to permit development of a common core curriculum (Gandal, 1996). The states also differ in how they use the standards as part of their accountability systems. Some states impose no direct consequences on either schools or students for mastery of the standards. Others reward or sanction schools based on their students' performance, and a few states currently require that students meet the content standards as a condition for high school graduation.

Along with content and performance standards, student testing is typically a central component of state reform initiatives. Large-scale assessments, administered by the states, are designed to measure the extent to which students' mastery of content standards is at a level specified in state performance standards. Coincidental with the implementation of standards-based reform has been a move to diversify the format of these assessments and to expand beyond a sole reliance on multiple-choice items. The most typical pattern has been to combine multiple-choice items with open-ended responses and writing samples.[4] About five states are including performance tasks in their assessments, and an equal number have student portfolios as part of their assessment process.[5] However, in their analysis of state mathematics and science curriculum frameworks, Blank and Pechman

---

[3]Professional associations representing those who teach in the different subject-matter disciplines have influenced the pace with which the states have developed content standards. Largely because the National Council of Teachers of Mathematics was the first professional group to develop a set of academic standards, mathematics standards are the most well developed among state content standards. In contrast, for standards in disciplines in which the national development process undertaken by the subject-matter groups has been slower or more problematic (e.g., language arts, history), states tend not to be as far along in their implementation.

[4]A total of 17 states have assessments that consist of multiple-choice items and a writing sample, and 16 others include open-response items of some type, in addition to the multiple-choice items and the writing sample (Bond et al., 1996).

[5]Of the five states with portfolios, however, two are voluntary, one is locally determined, and one is not scored (Bond et al., 1996).

(1995) found that only 10 of 40 recent frameworks show a clear linkage between the framework and the state assessment.

The states also vary in their scoring systems and units of accountability. In keeping with the standards-based notion of performance levels, more than half the states with assessments report results using either the percentage of students reaching each of three or more performance levels or the proportion attaining a state goal (National Education Goals Panel, 1996). Kentucky, for example, has four performance levels, with the second-highest representing the proficient level that the state expects all students to attain within 20 years. The proficient level is meant to indicate that a student understands the major concepts embodied in the state standards or "academic expectations," and that he or she can perform almost all of a task that requires application of those concepts and can communicate the concepts clearly. Other states, for example Delaware and Illinois, report assessment results in terms of the proportion of students who exceed state goals, who meet them, and who do not meet them.

In most states, the unit of accountability is the school, the individual student, or both. Assessment results are used as school accountability measures in 40 states, and in 27 of them results may have consequences for schools, including potential rewards in the form of additional funding and recognition or sanctions such as funding losses, probation, reduced autonomy, and loss of accreditation. In all, 30 states have made students accountable: 18 require that they receive a passing score on a state assessment as a condition for high school graduation;[6] 5 base student promotion decisions on the state assessment; and 12 use their assessment system to provide students with awards or recognition (National Education Goals Panel, 1996; Bond et al., 1996).

Despite the innovations in state assessments over the past decade, there is some indication that even these changes do not sufficiently address the expectations in federal policy or the requirement to include students with disabilities in state assessments. A recent survey of state assessment programs conducted by the Council of Chief State School Officers and the North Central Educational Laboratory (Bond et. al., 1996) found that, as of 1995, only seven states had plans for testing Title I students' mastery of state standards.[7] Although they have until 2000 to implement the required Title I standards and assessments, many states reported having difficulty in complying because of what they perceive to be a lack of firm guidelines on how to set performance standards or assess students who may require accommodations. Consistent with this lack of clear guidance,

---

[6]Until recently, most of the assessments that states have used to test students for high school graduation measure their mastery of basic literacy and numeracy skills, with the tests often calibrated to measure the skill levels expected of eighth graders. However, some states, for example Maryland and New York, are now in the process of implementing high school graduation assessments tied to the state standards and requiring higher mastery levels of more complex skills.

[7]The states were Kansas, Kentucky, Maryland, New York, Ohio, Tennessee, and Texas.

the survey found that states vary in whether they permit testing accommodations for students with disabilities and in the types of accommodations afforded them.[8]

As this brief overview of state policies illustrates, the notion of standards-based reform is likely to have a wide range of meanings and to be implemented in very different ways across the 50 states.[9] How standards policies function in each state depends on the historical level of state direction over local districts, its current fiscal capacity, and the extent to which key state officials view standards-based reform as an effective strategy for educational improvement.

Rationale Behind Standards Policies

As with most education policies, arguments in favor of standards reforms rest on a combination of value appeals, inferences derived from research, and lessons learned from the implementation of prior reform initiatives. The policy framework for standards-based reform is at once a straightforward and a complicated one. The major idea animating it is a simple belief that all students can meet high standards if those standards are clearly articulated and if teachers teach to them.

The tangible inducements for change are modest. Although the refocusing of Title I funds represents a sizable financial incentive for states and localities, the Goals 2000 funding represents only a small catalyst. With a few notable exceptions, for example Kentucky, most states have not accompanied their foray into standards-based reform with either significant new funding or a redirection of existing monies. As a result, the capacity-building costs associated with a major new initiative, such as staff retraining and planning time, have been largely pushed down to local districts and schools.

In some sense, the major incentive to buy into standards-based reform may not be the financial resources provided by higher levels of government, but rather the intangible one represented by a vision of teachers teaching to and students learning to common standards. Behind that vision are a host of other values that include the quest for a new "common school," a belief that American students should be the equal of or better than those around the world, a hope that opportu-

---

[8]As examples of the variation among states, two states (Connecticut and Georgia) require students with disabilities to take tests without accommodations; 41 states currently allow students with IEPs to be excluded from state assessments; and 39 permit some type of accommodations. The most common adaptations permitted for students with disabilities are large print (34 states) and braille or sign language (33 states) (Bond et al., 1996).

[9]Goertz and Friedman (1996) summarize the different ways that the content of state standards differs as one illustration of the extent of state variation. Some states have chosen to concentrate on a set of generic skills, such as listening actively, organizing information, and applying knowledge in new situations. Other states emphasize student outcomes in specific disciplines, such as mathematics and language arts, whereas others have included both generic and disciplinary-specific outcomes in their standards. Still others have also included outcomes that are not strictly academic, such as physical fitness and a sense of personal competence.

nity to learn embodies a more effective strategy for achieving equity, and a conviction that schools should be held publicly accountable for their performance. Any or all of these values may serve as a stronger incentive for standards-based change than the nominal resources that have been offered as incentives. But the power of values to shape policy outcomes depends not on their veracity, but on how widely they are accepted by educators, parents, students, and the public.

In addition to a call on shared values, standards-based reforms have also been justified by evidence from both research and practice. The empirical basis for assuming that a focus on content standards will improve student outcomes is an indirect one. Yet there is a widespread belief among standards advocates that this strategy is consistent with research documenting a relationship between student achievement and the types, content, and level of courses taken. In their view, some of the most compelling evidence about the link between achievement and curricular content comes from the Second International Mathematics Study (SIMS), which documented national differences in the intensity of curricula and content coverage and its relationship to student achievement. One finding that helped explain the poor showing of U.S. students was the superficiality of topic coverage in the U.S. curriculum, compared with Japan, France, and Belgium. The U.S. curriculum is characterized by extensive repetition and review and little intensity of coverage. Low-intensity coverage means that individual topics are treated in only a few class periods, and concepts and topics are quite fragmented (McKnight et al., 1987).[10]

Research focused solely on U.S. students seems to reinforce the international findings. These studies show a correlation between the number and level of mathematics courses taken and student achievement, even when background variables such as home and community environment and previous mathematics learning are taken into account (Hoffer et al., 1995; Raizen and Jones, 1985; Jones et al., 1986). For advocates of content standards, the implication of this research is that a set of curricular standards that applies to all students will increase their opportunity to learn and hence their achievement. Although this evidence is suggestive, the inferences that can be drawn from it are limited by significant data constraints. With few exceptions, studies of content coverage are confined to samples of high school students; most of the research focuses on mathematics courses and primarily considers content coverage. It does not focus on the type or quality of instruction or the effects of different curriculum requirements on students' achievement, and it does not look specifically at students with disabilities.

---

[10]Although analyses of the relationship between content coverage and student achievement are not yet available from the recently released Third International Mathematics and Science Study (TIMSS), the initial findings indicate that the eighth grade mathematics curriculum in the United States is less focused that that of other countries. U.S. schools are still teaching a greater number of topics at a lower level of intensity than their counterparts internationally, and the U.S. mathematics curriculum is not as advanced as that of Japan and Germany. The U.S. science curriculum, however, more closely resembles that of other countries (U.S. Department of Education, 1996c).

The argument that standards-based reform addresses the identified shortcomings of past education policies may be a stronger rationale than arguing that it is derived from research on student achievement. One of the primary reasons that Smith and O'Day (1991) and others advocate comprehensive or systemic reform, with curriculum standards at the core, is because they view it as a way to address a major disadvantage of the United States' decentralized approach to educational governance and policy making: "We argue that a fundamental barrier to developing and sustaining successful schools in the USA is the fragmented, complex, multi-layered educational policy system in which they are embedded. . . . Indeed, the fragmented policy system creates, exacerbates, and prevents the solution of the serious long-term problems in educational content, pedagogy, and support services that have become endemic to the system" (p. 237).

Systemic reform, with its emphasis on curriculum standards, is portrayed as a solution that "seeks to combine the vitality and creativity of bottom-up change at the school site with an enabling and supportive structure at more centralized levels of the system" (Smith and O'Day, 1991:245). From this perspective, standards are viewed as a way to avoid the dilemma of past top-down reform policies, which failed to reach far enough into the classroom to change the teaching and learning process, and bottom-up reforms, which had a limited impact because they never influenced more than a few schools or local districts at a time.

Even though standards-based reform was conceived as a way to compensate for the fragmented system that governs education in the United States, the institutional arrangements it espouses still reflect that fragmentation. All three levels of government are involved, with the federal government essentially serving as a "bully pulpit," exhorting states and localities to move in a new direction, states choosing to play roles that range from strict regulator of local behavior to cheerleader for reform, and local communities responding to federal and state initiatives while still trying to maintain their own agendas.

But standards-based reform includes more than just the three levels of government. Its prominence on the national education policy agenda means that it has also involved the two political parties, major education interest groups such as the teacher unions, groups representing professional disciplines such as mathematics teachers, and organizations representing business interests such as the Business Roundtable. For example, the National Council of Teachers of Mathematics framed and published voluntary national mathematics standards (National Council of Teachers of Mathematics, 1989). The National Science Foundation and the American Association for the Advancement of Science (American Association for the Advancement of Science, 1989) developed materials and ideas that influenced the eventual development of voluntary national science standards by the National Academy of Sciences (National Research Council, 1996). Both these efforts have served as models for standard setting at the state and local levels (Lewis, 1995; McLaughlin and Shepard, 1995).

The need to choose among curricular values also means that standards-based reform has mobilized diverse ideological interest groups, such as the Eagle Forum and People for the American Way. Its reliance on new curricular approaches and forms of assessment has involved testing companies and textbook publishers. Consequently, to talk about the institutional arrangements assumed in the standards-based policy framework is to pose a question about who has authority to define and implement standards and to ask whether consensus is possible among all these different interests.[11]

New forms of assessment are also seen as a solution to the shortcomings of past policies. Largely in response to the growing state use of minimum competency tests for high school graduation, beginning in the 1970s, a number of testing and measurement experts analyzed the problems associated with the policy uses of assessment (e.g., Airasian and Madaus, 1983; Frederiksen, 1984; Haertel, 1989). Their critiques of traditional multiple-choice tests are now well known. They questioned the disjuncture between the actual curriculum in schools and what was being tested, the assessment's emphasis on basic skills at the expense of more challenging content, the lack of opportunity for some students to gain even the basic knowledge and skills needed to score well on these tests, and the corruption of the tests as valid and reliable measuring devices because of the strong sanctions keyed to their results. Experts argued that tests whose results determined whether students graduated from high school or whether schools received extra resources would change school behavior and, in the process, the tests themselves would be altered as valid measures of student achievement.

To a large extent, new forms of assessment were developed in response to the identified shortcomings of multiple-choice tests. In fact, if one looks at some of the recommendations coming from critics of traditional tests, one finds an almost direct correspondence between those recommendations and the goals of alternative assessments. For example, Haertel (1989:31) recommends that other kinds of learning outcomes be recognized, including "not only better tests of critical thinking and higher order skills, but also ways to recognize students' exceptional individual accomplishments, from written works or science fair projects to artistic creations." Those who espouse the use of such assessment devices as student portfolios see themselves as having responded to the identified shortcomings of more traditional forms of student assessment (e.g., see National Council on Education Standards and Testing, 1992:28).

---

[11]In contrast to analysts such as Smith and O'Day (1991), who assume that systemic standards policies can overcome the effects of fragmentation, others such as Cohen (1996) argue that distinctive features of the U.S. system limit the potential for translating such reforms into a coherent system of instruction. He points out that our history of fragmented governance and contentious education politics creates many opportunities to oppose policies, a particular problem for standards-based reform in which political divisions are overlaid with cultural differences. In other words, fragmented structures create a political climate that makes implementation of centralizing policies, especially those grounded in contested social values, very difficult.

Guiding Assumptions and Whether They Will Be Met

The idea that common standards will serve as a powerful catalyst for improved educational outcomes can work as intended only if a number of key assumptions are true. In this section, we analyze five assumptions that undergird the standards policy framework. We consider available evidence as a basis for determining whether these assumptions are likely to prove valid as standards policies are implemented in a variety of forms across states and local communities.

Unfortunately, we cannot determine at this point whether any of the standards movement's guiding assumptions are correct, nor can we say whether these policies will produce their expected effects. Even early implementers, for example Kentucky and Maryland, have had their programs fully in place for less than five years, and, in the case of standards-based reform, the implementation process is longer than for most education policies. For example, Goertz and Friedman (1996) report that, in the 18 states they studied, the standards-setting process took between 2 and 4 years from the time that legislation was enacted to final approval of the standards. Additional time was then needed for states to develop curriculum frameworks. Similarly, the initial development and subsequent modifications of new state assessments can also consume several years.[12] Nevertheless, even though we cannot draw any conclusions about the effectiveness of standards policies, the experience of the early implementers does illustrate some of the potential barriers. Our analysis indicates that, unless the first four of the five assumptions discussed below are valid, standards-based reforms are likely to encounter serious implementation problems or perhaps even fail to achieve their purpose.

Standards Should Apply to All Students

The disparities in achievement among students of different demographic and socioeconomic groups represent one of the most significant problems in American education. The concept of high standards for all is viewed as one solution to this problem (Ravitch, 1995). The assumption is that, by clearly communicating the notion "all students can learn to high standards," teachers and students alike will understand what is expected of them and schools will move to equalize students' opportunities to learn. Consequently, the Goals 2000 legisla-

---

[12]The difficulties associated with making premature judgments about the effects of standards-based reforms is illustrated by the case of Kentucky. The U.S. Department of Education notes in its recent report on Goals 2000 (U.S. Department of Education, 1996b) that comprehensive reform in Kentucky is beginning to pay off, with the percentage of students in tested grades scoring at the proficient or distinguished levels having increased significantly between 1993 and 1995. However, a panel of testing experts who evaluated the Kentucky assessment concluded that, among other technical problems, errors in equating across assessments make year-to-year comparisons of test results of questionable validity (Hambleton et al., 1995).

tion is explicit about standards applying to all students, and some states, for example Kentucky, have made this assumption a central tenet of their reforms. Nevertheless, moving from the rhetoric of "all children can learn" to everyday classroom practice poses serious political challenges—including the need to equalize instructional resources—as well as philosophical and logistical issues, such as balancing high, uniform standards with students' unique educational needs and abilities.

The assumption that standards should and can apply to all students is of particular relevance to students with disabilities. Unfortunately, the information available on how students with disabilities are being addressed in standards policies is minimal. One research project, currently under way, is using state and local case studies to examine the interaction between general and special education policies and their impact on students with disabilities (Goertz and Friedman, 1996). Some information is also available from general studies of state systemic reforms (e.g., Goertz et al., 1995). In addition, the committee reviewed a small sample of state standards documents.

The picture that emerges from these limited and nonrepresentative sources is of states acknowledging their responsibility to include students with disabilities in standards-based reforms, but unsure of exactly what that means or how to accomplish it. Most of the state Goals 2000 plans that we reviewed specifically mention students with disabilities, and a number list special support services for these students, such as preschool programs. Some states, for example Vermont, have changed the way they fund and regulate services for students with disabilities as a way of creating incentives for local schools to serve them in regular classrooms with appropriate instructional support systems, and to do so without labeling or classification.

States that are developing new forms of assessment are paying greater attention to ensuring that students with disabilities are included in assessments and that reasonable accommodations are provided. Kentucky and North Carolina are two states that have created strong incentives to minimize local exclusion of students with disabilities from the state assessment. For example, in North Carolina, schools must test 95 percent of the students eligible for state testing or face having "chance scores" added to their performance reports. Those scores represent what a student would receive if he or she answered test questions at random. In Kentucky, only students with severe disabilities who do not follow the regular curriculum are included in an alternate portfolio assessment system, and the state estimates that only 1 percent of Kentucky students take this alternate test (Schnaiberg, 1995b). In both states, the assumption is that, if local schools have to include students with disabilities in the state assessment, they will also include them in the curriculum on which they are tested.

Implementing appropriate support services and creating incentives for including students with disabilities in the mainstream curriculum and assessment will continue to challenge states and local districts. But what seem to be an even greater challenge and a major source of ambiguity are the prior issues of deciding to which standards students with disabilities are to be held, whether those standards are common to all students or whether there can be differences within some general parameters, and how students with disabilities are to be taught effectively in a standards-based curriculum. Part of the problem seems to stem from the historical divide between general and special education personnel. Goertz and Friedman (1996:18) report: "based on our interviews with state special education directors and state directors of curriculum and instruction, it appears that special education has not played a major role in the development of either state content standards or specific curriculum frameworks in most states. Rather, special education's involvement has generally been limited to a review of standards and curriculum documents prepared by other educators—if that." However, these researchers did find a few notable exceptions to this pattern. For example, in Missouri, state special education staff have developed sample instructional activities to illustrate how state performance standards can be applied to students with cognitive disabilities.

Leaders of interest groups representing students with disabilities, professional educators, and policy makers have also expressed uncertainty about the specifics of standards-based reform. At an October 1995 workshop sponsored by the committee as part of its information-gathering activities, groups that advocate on behalf of students with disabilities argued that standards-based reforms embody a potentially effective strategy for improving educational opportunities for the students they represent (see Appendix B). Representatives from groups including the Council for Exceptional Children, the United Cerebral Palsy Association, and the National Association of State Directors of Special Education argued that educators and the public often hold low expectations for students with disabilities; including them in standards-based reform would raise expectations and allow these students to accomplish more in school. They also maintained that placing students with disabilities in a state's or local community's standards framework would require school systems to be more explicitly and publicly accountable for them. Those making workshop presentations on behalf of groups representing educators and policy makers, such as the National Education Association, the Council of Chief State School Officers, and the National Governors' Association, concurred in the view that standards-based reform could serve as a vehicle for improving the educational opportunities of students with disabilities.

However, their clarity about the potential benefits of standards-based reform was not matched by equal precision about how the standards framework might be implemented for students with disabilities. Most presenters acknowledged that they and their constituents lack sufficient experience with the reform to suggest concrete strategies for how students with disabilities might effectively participate in curricular standards and the accompanying assessments. There was general uncertainty about the extent to which standards would need to be individualized; whether this individualization should apply to the content standards or just to

performance levels on the common content standards; the extent to which accommodations would apply to the curriculum as well as to assessments; and who
ought to make decisions about participation in or exclusion of students with disabilities from the common standards framework. Presenters from groups representing state and local policy makers also questioned whether special education
policy has created a dual system that makes integrating students with disabilities
into the common standards more difficult.

The interest groups' lack of specificity about the relationship between special education and standards-based reform further illustrates a central fact about
standards policies at this time: systematic efforts to determine whether state content standards are appropriate for all or most students with disabilities and to
identify the conditions under which these students might be taught and assessed
according to those standards are not yet an integral part of state policy frameworks. Consequently, even with the limited data available, it seems reasonable to
conclude that the assumption "all children can learn to high standards" has not
yet been adequately defined in policy, much less implemented.

Two recent surveys of Kentucky and Maryland teachers suggest that translating the call for high standards for all students into classroom practice will also
require that teachers first be persuaded of the veracity of that claim. The Kentucky teachers surveyed were evenly divided about whether or not they agreed
with the tenet "all children can learn to a high level." An overwhelming majority
(83 percent) agreed that, regardless of whether it is possible for all students to
learn to that level, it is an appropriate message to send Kentucky students. However, very few (9 percent) agreed that all students can reach the *same* high level of
performance, with most teachers in the sample (90 percent) saying that novice,
the lowest performance level in the Kentucky system, is a high level for some
students (Koretz et al., 1996b). The results from the Maryland sample are essentially similar, except that a slightly higher proportion of teachers (21 percent) felt
that students could learn to the same high level (Koretz et al., 1996a).

Content and Performance Standards Can Be Defined

The effectiveness of a standards approach to school reform initially depends
on a clear definition of exactly what is important for students to learn. The definitional process is likely to be both a technical, professional one—translating rhetorical goals into specific curricular objectives—and a political one, because a
broad consensus on the standards is needed among policy makers, educators,
parents, and the public. Ravitch (1995:12) outlines the criteria that content standards should meet:

> A content standard should be measurable, so that students can demonstrate their
> mastery of the skills or knowledge; if mastery of the standard is neither measur-
> able nor demonstrable, then it is probably so vague that it has little meaning or

value for teachers and students. Content standards should be specific enough to be readily understood by teachers, parents, students, and others. They should be clear enough so that teachers know what students are supposed to learn and can design lessons to help them learn what is expected.

Once content standards are defined, then standards must be set for what constitutes inadequate, acceptable, and outstanding performance in demonstrating mastery. The traditional approach to large-scale assessments in the United States requires that students' general knowledge be assessed across some broadly defined areas of achievement and their performance ranked and compared on numeric scales. In contrast, the new performance standards require that student performance be evaluated in relation to absolute standards (Taylor, 1994).

Promulgating clear and precise content standards depends on the ability of policy makers, educators, subject-matter experts, and the public to reach a consensus on what those standards ought to include. Basically, the relevant community needs to agree on what constitutes the valuable knowledge that students should learn. However, the data on which to draw inferences about the degree of public and elite support for the concept of standards and for specific types of standards show a mixed picture. An overwhelming majority of the American public supports having local schools conform to a set of national achievement goals and standards and requiring that standardized tests be used to measure student achievement on those standards (Elam et al., 1991, 1992). A majority also sees raised standards as a way to encourage students, including ones from low-income backgrounds, to do better in school (Elam and Rose, 1995).

Similarly, based on the initial response to the mathematics standards, a sample of federal and state policy makers interviewed in 1991 thought that a broad-based consensus could be reached on curriculum standards (McDonnell, 1994). A few acknowledged that agreement might be considerably more difficult to reach in subjects such as science, English literature, and social studies—some of whose content reflects geographic, ethnic, and ideological divisions in society. A few observers have also raised the question of who has the right in a democracy to set educational standards. Sizer (1992), for example, questioned whether subject-matter experts who are neither elected nor representative of the interests of all parents and citizens and who operate at a distance from most local communities should be the ones to decide what students should learn. But most policy makers in the 1991 study agreed with a respondent who argued that "if we had a referendum on what topics should be included in standards, there would be agreement on content. People tend to overstate the disagreement."

By 1994, however, the belief that a consensus could be easily reached on curriculum standards had proven overly optimistic. The continuation of the California Learning Assessment System (CLAS), widely touted as a model performance assessment, had been vetoed by the governor after strong opposition to the content and format of its language arts test. A small but vocal group of opponents in Kentucky was lobbying to have that state's assessment terminated or significantly modified. Other states, for example Pennsylvania, were experiencing serious opposition to efforts aimed at specifying a set of intended outcomes for students (Ravitch, 1995). At the national level, the U.S. Senate, on a vote of 99 to 1, passed a resolution early in 1995 condemning voluntary national history standards that had been drafted by a group of subject-matter experts and classroom teachers (Lewis, 1995).

These controversies, along with public opinion data, suggest that consensus breaks down once the public moves beyond a general belief in the need for standards and assessments to questions about what those standards should be and how students should be taught and tested. Groups representing religious conservatives have been the most visible opponents of recent curricular innovations and new forms of assessment, questioning their content and format (McDonnell, 1997). But public opinion data indicate that some of the questions these groups are raising reflect broader public concerns. For example, recent surveys about the teaching of mathematics and writing point to fundamental differences between the curricular values of education reformers and large segments of the public. These are reflected in differences of opinion about when students should be allowed to use calculators, the relative importance of grammar and spelling, and the value of teaching students in heterogeneous ability groups (Johnson and Immerwahr, 1994).[13] Differences between education reformers and parents have been reinforced by recent controversies over the use of "whole-language" pedagogy, which deemphasizes phonics and emphasizes the use of literature in reading instruction. In admitting that reading instruction had swung too far in what had been considered the reform direction and that a balance now needs to be struck between traditional and whole-language methods (California Department of Education, 1995; Jolley, 1996), state education officials in California appeared to validate parental concerns that their children are not learning the building-block skills needed to read well and that "invented spelling" and a lack of knowledge of grammar rules will hinder their writing ability.

Those advocating standards-based reform can draw a number of inferences from public opinion data and case study research on state efforts to reach consen-

---

[13]In a Public Agenda survey conducted in August 1994, 86 percent of the respondents in a national sample said that students should learn to do arithmetic "by hand"—including memorizing multiplication tables—before starting to use calculators. This opinion contrasts with 82 percent of mathematics educators responding to an earlier survey who said that "early use of calculators will improve children's problem-solving skills and not prevent the learning of arithmetic" (Johnson and Immerwahr, 1994:17). Sixty percent of those in the Public Agenda sample rejected the educational strategy that encourages students to write creatively without a prior concentration on spelling and grammar. Instead, most respondents endorsed the idea that "unless they are taught rules from the beginning, they will never be good writers" (p. 18). Similarly, the Public Agenda poll found that "only 34 percent of Americans think mixing students of different achievement levels together in classes—'heterogeneous grouping'—will help increase student learning. People remain skeptical about this strategy even when presented with arguments in favor of it" (p. 18).

sus. Some conclusions relate to the importance of state political leadership that is strong in its support of standards-based reform, yet flexible enough to make needed modifications as technical and political problems arise.[14] But for our purposes, two other inferences are perhaps more important. First, consensus about the specific content of standards and assessment is proving much more difficult to reach than reform advocates had initially assumed. Moving from a widespread belief in the idea of standards to the detail of what should be taught and tested is a challenging task, not only because it touches on deeply held religious, cultural, and political values, but also because it tests competing beliefs about what the purpose of education should be. The prominent role of societal values in reaching a consensus leads to the second inference: the development of new curriculum standards and assessments is likely to encounter problems if it is solely a technical process with participation limited to experts. The contrasting experiences of Vermont, with its more open, participatory approach to standards development, and California, where curriculum and assessment design was confined to teachers and other experts, suggest how critical the nature of the standards development process is to whether or not the consensus assumed in standards-based reform can be reached (Goertz et al., 1995; McDonnell, 1997).

Student Performance Can Be Measured Validly and Reliably

If students are to be held to a certain performance level on a set of curriculum standards, then they have to be assessed in a way that is cost-efficient and comparable across large numbers of students. Historically, these two criteria have led states and local districts to rely on standardized, multiple-choice tests because they offer a variety of practical and measurement advantages. They can be administered and scored at relatively little cost in time and money. They eliminate subjectivity of scoring—a concern that initially contributed to their development and popularity. Because of the short time required to administer each item, these tests can be sufficiently long to be acceptably reliable and to cover a wide range of content. The validity of inferences based on many of these tests was bolstered by attention to content coverage, the performance of individual items (e.g., their discriminating power and freedom from bias), the quality of reporting scales, and other factors. Now, although policy makers and testing experts disagree about the difficulty of designing assessments that measure more rigorous curriculum standards, they do agree that traditional multiple-choice tests alone are inadequate (McDonnell, 1994; Taylor, 1994).

---

[14]California and Kentucky represent contrasting cases. Both states faced political opposition to their assessment programs, but Kentucky was able to maintain its program, whereas California's was discontinued. One of the major factors explaining these different outcomes was the response of state political leaders to the controversy. (For a comparative analysis of the politics of testing in the two states, see McDonnell, 1997.)

But the move to alternative forms of testing that are based on a precise set of standards and parallel real-world tasks presents a number of technical challenges, which are discussed in greater detail in Chapter 5.[15] In contrast to multiple-choice items that require only a few minutes or less for students to answer, some performance tasks may take 30 minutes or even an hour to complete. As a result, unless the testing time is greatly increased, it is difficult to test the entire domain of what students are expected to know (Linn, 1993). Furthermore, alternative assessments cannot be machine-scored in the way that multiple-choice tests are. As a result, cost and reliability become more of a challenge as expert scorers must be trained and monitored to apply the same set of scoring rubrics across thousands of individual assessments. Although acknowledging these technical challenges, policy makers have continued to believe that they can be overcome. Officials in a number of states have chosen to move ahead before public and media attention shift and the opportunity for significant change is lost (McDonnell, 1994). The metaphor governing assessment design in the most innovative states has been "building the airplane while we fly it."

Instruction Consistent with the Standards Can Be Implemented in Individual Schools and Classrooms

Curriculum reformers and their allies in the policy community assume that content standards, coupled with the appropriate assessments, will change classroom instruction. Although the accountability purposes of student testing remain prominent, assessments are also now intended to serve as powerful forces for curricular change. Despite this strong expectation that classroom teaching consistent with standards and assessment policies will occur, reform advocates also assume that content standards will serve only as a general guide to instruction, and that teachers will use their professional judgment in customizing the standards to their individual classrooms. Yet some of the content represented in the new standards differs significantly from what is traditionally covered in most courses.

In addition, as Chapter 4 explains, many of these standards embody assumptions about pedagogy as well as content, and many of the accompanying assessments are geared toward instruction that emphasizes student writing, learning by discovery, and collaborative student work. However, schooling in the United States has traditionally been characterized by teacher-directed instruction that relies on only a few strategies such as teacher lecture, boardwork, and students working individually on assignments (e.g., see Oakes, 1985; Gamoran and Nystrand, 1991; Burstein et al., 1995). Despite this persistent and enduring pattern of instruction, the standards movement assumes that teachers will accept

---

[15]Chapter 5 also analyzes the assumption of the standards policy framework that performance on content standards can be measured reliably and validly, with particular attention to its implications for students with disabilities.

different content and pedagogical approaches as preferable to current practice, and that they will have the ability to make the necessary changes.

Because most studies of the impact of the standards movement on classroom teaching are still ongoing, we do not yet know whether standards-based reform can be successfully implemented in the way that its proponents assume. However, several studies provide insight into two of the major challenges involved. The first is translating curriculum standards into classroom practice. For example, teachers in California and Kentucky have found themselves in somewhat of a bind. On one hand, state officials formulated curriculum and performance standards on which students will be assessed. On the other hand, they have avoided specifying too detailed or prescriptive a curriculum in order to defer to teachers' professional judgments about how best to customize instruction to their own students. Although teachers may appreciate having their professional status acknowledged, this strategy has often left them with little direction. Further complicating the problem is that instructional materials reflecting the new standards are not yet widely available, and teachers have been left to patch together new materials from a variety of different sources.

A second problem is that the new curriculum standards expect teachers to teach very different content from that of the past and to teach it in fundamentally different ways. As Cohen and Peterson (1990:233) ask in their study of the implementation of the California mathematics frameworks, "How can teachers teach a mathematics that they never learned in ways they never experienced?" These researchers and their colleagues studied a group of elementary teachers, some of whom have embraced the mathematics frameworks and believe that they have revolutionized their teaching. However, classroom observations indicated that teaching innovations were often filtered through a very traditional approach to instruction, so that the new curriculum was used "in a way that conveyed a sense of mathematics as a fixed body of right answers, rather than as a field of inquiry in which people figure out quantitative relations" (p. 313).[16]

Although most studies of the effect of new standards and assessments on classroom teaching and learning are still limited, the few available do suggest that teachers are making changes, but that those changes are not yet as deep or extensive as reformers expect.

---

[16]In their study of the implementation of mathematics and science reforms in nine local districts in Michigan, Spillane and his colleagues (1995) also found that, at the district level, officials responsible for promoting curriculum innovations used terms common to the reform movement (e.g., problem solving, integration, hands-on), but that their conceptions of key reform terms were "rather thin" and differed significantly from the ideas promoted by state and national reformers. The researchers noted: "A troubling issue here is that many local educators believed they understood and were pressing for the enactment of ideas about mathematics and science education that were analogous with those advanced by AAAS, NCTM, and others. . . . The reform rhetoric of local educators, then, masks significant variability across and within school districts. It can easily deceive policy analysts and researchers, especially those who fail to dig beneath the surface of labels, leading them to make inflated judgments about the success of recent reform efforts" (p. 78).

Surveys of educators in two states implementing standards-based reforms indicate that, although teachers express reservations about some aspects of standards and assessment policies, the majority support the reform concept and report that these policies have changed their instruction. In their 1995 statewide survey of Maryland principals and teachers in two of the three grades in which the Maryland School Performance Assessment Program (MSPAP) is administered, Koretz and his colleagues (1996a) found that 81 percent of the principals believe it has been a useful tool for encouraging positive change among teachers resistant to modifying their instruction. The overwhelming majority of fifth-grade teachers (83 percent) and eighth-grade mathematics teachers (63 percent) in the sample reported that MSPAP has had positive effects on instruction in their schools; about half believe that it has caused some teachers who are resistant to change to alter their instruction. A total of 55 percent of the fifth-grade teachers and 33 percent of the eighth-grade mathematics teachers reported focusing "a great deal" on improving the consistency between their instructional content and the MSPAP. Other examples of reported changes in instruction include more instructional time devoted to writing by the fifth-grade teachers, with a greater proportion of that time spent on writing for a variety of purposes, analysis of text, and literary comprehension and less emphasis on spelling, punctuation, and grammar. The eighth-grade teachers reported an increased emphasis on data analysis, communication of mathematical ideas, and problem solving, with decreased attention to computation and algorithms.

The second study surveyed Kentucky principals and teachers from two of the grade levels tested by the Kentucky Instructional Results Information System—KIRIS (fourth-grade and eighth-grade mathematics), and it presents a similar picture of educators' responses. Koretz and his colleagues (1996b) found that close to 90 percent of the Kentucky teachers reported focusing "a moderate amount" or "a great deal" of attention on improving the match between the content of their instruction and what is tested on KIRIS. The specific curricular changes that they reported parallel those of the Maryland teachers—e.g., more classroom time spent on writing and a greater emphasis on communicating mathematical ideas and solutions and less attention to computation.[17]

---

[17]A third statewide survey, conducted in 1994 on teachers' responses to the Arizona Student Assessment Program (ASAP), found somewhat different results. About 50 percent of the respondents reported that ASAP has had little or no effect on their teaching, and only 30 percent agreed with the statement that "as a result of ASAP, major changes in curriculum have been made at this school" (M.L. Smith, 1996:50). There may be a number of reasons for the differences between the Maryland and Kentucky findings and the Arizona results (which were also confirmed by multiyear, comparative case studies of four schools). Possible reasons relate to the broader scope of the Maryland and Kentucky reforms and to the "virtually nonexistent" investment in teacher capacity-building by Arizona (M.L. Smith, 1996:102). However, the strongest explanation for the differences may be that Arizona suspended ASAP after only two years of administration. As of 1996, the state had not issued new standards and the legislature had mandated the return to an assessment system of standardized, norm-referenced tests in grades 3-12.

But as a number of researchers have found (e.g., Cohen and Peterson, 1990; Spillane et al., 1995; Burstein et al., 1995), there is often a substantial gap between what teachers report they are doing in response to new policy initiatives and what researchers find when they analyze their classrooms. These classroom studies, however, are typically based on either observational data or a content analysis of class assignments collected from a small sample of teachers. Consequently, they are less generalizable than teacher surveys based on state-representative samples, but they can enhance our understanding of the lag between teachers' acceptance of the language of reform and translation of it into instructional practice. A recent content analysis of approximately 35 classroom assignments from each of 24 teachers in Kentucky and 24 in North Carolina illustrates the type of responses to standards-based reform that can be expected from teachers in the first few years of implementation. McDonnell and Choisser (1997) found that teachers' assignments are reasonably consistent with state standards in the types of classroom activities they use, but not in the concepts they stress. In their assignments and classroom activities, teachers are using some strategies associated with standards reforms, such as encouraging active student participation and inquiry through group work, but they are also relying in equal measure on more traditional activities, such as whole-class instruction and review. In both state samples, teachers have combined the old and the new, adding those aspects of reform that make sense to them, while still relying on the traditional strategies with which they are most comfortable and that they believe have been effective in the past.

Teachers' willingness to use instructional strategies consistent with standards-based reform is not matched by equal attention to the concepts embodied in the two states' standards. For example, the Kentucky teachers included in only a few of their assignments the state learning goals that stress thinking critically, developing solutions to complex problems, and organizing information to understand concepts. Similarly, low-end content standards such as understanding computational procedures and reading comprehension were more likely to be reflected in assignments than complex standards such as understanding space and dimensionality and using reference tools appropriately. Teachers were also asked to select from among their assignments those that they consider to be most similar to the state assessments in purpose and format. Only 32 percent of the North Carolina "most similar" assignments and 53 percent of the Kentucky ones were judged by coders to be similar. Teachers' misjudgment about the similarity of their assignments typically stemmed from their not recognizing the full complexity of the skills being measured on the state assessment.[18] Since these assign-

---

[18]For example, a North Carolina seventh grade mathematics teacher submitted assignments that she thought most closely approximated the state assessment. They required students to make basic mathematical computations, with no effort to gauge whether they understood underlying concepts, the solution process, or how they might apply the algorithms in unfamiliar situations.

ments represent teachers' own judgments about which aspects of their teaching most closely mirror the purpose, content, and format of the state assessments, it seems reasonable to assume that these teachers lack adequate information about the objectives of the state standards and assessments.[19]

Although past research on the implementation of curricular reforms would suggest that these findings are not surprising, it should be noted that, in some sense, Kentucky may be a best possible case. The reforms in Kentucky are quite far-reaching and much has been expected of teachers there, and the state has provided far more in resources for teacher training than is typically the case. School districts have been allowed to use up to nine days a year for professional development; in addition, $400 per teacher was allocated for professional development, with 65 percent of that sum under the control of the local school site. Even this substantial resource commitment has been insufficient. In eight focus groups of teachers conducted around the state by the Appalachia Educational Laboratory (1995), teachers reported that training opportunities for curriculum development and alignment are limited and the quality mixed. They also indicated that they were uncomfortable developing curriculum at the local level and aligning it with the state standards because they were accustomed to its being done by textbooks. In addition, the teachers in the focus groups reported needing much greater guidance about how to apply the state's academic expectations to specific grade levels.

Whether the type of instruction that reformers advocate can actually be implemented in most classrooms remains unknown at this time. However, before any significant progress can be made, investments in capacity-building will need to be increased substantially.

Standards Reform Is One Component of a Broader Strategy for School Improvement

Standards-based reform is often viewed as one element of what has come to be known as systemic reform (Smith and O'Day, 1991). This strategy advocates a unifying vision based on educational goals that are consistent at the national, state, and local levels, as well as a coherent system of state policy guidance based on a set of curriculum standards that inform related policies dealing with teacher training and licensure, curricular materials, and student assessment. In addition, systemic reform also assumes that governance changes will simultaneously promote clearer state guidance and support along with greater school-site autonomy, thus giving teachers more of a role in deciding how best to tailor the curriculum to individual student needs.

---

[19]This study also found that the instructional responses of the Kentucky and North Carolina teachers were very similar, despite the fact that the North Carolina assessment is more traditional in its format and has few consequences, whereas KIRIS is a more innovative, high-stakes assessment.

Goals 2000 strongly encourages a systemic approach to reform in legislative language detailing what should be included in state improvement plans. States are encouraged to describe the process they will use to align curricular materials with state content standards, provide professional development to teachers, ensure that decisions about meeting content standards are made closest to individual learners, encourage parental participation, and increase student access to needed social services. Although a number of states have adopted some of the individual elements included in systemic reform, only one, Kentucky, has implemented a comprehensive policy that includes all the major components.[20] Nevertheless, there remains a widespread assumption that standards and assessment policies will be linked (at least informally) to policies that decentralize more authority over funds, curriculum, and personnel to individual schools and that enhance teachers' professional skills.

We leave this examination of the standards policy framework with many unanswered questions. It is clear that standards-based reform is still viewed by many—including national and state political leaders, influential groups such as The Business Roundtable, and the public—as a promising strategy for effecting improved student achievement. However, standards-based reform poses serious challenges for which there are no obvious or easy solutions. It attempts to influence teaching and learning, even though research has demonstrated the limited ability of top-down policy to change classroom practice. In addition, standards-based reform seeks to minimize direct regulation by giving teachers and other education professionals discretion in how they translate curriculum standards into practice. Yet with its strong emphasis on both accountability and a particular instructional approach, standards-based reform expects teachers to produce better results from their teaching, often with little guidance about how to surmount the practical difficulties associated with such a transformation. Standards-based reform also rests on a set of assumptions that have not yet been proven true in practice, and the political and technical challenges facing implementers are formidable. None is perhaps more demanding than demonstrating that all children can indeed learn to high standards.

---

[20]The comprehensiveness of the Kentucky reforms stems from a set of circumstances unique in American history. In 1989, in response to a lawsuit challenging the constitutionality of the state's school finance system, the Kentucky supreme court ruled not only that the finance system was unconstitutional, but also that the entire state school system was unconstitutional. The court ordered the legislature to redesign Kentucky's education system in its entirety. The Kentucky Education Reform Act, signed into law in April 1990, pumped over $700 million in new funds into the system in its first two years of implementation. The law made a number of sweeping changes that range from how the duties of local school boards are defined to how teachers are licensed and what is taught in classrooms. It required that elementary schools teach younger children in "ungraded primaries" that combine students from kindergarten through third grade in the same classrooms; it mandated that each school establish a site council to govern its curricular, personnel, and budgetary decisions; and it created a network of family service and youth service centers located at or near schools with large concentrations of poor students.

For students with disabilities, one obvious question is whether the special education policies that have been designed to ensure an appropriate education can aid in integrating these students into a standards-based curriculum. We turn to that question now by examining the special education policy framework and its implications for the standards movement. In doing so, we compare federal and state laws that start with premises different from most standards policies. Whereas the standards framework emphasizes common benchmarks for all students and public accountability for their attainment, the special education framework focuses on the individual student and the educational services most appropriate for his or her particular needs. As such, it not only creates very different incentives for schools in deciding how to serve such students, but it also forces them to balance diverse learning goals in an environment of constrained resources.

SPECIAL EDUCATION

Federal Initiatives

Federal statutes and regulations, along with judicial interpretations of the constitutional due process and equal protection clauses, have played a preeminent role in the education of students with disabilities for the past 25 years. These federal policies are mirrored in state law and regulations and in many state court decisions, some of which expand the protections afforded individuals with disabilities beyond those offered in the federal laws.

Individuals with Disabilities Education Act

The Individuals with Disabilities Education Act (IDEA) is the primary federal law providing funding and policy guidance for the education of students with disabilities; its major policy goals have remained constant since the IDEA's predecessor, Public Law 94-142, was enacted in 1975. The IDEA is basically a grants program that provides funds to states to serve students with disabilities in need of special education on the condition that the states ensure an appropriate education for them. The IDEA is also a civil rights law extending the constitutional right to equality of educational opportunity to students with disabilities needing special education. The law sets out three basic requirements with which states and local districts must comply:

• All children with disabilities and in need of special education must be provided a free, appropriate public education.
• Each child's education must be determined on an individualized basis and designed to meet his or her unique needs in the least restrictive environment.
• The rights of children and their families must be ensured and protected through procedural safeguards.

The primary mechanism for ensuring that the educational objectives of the IDEA are met is the individualized education program (IEP) that must be prepared for each child identified as having a disability and in need of special education. The IEP is a written statement that describes the child's current level of educational performance, the annual goals and short-term objectives that have been established for him or her, the specific educational and related support services to be provided, and procedures for evaluating progress on the stated goals and objectives.

The IDEA is the second-largest federal program supporting elementary and secondary education and currently provides about $2.3 billion a year to help fund the extra costs associated with educating students with disabilities. When Public Law 94-142 was passed, the initial funding to states was 5 percent of the estimated excess costs of special education. The legislation authorized the phasing in of additional support, with the goal that the federal government would fund 40 percent of the average excess costs of special education by 1981. That objective has never been met. At its highest level, in 1979, the federal appropriation reached 12.5 percent of the excess costs. Currently, federal aid provides about 7 percent of the excess cost, with states and localities responsible for the remainder (Box 2-1).

The centerpiece of the law is Part B, which authorizes the grants to states and outlines the requirements that states and districts must meet as a condition of funding. Part B is permanently authorized. However, other sections of the IDEA, which authorize funding for various discretionary grant programs, expire every 3 to 5 years.

Although the IDEA is both a civil rights statute and an education statute, the line between the two aspects is blurred. As one commentator has suggested, its legislative history shows that Congress clearly intended not to choose between these two goals and purposely left to state and local officials the responsibility for defining an appropriate education and deciding various policy issues, such as the resource trade-offs between groups in meeting excellence and equity goals. Furthermore, Congress purposely left resolution of these matters to evolve over time rather than setting specific national educational priorities (Yudof, 1984). The advent of standards-based education reform is a prime opportunity for testing how the excellence and equity goals for students with disabilities that were sought by Congress have evolved over time.

Section 504 of the Rehabilitation Act of 1973

Because the IDEA is essentially a federal grants program, state participation is voluntary and the act's requirements are imposed on states and local districts only if they choose to accept the funding. All states are currently accepting IDEA funding. However, even in its absence, school districts would still have a legal obligation to serve students with disabilities because of two federal civil rights

BOX 2-1   Special Education Costs and Financing

The exact amount spent on the education of students with disabilities is unknown. The federal government no longer requires states to report the statewide cost of their special education programs, and many states do not collect this information. The most recent national study of the cost of special education found that the expenditure for the average special education student is 2.3 times that of the average general education student, but this study is based on 10-year-old data (Moore et al., 1988). Using this cost ratio, the Center for Special Education Finance has estimated that the *marginal* cost of special education was $32.3 billion for the 1993-94 school year, about 14 percent of total education spending in that year (Parrish, 1996).

The lack of precise information about special education costs has meant that public perceptions of these costs vary considerably. Recent articles in the education and popular press have described the growing proportion of local district budgets spent on special education, often focusing on the small group of special education students who are the most expensive to educate or who attend private special education schools at public expense (e.g., Toch, 1995; Schnaiberg, 1995a; Stanfield, 1995). Such articles have generated calls for greater attention to these costs and for financing methods that are less burdensome on local districts. At the same time, however, national public opinion data indicate that the overwhelming majority of the American public does not know how much special education services cost or what proportion of students receive them. Only 7 percent estimated that the average special education student costs at least twice as much as the average general education student; 75 percent assumed the differential to be much lower; and 44 percent assumed that over 20 percent of all students are receiving these services (Elam et al., 1996). So, although special education costs continue to be a factor in policy debates and local district resource decisions, they are typically not informed by current, accurate data.

Although it is difficult to document levels of and trends in spending on programs for students with disabilities, two recent studies of a small number of school districts and one state suggest that special education expenditures have grown more rapidly than those for general education. Both studies, which examined the allocation of spending increases, found that 38 percent of new education dollars spent in the 1970s and 1980s were allocated to special education (Lankford and Wyckoff, 1995; Rothstein and Miles, 1995). However, a decomposition of changes in special education expenditures in one of the studies shows that most of this growth was attributable to increases in special education enrollments. Although enrollment growth accounted for most of the cost increase, changes in the *composition* of special education enrollments over time in New York also drove changes in the cost of that state's program (Lankford and Wyckoff, 1996). Parrish (1996) estimates that, even when adjusted for changes in enrollment, special education costs have risen 20 to 100 times faster than costs for the general education student. Regardless of the reasons for increased special education costs, when budgets were tight in New York in the early 1990s, spending on students with disabilities absorbed most of the few new dollars available to local school districts (Lankford and Wyckoff, 1995).

The categorical nature of much special needs funding is another issue in special education financing. Historically, state and federal funds for special needs students—students with disabilities, students who are economically or educationally disadvantaged, and students with limited English proficiency—have come with conditions attached to ensure fiscal and programmatic accountability. For example, school districts must ensure that special needs funds supplement and do not supplant general operating funds and that they are used for special education services and students. These fiscal accountability rules have served as an incentive for schools and districts to segregate special education services and students to maintain a clear audit trail (Moore et al., 1983; Knapp et al., 1983), and they appear to limit local program flexibility. In addition, many researchers and policy makers have argued that the structure of federal and state special education funding formulas creates an incentive for school districts to place students in more, rather than less, restrictive placements. Research on the actual impact of state funding formulas on special education services is limited and reports mixed results (e.g., Hasazi et al., 1994, cited in Parrish, 1995; Coleman et al., 1994; O'Reilly, 1996). Nevertheless, a few states have enacted census-based funding formulas, which allocate funds to local districts based on an assumed proportion of students with disabilities (e.g., 10 percent of total enrollment) rather than on the actual number of students identified as having disabilities and needing special education. This change is viewed as a way to discourage districts from over-identifying special education students.

statutes: Section 504 of the Rehabilitation Act of 1974 and the Americans with Disabilities Act of 1990.

Section 504 prohibits discrimination, solely on the basis of disability, against otherwise qualified persons in federally assisted programs and activities. It applies to virtually all public schools, since the overwhelming majority receive some form of federal assistance. In the context of elementary and secondary education, the regulations implementing Section 504 require that local districts provide a free, appropriate public education to each school-age child, regardless of the nature or severity of the person's disability.

Although many of the steps taken to comply with the IDEA's requirement for a free and appropriate public education also meet some of the requirements under Section 504, Section 504 differs from the IDEA in four significant ways. First, Section 504 applies to any educational institution, public or private, that receives any type of federal funding, making its reach broader than that of the IDEA. Second, as a civil rights statute designed to ensure nondiscrimination and equality of opportunity, Section 504 requires that comparable educational benefits be provided to individuals with and without disabilities. Third, whereas the IDEA addresses individuals with disabilities who need special education, Section 504 defines and protects a broader category of these individuals, whether or not they require special education programs or related services. So, for example, elementary and secondary students requiring only special accommodations but not special education are covered by Section 504. Fourth, Section 504 requires the provision of reasonable accommodations for individuals with disabilities who are otherwise qualified to participate in an educational program or activity.

Americans with Disabilities Act

The Americans with Disabilities Act of 1990 (ADA) is a comprehensive federal civil rights statute that provides a "national mandate to end discrimination against individuals with disabilities in private-sector employment, all public services and public accommodations, transportation, and telecommunications" (Hardman et al., 1996:13). The ADA requires "reasonable accommodations," a term that has not yet been definitively interpreted by the courts. Perhaps the greatest impact of the ADA on the education of students with disabilities is the increasing availability of accommodations for persons in the private sector in employment, recreation, living arrangements, and mobility, thus necessitating a more comprehensive effort to prepare students for greater participation in community settings.

The ADA's Title II mirrors the nondiscrimination provisions of Section 504. It extends civil rights protections for otherwise qualified persons with disabilities to include services, programs, and activities provided by "public entities," which include state and local governments and their instrumentalities. Consequently, access to state and local programs must be provided irrespective of the receipt of federal funding. Thus, even public schools not covered by other federal laws governing special education must comply with the ADA.

State Laws

In addition to the federal laws governing the education of students with disabilities, all states and many local governments have enacted statutes and regulations designed to promote the rights of students with disabilities. Since states must have a plan to qualify for IDEA funds, all have enacted special education statutes that incorporate the major provisions of the IDEA. Some state laws, however, extend beyond the federal criteria for an appropriate education. Melnick (1994) notes, for example, that Massachusetts law refers to the "maximum possible development of handicapped children" and that New Jersey's statute establishes the principle that all students "be assured the fullest possible opportunity to develop their intellectual capacities" (p. 174). The First, Third, and Ninth U.S. Circuit Courts have all argued that the IDEA should be interpreted to include such state laws.

Because the U.S. Constitution does not create a fundamental right to education (*San Antonio Independent School District* v. *Rodriguez*, 411 U.S. 1, 1973), the constitutions of all 50 states contain provisions setting forth each state's responsibilities for educating its citizens. Over the past 25 years, lawsuits have been brought in 27 states alleging that the state system for financing and operating public schools violates these constitutional mandates. Early cases focused solely on funding inequities, aiming to increase and more equitably distribute resources among local school districts. Some recent cases have gone further, challenging the substantive adequacy of state education support. These required state courts to assess the impact of state constitutional language specifying the parameters of an adequate education. In six states, a constitutionally adequate public education system has been defined as one that enables students to meet the broad educational outcomes anticipated by the relevant state constitutional provisions. In five others, the courts have held states to a less precise standard, but one that still requires the public schools to provide students with an education sufficient to allow them to function in society (McCusic, 1991; Underwood, 1995). [21]

The outcomes articulated in this subset of school finance cases are part of what constitutes an appropriate education in a particular state for the purposes of the IDEA's definition of free, appropriate public education. In Kentucky, for example, the state supreme court held that the Kentucky constitution, which requires that the legislature "provide for an efficient system of common schools throughout the state," means that "*every* child . . . must be provided with an equal opportunity to have an adequate education"; the court then went on to specify a

---

[21]Not all plaintiffs have been successful, however, in challenging the constitutionality of state funding systems. Over the past eight years, plaintiffs were unsuccessful in six states.

number of outcomes that could be expected for educated persons (*Rose* v. *Council for Better Education*, 790 S.W. 2d 186, 1989). In another state case that specifically assessed school finance issues affecting students with disabilities, the Alabama supreme court held that constitutionally adequate education for students with disabilities was the same as that for all children, in addition to whatever special education law required (*Alabama Coalition for Equity* v. *Hunt*, 19 IDELR 810; see also *Opinion of the Justices of the Alabama Supreme Court* no. 3, 624 So. 2d 107, 1993). These outcomes can also serve as a baseline against which the opportunities afforded children with disabilities may be compared for purposes of determining if the state meets the provisions for nondiscrimination required under the ADA and Section 504 (Ordover et al., 1996).

Rationale Behind the Special Education Policy Framework

Current policy frameworks for special education were initiated by an alliance of families and professionals working with individuals with disabilities and advocacy groups dedicated to disability rights. Special education policy in the United States over the past 25 years is a direct response to a history in which students with disabilities were either excluded entirely from educational opportunities or were often segregated in inadequate programs in inadequate facilities (Sarason and Doris, 1979; Minow, 1990). Current special education policy also reflects the evolving professional practices, knowledge base, and interests of educators and other professionals working with persons with disabilities.

As one commentator has noted, "The history of special education has been a tale of exclusion—the exclusion of the handicapped from schools and the exclusion of their representatives from participation in educational policymaking" (Tweedie, 1983:48). Even the advent of compulsory attendance laws in most states in the period between 1852 and the end of World War I allowed local school officials to routinely exempt from attendance requirements students who were deemed "uneducable" (Mayer, 1975; Lazerson, 1983). In addition to, or as a part of, compulsory attendance laws, many states maintained statutes that permitted the exclusion of certain types of educationally difficult children from school (Trudeau, 1971). Although a number of private schools were established in the nineteenth century for children with certain types of disabilities, particularly deaf and blind children, little public schooling was available for students with disabilities before 1900.

By the early twentieth century, public education programs for students with disabilities gradually began to be implemented. However, a 1972 report estimated that only 40 percent of all children with disabilities were being provided educational services (Weintraub et al., 1971), and congressional committees, during the debate leading to the passage of Public Law 94-142, concluded that more than half of the children with disabilities in the country were not receiving an education appropriate to their needs (Aleman, 1995).

The first goal for special education policy in the second half of this century has been access to education for all students with disabilities. Between 1966 and 1974, 38 states and the U.S. Congress passed statutes that began to address this goal. Access to education was expanded to embrace several key policy goals: "zero reject," the concept that every child with a disability is educable; the principle that, to the maximum extent appropriate, students with disabilities should be educated in the same settings and classrooms as their peers without disabilities; the provision of individually appropriate education for all students with disabilities; and the use of procedural safeguards to protect the rights of students with disabilities (Minow, 1990; Tweedie, 1983; Sarason and Doris, 1979; Butts et al., 1953).

The most significant early victories of the disability rights advocates occurred in two pieces of litigation: the 1971 case of *Pennsylvania Association for Retarded Children (PARC)* v. *Commonwealth of Pennsylvania* (334 F. Supp. 1257 E.D. Pa., 1971, 343 F. Supp. 279 E.D. Pa. 1972) and a 1972 case, *Mills* v. *Board of Education of the District of Columbia* (348 F. Supp. 866, 1972). The settlement agreement reached by the parties in the *PARC* case and the court decision in the *Mills* case served as models for many state legislatures and for Congress as they wrote new legislation to ensure equality of educational opportunity for children with disabilities. The U.S. Supreme Court affirmed that these state efforts and the IDEA were means to aid states in "complying with their constitutional obligations to provide public education for handicapped children" (*Smith* v. *Robinson*, 468 U.S. 992, at 1009, 1984).

Guiding Assumptions and Whether They Are Being Met

State and federal policies for the education of students with disabilities are based on a common set of assumptions that were first embodied in the legislative and judicial determinations of the early to mid-1970s. Here we describe the assumptions undergirding special education policy, assess available evidence about their current status, and consider the impact of standards-based reform on these assumptions.

All Students Can Learn

The most fundamental assumption of state and federal special education policy is that all students with disabilities can learn and that all, no matter the nature or severity of their disability, should be given access to an appropriate public education. Neither the federal nor any state statute has attempted to specify *what* children with disabilities could or should learn. Instead, an individual determination is to be made for each student, guided by the requirements of the IDEA.

One of the benchmarks for assessing whether the goal of education for all students with disabilities is being met is participation rates. In the 1992-93 school year, almost 4.5 million children with disabilities were served by programs aided with IDEA funds (Aleman, 1995:35). As noted by the Congressional Research Service (Aleman, 1995:8), "wholesale numbers of children with disabilities are no longer being denied equal access to public education." There are, however, some areas for concern about the participation of students with disabilities in elementary and secondary education. For example, high school dropout rates are higher for students with disabilities than for those without (see Chapter 3). There are also concerns in many states, such as Massachusetts, that students with disabilities are increasingly denied access to education because of disciplinary exclusions from school through long-term suspensions and permanent expulsions (Aleman, 1995). There remain considerable disagreements over the quality of the services provided to groups of students and individuals.

No one disputes that access to educational services for students with disabilities has improved dramatically. To the extent that large numbers of students with disabilities were excluded from schooling entirely when the federal laws were first passed, the goal of greater inclusion of students with disabilities in elementary and secondary education programs began to be realized within the first decade of the statute's passage. However, concern over educational outcomes for students with disabilities began growing in the mid-1980s, with the publication of follow-up studies documenting high unemployment and social isolation among former special education students (Edgar et al., 1986; Hasazi et al., 1985; Mithaug et al., 1985). Studies such as the National Longitudinal Transition Study (Wagner et al., 1993; see Chapter 3 for further discussion) focused attention on the long-term outcomes of special education.

As a result, attention has shifted away from questions of access to ones about the quality of education received by students with disabilities (Aleman, 1995). Consistent with this focus, attention has also shifted to how students with disabilities have fared during their school careers and the extent to which they are included in assessment and accountability systems (McLaughlin and Warren, 1992; National Center on Educational Outcomes, 1992; Brauen et al., 1994). Similarly, attention has turned from a focus on the IEP as an instrument for documenting procedural compliance to the IEP as a vehicle for ensuring school district accountability for student outcomes.

Students with Disabilities Can Be Accurately Identified for Education Services

The provisions of the federal IDEA and Section 504 and the requirements of most state special education laws that require an individualized, appropriate education for students with disabilities rest on two key assumptions about student evaluation and identification. First, students are not eligible for coverage under the laws unless they have either been identified as "disabled" and in need of special education or, under Section 504, are either "disabled" or "regarded as being disabled." Consequently, a process has to be undertaken to determine whether each individual is eligible for the procedural protections or services each law provides. Second, the laws require a process to evaluate each individual with a disability in order to identify the student's capabilities and needs and the appropriate programs and services. Whether the current technology for student identification is sufficient to meet these two assumptions is an issue worthy of further inquiry (see Chapter 3).

Under the IDEA and most state special education laws, a student is either eligible or not under the statute, a distinction that is somewhat at odds with current professional practice, which assumes more of a continuum of disability dimensions.

The federal regulations implementing the IDEA note that the statute applies only to students with learning problems based on a disability and not to students whose special needs stem from "environmental, cultural, or economic disadvantage" (CFR, Title 34, Subtitle B, Chapter III, Section 300.7 [b][10]). These distinctions are not always easily made or even possible, given that such factors as prenatal nutrition and environmental pollution can lead to bona fide disabling conditions.

As we discuss in greater detail in Chapter 3, there is a great deal of variability from place to place in the criteria used to define disability and in the local implementing conditions for deciding who qualifies as having a disability. For some students with disabilities (e.g., those with physical or sensory disabilities), the criteria are clear. However, for those with disabilities, such as learning disabilities, mild mental retardation, and serious emotional disturbance, the criteria are much less clear and the implementation practices more variable. Furthermore, research on the extent to which students with mild forms of these disabilities can be distinguished reliably from other students variously called "low-achieving" and "educationally disadvantaged" is mixed (e.g., Lyon, 1996; Kavale et al., 1994). Consequently, decisions about which children have disabilities cannot be made reliably or consistently for some categories of disability. Furthermore, it is not clear that the current research base is adequate to allow such distinctions to be made. Although difficulties with eligibility policy and practice are widely acknowledged among special education researchers and practitioners, there is little consensus about solutions.

Besides a lack of consistent identification practices across schools, educators also face competing incentives in serving students who may have disabilities. For example, financial pressures on school districts and a lack of adequate federal and state support may make local officials reluctant to refer students for special education services even when they appear to meet relevant eligibility criteria. At the same time, some schools may view their special education program as a kind of organizational safety valve that allows inexperienced teachers to remove disruptive students from their classrooms, or that responds to the demands of vocal parents wanting additional assistance for their children. Consequently, they may refer students for special education services when other remedies are more appropriate. Although none of these reasons is an adequate or even legitimate basis for deciding whether students are eligible for services, they represent the realities of local implementation. Educators' efforts to balance their responsibilities by simultaneously serving all students, interpreting applicable legal requirements for individual children, working within existing fiscal and organizational constraints, and responding to parental concerns may result in some students receiving services in one school and being ineligible for them in another.

Students with Disabilities Are Entitled to an Appropriate Education

The IDEA rests on an assumption that the best way to achieve an appropriate education for students with disabilities is to design a program of education and related services through the IEP process. The process of teachers, other service providers, and parents working together to define an appropriate program and services is as important as the IEP document itself (Zettel, 1982). Consequently, parents and educators have come to rely on the IEP as the keystone of special education, and the IEP process and the resulting document have become integral parts of special education, irrespective of the legal mandate (S. Smith, 1990). The IEP process includes both substantive protections governing a student's educational program and procedural requirements fostering a parental role in educational planning and ensuring an independent review mechanism if irresolvable disputes arise between educators and the family over how or where to educate the student.

Research has documented several shortcomings of the IEP, particularly as an accountability tool. Persistent concerns relate to the lack of parental participation and the effectiveness of that participation (Harry et al., 1995; Singer and Butler, 1987; see Chapter 3); limited instructional usefulness (Giangreco et al., 1994; S. Smith, 1990); and a lack of connection to the general education curriculum and instruction (Giangreco et al., 1994; Pugach and Warger, 1993; Sands et al., 1995). These problems may be due not to flaws in the basic concept of individualized educational planning, but to logistical issues such as lack of time for development or excessive paperwork burdens.[22] Similarly, the limited utility of many current IEPs may also be attributable to a lack of clarity about the curricular function of the IEP or confusion about the nature and extent of standards-based reform in educational decision making for students with disabilities. Some studies have indicated that teachers find that the IEP is not useful as a classroom pedagogical device (Smith and Brownell, 1995), although it was not really intended to be that.

The IEP requirement for individualization has also led to variability in the

---

[22]Although one study reported that, 10 years into the implementation of the law, districts had begun to overcome the paperwork burden resulting from the IDEA (Research Triangle Institute, 1980; Stanford Research Institute, 1982; Singer and Butler, 1987).

implementation of the IDEA. Evaluation, placement, and programming decisions for students with disabilities are intended to be idiosyncratic. And, although bureaucratic efficiency promotes standardization, individualization and
parental input exert counterpressures.

The state and federal courts have played a role in refining the IDEA's statutory and regulatory requirements for appropriate and individualized education for
students with disabilities. Several cases are particularly important in the context
of standards-based reform. The first case under the IDEA considered by the U.S.
Supreme Court was *Board of Education of Hendrick Hudson Central School District* v. *Rowley* (458 U.S. 176, 1982). The case involved Amy Rowley, a deaf
elementary school student with excellent lip-reading skills who performed above
average educationally and advanced easily from grade to grade; the focus of the
dispute was a conflict over the extent of related services required. The Supreme
Court held that, in order to be "appropriate," the package of special education and
related services provided to a child with disabilities must be designed in conformity with the IDEA's procedural requirements and must be reasonably calculated
to enable her to receive educational benefits. The Court also held that, to assess
appropriateness of education (458 U.S. at 188-89, emphasis added):

> Almost as a checklist for adequacy under the Act, the definition requires that
> such [specially designed] instruction and services be provided at public expense
> and under public supervision, *meet the State's educational standards*, approxi-
> mate the grade levels *used in the State's regular education*, and comport with
> the child's IEP. . . . Thus, if personalized instruction is being provided with
> sufficient support services to permit the child to benefit from instruction, *and the
> other items on the definitional checklist are satisfied*, the child is receiving a
> "free appropriate education" as defined by the Act.

The Court expressly declined to establish any one test for appropriateness, but
since Amy Rowley was receiving substantial special services and was performing
above average in a regular classroom, it limited its analysis to that situation and
concluded that she was receiving an appropriate education.

The *Rowley* case received considerable attention, but it was in many ways a
poor case to guide educators and judges in future disputes since it involved a
student who, despite her parent's requests for more special education services,
was doing quite well. However, for several years the case was the only Supreme
Court precedent to provide guidance in interpreting and applying the IDEA.

When lower courts have applied the *Rowley* test to the facts in individual
cases, they have had no difficulty judging the procedural due process portion of
the test. The issue of what constitutes a beneficial education has been more
difficult, but the lower courts have followed the Supreme Court standard and
have not substituted their judgment for that of educators on pedagogical or meth-
odological questions; school districts have generally been successful in court if
they could demonstrate that they made an earnest attempt to do all they could for
a student (Broadwell and Walden, 1988).

The biggest problem for parents, educators, hearing officers, and judges trying to implement the *Rowley* standards is that the case was simply unclear on how to deal with much more difficult issues, such as the meaning of the IDEA's requirement for education in the least restrictive environment, access to year-round schooling, and the provision of services to students who, unlike Amy Rowley, were not in general education and performing above average compared with their peers.

Initially, lower courts reacted in most cases to *Rowley* by holding that the IEP, and the educational programs called for in the IEP, were appropriate if they resulted in at least some educational benefit for the student, even if the benefit was minimal (Osborne, 1996). Eventually, the lower courts began to expand their interpretations of the "educational benefit" criteria, as did the U.S. Supreme Court in a subsequent decision (*Irving Independent School District* v. *Tatro, 468 U.S. 883, 1984*, relying heavily on an equality of opportunity approach in giving a broad definition to the term *related services*; see Wegner, 1985; Gallegos, 1989). However, all the federal courts were uniform in determining that maximization of educational benefit for a student with disabilities was not required unless this higher standard of service had been adopted by a state legislature (Osborne, 1996; Rothstein, 1990; Strope and Broadwell, 1990; Wegner, 1985).

Some commentators have asserted that the lower federal courts have not been uniform in following the *Rowley* standard (Neal and Kirp, 1985; Wegner, 1985; Melnick, 1994; Weber, 1990). Others have argued that the courts have utilized the *Rowley* standard and applied it to the disputes about individualized appropriateness before them (Broadwell and Walden, 1988; Gallegos, 1989; Rothstein, 1990; Strope and Broadwell, 1990; Turnbull, 1993; Osborne, 1996). At least one prominent commentator, assessing the impact of the post-*Rowley* cases, has noted that the lower courts have widely applied the essence of that decision, the standard of requiring that a student be provided educational benefit, but not a benefit that would maximize the student's potential. These courts apply the educational benefit standard on a case-by-case basis, with the student's present placement, diagnosis, disability, and capability all taken into account to make an individualized determination of what is appropriate for the student. In the inevitable determinations that courts must make in choosing between at least two different proposed placements or programs, the courts have tended to follow a "balancing of benefits" approach. In this approach, the courts consider the student's capability to make educational progress; appropriate education and educational benefits requirements are met whenever one placement is likely to result in higher outcomes for a student than another and the program uses appropriate curricula to meet the student's needs. Only a minority of cases, most of them less recent, reject the balancing of benefits approach (Turnbull, 1993).

Despite some disagreement among commentators on the impact of the *Rowley* decision on the lower courts, a legal analysis prepared for the committee indicates that the *Rowley* criteria provide clear guidance for defining an appropriate education for students with disabilities under standards-based reform. Under the *Rowley* standards, an appropriate education should include elementary and secondary education as defined by state standards and should be designed to provide educational benefit. In a standards-based system, then, a free and appropriate education includes the special education and related services necessary to allow students to attain the outcomes set forth for them, as well as any programming needed to address their supplemental, individualized educational needs (Ordover et al., 1996).

Students with Disabilities Should Be Educated in the Least Restrictive Educational Environment

In addition to decreasing the number of students with disabilities who are excluded from education, federal laws also sought to ensure that, whenever possible, participation in special education classes would be reduced in favor of placement in the regular classroom (Benveniste, 1986). The requirement for educating students with disabilities in the least restrictive environment is rooted in the belief that the approach will remove stigma from these students, enhance and normalize their social status (e.g., Nirge, 1970; Wolfensberger, 1970), facilitate modeling of appropriate behavior, provide a richer educational environment, be more flexible and cost-effective, and enhance broader public acceptance of people with disabilities (Weatherley, 1979; Minow, 1990).

The issue of what constitutes education in the least restrictive environment is one of the more controversial issues currently confronting special education, particularly among educators, some parents, and more than a few public officials. State and federal statutes specify that, in determining what constitutes the least restrictive environment, the IEP team is to begin with the general education classroom and consider which supports or accommodations can be made; only after determining that this environment would not afford appropriate education should more restrictive placements be considered. School districts must maintain or make available a continuum of placements, including special classrooms, schools, and even residential or other instruction. Students with disabilities should be removed from general education settings only to the extent essential to meet their individual needs.

Many students with disabilities are currently being educated in general education classrooms for a large part of their school day. Recent data indicate that more than 70 percent of students with disabilities spend at least 40 percent of the school day in the regular classroom (U.S. Department of Education, 1996a; see also Chapter 3). The issue of least restrictive environment for these students is not whether they can access the general education classroom, but whether appropriate types and levels of support will be provided entirely in the general education classroom or partially in a specialized environment such as a resource room, pullout program, special classroom, or separate school. In the past 10 years, there have been many calls to include students with disabilities more fully in general education (Will, 1986; Gartner and Lipsky, 1987; Stainback and Stainback, 1984; Wang et al., 1986).

Nevertheless, some parents and advocates, as well as students themselves, view separate and specialized support services as necessary for students with disabilities to meet the demands of the general education curriculum or to attain adequate levels of essential skills. They maintain that a continuum of placement options should be available, and one should be selected only after educational appropriateness is determined (Bateman, 1994; Learning Disabilities Association of America, 1993; Kauffman and Lloyd, 1995). The educational goals defined for many students with disabilities include increased academic competence and emotional well-being or positive social behaviors. Since research has yet to demonstrate that these important outcomes can always be obtained in general education classrooms (e.g., Fuchs et al., 1993; Jenkins et al., 1991), the resulting tension between those advocating inclusion and those wanting to maintain a continuum of placements is strong (Fuchs and Fuchs, 1994; Kauffman and Hallahan, 1993; Shanker, 1994).

From the perspective of standards-based reform, however, the issue is not *where* students with disabilities receive their education, but whether they have access to a challenging curriculum and high-quality instruction consistent with state and local standards. Most disability advocates seek the participation of students with disabilities in key reform initiatives, such as high common standards, large-scale assessments, and curricular reforms, regardless of what stance they take on the general inclusion issue. These advocates endorse higher standards and higher expectations for all students and seek to give students access to a broad and balanced curriculum.

Generally, the courts have held that the least restrictive environment mandate is secondary to provision of an appropriate program and services, and that both program and placement decisions should be individualized. Thus, the degree of integration into general education is intertwined with determinations of what the educational goals should be and whether specialized services can be effectively provided in general education environments. A number of recent lawsuits have focused on the standards and criteria for assessing whether the least restrictive environment requirement has been met for a particular child (e.g., *Board of Education, Sacramento City Unified School District* v. *Holland*, 14 F. 3d 1398, 9th Cir. 1994; *Oberti* v. *Board of Education of Borough of Clementon*, 995 F. 2d 1204, 3rd Cir. 1993; *Daniel R.R.* v. *State Board of Education*, 874 F. 2d 1036 [5th Cir. 1984]). These cases support the right to full participation of students with disabilities in the general education environment.

Another related issue of increasing concern is the large number of students with disabilities who are exempted from local and statewide accountability systems used to evaluate school and district effectiveness in helping students meet desired educational outcomes (Brauen et al., 1994). These systems employ a

variety of accountability measures related to student participation (e.g., attendance, promotion/retention, suspension/expulsion, and graduation) and student
performance (e.g., attainment of minimum competency or common standards).
Excluding large numbers of students with disabilities from these systems has
resulted in a lack of accountability for the success of their educational programs.

In conjunction with the requirement for the least restrictive environment, the
IDEA's definition of an appropriate education requires that the goals and content
of specially designed instruction and related services be designed with reference
to public education, as defined by state law and practice. The IDEA and its
implementing regulations require states and local school systems to adopt and
implement a goal of providing "full educational opportunity" to all children with
disabilities (20 U.S.C. 1412[2][a], 1414[a][1][c]; 34 C.F.R. 300.304). When
states adopt content and student performance standards and aligned curricula,
these define "an appropriate . . . elementary or secondary education in the State
involved," pursuant to the IDEA requirements.

Accommodations Should Be Provided

In order to afford students with disabilities a fair and even playing field, the
laws specify that accommodations in educational services should take into account students' needs stemming from their disabilities. These accommodations,
however, must be reasonable and are required only for students who are otherwise qualified to participate in an educational program or activity. Courts have
held that the provisions of Section 504 do not require states or schools to alter the
content of a minimum competency test used to award high school diplomas, in
that a substantial modification would unreasonably alter the graduation requirement, but they do require the implementation of IEPs that facilitate successful
participation by students with disabilities (*Brookhart* v. *Illinois State Board of
Education*, 697 F. 2d; see also *Board of Education of Northport-East Northport
Union Free School District* v. *Ambach*, 60 N.Y. 2d 758).

Although states or school districts using assessments for high-stakes purposes, such as the awarding of high school diplomas, are not required to modify
the educational content they measure, they can be required to provide accommodations in administering a test or assessment. For example, the Office for Civil
Rights of the U.S. Department of Education has required, under Section 504, that
Hawaii provide a reader for a student with a learning disability during a high
school graduation examination, as it has provided readers for blind students. It
ruled that the state discriminated against the student in violation of Section 504
because it failed to provide him adjustments necessary to offer him an equal
opportunity to pass the test; the Office for Civil Rights noted that "equal opportunity to obtain the same result" on the test, required under Section 504 regulations,
necessitates that the tests be administered so as to measure the student's proficiency in the subject tested, rather than his or her unrelated disability.

Parental Participation Should Be Encouraged
Consistent with Procedural Protections

Parental involvement in the education of children with disabilities is a key principle of the IDEA. The legislation gives parents many procedural rights, responsibilities, and opportunities to shape the education of their children with disabilities. Both the state and federal laws include procedural protections for families during the special education evaluation and placement processes to ensure a mechanism for family participation in decision making and for impartial review of disputes that may arise between a family and educators about the education of a student with a disability. As the U.S. Supreme Court noted in the *Rowley* case, educators' compliance with procedural protections is a crucial element for ensuring that the appropriateness requirements of the IDEA are met.

The IDEA requires parents to be notified before their child is evaluated for special education services and requires their consent prior to an initial evaluation for placement in a special education program. Parents have the right to participate in planning their children's instructional program, to review educational records, and to obtain independent educational evaluations. They also have the right to receive prior written notice of significant school decisions and to file a complaint regarding decisions or actions with which they disagree. Parents are entitled to have an administrative due process hearing on all such complaints and to file a lawsuit if they do not prevail (Ordover et al., 1996:109).

Many special educators believe the parents' role in developing the educational program, particularly the IEP, is the cornerstone of parental involvement in special education. The IEP creates opportunities for parents and professionals to develop individualized approaches for every student's education, including setting long-term goals and short-term objectives, specifying evaluation measures, determining the related services to be provided and accommodations required, and deciding on student placement and involvement in the general curriculum.

The IDEA parental provisions have multiple objectives. First, the law recognizes and seeks to reinforce the positive effects that parents can have on learning and school success for children with disabilities, just as all parents can do for their children. (See Chapter 3 for further discussion of parental involvement and the educational experiences of children with disabilities.) Second, the IDEA acknowledges the critical caretaking responsibilities, support functions, and strong concerns about their children's futures assumed by parents of children with disabilities. Third, the legislation recognizes that parents, above all others, have a deep, abiding interest in the quality of their children's education and their general well-being; therefore, the law places the major burden of enforcement and accountability on parents.

This advocacy role for parents is the culmination of an evolutionary process. Public Law 94-142 broke new ground in 1975 by granting active decision-making rights to parents of children with disabilities. In doing so, Congress accepted the basic premise that public schools may not always, of their own accord, provide an appropriate education for children with disabilities and may need prodding from parents, who have the strongest incentives to ensure that their children receive the services and rights to which they are entitled. No longer were parents expected to be passive recipients of professional decisions about their children, but instead they were to become decision makers and monitors of their children's education (Turnbull and Turnbull, in press).

One of the most significant factors in the implementation of state and federal special education policy is that the burden of enforcement largely rests on parents and advocacy groups. Yet parents have generally been reluctant to pursue procedural protections (Weatherley, 1979; Engel, 1991). With a few exceptions when advocacy groups have become involved, most of those who have pursued procedural remedies have been more affluent families.

Standards-based reform may trigger disagreements between individual parents and educators about appropriate IEP goals and objectives, the content of instruction, and the use of alternate performance standards or assessments. Some parents may also invoke their procedural rights when such disputes arise—whether through participation on the IEP team or the filing of a complaint. Parents invoking these rights will do so within the substantive framework of the child's right to receive a free, appropriate public education as defined by the IDEA, with maximum appropriate integration with nondisabled peers.

The use of procedural protections to ensure students with disabilities access to appropriate education has resulted in the "legalization" of special education (Neal and Kirp, 1985; Yudof, 1984). By 1982, there had been nearly 300 federal and state court cases bearing on the meaning of Public Law 94-142, mostly concerning disputes over IEPs (Yudof, 1984). One study estimated that, during the 1980s, there were 342 reported federal cases and 99 reported state cases under the predecessor legislation to the IDEA (Zirkel and Richardson, 1989).

Although several commentators have decried what they perceive as a frightening increase in litigiousness on special education issues (Melnick, 1994; Zirkel and Richardson, 1989), the total number of administrative hearings and court cases seems quite small given the millions of students receiving special education under the IDEA and the detailed substantive and procedural protections built into this law. Concerns about the volume of hearings and court activity are also offset by the fact that the majority of the cases have been won by school districts (Kuriloff, 1985; Winnick, 1987). Several studies have indicated that parents win only a minority of the hearings; according to one study of four years of hearings in Pennsylvania, parents achieved some form of victory in only 35 percent of the hearings, a percentage paralleled in a Massachusetts study and in a nationwide survey of 42 states (Kuriloff, 1985).

A more pertinent question is what effect legalization has had on the daily activities of educators, the relationships between educators and families, and the educational opportunities of students with disabilities. Studies of the implementation of the 1972 Massachusetts legislation, one of the first state statutes designed to ensure the provision of equality of educational opportunity for students with disabilities and a prototype for Public Law 94-142, concluded that teachers and administrators incorporated the new legal requirements into their daily practice, in effect making new policies consistent with, and easily accommodated into, their existing practices and procedures (Weatherley and Lipsky, 1977; Weatherley, 1979; see also Wise, 1979).

However, the efforts of well-meaning educators to cope with the added demands of the new policy requirements when resources are limited has resulted in priorities that have often benefited the affluent and penalized the poor (Budoff and Orenstein, 1982; Weatherley, 1979; Singer and Butler, 1987; Neal and Kirp, 1985). It has been easier for educators to comply with the procedural rather than substantive components of IEP requirements (Smith and Brownell, 1995; see also Clune and Van Pelt, 1985; Neal and Kirp, 1985). The combination of detailed legal requirements and insufficient resources has forced local educators to ration resources, sometimes by "slotting" or mass processing students into categories for diagnosis and service to promote administrative efficiency and keep down the cost of services (Weatherley, 1979; Handler, 1986). In these situations, the IEP process often becomes one of political bargaining, with enormous pressures on parents to comply with educators' recommendations. The collective result is considerable momentum against the high level of individualization required by state and federal laws (Weatherley, 1979; Handler, 1986).

CONCLUSIONS

The two policy frameworks that define standards-based reform and the education of students with disabilities embody potentially compatible goals. However, before those ideals can be melded into effective classroom practice, two major barriers must be overcome.

First, the expectations of those advocating standards-based reforms currently exceed the limits of existing professional practice and expert knowledge. Standards-based reform assumes that rigorous curriculum content, conveyed through sophisticated pedagogy, can be provided to students with diverse needs and abilities by teachers of varied experience and training. Yet research on the implementation of past education reforms and the experience of early implementers of standards-based policies indicate that translating these initiatives into widespread practice will require considerably more time and a greater investment in professional training than many states have been willing to expend. Similarly, one of the key assumptions of standards-based reform is that student performance can be accurately measured by new forms of assessment that will serve as both credible accountability mechanisms and strong instructional guides. Yet the transition away from a sole reliance on multiple-choice assessments has posed a host of technical challenges. Considerable progress has been made in addressing those problems, but technical solutions have come more slowly than the deadlines imposed by policy makers anxious to implement alternative assessments.

The professional and technical problems associated with standards-based reform are compounded when it is melded with special education. Some of these challenges, such as the curricular ones discussed in Chapter 4, stem partly from the historical separation between general and special education, each with its own research base and norms of professional practice. Other challenges are due to the different institutional arrangements that flow from the centrality of the IEP in special education and the emphasis on a common curriculum and public, aggregated forms of accountability in standards-based reform. Still other challenges flow from a lack of experience with the practices necessary for students with disabilities to participate in the standards movement. One example is the design of valid testing accommodations discussed in Chapter 5.

All these challenges are further complicated because they must be addressed within the rights-based framework of special education, which also has professional and technical limitations. For example, substantive decisions about the participation of students with disabilities in content standards must be made within an IEP process that has become increasingly routinized and procedural in its emphasis. Similarly, assessment accommodations for some students, such as those with cognitive disabilities, will be determined on the basis of a taxonomy of disability that lacks clear and objective identification criteria. Above all, standards-based reform brings into sharp focus the major challenge of special education: ensuring that students with disabilities have access to an appropriate education, with the particular content of that education specified not in law but individually through the IEP process. The challenge is to preserve the rights of individual students within the framework of common standards, with only general guidance from legal precedents and professional practices that have not yet been tested in the evolving context of standards policy.

Unfortunately, there are no quick or simple solutions to these professional and technical challenges. Most of them are likely to be solved or at least made more tractable over time. But progress will not occur without a continued investment in professional capacity-building and in clinical and psychometric research.

In its articulation of curricular standards and the design of new forms of assessment, the standards framework emphasizes the professional judgment of classroom teachers as well as that of subject-matter and testing experts. The special education framework has a set of legal entitlements at its core, but it too relies heavily on professional judgment to determine which educational services are appropriate to meet the needs of individual children. But politics, broadly defined, also shapes both policy frameworks, primarily through public values about what constitutes a good education, who is entitled to that education, and what kinds of resources should be devoted to it.

Consequently, the second barrier is a perceptual and political one that must also be overcome if students with disabilities are to participate in standards-based reform. *The broad range of people involved in the educational enterprise need to understand and to agree on what the phrase "all students can learn to high standards" really means. Survey data from teachers and the public suggest that, at a symbolic level, the idea is accepted. But there is considerably less agreement about its operational meaning—how the idea should be applied to individual students and implemented in classrooms, and what consequences should be imposed for nonattainment of the standards.*

The thorny issues of defining and operationalizing "all students" and "high standards" constitute one dimension of the political challenges facing standards-based reform. *Reaching consensus on what the specific standards should be—whether or not they are truly high or apply in the same way to all students—is an equally critical dimension.* The events of the past few years have demonstrated that the schools remain a major focal point for debates over the cultural values that divide Americans. Yet by definition the standards movement rests on the notion of common standards reflecting what the broader community wants its children to know and be able to do. Debates over the purposes of public schooling are a healthy part of the democratic process if they do not disrupt or impede children's education. Consequently, ways must be found to have those debates while still seeking consensus.

One lesson that emerges quite clearly from the experience of the states that implemented standards reforms early is that the development of new curriculum standards and assessments cannot be solely a technical process with participation limited to experts. Decisions as significant as what knowledge is most important for students to learn and how they should be tested on their mastery of it require open, public deliberation. That participation can be organized in any number of ways, including state-level review committees, forums in local communities sponsored by the Parent-Teachers Association or the League of Women Voters, informal gatherings in people's homes, and op-ed exchanges in local newspapers and on radio and television programs. Widespread participation should be encouraged from those representing the general and special education communities, from those with school-age children and those without, and from supporters and opponents of standards-based reform.

Because deliberation depends on the primacy of talk, it requires time and the willingness of participants to be open to viewpoints different from their own.[23]

---

[23]Clearly, deliberation alone does not ensure either consensual or productive decisions. Nevertheless, a variety of empirical evidence from social psychology, political science, and public opinion research indicates that individuals are more likely to approve of the decision-making process, understand outcomes better, and support them—even if they initially disagreed—if the decisional process is one that allows for all sides to speak and be considered (e.g., Tyler et al., 1989; Gamson, 1992). Perhaps the best-known recent demonstration of the impact of deliberation was the National Issues Convention, a gathering of 600 randomly selected, nationally representative citizens who discussed key issues with each other and with candidates running in the 1996 presidential primary elections. Opinion data were collected from participants before and after their deliberations, and the results

Such openness to new approaches may be especially difficult in special education, because the policy framework and professional practice are well established. Similarly, those outside special education have not really had to confront exactly what their exhortation for common standards really means for students with unique educational needs. Just as standards advocates have had to listen to and accommodate the preferences of those with different cultural values, so they must be open to students whose educational needs do not completely conform to their prior assumptions. Deliberation is difficult, but not to talk constructively across interests and communities is to mock the notion of common standards for public schools.

---

show that many changed their views on the interpretation of social and economic problems and on their preferences for government action. Participants' level of information about national issues increased and they reported feeling more politically efficacious. (Information about the National Issues Convention is available on the Internet at http:/www1.pbs.org/nic_background.html. Results of the pre- and post-deliberative polls are available at http://www1.pbs.org/nic/poll_results.html.)

3

The Diversity of Students with Disabilities

This chapter describes the tremendous diversity that characterizes students with disabilities. Most of these students are eligible to receive special education services provided by the public schools. Yet, as this chapter shows, one cannot really speak of them as a group in a meaningful way, except perhaps with respect to the rights that all are accorded under the Individuals with Disabilities Education Act (IDEA), Section 504 of the Rehabilitation Act of 1973, and the Americans with Disabilities Act (ADA) by virtue of their having a disability.

Some students with disabilities are never taken out of general education classrooms; others never enter a regular school building. Some have very mild disabilities observed only in school settings; others have multiple severe disabilities that affect many aspects of their lives. Some spend only minutes each week with a specially trained teacher, others the whole day. Some graduate from high school with a full academic courseload and go on to highly competitive colleges; others drop out of high school entirely; and still others receive special diplomas or certificates of attendance. Some have parents who are deeply involved in advocating and planning their individualized programs; others have parents who have never attended an IEP meeting.

Meaningful discussion of standards, curriculum, assessment, and outcomes cannot occur without some attention to the varied characteristics of these large numbers of children. This chapter examines how their extraordinary diversity complicates efforts to identify and categorize children with disabilities and to design effective educational policies for them. It also analyzes how disability variously affects the school experiences of these students, the roles their parents play in that schooling, and the possible implications for standards-based reform.

WHO QUALIFIES FOR SPECIAL EDUCATION?

Identification

The process of identifying students with disabilities is important because it determines who among the general student population is entitled to unique and specific legal and educational rights as well as access to extra resources and services. As explained in Chapter 2, these rights involve extensive due process protections, designed to ensure fundamental fairness in all aspects of the identification and placement of students with disabilities and to prevent misclassification.

Once a child is identified as having a disability, then a determination is made as to whether he or she qualifies for special education and related services. Under the IDEA, eligibility for special education services is based on two criteria: first, the student must meet the criteria for at least one of the 13 disabilities recognized in the IDEA (or the counterpart categories in state law) (Reschly, 1987a) and, second, the student must require special education or related services in order to receive an appropriate education (*Board of Education of the Hendrick Hudson Central School District* v. *Rowley,* 458 U.S. 176, 1982; Reschly, 1987a). According to the most recent data collected by the U.S. Department of Education (1996), approximately 4.7 million children between the ages of 6 and 17 qualified for special education services in school year 1994-95; this represents 10.4 percent of the total student population.

This two-part definition means that not all students with disabilities are eligible to receive special education services. For example, students with medical or physical disabilities do not qualify for special education unless they also demonstrate educational need. These children are still protected by Section 504 of the Rehabilitation Act of 1973, which governs all publicly supported agencies. This statute entitles students with disabilities to reasonable accommodations in educational settings to permit them to overcome impairments in critical life activities— even if they do not qualify for special education services. Currently the number of these students, who are covered by Section 504 but are not in special education, is unknown.[1] Nevertheless, the legal rights accorded them have the potential to affect the implementation of standards-based reform. For example, an increase in the number of Section 504-eligible students requesting accommodated assessments under standards-based reform would complicate interpretations of the meaning of assessment data.

Some children enter kindergarten already identified and receiving special education services. Many others are identified in their first few years of elementary school because they encounter difficulties in general education classrooms.

---

[1] Available data about the numbers and characteristics of children with disabilities, which are discussed in this chapter, are collected for IDEA-eligible children and thus do not include noneligible students with disabilities.

The process of identifying students with disabilities and determining their eligibility for special education typically involves three steps: referral, evaluation, and placement. Referral (usually by teachers) is the primary method through which children begin to be considered for a disability diagnosis. Most of these children are referred by their teachers for "repeatedly poor academic performance or poor social adjustment" (Heller et al., 1982:38). Thus, the performance of these students suggests they may need special education services, but they will qualify only if they are found to have a disability.

The IDEA is explicit and detailed about testing and assessment procedures used to qualify students for special education. A number of legislative provisions are designed to protect students and ensure the fair, nondiscriminatory use of tests. These provisions stipulate that decisions about children must be based on more than a single test, that tests must be validated for the purpose for which they are used, that students must be assessed in all areas related to a suspected disability, and that evaluations must be made by a multidisciplinary team. Children are generally tested in one-to-one situations with various school professionals (e.g., a school psychologist, an occupational therapist, a speech and language therapist) on tests that can be individually adapted to match the child's level. This type of highly individualized testing differs considerably from the large-scale, group-administered assessments usually tied to standards-based reforms.

The costs associated with conducting eligibility and other mandated assessments have raised concern. Data from several finance studies (Chambers and Parrish, 1983; Moore et al., 1988) indicate that these initial assessments, as well as the requisite triennial reevaluations of students, are very expensive, each costing an estimated $2,000 (Chaikind et al., 1993). Furthermore, research indicates that far too often these evaluations are used to classify a student within a specific diagnostic category rather than to determine specific instructional interventions (Merrill, 1990; Shinn et al., 1988; Smith, 1990).

If both the disability diagnosis and special education need are confirmed, then the student has rights to an individualized education program (IEP) designed to improve educational performance and expand opportunities. Evaluation results are used to develop an IEP that specifies the general goals and particular instructional objectives for the child; results are also used to design instruction and related services and to monitor the child's progress toward objectives and goals. A yearly meeting must be held to update and revise the IEP. Every three years, a student goes through a complete reevaluation; a battery of tests and assessments is again given by a multidisciplinary team and an eligibility meeting held to determine whether the student still has a disability and requires special education services.

Thus, students can and do move into and out of the special education system as they pass through the elementary and secondary school years. Little is known about the average length of time students stay in the system, but data indicate considerable movement. Available data suggest that, over a 1-year period at the secondary level, about 4 to 5 percent of eligible students are declassified and return to general education full time (Wagner et al., 1991; U.S. Department of Education, 1996). One longitudinal study of elementary schools in three urban districts suggested a slightly higher declassification rate during elementary school of 17 percent over a 2-year period (Walker et al., 1988).[2]

National enrollment data by age cohort suggest that enrollments in special education increase substantially between ages 6 and 8, peak for children at ages 9 and 10, and drop off steadily as students get older. This pattern varies, however, across disability categories, with some enrollments remaining relatively stable, whereas others (e.g., speech and language) decrease steadily with increasing age.

Special education referral rates can be affected by other policies and practices in a school system. Some have argued, for example, that, in some schools and districts, policies that raise the consequences tied to test scores have led to increased numbers of students being identified as having a disability (Allington and McGill-Franzen, 1992), since special education students, many of whom tend to score lower, are commonly excluded from schoolwide reporting of test scores. The availability of other special programs, like remedial reading and Title I services, can affect the number of students referred for special education (Keogh and MacMillan, 1996). Others have suggested that fiscal incentives, such as basing allocations on counts of students with disabilities, can directly influence the number of students who get referred and placed in special education (Mehan, 1995). In a climate of reform aimed at raising academic standards, many are concerned that special education referral rates may go up if children with disabilities are exempted from certain aspects of reform or treated differently for accountability purposes. Unfortunately, at the current time, no systematic data are available on referral or placement rates that would allow monitoring of these trends over time.

Defining Disability

A number of comprehensive systems exist for classifying various kinds of disabilities, and these have influenced classification in special education to varying degrees (American Psychiatric Association, 1994; Luckasson et al., 1992; MacMillan and Reschly, in press; Reschly, 1992; World Health Organization, 1994). There is, however, no official special education classification system that is used uniformly across U.S. states and regions.

Thirteen disabilities are mentioned in the federal IDEA and defined in the accompanying regulations (IDEA 1991, 34 C.F.R. 300.7). Box 3-1 shows the federal definitions of disability categories along with the additional regulatory criteria for SLD. Brief definitions are provided for the following categories of disabilities: autism, deaf-blindness, deafness, hearing impairment, mental retar-

---

[2]In this study, students classified with speech and language disorders and specific learning disabilities were the most likely to move out of special education.

BOX 3-1   Definitions of Disabilities in Federal Regulations

300.7   Children with disabilities

(a)(1) As used in this part the term "children with disabilities" means those children evaluated in accordance with ßß300.530-300.534 as having mental retardation, hearing impairments including deafness, speech or language impairments, visual impairments including blindness, serious emotional disturbance, orthopedic impairments, autism, traumatic brain injury, other health impairments, specific learning disabilities, deaf-blindness, or multiple disabilities, and who because of those impairments need special education and related services.

(b) The terms used in this definition are defined as follows:

(1) "Autism" means a developmental disability significantly affecting verbal and nonverbal communication and social interaction, generally evident before age 3, that adversely affects a child's educational performance. Other characteristics often associated with autism are engagement in repetitive activities and stereotyped movements, resistance to environmental change or change in daily routines, and unusual responses to sensory experiences. The term does not apply if a child's educational performance is adversely affected primarily because the child has a serious emotional disturbance, as defined in paragraph (b)(9) of this section.

(2) "Deaf-blindness" means concomitant hearing and visual impairments, the combination of which causes such severe communication and other developmental and educational problems that they cannot be accommodated in special education programs solely for children with deafness or children with blindness.

(3) "Deafness" means a hearing impairment that is so severe that the child is impaired in processing linguistic information through hearing, with or without amplification, that adversely affects a child's educational performance.

(4) "Hearing impairment" means an impairment in hearing, whether permanent or fluctuating, that adversely affects a child's educational performance but that is not included under the definition of deafness in this section.

(5) "Mental retardation" means significantly subaverage general intellectual functioning existing concurrently with deficits in adaptive behavior and manifested during the developmental period that adversely affects a child's educational performance.

(6) "Multiple disabilities" means concomitant impairments (such as mental retardation-blindness, mental retardation-orthopedic impairment, etc.), the combination of which causes such severe educational problems that they cannot be accommodated in special education programs solely for one of the impairments. The term does not include deaf-blindness.

(7) "Orthopedic impairment" means a severe orthopedic impairment that adversely affects a child's educational performance. The term includes impairments caused by congenital anomaly (e.g., clubfoot, absence of some member, etc.), impairments caused by disease (e.g., poliomyelitis, bone tuberculosis, etc.), and impairments from other causes (e.g., cerebral palsy, amputations, and fractures or burns that cause contractures).

(8) "Other health impairment" means having limited strength, vitality or alertness, due to chronic or acute health problems such as a heart condition, tuberculosis, rheumatic fever, nephritis, asthma, sickle cell anemia, hemophilia, epilepsy, lead poisoning, leukemia, or diabetes that adversely affects a child's educational performance.

(9) "Serious emotional disturbance" is defined as follows:

    (i) The term means a condition exhibiting one or more of the following characteristics over a long period of time and to a marked degree that adversely affects a child's educational performance—

        (A) An inability to learn that cannot be explained by intellectual, sensory, or health factors;

        (B) An inability to build or maintain satisfactory interpersonal relationships with peers and teachers;

        (C) Inappropriate types of behavior or feelings under normal circumstances;

        (D) A general pervasive mood of unhappiness or depression; or

        (E) A tendency to develop physical symptoms or fears associated with personal or school problems.

    (ii) The term includes schizophrenia. The term does not apply to children who are socially maladjusted, unless it is determined that they have a serious emotional disturbance.

(10) "Specific learning disability" means a disorder in one or more of the basic psychological processes involved in understanding or in using language, spoken or written, that may manifest itself in an imperfect ability to listen, think, speak, read, write, spell, or to do mathematical calculations. The term includes such conditions as perceptual disabilities, brain injury, minimal brain dysfunction, dyslexia, and developmental aphasia. The term does not apply to children who have learning problems that are primarily the result of visual, hearing, or motor disabilities, of mental retardation, of emotional disturbance, or of environmental, cultural, or economic disadvantage.

(11) "Speech or language impairment" means a communication disorder such as stuttering, impaired articulation, a language impairment, or a voice impairment that adversely affects a child's educational performance.

continued

BOX 3-1—Continued

(12) "Traumatic brain injury" means an acquired injury to the brain caused by an external physical force, resulting in total or partial functional disability or psychosocial impairment, or both, that adversely affects a child's educational performance. The term applies to open or closed head injuries resulting in impairments in one or more areas, such as cognition; language; memory; attention; reasoning; abstract thinking; judgment; problem-solving; sensory, perceptual and motor abilities; psychosocial behavior; physical functions; information processing; and speech. The term does not apply to brain injuries that are congenital or degenerative, or brain injuries induced by birth trauma.

(13) "Visual impairment including blindness" means an impairment in vision that, even with correction, adversely affects a child's educational performance. The term includes both partial sight and blindness.

§ 300.541   Criteria for determining the existence of a specific learning disability.

(a) A team may determine that a child has a specific learning disability if—

(1) The child does not achieve commensurate with his or her age and ability levels in one or more of the areas listed in paragraph (a)(2) of this section, when provided with learning experiences appropriate for the child's age and ability levels; and

(2) The team finds that a child has a severe discrepancy between achievement and intellectual ability in one or more of the following areas—

    (i) Oral expression;
    (ii) Listening comprehension;
    (iii) Written expression;
    (iv) Basic reading skill;
    (v) Reading comprehension;
    (vi) Mathematics calculation; or
    (vii) Mathematics reasoning.

(b) The team may not identify a child as having a specific learning disability if the severe discrepancy between ability and achievement is primarily the result of—

    (1) A visual hearing, or motor impairment;
    (2) Mental retardation;
    (3) Emotional disturbance; or
    (4) Environmental, cultural or economic disadvantage.

(20 U.S.C. 1411 note).

dation (MR), multiple disabilities, orthopedic impairment, other health impairment, serious emotional disturbance (SED), specific learning disability (SLD), speech or language impairment (Sp/L), traumatic brain injury, and visual impairment. Classification criteria are not provided for any of these disabilities except learning disabilities (see IDEA 1991, 34 CFR 300.541).

States and school districts do not have to adopt the disability categories in the federal law and regulations. Indeed, classification practices vary significantly from place to place, including names for categories, key dimensions on which the diagnosis is made, and criteria for eligibility determination (Mercer et al., 1990; Patrick and Reschly, 1982; Singer et al., 1989; Smith et al., 1988). These differences have the greatest impact on students with mild disabilities. As a result, it is entirely possible for students with identical characteristics to be diagnosed as having a disability in one state but not in another, or to have the categorical designation change with a move across state lines (Box 3-2).

Many reasons have been given for the high degree of variability in the classification rates. Some of this variation stems from the different ways that the law has been implemented or that professional practice has been conducted in different jurisdictions. States and districts differ in referral practices, effectiveness of child-find programs, and definitions of disability used. In addition, identification rates are affected by factors such as the strength of professional and special interest groups, the proclivity and capacity of parents to seek services, the availability and cost of services, the stigma attached to various disability designations, and the history of litigation in different places (Singer et al., 1989).

Severity of Disabilities

The degree of an individual's disability can range from mild to severe within a category. This means that students who may be considered as having a specific disability, such as learning disability or mental retardation, can be very different from one another. Severity is influenced by: (a) the *size* of the deficit(s) in behavior along such key dimensions as intelligence, academic achievement, communication/language, motor skills, and emotional adjustment; (b) the *number* of areas in which there are deficits; and (c) the *complexity* of developing educational interventions. The adjectives mild, moderate, and severe are usually used to denote the degree of severity of disabilities.

People with mild disabilities typically have smaller deficits on the key dimensions, have deficits in fewer areas, and can function without assistance in most normal daily activities. Most students with mild disabilities demonstrate no evidence of physical or health anomalies that cause deficits in behavior. For this reason, mild disabilities are largely a school-age phenomenon. Identification occurs *after* school entrance through a preplacement evaluation, which usually occurs because a teacher has referred the child due to severe and chronic achievement problems (Reschly, 1987b). Persons with mild disabilities typically require

---

BOX 3-2   State Variation in Classification Policies

States use diverse classification practices in special education. The category of mental retardation illustrates some of these differences. In the MR category, enormous differences exist among states in terminology (some of the terms used to refer to mental retardation include *mental handicap, mental disability,* and *significantly limited intellectual capacity*), key dimensions (e.g., some states do not include adaptive behavior in the conceptual definition), and classification criteria (e.g., the IQ score criterion varies from a low of 69 to a high of 85).

State differences have the greatest impact on students with mild disabilities; prevalence differences are negligible for the more severe disabilities. Consider these prevalence figures: SLD varies from 2.86 percent in Georgia to 9.27 percent in Massachusetts; MR varies from 0.31 percent in New Jersey to 3.11 percent in Alabama; Sp/L varies from 1.28 percent in Hawaii to 3.94 percent in New Jersey; and SED varies from 0.05 percent in Mississippi to 2.06 percent in Connecticut. To cite another example, the Sp/L prevalence in New York is only 1.36 percent, whereas in the adjacent state of New Jersey it is nearly 4 percent (U.S. Department of Education, 1996:A-40).

The idea that such variations could reflect genuine differences in student populations stretches the imagination. It is highly unlikely that there are over nine times as many students with mental retardation in Alabama as New Jersey; that there are over three times as many students with SLD in Massachusetts as in Georgia; or that there are 40 times as many students with SED in Connecticut as in Mississippi. State prevalence of all disabilities for children and youth ages 6 to 17 vary from a low of 7.34 percent in Hawaii to 14.98 percent in Massachusetts (U.S. Department of Education, 1996). These variations are more likely to be related to unique state-by-state practices regarding how children and youth are identified as disabled than to real differences in student populations.

---

part-time special education programs that are delivered by special resource teachers or in special classes for part of the school day. During the adult years, the vast majority of these persons will not be officially designated as having a disability and will become self-supporting, independently functioning citizens in the community. Their needs for supportive services as adults are generally intermittent and restricted to particular activities or events.

Because a disability is mild does not mean that it is trivial or that it magically disappears at age 18 or 21. Students with SLD, for example, are seriously impaired in one of the most important developmental tasks in a technologically complex society: acquiring literacy skills and using them to master bodies of knowledge. Poor reading skills in particular constitute formidable barriers to academic progress and significantly limit adult career opportunities.

People with disabilities at the moderate to severe levels typically have a large deficit on at least one of the important behavioral dimensions, as well as moderate to large deficits in one or more of the other dimensions. These deficits tend to have a biological or physiological basis, and affected persons usually carry physical symptoms that influence their appearance. Disabilities at the more severe levels are typically diagnosed initially in the preschool years, often by medical personnel. During the school-age years, people with moderate or severe disabilities typically require assistance with certain daily living activities, such as self-help skills, mobility in the community, basic communication skills, and recreation. Special education programs for these students usually involve extensive assistance, whether in special classes with a very low student-to-teacher ratio (e.g., 5:1) or in general education classrooms with a full-time teacher or aide. Most people with disabilities at the moderate or severe level require lifelong assistance with one or more of the everyday activities of work, recreation, mobility, and self-care.

People with disabilities at the most severe level typically have large deficits, often in two or more areas, that result in poor educational performance and require extensive and consistent support. Mental retardation is often a primary disability for people with severe multiple disabilities; for example, approximately 60 percent of people with cerebral palsy have mental retardation (Batshaw and Perret, 1986). In educational contexts, the focus of defining severe disabilities has moved from describing negative behaviors (e.g., self-mutilation, self-stimulation, loss of contact with reality) to describing developmental levels of functioning. This latter approach emphasizes the discrepancy between what is expected in "normal development" and actual student performance (e.g., a student's developmental level is 50 percent lower than what is expected for his or her chronological age) (Abt Associates, 1974; Justen, 1976). Individuals with the most severe disabilities are far below normal development and require continuing assistance, in childhood and adult years, with very basic self-survival skills.

Disability Dimensions

The 13 disability categories in the federal regulations are based to varying degrees on 8 dimensions of behavior or individual characteristics: academic achievement, intelligence, adaptive behavior, emotional adjustment, communication/language, sensory status, motor skills, and health status, (Reschly, 1987b). As explained in the following pages, each dimension affects how children are identified and served in special education.

Academic Achievement. Assessment of achievement in such core academic subjects as reading, writing, and math is nearly always part of the full and individual evaluation provided to children referred for special education, regardless of which of the 13 categories of disability is being considered. A high percentage of children in special education exhibit low achievement in at least one academic area.

Achievement as a dimension of disability has important implications for standards-based reform. Serious debate exists about the relative importance of traditional academic literacy skills for students with severe disabilities and for many middle- and high-school-age students with moderate and mild disabilities. The majority of students with severe disabilities will not reach basic levels of academic literacy as they are understood in standards-based reforms. Furthermore, students with mild disabilities may reach plateaus in academic achievement, or, if not actual plateaus, then stages in skill acquisition, at which further progress is extremely slow. As we discuss in Chapter 4, the low achievement of some children with disabilities raises difficult issues about whether an academically oriented curriculum is the most appropriate emphasis, particularly if it takes time away from teaching social and functional competencies and vocational skills.

Intelligence.   General intellectual functioning is typically assessed as part of the evaluation for special education, usually with a standardized IQ test individually administered by a psychologist. Intellectual functioning is a key criteria for classifying students as MR and SLD in most states. Federal regulations define mental retardation as "significantly subaverage general intellectual functioning existing concurrently with deficits in adaptive behavior" (34 CFR 300.7). Federal regulations for diagnosing specific learning disabilities require that there be a "severe discrepancy between achievement and intellectual ability" (34 CFR 300.541); most states have established procedures for determining what constitutes a severe discrepancy. Recent research, however, has challenged the validity of using an intelligence-achievement discrepancy to define SLD (see Morison et al., 1996).

Although the meaning of the construct of intelligence continues to provoke debate, especially as it relates to achievement, some features of intelligence are reasonably well established. Intelligence is related to efficiency in information processing, the ability to learn abstract concepts, the spontaneous use of strategies to acquire and remember information and solve problems, and the capability to learn from incomplete instruction. Generally the lower the levels of intelligence (and achievement), the greater the need for more concrete, less abstract instruction that proceeds in small steps and includes ample demonstration and practice (Campione et al., 1982; Neisser et al., 1996). Intelligence is related to school performance and academic achievement, but the relationships are complex and difficult to separate (Neisser et al., 1996). Intelligence is both a predictor and an outcome of school achievement—that is, schooling both affects and is affected by general intellectual functioning.[3]

Adaptive Behavior. Adaptive behavior, also referred to as adaptive skills or social competencies, is traditionally defined as "the effectiveness or degree with which individuals meet the standards of personal independence and social responsibility expected for age and cultural group" (Grossman, 1983:1). Included in this concept are domains of behavior such as: (1) *independent functioning*—examples at the most basic level include toileting, eating, dressing, avoiding danger, getting around the community, handling money wisely; (2) *social functioning*—e.g., orienting to human contact, complying with rules and expectations, refraining from behaviors that destroy property or injure others, working cooperatively; (3) *functional academics*—e.g., acquiring language to communicate needs and to interact with others, using basic literacy skills in everyday activities, mastering concepts of time and number used in everyday environments; and (4) *vocational-occupational skills*—e.g., exhibiting good work habits and positive attitudes, mastering skills related to employment.

The mental retardation diagnosis explicitly requires a determination of adaptive behavior deficits and cannot be made solely on the basis of an IQ score. Diagnosis of SED also involves adaptive behavior domains; conduct disorders involving aggression against persons and property and refusal to comply with societal norms and rules are the most frequent kind of SED. Because adaptive behavior expectations vary by age, setting, and cultural group, they are sometimes difficult to assess. But adaptive behavior is essential to every disability category, and adaptive behavior competencies are widely recognized as crucial to the adjustment of students with disabilities, especially as they mature into adults.

Emotional Adjustment. Emotional adjustment involves attitudes, values, and emotions that can facilitate or interfere with academic and social behaviors in a variety of settings. A relatively small number of students with SED have problems with emotional adjustment called internalizing disorders. These disorders involve patterns of behavior, such as excessive anxiety, dysphoric mood, and repetitive ritualistic behaviors, that cause distress to the individual and interfere with everyday performance. Depending on state and local practices, children and youth with internalizing disorders may receive related services such as counseling.

Communication/Language. Communication skills and language development are central to several disabilities, particularly the Sp/L category. Sp/L disorders vary markedly, from relatively straightforward misarticulation difficulties

---

[3]Because the dimensions of achievement and intelligence are so closely related, we use the term *cognitive disability* throughout the rest of the report to describe disabilities that affect students' learning and thinking processes.

(such as slurring "s" and "sh" sounds) that may be resolved through short-term treatment, to severe stuttering that markedly interferes with normal communication and requires years of speech therapy. Understanding and using language to communicate also is crucial to determining the level of disability in other categories and is a central focus of special education programming for many students with disabilities.

Sensory Status.   Sensory status, particularly auditory and visual acuity, is the basis for the disability categories of deafness, hearing impairment, deaf-blindness, and visual impairment. Screening for sensory deficits is routinely included in full and individual evaluations for special education. Sensory deficits often accompany other disabilities, especially at the multiple and/or severe levels.

Motor Skills.   Special education and related services are often needed by students with motor disabilities to compensate for their motor limitations and to treat associated problems such as speech production difficulties. Motor skills limitations also can influence participation in activities associated with the general education curriculum and standards-based reform. For example, many students with motor limitations have difficulties with the response formats required on standards-based assessments (e.g., group-administered paper-and-pencil tests).

Health Status.   A wide variety of health problems, some of which are life threatening, can result in a disability diagnosis and referral to special education. Some students are so ill that they cannot participate in the general school curriculum or activities associated with standards-based reform. Students with severe head injuries, for example, who are attempting to regain very basic cognitive functions such as awareness and memory, can hardly be expected to participate meaningfully in standards-based reforms. A few students have health problems that are so severe and chronic that their special education and related services do not incorporate any skills that would be included in the general education curriculum at the lowest grade levels.

Different Models of Disability

The current special education classification system mixes two different ways of thinking about the nature and origin of disabilities: the medical and the social system models of deviance (Mercer, 1979; Reschly, 1987b). Each model implies different assumptions about etiology, identification, assessment, and treatment.

The medical model generally applies to disabilities that have known biological bases; retinopathy caused by premature birth as a cause of blindness is an example (Mercer, 1979; Reschly, 1987b). Medical model disabilities are generally lifelong, can be observed across most if not all social roles and settings, and are likely to be identified regardless of cultural context. Medical model disabilities typically are identified by medical personnel during the preschool years, often in the first year of life. Treatment focuses on eliminating the underlying cause, if possible, or compensating for its effects on daily activities to the extent feasible.

In contrast, the social system model typically refers to disabilities that are socially constructed and relevant to some but not all settings. In the social system model, disorders are defined as discrepancies from expected patterns or normative standards of performance on important dimensions of behavior. In children, many such disabilities are evident only after a child enters school and begins to have difficulty with academic learning. Statistical indices such as percentile ranks and discrepancy scores are used to quantify the amount of divergence from age or grade-level averages. Often a point or two in these discrepancy scores can determine whether a student receives special education services and whether additional thousands of dollars are spent on the child's education.

The 13 disability categories in the IDEA reflect to varying degrees these two models of deviance. The medical model is useful for describing such categories as deafness, deaf-blindness, hearing impairment, multiple disabilities, other health impairment, traumatic brain injury, visual impairment, and the moderate or severe levels of mental retardation. Nearly all of the children and youth with these types of impairments have identifiable biological and observable physiological anomalies that are permanent and that have a direct relationship to impairments in behavior.

Disabilities at the mild level in the categories of SLD, Sp/L, SED, and MR are understood best from the social system model of deviance because there is no clearly identifiable biological basis for the disability; the impairments in behavior are restricted to particular roles in specific contexts, and effective treatment focuses on symptoms rather than underlying causes.

The mixture of the medical and social system models has the most serious consequences in the area of SLD; there often is confusion over the relative importance of underlying causes and symptoms in the assessment, identification, and treatment of this disability. The conceptualization of learning disabilities as a problem with psychological processing emerged in the 1960s. Various definitions have evolved over time, and most incorporate the ideas that learning disabilities (1) are different from other achievement-related conditions such as mental retardation or slowness in learning, (2) can be expressed as unexpected difficulties in a range of basic ability domains, such as thinking and spoken or written language, and (3) are caused by something within the individual, often presumed to be an underlying neurological condition (Keogh and MacMillan, 1996). The most widely used definition states that SLD is "a disorder in one or more of the basic psychological processes involved in understanding or using language" and refers to such conditions as "perceptual disabilities, brain injury, minimal brain dysfunction, dyslexia, and developmental aphasia" (Mercer et al., 1990; IDEA, 34 CFR 300.7[a][10]). However, the majority of students with SLD do not show identifiable signs of neurological deficits (Hammill, 1990). Furthermore, recent research on at least one kind of reading disability challenges the notion that it is a discrete diagnostic entity; instead, these authors (Shaywitz et al., 1992:148) argue that:

> Dyslexia occurs along a continuum that blends imperceptibly with normal reading ability. These results indicate that no distinct cutoff point exists to distinguish children with dyslexia clearly from children with normal reading ability; rather, the dyslexic children simply represent the lower portion of the continuum of reading capabilities.

Different perspectives on the definitions and key criteria are not the only complication in the area of learning disabilities. Problems in its implementation in the school context include unsound diagnostic practices, unreliable measures, different choices of discrepancy models for operationalizing the definition, different understandings of SLD by those making referrals, and preference for the SLD diagnosis because it incurs less stigma than some other categories (Keogh and MacMillan, 1996; Lyon, 1996). Thus, "the heterogeneity evident in any identified group of learning disabled individuals is a function of both conceptual and operational inconsistencies" (Keogh and MacMillan, 1996:316).

Eligibility Policy

Proper diagnosis of disabilities is complicated by the nature of current policy requirements, especially the all or none character of eligibility—that is, a student must be deemed either to have or not to have a disability for educational purposes. In fact, the capabilities and needs of many students do not fit into such a neat dichotomy but rather exist on a broad continuum, often lacking clear demarcations between students with disabilities and those without.

Problems with the current classification system were recognized at least 20 years ago in the massive federally funded exceptional child classification project. Hobbs (1975:102) characterized the conventional categories and the procedures for arriving at them as follows:

> They are imprecise: They say too little, and they say too much. They suggest only vaguely the kind of help a child may need, and they tend to describe conditions in negative terms. Generally, negative labels affect the child's self concept in a negative way, and probably do more harm than good.

Some of the assumptions behind the current categorization system were again questioned in a later report issued by a National Research Council panel on selection and placement of students in programs for the mentally retarded (Heller et al., 1982:21):

> To what extent must children be classified and labeled according to a generic class of deficiencies in order to receive special education services? Diagnostic categories such as EMR [educable mentally retarded] may be more an administrative convenience than an educational necessity, allowing schools to count the

number of children in this and other special programs in accord with federal requirements. If categorical labels are required for administrative purposes, they could be chosen to reflect the educational services provided, thereby emphasizing the responsibilities of school systems rather than the failings of the child.

Following are brief descriptions of some of the problems involved in classifying disabilities, with selected references for further reading.

Social Stigma

The degree to which classification or labeling, as it is sometimes called, produces lifelong, permanent negative effects is still disputed. Certainly, the more extreme claims made by critics of classification procedures in the late 1960s and early 1970s (e.g., Mercer, 1973) are not supported by empirical evidence. Nevertheless, the common names of MR and SED used for students with those disabilities have negative connotations. An earlier, now classic, review (MacMillan et al., 1974) reported two well-established facts concerning the effects of traditional classification categories: there is widespread misunderstanding of their meanings by professionals and the lay public (Goodman, 1989) and the bearers of labels find the classification uncomfortable and, very often, objectionable (Jenkins and Heinen, 1989). Concerns about the effects of classification on individuals have led to calls for the elimination of the common classification categories (National Association of School Psychologists, 1986). A concern for stigmatization has been cited as one of the reasons for the growth in the numbers of children diagnosed as SLD, as this label is thought to be more socially acceptable than MR or SED (Lyon, 1996). Although this literature is complex, one conservative conclusion is that categorical classification should be used as sparingly as possible, should use terms with as few negative connotations as possible, and should focus on skills rather than presumed "inherent attributes" or internal characteristics of the individual.

Imprecision of Disability Categories

Current diagnoses using traditional categories are frequently unreliable, for several reasons. First, the characteristics of students in such categories as SLD and MMR (mild mental retardation) often do overlap (Epps et al., 1984; Gajar, 1979; Kavale, 1980; Neisworth and Greer, 1975; Shinn et al., 1986; Ysseldyke et al., 1982a). Second, teachers vary in their tolerance for student differences, and different screening and placement practices exist within and between districts (Hersh and Walker, 1983; MacMillan et al., 1980). Third, the quality of the assessment measures varies, and most cannot reliably differentiate among the high-incidence populations of SLD, SED, and MMR (Coles, 1978; Shepard, 1983; Ysseldyke et al., 1983). Fourth, as explained above, classification criteria vary among and within states. A number of researchers have long noted the degree of overlap among these categories and have suggested that efforts to maintain a strict categorical approach to programming is neither feasible nor necessarily educationally advantageous (Gajar, 1979; Hallahan and Kauffman, 1977; MacMillan and Hendrick, 1993; Reschly, 1988).

Research also suggests that current disability classifications have some limitations in validity. A disability category is considered valid if it provides information that is relevant to prevention and/or to decisions about kinds and outcomes of treatment. A category is also considered valid if the information used to classify the student is useful to the individual's prognosis or outcomes.

For example, information needed to determine whether a student is eligible to be classified as SLD, MMR, or SED typically does not relate closely to treatment decisions, especially decisions about the student's general educational goals, specific objectives, or educational interventions, nor is it particularly useful in evaluating outcomes. Some evidence now suggests that the educational interventions provided to students in the different disability categories are far more alike than different (Algozzine et al., 1988; Boucher and Deno, 1979; Epps and Tindal, 1987; Haynes and Jenkins, 1986; Jenkins and Heinen, 1989; Jenkins et al., 1988). This same research and other reviews also indicate that traditional categories do not have a demonstrable relationship to specific outcomes or to prognoses (Epps and Tindal, 1987; Kavale, 1990; Kavale and Glass, 1982).

Another difficult question, one that has important implications for eligibility policy, is whether some students with mild cognitive disabilities can be reliably and validly distinguished from other students who are alternately termed "low achieving," "slow learners," or "educationally disadvantaged." As noted earlier, these categorizations and distinctions are not implemented reliably in many places. Under current practice, although it is virtually impossible for a student whose achievement level is average or near average to be diagnosed in a category like SLD, it is not clear-cut how to distinguish between various degrees of below-average achievement and SLD or MMR.

Research evidence that could guide these decisions is mixed. For example, a growing body of evidence indicates that a significant number of students identified as SLD do not differ on any psychometric or functional dimensions from other low-achieving students (Keogh, 1990; Ysseldyke et al., 1982a; Shaywitz et al., 1992; Lyon, 1996). Other researchers, however, have found that reliable and large differences exist on multiple dimensions between students who are identified as SLD and low-achieving students who are not so identified (Bursuck, 1989; Kavale et al., 1994; Merrill, 1990; Shinn et al., 1986; Tur-Kaspa and Bryan, 1994).

Similarly, research evidence is mixed on whether the two groups respond differently to educational treatments. Some studies have indicated that effective instructional programming or psychological treatment uses the same principles and often the same procedures regardless of whether the student is classified SLD, MMR, SED, slow learner, or educationally disadvantaged (Carter, 1984; Epps and Tindal, 1987). Other research has suggested that SLD and low-achieving non-SLD learners show differential responses to general education treatments (Fuchs et al., 1994; Fuchs et al., in press; Tateyama-Sniezek, 1990).

The validity of a given classification is strongly related to the use or purpose to which the category is put. Our discussion has mentioned the importance of a valid taxonomy for two different purposes: making eligibility determinations and making treatment decisions. As described earlier, evidence suggests that the existing classification system largely serves the first purpose at the expense of the second. For this reason, some have suggested moving to a more global category system for determining eligibility (e.g., students with disabilities and other students). But, as this chapter suggests, some method of categorizing different disabilities is important for research purposes, because research indicates that achievement and outcomes vary dramatically for children with different kinds of disabilities and at differing levels of severity. In addition, as Chapter 5 suggests, some kind of taxonomy of functional characteristics related to disability will be needed to design valid assessment accommodations. A taxonomy that is useful or valid for one of these purposes may not necessarily be valid for the others.

A possible resolution to the problem of eligibility and treatment decisions is to establish diagnostic constructs based on a child's placement along a number of continuous dimensions of disability, rather than an either-or dichotomy. Reschly (1996) proposed a model for determining eligibility that would recognize a broad continuum of need and produce levels of funding based on degree of need. In this model, degree of need is ascertained by determining: (1) the number of discrepancies from average levels of performance using the eight dimensions described earlier in this chapter; (2) the size of the discrepancy on each of the dimensions; (3) the complexity of the treatment required (kind of professional assistance and equipment or special environments); and (4) the intensity of the treatment (amount of time per day and the length of treatment) needed to provide an appropriate education. These four variables could also be used as weighting factors in a regression equation that would yield a total number of dollars available to support the special education of a particular student. Approaches like this may result in a more consistent classification system that could be implemented at all stages of the special education process, including screening, prereferral intervention, classification, programming, and funding.

The variety of issues surrounding eligibility has prompted calls for a more flexible taxonomy. Congress and the Clinton administration have considered proposals to use a generic category, such as "developmentally delayed," for children through age 9, which in effect would eliminate the federal requirement for categorization of younger children. Other proposals would abolish the requirement to define disability at all and would send special education funds to states and local districts based only on some proportion of the school-age population, to be used for whichever children they see fit. But, although the difficulties with current eligibility policy and practice are widely acknowledged within special education, there is little consensus surrounding the solutions.

In sum, there is no single accepted taxonomy, or classification system, for identifying which children have disabilities or describing the functional characteristics of various disability dimensions. The categories specified in federal regulations are general and are not universally used. The most commonly used taxonomies combine medical and social approaches in ways that are not always clear-cut. Nevertheless, some national data are available about the numbers and characteristics of children in each of the 13 federal categories. These data are reviewed in the next section.

STUDENTS AND SCHOOLING CHARACTERISTICS

Available data on the number of students with different kinds of disabilities come almost exclusively from the Office of Special Education Programs (OSEP) in the U.S. Department of Education. These data are collected on a yearly basis from states and aggregate the number of children being served in special education programs across the 13 categories of disability.[4] There are no other population-based data on the prevalence of disabilities among children against which to compare the OSEP data. Although other kinds of national surveys have been done, they often rely on parent reports of disability characteristics and specific educational problems and do not provide reliable prevalence estimates (Lewit and Baker, 1996).

Table 3-1 provides a summary of disabilities by key category for children ages 6-11 and 12-17 for school year 1994-95 (U.S. Department of Education, 1996). [5] Several important trends can be identified from the table. The prevalence of disabilities varies by age and category. The prevalence of Sp/L disabilities declines substantially in the older age interval. SLD is the most frequently occurring disability at both age intervals, and it is particularly prominent at the 12-17 age interval. Approximately 90 percent of the children classified as having disabilities in school settings are accounted for by just 4 of the 13 categories: SLD, Sp/L, MR, and SED. Specific learning disabilities now account for over half of all students classified as having disabilities. Indeed, the SLD category has grown substantially since 1976, when the department began collecting classification data.

Although one disability is usually designated to be the primary disability (and thus a student is counted in that category in Table 3-1), many students have

---

[4]State counts of the total number of children served under the IDEA on December 1 of each school year (as reported in the Annual Reports to Congress on the IDEA) are auditable because they are used to provide IDEA, Part B, monies to states. As a result, states believe these total counts are highly accurate. In contrast, states define their own eligibility criteria for each disability category; although the data are aggregated across states to get national totals in each of the 13 categories, the comparability of characteristics of students in each category is unknown.

[5]The data discussed here apply only to students ages 6-17 with disabilities who are served under Part B of the IDEA.

TABLE 3-1   School-Age Children with Disabilities, 1994-95 (percentages in parentheses)

Category	Ages 6-11	Ages 12-17	Total	Percentage of Overall Population	State Ranges (%)	
SLD	1,040,972 (41.39)	1,345,657 (62.58)	2,386,629 (51.16)	5.34	2.86 to 9.27 (GA)	(MA)
Sp/L	906,380 (36.03)	110,937 (5.16)	1,017,317 (21.80)	2.28	1.28 to 3.94 (HI)	(NJ)
MR	228,952 (9.10)	278,676 (12.96)	507,628 (10.88)	1.14	0.31 to 3.11 (NJ)	(AL)
SED	144,668 (5.75)	260,251 (12.10)	404,919 (8.68)	0.91	0.05 to 2.06 (MS)	(CT)
Other	194,171 (7.72)	154,615 (7.19)	348,786 (7.48)	0.78		
Total	2,515,143 (100)	2,150,136 (100)	4,665,279 (100)	10.45	7.34 to 14.98 (HI)	(MA)

NOTES: The data in this table were compiled from U.S. Department of Education (1996: Tables AA3, AA4, and AA13) for the 50 states, Puerto Rico, and the District of Columbia. The percentages are based on a total estimated enrollment of children age 6-17 of 44,643,818.

SLD = specific learning disability; Sp/L = speech or language impairment; MR = mental retardation; and SED = serious emotional disturbance.

"Other" is the prevalence of autism, deaf-blindness, deafness, hearing impairment, multiple disabilities, orthopedic impairment, other health impairment, traumatic brain injury, and visual impairment.

more than one disability—19 percent, according to one nationally representative study of secondary school youth with disabilities. The most frequently reported additional disabilities in that study were mental retardation and speech impairment (Wagner et al., 1991).

Although there are wide variations among students in each of the 13 categories of disabilities, some general trends occur. The high-incidence disabilities such as SLD and Sp/L are nearly always mild. The level of disabilities in MR and SED can vary from mild to severe; however, at least half of the students with MR and SED function at the mild level (Grosenick et al., 1987; Kauffman et al., 1987; MacMillan, 1988). In contrast, the disabilities in the category of "other" in Table 3-1, which account for about 7 percent of the school-age population with disabilities and about 1 percent of the overall population, are much more likely to cause moderate or severe levels of impairment. These include the categories of autism, deaf-blindness, orthopedic impairment, multiple disabilities, hearing impairment, visual impairment, traumatic brain injury, and other health impairments.

Characteristics Related to Disability Status

Other than age, OSEP does not collect any demographic information from the states concerning students with disabilities. The data that exist come from other sources.

Most data on school-referred samples of children indicate that boys are identified for special education at higher rates than girls (Heller et al., 1982; Wenger et al., 1996). For example, about two-thirds of the sample of secondary students with disabilities identified for the National Longitudinal Transitional Study of Special Education Students (NLTS) were male (Wagner et al., 1991); only in the categories of deaf-blindness and hearing impairment was the gender distribution approximately equal. However, recent data using clinically identified samples of students suggest that approximately the same number of girls and boys are identified when functional characteristics are assessed (e.g., Lyon, 1996).

Since the 1960s, there have been concerns about higher proportions of minority children being identified as having disabilities, particularly for the category of mental retardation. This concern about overrepresentation of minorities provoked numerous cases in which the federal courts scrutinized the professional practices of special educators and school psychologists, as well as the validity of IQ tests in making disability diagnoses (see Morison et al., 1996).

The only national data regarding race/ethnicity and disability category are collected by the Office for Civil Rights (OCR) in the U.S. Department of Education. Table 3-2 presents data from the 1978, 1986, and 1990 OCR surveys of school districts. These data should be viewed with an understanding that they are not a representative sample, do not use the same sampling methodology over time, and do not include all 13 IDEA categories.[6]

Data from the 1990 OCR survey suggest that, over the four categories included in the survey (MMR, SLD, SP/L and SED), 11 percent of both African American and Native American children receive special education services; this is somewhat higher than identification rates of other racial/ethnic groups (9.5 percent of whites, 8 percent of Hispanics, and 4 percent of Asian/Pacific Island-

---

[6]Although the OCR sampling unit is the school district, OCR surveys are not a representative sample of school districts in the United States because the sampling includes all of the "large" districts and a sample of "smaller" districts. Furthermore, the OCR sampling strategy has changed over the surveys reported in Table 3-2, and it is impossible to determine with certainty the effects of these changes on the representativeness of the OCR results. Finally, OCR collects data for only 5 of the 13 categories recognized in the IDEA. The most emphasis is placed on three "judgmental categories" (mental retardation, specific learning disability, and serious emotional disturbance), that is, the categories in which a degree of professional judgment is required in diagnostic decision making (Gelb and Mizokawa, 1986).

TABLE 3-2   Percentages of African American, Hispanic, and White Students Classified with Mild Disabilities

Year and Ethnic Category	Disability Category			
	MMR	SLD	SED	Total
1978				
African American	3.46	2.23	0.50	6.19
Hispanic	0.98	2.58	0.29	3.85
White	1.07	2.32	0.29	3.68
1986				
African American	2.30	4.43	1.04	7.77
Hispanic	0.56	4.31	0.46	5.33
White	0.87	4.29	0.57	5.73
1990				
African American	2.10	4.95	0.89	7.94
Hispanic	0.65	4.68	0.33	5.66
White	0.81	4.97	0.69	6.47

NOTE: Data in the table represent the percentage of the total number of students in each ethnic minority group who are classified in the particular category given. MMR= mild mental retardation; SLD= specific learning disability; and SED= serious emotional disturbance.

SOURCE: 1978 data based on Finn (1982:324-330). 1986 data based on analyses by Reschly and Wilson (1990), using 1986 OCR survey data compiled by the National Council of Advocates for Students. 1990 data based on U.S. Department of Education (1994:198, 201, 202).

ers). Data across time suggest that, although overrepresentation of African American children in some categories still occurs, it has decreased in the past 20 years.

Several trends regarding minority participation in special education are apparent from the data on African American, Hispanic, and white students presented in Table 3-2. The overall rates of identification in these mild categories have increased for all three racial/ethnic groups since 1978; the biggest proportional increases have occurred for white children (from under 4 percent identified in 1978 to over 6 percent in 1990). The most recent data suggest that patterns of disproportion vary by disability category. The most common disability across all three racial/ethnic groups is SLD, with approximately similar rates for each group (just under 5 percent of all students in 1990). Hispanic children show the lowest rates of identification across all three mild disability categories. Most of the overrepresentation of African American children is due to the larger percentage labeled MMR, although African American children also show slightly higher rates of identification as SED.

Some analysts have argued that other variables, such as socioeconomic status and poverty status, which are confounded with race and ethnicity, may account for at least some of the variation in special education identification rates.

Poverty has long been associated with special education placement rates (e.g.,

Dunn, 1968). It is rare, however, to find analyses and publication of data concerning the actual relationship of poverty to the incidence of disabilities and special education placement. Appropriate data for these analyses were available from four school districts (*Coalition to Save Our Children v. Board of Education et al.,* U.S. District Court, District of Delaware, Civil action no. 56-1816-1822, 1994). In all four districts, both African American and white students who were poor, as gauged by eligibility for subsidized school lunch, were much more likely to be classified as disabled and placed in special education. In three of the four districts, African American and white students in poverty circumstances had essentially the same rates of diagnosis for and placement in special education—about 19 percent on average. In the four districts, children who were not eligible for subsidized lunch were placed in special education at much lower rates—ranging from 7.3 to 9.2 percent for African Americans and from 5.3 to 7.3 percent for whites; even so, the placement rates for nonpoor African American students were slightly higher. Poverty is a plausible explanation for much of the special education overrepresentation of minority children, although additional studies are needed on the relationship of poverty to disability diagnosis and special education placement.

Data from the NLTS, a longitudinal study of secondary school youth with disabilities, provides data on several socioeconomic and household characteristics. Table 3-3 presents some of these data as well as approximately comparable numbers for the general population (Wagner et al., 1991). These data suggest that students with disabilities are more socioeconomically disadvantaged than the general population—that is, more likely to come from single-parent households, to have a head of household with lower educational attainment, and to have lower household incomes.

Educational Placement

Having a disability, mild or severe, can affect a child's schooling in many ways. It can affect where children are educated, whether they have the same goals for schooling as children without disabilities, and whether they participate in all of the general education curriculum, some of it, or none. Furthermore, it can influence whether they can be taught by the same methods and with the same tools and equipment as other students, and whether they can be evaluated in the same ways. Many children with disabilities work toward the same high school diploma as other students, whereas some will seek a different credential or certificate of completion.

Very little systematic, representative data exist that describe the range and degree to which students with disabilities participate in the various aspects of general education. In part this is because individualized programs are the hallmark of special education services, making it hard to collect and aggregate data systematically about the school experiences of these students. In addition, re-

TABLE 3-3   Socioeconomic Characteristics of Secondary School Youth with Disabilities and Youth in the General Population

Socioeconomic Characteristics	Youth with Disabilities[a]		Percentage of Youth in the General Population[b]
	%	Standard Error	
Education of household head			
Less than high school	41.0	1.5	22.3
High school graduate	36.0	1.4	38.8
Some college/2-year degree	14.0	1.0	17.8
4 year degree or more	8.9	0.9	21.1
	n = 6,650		
Annual household income			
Under $12,000	34.8	1.5	18.2[c]
$12,000 to $24,999	33.5	1.5	20.6
$25,000 to $37,999	16.2	1.2	25.4
$38,000 or more	15.4	1.1	35.8
	n = 6,092		
Receiving public benefits			
Food Stamps	23.7	1.2	12.9[d]
Medicaid or similar coverage	21.6	1.2	12.6[d]
AFDC	12.5	1.0	12.6[e]
	n = 6,631		
Living in single parent households	36.8	1.4	25.6[b]
	n = 6,385		

[a]Data on youth with disabilities are from the NLTS.

[b]U.S. Bureau of Census (1988:Table 9, pp.45 ff). Data refer to youth ages 12 to 17 and living with at least one parent in March 1987.

[c]Note that categorical boundaries are set at $12,500, $25,000, and $40,000 rather than $12,000, $25,000, and $38,000.

[d]U.S. Department of Education (1988:34). Percentage of households with youth ages 0 to 18 (not youth ages 0 to 18 in households) in 1985.

[e]U.S. Department of Education (1988:32). Percent of youth ages 0-17 in 1985.

SOURCE: Adapted from: Wagner et al. (1991).

search is scarce on the longitudinal progress and development of students with disabilities, partly because they have been left out of large-scale longitudinal studies and databases or, in cases of mild disabilities, have been included but with no information on disability status. One analysis of major national education databases (such as the National Assessment of Educational Progress and the National Education Longitudinal Study) estimated that 40 to 50 percent of all school-age students with disabilities are excluded from these samples. Furthermore, exclusion criteria vary and exclusion rates are often not reported systematically (McGrew et al., 1993). In addition, the lack of consistent and reliable disability categories within and across studies makes it especially difficult to analyze how longitudinal pathways may vary by disability and to compare results from study to study (McGrew et al., 1995).

Among the important decisions made during the instructional planning and IEP development process are decisions about where the child will receive services. Some children need special education services in only one or two academic skill areas (e.g., spelling and written language), whereas others have IEPs that cover academic, behavioral, vocational, and social skill domains. For many children, then, placement decisions vary by skill or goal areas.

Views about the optimal educational settings for children with various kinds of disabilities differ. Over the past several decades, policies have shifted regarding whether students with disabilities should be educated in special or regular classrooms. Although since 1975, the IDEA has required that each student with a disability be provided with a free and appropriate education in the least restrictive environment (see Chapter 2), for many students with disabilities, debate still continues over what the most appropriate placement is. In addition, it is important to remember that "regular education is not one setting but many different settings that vary considerably from one classroom to the next" (Hebbeler, 1993:1-3). Furthermore, *where* a child is placed is not necessarily related to what curriculum and instruction he or she receives.

Data collected from all states for the 1993-94 school year (reported in Table 3-4) indicate that over 95 percent of students with disabilities served under the IDEA were served in regular school buildings (U.S. Department of Education, 1996), a slight increase since 1977, when data were first collected (Sawyer et al., 1994). The remaining 4.4 percent of students receive their education in either a separate day school, a residential facility, a hospital, or a homebound program. Students diagnosed with specific learning disabilities or speech/language impairments were the least likely to be placed outside the regular school building.

In a regular school building, students may receive services in one of several places: some are served largely in regular classrooms, others spend a significant part of their day in special education resource rooms, and still others spend the majority of their day in separate, self-contained special education classrooms. Although the data are reported in very broad categories and by somewhat different methods, aggregated state child count data give a general national picture of current placement trends (U.S. Department of Education, 1996).[7] As Table 3-4

---

[7]The intent of the placement data collected as required by Section 618 of the IDEA is to assess the extent to which students with disabilities are being served with their peers without disabilities. Because of state-regulated data collections and specific service configurations used by states, some states crosswalk their placement data with the OSEP placement categories; as a result, despite extensive federal support and technical assistance, the placement data reported in the Annual Report to Congress are less reliable than is the total count of students receiving special education under the IDEA.

TABLE 3-4　Educational Environments for Students with Disabilities 1993-1994 (percentage)

	Separate School	Regular School Buildings		
		Separate Class (less than 40% of the day in regular classroom)	Resource Room (40-79% of the day in regular classroom)	Regular Class (at least 80% of the day)
All Disabilities	4.4	22.7	29.4	43.4
6-11- year-olds	2.5	19.3	24.8	53.5
12-17-year-olds	5.6	25.9	35.2	33.3
Specific learning disabilities	0.8	18.8	41.0	39.3
Speech/language	0.4	4.5	7.6	87.5
Mental retardation	8.3	57.0	26.2	8.6
Serious emotional disturbance	18.5	35.3	25.8	20.5
Multiple disabilities	27.1	44.1	19.7	9.0
Hearing impairments	18.7	30.6	20.0	30.6
Orthopedic impairments	8.7	33.3	20.7	37.4
Other health impairments	11.6	21.3	27.0	40.0
Visual impairments	15.3	18.3	21.3	45.2
Autism	27.8	54.5	8.1	9.6
Deaf/blindness	50.1	34.2	7.9	7.8
Traumatic brain injury	23.9	30.2	23.5	22.3

NOTE: Students age 6-21. Separate schools include separate day schools, residential facilities, and hospital or homebound programs. Children are counted as being served in a separate day school if they spend more than 50 percent of the school day there. This includes private facilities attended by students at public expense.

SOURCE: Tables AB2, AB4, AB5, Eighteenth Annual Report. U.S. Department of Education (1996).

illustrates, in 1993-94, 23 percent of students with disabilities spent the majority of their time (more than 60 percent) in such separate, self-contained classrooms. Another 29 percent spent a substantial portion of their time in special education resource rooms, with the rest of their time spent in the regular classroom. About 43 percent of students with disabilities (or about 2 million) are classified as "regular classroom" students—meaning that they spend at least 80 percent of their day there. Many of this group of students are likely to be participating in the general education curriculum and in large-scale assessments, although perhaps with accommodations for both.

Data presented in the table indicate that the amount of time spent in the regular classroom varies by disability. Students with autism, deaf-blindness, mental retardation, and multiple disabilities are least likely to spend much time in the regular classroom. Data also suggest that elementary school students (ages 6-11) are more likely to be served for more time in regular classrooms than are secondary school students (ages 12-17).

Reflecting the national policy trend toward greater integration of students with disabilities into the least restrictive environment, placements in the regular education classrooms increased between 1985-86 and 1989-90 for almost all disabilities, and placements in resource rooms declined. Placements of children in separate classrooms in regular school buildings remained essentially unchanged (Sawyer et al., 1994).

Achievement and Post-School Outcomes

Concern over what happens to students with disabilities after they leave school has been growing since the mid-1980s. It began with the publication of a number of follow-up studies that documented the high unemployment and social isolation among former special education students (Edgar et al., 1986; Hasazi et al., 1985; Mithaug et al., 1985). Contributing to the concern was a 1986 Harris poll indicating that unemployment among persons with disabilities was higher and wages lower than for any other group of working-age Americans (Harris and Associates, 1986).

Almost no nationally representative data were available at that time to examine the post-school outcomes of special education programs for students with various kinds of disabilities. Reliable data on special education graduation and dropout rates are particularly difficult to obtain (U.S Department of Education, 1995; MacMillan et al., 1992). Problems with estimating dropout rates in general are well known; these problems are exacerbated in the case of special education by factors such as the different kinds of diplomas awarded special education students, the return of some portion of special education students to general education during any given year, the tendency of some special education students not to remain with their age or grade cohorts but rather to "age out" of school, and the tendency of others to drop out before ninth grade and never be counted in high school figures.

Because of these concerns, Congress directed the U.S. Department of Education to commission a study of "a sample of handicapped students, encompassing the full range of handicapping conditions, examining their educational progress while in special education and their occupational, educational, and independent living status after graduating from secondary school or otherwise leaving special education" (P.L. 98-199, sec. 618). The NLTS data collection began in 1987 with a sample of more than 8,000 youths with disabilities from more than 300 school districts nationwide. The sample consisted of special education students between the ages of 13 and 21 in the 1985-86 school year. Data were collected in 1987 and again in 1990, drawing on school records, parent and student interviews, and teacher and principal surveys (Wagner et al., 1992). Although these data are now a decade old and were collected prior to the transition requirements of the IDEA, they provide the only representative data about the secondary school achievement and post-school outcomes of special education students.[8]

High School Graduation

One of the most consistent and worrisome findings of research on educational outcomes has been the high dropout rates among students with disabilities. NLTS data confirm that graduating from high school has been problematic for many; about 8 percent of students with disabilities in the NLTS sample dropped out before the ninth grade, and an additional 30 percent dropped out in grades 9 through 12, a rate higher than the national average of 12 percent for students in the general population.[9] Among those who entered high school, less than one-fourth left before age 17, another third left at 18, and the remainder were 19 or older when they left, indicating that many of these students stayed in school until their age peers graduated. On average, however, dropouts with disabilities had accumulated slightly less than 10 credits, whereas students with disabilities who graduated averaged 22 credits; this low accumulation of credits can be accounted for, at least in part, by the high course failure rate among dropouts (Wagner et al., 1993a:2-9). Fewer than 5 percent of students with disabilities who dropped out of secondary school ever returned to earn a diploma (Wagner, 1993:S-2).

Dropout rates were particularly high for students with serious emotional disturbances; close to half of the SED students who started high school left by dropping out. Slightly less than 30 percent of students with learning disabilities, mental retardation, or health impairments dropped out of high school. Dropout rates were higher for minority students than for whites, and also higher for economically disadvantaged students.

---

[8]The NLTS sample included 303 school districts serving secondary students in special education and 22 special schools. Districts were selected randomly from the approximately 14,000 U.S. school districts serving secondary students in special education, stratified by region of the country, a measure of district wealth, and student enrollment. Students were selected from rosters of all students in special education in the 1985-86 school year who were in grades 7 though 12. Rosters were stratified into 3 age groups for each of 11 federal special education disability categories, and youth were randomly selected from each age/disability category so that approximately 800 to 1,000 students were selected in each category (except for the deaf-blind category, for which fewer than 100 students were served in the districts sampled). When possible, the study authors created a comparison group of the general population of youth using data from the National Longitudinal Survey of Youth. Further details regarding the sample and weighting procedures can be found in Wagner et al. (1991) and the sampling design in Javitz and Wagner (1990;1993).

[9]The cohort dropout rate was approximately 12 percent in the National Education Longitudinal Study of 1988 (NELS:88); this cohort is comparable to the NLTS cohort relative to the time period (Aleman, 1995).

In some places, special education students do not qualify for the standard high school diploma unless they have met the criteria for that diploma. Nineteen states require a specific number of credits for the diploma and hold students with disabilities to that same standard. In nine states, however, students with disabilities are awarded the standard diploma but without necessarily being held to the general criteria; instead, criteria are modified and the standard diploma is usually offered upon successful completion of the IEP.

In other states, some kind of test must be passed as one of the requirements for a diploma. In 1994-95, 17 states used this type of exam (along with successful completion of required coursework) to determine whether a student earned a standard diploma (Bond et al., 1996). Of the 17 states with graduation exams, 5 allowed special education students with IEPs to receive a graduation diploma without passing, or even taking, the exam. In these states, students with disabilities could be "exempted" from the assessment, yet still receive a diploma if coursework requirements were met (and these could be met through alternative, special education courses) (Thurlow et al., 1995). Analysts are concerned that such "exempt but graduate" policies could lead to increased referrals to special education (Allington and McGill-Franzen, 1992) or increases in the number of families moving their children to schools in "easy" graduation states (Thurlow et al., 1995).

Still other states award a modified diploma or certificate of completion upon successful completion of IEP goals and objectives. In a number of places, the certificate option is reserved for students with the most severe or profound disabilities. Many of these options are practices that the state has suggested to local education agencies. Since local education agencies have been given so much discretion in establishing requirements and practices, it is difficult to pinpoint exactly which policies are actually being used (Thurlow et al., 1995).

Data from the NLTS indicate that 75 percent of graduates with disabilities received regular diplomas. Diploma rates varied by disability, from 92 percent of graduates with a speech impairment, to 47 percent of those with mental retardation, to 33 percent of those with multiple impairments (Wagner et al., 1991:5-5).

The various state practices regarding graduation credentials for students with disabilities reflect legitimate differences of opinion about how best to meet the needs of students with disabilities. Some contend that differentiated diplomas perpetuate stigmatization; others argue that granting a standard diploma to students who do not achieve at the level represented by the diploma devalues the credential and corrupts the educational process (Destefano and Metzer, 1991). Further research is needed about the impact of differentiated diplomas on student motivation and employment potential.

Achievement

Data from the NLTS indicate that students with disabilities who earned dipomas had slightly lower grades than their peers, with an average grade point average (GPA) of 2.3 over four years of secondary school compared with 2.6 for the general population. (Note that 7 percent of students in regular schools and 55 percent of those in special schools did not receive course grades; they tended to be the students with the more severe disabilities.) Results also indicate that a sizable number of students with disabilities had markedly poor school performance; for example, close to two-thirds of students who completed high school failed at least one course during their four years. Students had better grades in special education classes than in regular education classes; in addition, failure rates were much higher in regular education classes than in special education classes. Students classified as deaf or orthopedically impaired earned the highest GPAs and failed the fewest courses; those with learning disabilities or emotional disturbances had the highest failure rates and the lowest GPAs (Wagner et al., 1993a:2-8).

Data from the NLTS also suggest that students with disabilities may have had to work harder to graduate. For example, almost one-quarter of graduates had attended summer school or taken an extra semester of high school. On average, graduates with disabilities were older than their peers, suggesting that they had had an extra year of school at some point in their academic careers (Wagner, 1993:S-2).

Preliminary analyses conducted for the committee of the *Prospects* study, a national study focused on districts with high concentrations of Title I students, suggest some interesting findings about achievement levels for students with disabilities in elementary school (see Appendix C for sample description and regression results). When their scores on fourth grade reading and mathematics tests are compared with those of their peers without disabilities, students with disabilities as a group scored considerably lower. However, if their third grade achievement levels are considered using "value-added analyses" that control for prior achievement, they showed the same rates of growth over time, suggesting that they were making progress commensurate with their classmates. Furthermore, when growth in achievement was analyzed for children in five different disability groups (emotional, learning, physical, speech, other), somewhat different results emerge. Students with learning disabilities showed slower rates of growth in reading achievement from third to fourth grade, suggesting that they may be falling further behind their peers (both those with and without disabilities). In contrast, with a broad set of variables included, students with speech disabilities actually showed more improvement in reading than other students (see Appendix C).

These preliminary results suggest that several factors will be important to examine in future research on achievement of students with disabilities. First, type of disability should be considered; overall achievement results, as well as the effects of some other independent variables, were different for children in different categories of disability. Second, longitudinal data should be collected that track change or progress in achievement over time: models that allow examination of growth and progress will be key to understanding whether achievement is rising, at what rates, and for which groups of children. Third, serious consideration should be given to using models that control for prior achievement in student assessment systems; this approach will better test the school's incremental contribution to student learning. In general, these results underscore the importance of more research on achievement and schooling that includes students with disabilities.

Postsecondary Education and Employment

The NLTS includes follow-up data on a subsample of about 1,800 students for three to five years after they had been out of school. Overall results of these data suggest much lower rates of participation for youth with disabilities in postsecondary school than in competitive employment (Wagner and Blackorby, 1996).

As Figure 3-1 shows, only 27 percent of youth with disabilities were enrolled in postsecondary education during this 3-5 year period, compared with 68 percent of the general population; among high school graduates, the rates were somewhat higher for both groups (37 and 78 percent, respectively). As the figure illustrates, however, postsecondary enrollment varied considerably for students with different kinds of disabilities—some had attendance rates close to those of the general population. When students with disabilities did go on to postsecondary schooling, it was most likely to be vocational training or attendance at a two-year college; only 4 percent had ever attended a four-year college by the time they had been out of high school for 3 to 5 years.

Youth with disabilities were competitively employed at lower rates than the general population (see Figure 3-1)—57 compared with 69 percent—not so large a gap as for enrollment in postsecondary schooling.[10] Youth in some categories of disability—learning disability and speech impairment—had employment rates at or near that of the overall population. Furthermore, among students with disabilities, high school graduates fared better than dropouts in the competitive job market (65 percent of graduates were employed compared with only 47 percent of dropouts).

Overall, then, available data on the outcomes of secondary schooling for special education students suggest that as a group they do not fare as well as youth in the general population. However, the outcomes vary tremendously within the group, especially by types of disability. This underscores the importance of policies and programs that are responsive to the wide variability of children and youth who fall under the protection of the IDEA. A diverse range of students is likely to require a diversity of educational options.

---

[10]Sheltered, supported (e.g., wages subsidized by public funds), and volunteer work were not included as competitive paid employment.

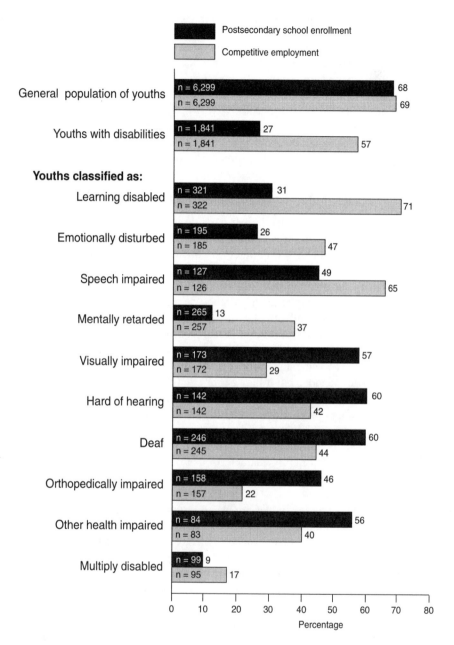

FIGURE 3-1   Postsecondary school enrollment and competitive employment of youths out of school three to five years. Adapted from: Wagner et al. (1992).

PARENTAL INVOLVEMENT

Parents play important roles in the schooling of students with disabilities: as contributors to their children's achievement, codevelopers of their children's educational program, and advocates of their children's rights. These roles are likely to become even more important under standards-based reform, which calls for higher achievement, necessitates additional educational decisions, and may create new legal issues. This section discusses the research evidence on parental involvement for students in general and for those with disabilities, as well as research evidence on parent participation in the special education process.

Effects of Parental Involvement on Achievement

Common sense tells us that higher parental involvement in a child's education should have a positive effect on his or her achievement. In general, research supports this conclusion; however, three complications or limitations arise. First, few studies are national in scope, and those that are, such as High School and Beyond (HSB) and the National Educational Longitudinal Study (NELS), provide information primarily at the high school level. We report evidence from a new elementary school study, the *Prospects* study, that offsets this bias. Second, the meaning of parental involvement must be broken down into relevant concepts, each of which may have differential impacts on achievement. For example, parental involvement in school organizations may have a number of positive outcomes for schools, but it may be far enough removed from an individual child's learning to have no direct link with the child's achievement. Or, a measure of the amount of parental contact with schools could indicate that the student is encountering problems in school, and thus could be negatively related to achievement (Muller and Kerbow, 1993:32-34). Third, parental involvement may be correlated with other family characteristics that also affect achievement, such as parental education and family income (e.g., Muller and Kerbow, 1993:Fig. 2.17) and family structure (Lee, 1993)—meaning that careful multivariate analyses that control for other variables are usually required to separate these effects.

Despite the limitations, several recent studies, using national-level data and sophisticated controls for other variables, indicate a positive relationship between parental involvement and achievement of children in general.[11] These studies overwhelmingly conclude that parental involvement, measured in terms of organizational involvement, parent-school contacts, parental monitoring of student activities, or parents working with students at home, is positively related to achievement as measured by standardized test scores, grades, high school completion, and the absence of behavioral problems. The one negative correlation was

---

[11]These include studies of High School and Beyond (Fehrmann et al., 1987; Astone and McLanahan, 1991) and a large set of studies using data from the National Educational Longitudinal Study (Lee, 1993; Muller, 1995; Sui-Chu and Willms, 1996).

for the measure of schools contacting parents, which, as noted above, was associated both with behavioral problems and lower achievement as measured by test scores and grades (Sui-Chu and Willms, 1996:Table 6). In addition, a number of these studies and several others (Milne et al., 1986; Madigan, 1994) found a positive relationship between high parental expectations for their children's education and achievement success.

These conclusions are supported by two other data sets, discussed in the next sections, which allow the examination of parent involvement specifically for students with disabilities.

National Longitudinal Transitional Study of Special Education Students

Parental involvement was measured in the NLTS by teacher ratings of parental involvement in school experiences, such as helping with homework and monitoring school progress. Study results show that students with disabilities whose parents were very involved in their education missed fewer days of school and were significantly less likely to fail a class than their peers with disabilities whose parents were not at all involved (Wagner et al., 1993c:5-9). Controlling for type of disability and other demographic factors, very involved parents were also more likely to see their children with disabilities attend postsecondary academic and vocational schools, become employed in the competitive labor market, and succeed in living independently (Wagner et al., 1993b:3-25).

Parental expectations, as measured by parent ratings of the likelihood that their children would attain specific goals (e.g., independent living, postsecondary schooling, competitive employment) also affect student school success, although the type of disability affected parental expectations.[12] Parents who held higher learning expectations for their children with disabilities (again, after controlling for type of disability, family socioeconomic status, and functional skill levels) were rewarded with greater student success in postsecondary enrollment, independent living, and community participation; employment prospects were unaffected. As the NLTS authors noted, "The influence of these aspects of parenting was powerful, more so than most of the other factors we have examined" (Wagner et al., 1993b:3-30).

The *Prospects* Study

Several relevant measures were obtained from the *Prospects* parent surveys (see Appendix C for more detail on this study): three questions on parental in-

---

[12]For example, the authors note that "only 3 percent of youth who scored low on the self-care scale were expected to live away from home unsupervised. Conversely, 84 percent of youth with high scores on the self-care skills scale and 92 percent of youth with high scores on the functional mental skills scale were expected to achieve residential independence" (Wagner et al., 1993c:3-26).

volvement (at home, through participation in school organizations, and through attendance at school events), number of school contacts, an index of school satisfaction, and a measure of parental academic expectations for their child. Parents of students with disabilities showed approximately similar levels of involvement as other parents. School dissatisfaction, however, appeared to be higher among parents of students with disabilities, especially parents of students with emotional problems. As anticipated, because the question on expectations was limited to academic alternatives, parents of students with disabilities showed considerably lower academic expectations overall, although there is quite a bit of variation depending on the type of disability.

The effects of these parental factors, as well as other relevant demographic factors, on fourth grade achievement in reading and math were examined using a model that also controls for previous educational achievement (as measured by third grade test scores). These analyses (see regression results in Appendix C) indicate that parental expectations for their children's education were a powerful predictor of achievement in both reading and math after controlling for race, gender, disability, and other family characteristics. For reading, the only other significant parental variable was frequency of school contacts, which was negatively related to reading achievement for the reasons explained above.

For math scores, several other variables were important. Parental involvement both at home and through school organizations had a positive and significant relationship with math achievement. In addition, higher school dissatisfaction had a negative relationship with lower math scores.

Although small sample sizes preclude doing these analyses exclusively for students with disabilities, the model does control for disability and, as noted previously, disability in general does not have a significant effect on growth in achievement (i.e., once previous achievement is considered).

Parental Involvement in the Special Education Process

As discussed in Chapter 2, the IDEA gives parents of students with disabilities important roles and responsibilities in the education of their children. Of particular note are the opportunities for parents to work with professionals to develop the IEP for their child.

Systematic research on the nature and quality of parent participation in the education of students with disabilities is very limited. As the point in the special education process at which parents and professionals have the greatest opportunity for collaboration and substantive input, the IEP conference has been the focus of much of the available research. Both research and parent reports (National Council on Disability, 1995) suggest that, for some parents, the IEP process has worked well: they are actively involved in key decisions regarding the education of their children, such as what goals the teacher should concentrate on and in what classroom setting the child should be educated. One mother's testimony describes her satisfaction with the IEP process (National Council on Disability, 1995:56): "A key to Michael's success has been the teamwork of all the educational professionals involved in Michael's program. The IEP process has allowed us to carefully plan and individually tailor Michael's educational goals and objectives." [13]

Evidence indicates that for some parents, however, the IEP process is a less positive experience. Some have found themselves in an adversarial relationship with schools when they do not agree with the recommendations made by the educators. Other parents have not participated at all in the IEP process and may not even be aware of the special role they are entitled to play. No systematic national data are available on participation rates of parents in IEP meetings or other factors, such as the number of parents who challenge IEP decisions. However, results of recent field hearings suggest that weak parent participation in decisions about appropriate education may be one of the most neglected problems in special education (National Council on Disability, 1995).

Barriers to Participation

Research has identified several barriers to effective parent participation in the IEP process. These include low parent attendance, time constraints, use of education jargon by school professionals, the undervaluing of parental input by school professionals, and a lack of parent skills and information.

Low attendance by parents at IEP meetings is reported to be a widespread problem (Goldstein et al., 1980; Leyser, 1985; Polifka, 1981; Scanlon et al., 1981). Some studies have suggested that parents are not well informed about the IEP (Christenson et al., 1992a); for example, one survey of 325 parents of students with disabilities found that 30-40 percent of the parents did not know what an IEP was (Leyser, 1985).

Studies have shown that the time allotted for meeting and developing IEPs is relatively brief for the amount of substantive work to be done. One qualitative research study (Silverstein et al., 1992) found that IEP meetings took one hour, but others (Vaughn et al., 1988; Ysseldyke et al., 1982b; Silverstein et al., 1992) found the time to be of much shorter duration. Parents did not necessarily desire longer formal meetings but instead wanted more time to process information, make decisions, and gain additional knowledge.

Evidence also suggests that the use of technical language and jargon, in both reports and conversations, is a barrier for parents at multidisciplinary team meetings (National Council on Disability, 1995; Mehan et al., 1986; Roit and Pfohl, 1984; Weddig, 1984; Ysseldyke et al., 1982b). Even without jargon, written and oral

---

[13]In the National Council on Disability Report of 1995, 400 witnesses, most of whom were parents or other family members of students with disabilities, testified in 10 field hearings across the United States on their experiences and recommendations for the IDEA.

language can pose a barrier for parents of students with disabilities. Research has found that special education documents are written at a fifth to eighth grade reading level, which may be too high for some disadvantaged or culturally different parents. Furthermore, if parents cannot understand critical documents, they may not actually be giving informed consent on important decisions (Lindle, 1992).

Yet another issue is the perception of some parents that school professionals are not responsive to their views during the IEP process. At the hearings held by the National Council on Disability (1995), many parents testified that they found the IEP process frustrating and intimidating, citing such problems as teachers who arrived at the meetings with completed IEPs or who did not respect their opinions on potential goals and objectives. Researchers have documented both superficial and low levels of parent involvement in the development of the IEP (Christenson et al., 1992a, Goldstein et al., 1980). As one mother testified, "I believe parents come to the IEP meeting as an unequal partner. Our signature means only that we were present at the meeting" (National Council on Disability, 1995:57).

Lack of good information about the sometimes complex IEP process appears to be one important reason why some parents of students with disabilities are not involved in educational decision making (Hoff et al., 1978; Goldstein et al., 1980; Leyser, 1985; Lindle, 1992). Research indicates that some parents lack familiarity with the IEP document and its contents (Leyser, 1985; McKinney and Horcutt, 1982). Even though some parents may not wish to participate in the decisions about their child's program, researchers have suggested that it is important that all parents be informed enough to choose the level of participation and to give meaningful consent (Turnbull and Turnbull, 1982, in press).

Special Needs of Minority and Poor Parents

Barriers to meaningful participation in educational decision making are often magnified for minority parents of students with disabilities, as well as for economically or educationally disadvantaged parents. Minority and poor parents may also encounter other obstacles stemming from cultural differences, language barriers, and lower educational attainment. These obstacles warrant attention, since African American and Native American children tend to be identified for special education at somewhat higher rates than other groups, and since parents of children with disabilities tend to be more socioeconomically disadvantaged than parents in general.

The research base on minority issues in special education is narrow and consists largely of qualitative research (e.g., Harry, 1992b,1992c; Harry et al., 1995). The available studies stress two features as central to the participation of minority parents in special education: (1) the influence of culture and socioeconomic status on the interactions between parents and professionals and (2) ineffective communication.

Research suggests that the typical modes and logistics of interactions between parents and schools may not be well attuned to differences in culture and economic circumstances. Education meetings in the United States are often characterized by efficiency, organization, and formality, which may contrast with the slower, more personalized approaches of other cultures (Harry, 1992a). Logistical matters, such as transportation, child care, and work schedules, often become a deterrent for parents who cannot make the necessary arrangements to attend education meetings (Harry, 1992a). These logistical barriers are not specific to minority parents; indeed, they can create problems for any single-parent, low-income, immigrant, or homeless family.

Research has also emphasized the importance of oral and written communication in minority parent participation. Parents for whom English is not the primary language may have difficulty comprehending plain English, let alone the educational jargon that is often part of such meetings (Harry, 1992a, 1992b; and Harry et al., 1995). There is also evidence that other cultures may have different views of specific terms such as "disability" or "handicapped," which may present problems for parents who are trying to understand the exact nature of their child's disability (Harry 1992a, 1992c).

Written communication is the primary means of providing information, recording decisions, and procuring parental permission in special education. Documents are usually written in English at a middle-grade reading level, are presented to parents without much discussion, and contain many unfamiliar words. Harry (1992a) has suggested that the presence of an interpreter and a special education family liaison worker may help to remove barriers for minority families who have differences in languages, experiences, and expectations.

PARTICIPATION IN STANDARDS-BASED REFORM: ISSUES AND CASE EXAMPLES

As the preceding sections have illustrated, the characteristics of students with disabilities are very heterogeneous, and their variety affects how they currently participate in general education. One can reasonably assume that this heterogeneity will also affect the nature and level of their participation in standards-based reform. A carefully considered approach to participation is consistent with the individualization of curricular goals, instructional objectives, teaching methodology, and assessment of progress that characterizes special education practice and the interpretation of legal mandates. For a number of students with disabilities, the general education goals and instructional objectives associated with standards-based reforms are likely to be compatible with their individualized educational programs. Clearly, these students should participate in the standards, curriculum, instruction, and assessments associated with the standards-based reforms.

For some other students with disabilities, participation in the common standards and the general education curriculum is likely to require some modification or adaptations. For example, some students who need special education in only one academic area (e.g., mathematics) may be able to participate fully in all other standards but may require adaptations in mathematics standards and curricula. Other students may need to move through the curriculum at a slower pace, necessitating adaptations. Some students will need instruction in areas not covered by the common standards. A small proportion of students with severe disabilities may require a curriculum that is very different from the curriculum based on the common standards. Issues related to standards, curriculum, and instruction are discussed further in Chapter 4.

Some students with disabilities will be able to participate fully in the common standards but will require adaptations or accommodations to participate in common assessments. Because of the nature of their disabilities, some of these children simply cannot take the tests as designed, for example because they cannot hold a pencil or see the test booklet. These children require testing accommodations, such as braille or large print versions of the test, oral reading of directions, use of a typewriter or computer, or a method to point to correct answers. Other students, such as some with learning disabilities, sometimes need accommodations such as extended time, more breaks during testing sessions, or a separate setting in which to take the test. Chapter 5 focuses on issues in the assessment of students with disabilities participating in standards-based reforms.

For an individual student with a disability, the curricular emphasis in the IEP will be one of the most important considerations in determining whether the common content standards and assessment procedures will be suitable. Depending on the number of behavioral dimensions affected by the disability and the severity of those effects, students' IEPs may or may not include goals that are consistent with standards-based reform. In the section below we present three case examples to illustrate these principles.

Case I: Student with a Mild Disability

Mary is a tenth grade student with an attention deficit disorder and a learning disability in the areas of reading recognition and reading comprehension.[14] She currently reads at the fourth grade level in one-to-one assessment trials with her resource room teacher. Her reading skills continue to improve with individualized, one-to-one instruction, but the pace of improvement is slow. The time she must devote to reading instruction in her daily schedule means there are other academic courses she cannot take.

In other academic areas, Mary performs at a below-average but passing level. Her mathematics skills, depending on how they are assessed, are near average for students her age. Her performance on measures of general intellectual functioning has varied within a narrow range, indicating low average overall abilities.

---

[14]Although her name has been changed, the description of Mary is based on a real child.

Overall, her motor abilities and adaptive behavior are normal; however, she has some difficulties with social skills and emotional adjustment. She does not react constructively to pressure to perform well or on timed academic exercises. She typically does very poorly on any kind of group-administered standardized test. She does considerably better on standardized tests if they are administered on a one-to-one basis or in a small group and on tests that do not require her to read complex narratives as part of solving problems. Mary's special education team and parents prefer that she be excused from group-administered standardized tests or that such tests be given to her in a small group setting with extended time limits.

Although the details vary from case to case, there are a relatively large number of students with cognitive disabilities like those described for Mary. Generally, these students do not have impairments on the dimensions of sensory acuity, motor skills, or health status. General intellectual functioning, speech/communication, and academic achievement typically are below average, but above the level that would lead to a diagnosis of mental retardation. Adaptive behavior in the sense of caring for one's self is normal or close to normal, but social skills generally are slightly below average, as is overall emotional adjustment.

Increasingly, over the last two decades, many students with these characteristics have been diagnosed as having specific learning disabilities in school settings, although there are many more students with some of these characteristics who are not referred and therefore never considered for special education eligibility. Indeed, depending on the state and, within states the school district, students like Mary may or may not be diagnosed as having a disability and qualify for special education.

The most difficult questions about participation in standards-based reform occur with students like Mary: students with real and significant educational problems that may or may not lead to a formal designation as having a disability. These students often devote some part of their school day to specially designed instruction to help remediate areas of academic difficulty; this makes it hard for them to participate fully in the rest of the curriculum and creates competing priorities for how they should spent their time in school.

Designation as having a disability triggers certain protections and rights under the IDEA and Section 504. Do these protections and rights include alternatives to the common curriculum, especially in areas of academic difficulty? Should they? Or is it more important that people with mild disabilities be included in the common curriculum, to ensure that the education system serves these students well and that they have access to curricula that meet high standards? If the answers to these questions are affirmative, then there is the further dilemma over assessment procedures: Should accommodations be available to students who read poorly, have difficulty meeting time limits, or are inattentive in larger groups? Accommodations almost inevitably change the assessment task in significant and often unknown ways, as we discuss further in Chapter 5.

Case II: Student with Multiple Disabilities of Varying Severity

Jerry (also a real child with the name changed) was diagnosed at the age of 6 months at a university clinic as having cerebral palsy that affected all four limbs as well as speech production. Preschool services for children with disabilities were provided beginning at age 1 and continuing until Jerry entered kindergarten in a general education setting. Although assessments of intelligence and achievement are difficult due to Jerry's disabilities related to movement and speech production, it appears that he has at least average cognitive ability. Jerry's IEP specifies that he receive the services of a one-to-one instructional assistant in the classroom to aid him with communication and mobility activities. Jerry also receives the related services of physical, occupational, and speech/language therapy. He participates in all academic activities in his first grade classroom and is acquiring academic skills in core areas such as reading and math at an average to above-average level. He is pursuing the goals in the general education curriculum adopted by his school district for children his age.

From what is known about Jerry, the common curriculum appears suitable for his abilities, and he is likely to make good progress in acquiring academic skills. Assessment of his skills and abilities is difficult; for example, he cannot write his answers because of his severe motor skills impairments. Testing accommodations are likely to require more time as well as help from his instructional assistant. Few would argue about whether he should receive such accommodations in assessment, but the meaning of his accommodated performance in relation to the performance of other students is uncertain. Furthermore, the way in which his performance should be included in high-stakes comparisons involving his classroom, school attendance center, or school district is even more uncertain. But Jerry clearly should have access to the general education curriculum, and assessment of progress in that curriculum is part and parcel of that access. Many would argue that, unless he is included in such assessments, general education will not be held accountable for his progress.   Resolution of the problems associated with Jerry's participation in the standards-based assessments will not be easy or straightforward. But resolution is necessary, and different options will have varying effects on him and his school.

Students like Jerry with normal cognitive ability and severe motor or sensory impairments are extremely rare—well under 1 percent of the overall student population. No matter what is done for Jerry and students like him, there will be little effect on the high-stakes comparisons of performance at the building, district, or state levels; the much larger group of students with mild to moderate cognitive disabilities, who make up 5-8 percent of the overall student population, have the potential to affect these high-stakes comparisons.

Case III: Student with Multiple Severe Disabilities

In any school district of more than a few hundred students, there are likely to be children with multiple severe disabilities who perform far below their age peers on several important dimensions of behavior. The number of disabilities, the severe discrepancies from developmental norms, and the complexity of their special education needs are likely to render at least some of them unable to participate in any meaningful way in the activities associated with standards-based reform. Consider the case of Tom, a child who has multiple and very severe disabilities, including extremely limited mobility, deafness, and profound mental retardation. He is not able to learn even rudimentary skills associated with the standard curriculum, e.g., basic letter-sound relationships, recognition of words by sight, knowledge of basic temporal relationships. He is nevertheless entitled by law to special education and related services. Tom's IEP might address such fundamental learning activities such as basic self-care and communication skills. Tom is part of the public school population to whom standards-based reforms are applied and is ostensibly included in the legislative language that declares "All children can learn and achieve to high standards." Extremely rare cases like this present a challenge to the inclusive language of "all" in standards-based reforms.

Issues

As noted throughout this chapter, there are enormous variations in the population of students classified as having disabilities. A very small number of students—those with the most severe disabilities, such as Tom—will not be able to participate fully in all aspects of the general education curriculum, the common academic standards embedded in that curriculum, or the common assessment procedures. For some, full participation in the general education curriculum and common academic standards will be feasible, but some modification such as assessment accommodations will be required to overcome obvious impediments due to sensory or motor impairments (such as the case of Jerry). Many students with mild disabilities can be expected to participate in the common curriculum for most, if not all, parts of their educational programs. For many students with disabilities, however, the extent of participation in the common standards-based curriculum and assessments is likely to depend on the interpretation of legal rights and assumptions about the risks and benefits of participation (such as the case of Mary) as well as the nature of the standards. These students *may*—and we emphasize *may* because the legal requirements are not clear—have legal rights to assessment accommodations and, arguably, entitlement to the curriculum specified in their IEPs rather than the curriculum specified in standards-based reforms.

Two particularly complex issues regarding the participation of all students with disabilities in standards-based reforms are considered further in Chapters 4 and 5: the extent of participation in the general education curriculum and the need for accommodations in standards-based assessment activities.

CONCLUSIONS

Several themes emerge from this discussion of student identification, disability characteristics, and educational needs.

The number of students with disabilities is sizable, and they are extremely heterogeneous. More than 5 million school-age students—or about 10 percent of the school-age population—qualify for special education services, constituting a significant population. Students served by special education vary widely in severity of disability, educational goals, and participation in the general education curriculum. These variations affect many aspects of their schooling. In addition, there is evidence that students with disabilities as a group are at socioeconomic disadvantage compared with their peers without disabilities.

Currently the criteria for identifying many of the categories of disability are not well defined or reliable, even though these criteria affect important decisions about which students are eligible for legal rights and special education services under the IDEA. Disability categories are defined largely by state policies; identification rates vary a great deal from state to state, and very different criteria are used in different places. Interpretation and implementation of the disability criteria is largely a district-level concern; no systematic data are available about how the criteria may be interpreted and therefore which students get into which categories and on what basis. Currently, to qualify for special education, a yes-no determination of the presence of a disability has to be made, although disability varies along a number of dimensions, each of which is best described as a continuum of severity. Clear-cut decisions about which children should be served are not easily made. Some children who qualify for special education in one school would not qualify elsewhere. Conversely, some children are not identified as disabled who are likely to have the same educational needs as those who are identified. The implications of standards-based reforms for these children—low-achieving but not currently identified for special education—is beyond the scope of this committee's work but nevertheless should be considered in implementing and monitoring the effects of standards-based reforms.

Meaningful discussion of standards, curriculum, assessment, and outcomes cannot occur without thoughtful consideration of the varied characteristics of the large and diverse number of students with disabilities. *The nature of the participation of students with disabilities in the common aspects of standards-based reform is likely to vary depending on their individual characteristics and educational needs.* Over the past 20 years, students with disabilities have been participating more and more in general education classrooms and curricula. For some students with disabilities, participation in the general education curricula and therefore in standards-based reforms is already a reality and will require minor or no individualized adaptations. The small group of children with very severe cognitive disabilities will present particular challenges for standards-based reforms and are likely to require major adaptations to standards-based curricula and assessments. For another group—largely those with mild to moderate cognitive disabilities—participation in common standards and assessments can be expected to increase considerably as the frameworks are put into place. These children may require some modifications to the common standards, curricula, or assessments to ensure compatibility of their individualized education programs with the standards frameworks.

The number of students with disabilities who may need accommodations or other modifications in standards and assessments is unknown and will depend on such factors as behavioral characteristics and severity of disability, extent of participation in the general curriculum, and the instructional needs of students. Nationally representative data are lacking about the population of students with disabilities on any of these factors. The need for accommodations and other modifications will also depend on the nature of a district's or state's particular content standards, performance standards, and assessments—which vary significantly from place to place.

The role of parents will be key in ensuring the successful participation of students with disabilities in standards-based reforms. Parental involvement and expectations are strongly related to the achievement of their children, even after taking into account the effects of related variables, such as parental education and socioeconomic status; these relationships appear to hold for students with and without disabilities. In addition, parents of students with disabilities have a unique role to play in the process of designing their children's educational programs. Although the IEP process is the cornerstone of parental involvement, evidence indicates that it has not worked well for all parents. Concerns regarding the IEP process are exacerbated for minority or economically disadvantaged parents. Resolving the barriers to parental involvement takes on even greater importance in the era of standards-based reform, particularly in light of the research evidence indicating its effects on improving achievement. The legal provisions guaranteeing the rights and responsibilities of parents in special education are potentially powerful tools that parents can use to bring about the successful integration of children with disabilities into a standards-based educational environment. At the same time, standards-based reform may place even greater demands on parents, in terms of decision-making responsibilities, participation requirements, and training and information needs.

Very few systematic, nationally representative data are available about students with disabilities. As a result, we know very little about the population served by special education—how many children move in and out of special education, how definitions of disability categories are interpreted by individual school staff, how many children are referred but not found eligible, how many have a disability but do not need special education, what the demographic characteristics of eligible children are, how many students complete full requirements for a diploma, how many leave school on some other basis, and so on. Counting and keeping track of data related to the disability status, outcomes, and performance of students with disabilities are complicated by a number of factors specific to this population—for example, many cannot take group-administered tests (usually the primary outcome measure) under standardized procedures, many split their time between general education classrooms and special education classrooms, some are served in separate schools not sampled in most data collection procedures, some do not remain with their age or grade cohort as they progress through school, and many move in and out of the special education system over time.

The exclusion of students with disabilities from these research and evaluation samples can affect the overall results of these studies. The results of any aggregated data pertaining to general education, and thus to standards-based reform, can be affected if these children are left out, especially since many students with disabilities have lower achievement. Furthermore, systematic, representative data are needed about the educational progress of students with disabilities relative to the larger group of general education students.

Without good data on such factors as special education referral and identification rates or graduation rates and types of diplomas, it will be hard to monitor some of the potential effects of standards-based reforms—both intended and unintended—for students with disabilities. Past experience has indicated that new policies often have systemwide effects that were not originally intended, such as increased dropout or retention rates. In addition, specific subgroups of children, such as those defined by gender or race/ethnicity, can be differentially affected. It will be very important to detect whether, for example, standards-based reforms are increasing the rates of referral to special education, changing the demographics of who gets identified, or affecting the dropout rates or types of diplomas obtained. Changes such as these have the potential to affect all students, not just those with disabilities.

4

Content Standards, Curriculum, and Instruction

Curriculum and instruction are the meat of the educational process. Real change in education comes with changes in the content that teachers teach and students learn, and in the instructional methods that teachers use. Both curriculum and instruction in turn are shaped by expectations about the kinds of educational outcomes that students should manifest by the time they graduate from high school.

Standards-based reform has been built around a specific set of assumptions about curriculum and instruction, embodied in the content and performance standards that are central to the reforms. Special education, for its part, has been built around a set of assumptions about valued post-school outcomes, curricula, and instruction that reflect the diversity of students with disabilities and their educational needs. Whether students with disabilities will participate successfully in standards-based reform will depend largely on the degree of alignment between these two sets of assumptions.

This chapter provides an overview of post-school outcomes and curricular and instructional issues for students with disabilities and their relationships to standards. We first review the key assumptions of standards-based reform concerning outcomes, curriculum, and instruction as embodied in existing state content standards. We then examine how these standards interact with the educational outcomes and curricular and instructional experiences that are valued for students with disabilities. We compare key characteristics, derived from research, associated with effective instruction for special education with the instructional assumptions of standards-based reform. The chapter ends with a discussion of the implications of including students with disabilities in the expected outcomes, curriculum, and instruction of standards-based reform and with conclusions about the alignment between standards-based reform and special education in these important areas.

CONTENT STANDARDS IN STANDARDS-BASED REFORM

As noted in Chapter 2, content standards are the main political tools of standards-based reform. They define the breadth and depth of valued knowledge that students are expected to learn, and they are intended to reduce the curriculum disparities existing across schools and school districts. For students with disabilities, the degree to which a set of content standards is relevant to their valued educational outcomes and consistent with proven instructional practices will determine how successfully they will participate in standards-based reform.

At the present time, 48 states and the District of Columbia have content standards or are in the process of developing them (Gandal, 1996). To provide a context for understanding the implications of these standards for the education of students with disabilities, this section examines the assumptions about post-school outcomes, curriculum, and instruction contained in current state content standards.

Purposes of Content Standards

As described in Chapter 2, content standards have three purposes, all intimately related to outcomes, curriculum, and instruction. First, they help frame the education reform debate by publicly identifying what is important for schools to teach and for students to be able to demonstrate (McLaughlin and Shepard, 1995). In a sense, then, content standards signal the outcomes that the public, policy makers, and educators consider valuable for students to exhibit at the end of their secondary schooling.

Second, content standards guide public school instruction, curriculum, and assessment in an organized and meaningful manner—essentially providing a map of where the curriculum should go and enabling schools and teachers to tailor their instruction to fit the needs of diverse learners. Finally—and ideally—they can guide the allocation of instructional resources by clarifying the goals of instruction and motivating districts to identify how to use their resources to achieve these goals (McLaughlin and Shepard, 1995).

Thus, content standards are not simply a list of important knowledge and skills. Rather, they are a "vision of what . . . curriculum should include in terms of content priority and emphasis. Content standards should provide a coherent structure to guide curriculum and instruction" (McLaughlin and Shepard, 1995:20). The emphasis is on *guiding*, not constricting, teaching, and learning (Council for Basic Education, 1996).

Varied Characteristics of State Content Standards

As discussed in Chapter 2, states are taking various approaches to developing content standards; consequently, their standards tend to differ by level of specificity and format. Some state content frameworks focus on big ideas rather than specifics (Elmore and Fuhrman, 1994). In civics, for instance, the Oregon Department of Education has developed relatively broad general guidelines; one example calls on students to "understand and apply knowledge about governmental and political systems, and the rights and responsibilities of citizens" (Oregon Department of Education, 1996:16). By comparison, the Michigan Department of Education has developed more prescribed content standards for civics, such as: "All students will identify the purposes of national, state, and local governments in the United States, describe how citizens organize government to accomplish their purposes, and assess their effectiveness" (Michigan Department of Education, 1995:22). Some state content standards are so specific as to designate a particular piece of literature that must be covered at a certain grade. Some states attach specific standards to grade levels; others provide more general outcomes that must be met at the elementary, middle, and high school levels.

The degree of variation among the state content standards and their politically charged nature have led states to call their content standards by different names, including goals, standards, examples, benchmarks, guidelines, and frameworks (Council of Chief State School Officers, 1995). A term being introduced by numerous states is *expectations*. The Kentucky Department of Education's state standards are actually called Kentucky's Learning Goals and Academic Expectations and consist of broad goals to be achieved and demonstrated prior to graduation (Kentucky Department of Education, 1994). Colorado defines its model content standards as setting "high expectations in these areas for all students" (Colorado Department of Education, 1995:3).

It is difficult to capture the extent of state variation in content standards. Extant surveys of state standards are limited by both the criteria used for reporting and evaluating the standards and when the data were collected. Two areas that were of particular interest to the committee were the content domains addressed by the standards and the pedagogical implications. Although there have been several national surveys of state standards development, the most recent evidence pertaining to areas in which standards are developed is available from the Council of Great City Schools (1996). Based on information obtained from 48 states, this survey indicated that almost every state was developing or had completed standards in the four core areas of mathematics, science, social studies, and language arts. These findings are corroborated by a survey by the Council of Chief State School Officers (in press). Far fewer states are developing standards in the arts (n = 31), health (n = 29), vocational/technical education (n = 16), or practical living skills (n = 9). Furthermore, only the core academic areas are currently being assessed.

The only in-depth analysis of the pedagogical implications of standards was conducted in the areas of mathematics and science by the Council of Chief State School Officers (Blank and Pechman, 1995). The results of this review of state standards indicated that recently developed state standards frameworks link math and science content to classroom practices and require different methods of teaching, different materials, and more active roles for students.

Despite the variation in the specificity, level of application, and labels used for content standards across the nation, similarities do occur across many states. For example, most states require students to be able to write well, apply prior knowledge to understand texts, demonstrate an ability to organize information, work with others, relate different experiences, integrate English skills throughout the curriculum, and demonstrate cultural sensitivity (Council for Basic Education, 1996).

To obtain a richer picture of the types of standards being developed by states across content domains, the committee examined more closely the content standards documents developed by seven states that represent both early and more recent developers of content standards, as well a regional mix.[1] We looked at standards documents to get a sense of whether they were strictly academic or more comprehensive. We then looked more closely at the standards documents in the areas of language arts/reading, mathematics, and social studies, to see whether they are generic or subject-matter-specific, what levels of knowledge they demand, and how explicit they are about pedagogy. The content standards we looked at include more than global statements of valued knowledge or skills; most are multilevel documents that begin with a goal statement, then further define the goals, sometimes through several levels of standards, expected performances, or sample demonstrations.

Our examination suggested that standards vary greatly across and within states in terms of organization and level of specificity. None of the standards documents seemed to provide the full scope and sequence required of a curriculum. Instead, all provide frameworks for defining the essential or enduring knowledge expected to be demonstrated by students at various stages in their education.

Mirroring the results of the state-by-state survey, the completed standards for the states we examined were predominantly academic. All seven states have completed math, science, and social studies standards as well as standards in areas of reading and writing or language arts. Three of these states have developed specific standards in the arts, health and/or physical education, and second languages. Two additional states embed the arts within other standards (e.g., communicating through music), and one state has specific content standards under development in the occupational and career areas.

Within the academic areas, the content standards seemed to range from a focus on basic knowledge and skills (e.g., arithmetic computation, use of phonics to recognize words) to more abstract applications of skills (e.g., problem solving; analyzing, interpreting, and evaluating ideas; writing to convey meaning). Most of the standards appeared to emphasize more abstract applications. For example,

---

[1]The states selected for review were Colorado, Kentucky, Maryland, Michigan, New York, Oregon, and Vermont.

reading standards commonly refer to reading for meaning, taking a critical stance, and interpreting texts. In only two states did reading standards include specific reference to basic literacy skills. One such standard, "Students read and understand a variety of materials," included the expectation that students will use comprehension skills (such as previewing, predicting, comparing and contrasting, re-reading, and self-monitoring) as well as word recognition skills (such as phonics, context clues, picture clues, word origins, and word order clues). In a second state, the standard, "Comprehend a variety of printed materials," included the ability to recognize, pronounce, and know the meaning of words using phonics skills, language structure, context clues, and visual skills. Across all seven states, social studies, history, and related standards included references to specific knowledge or skills, such as "relate historical events of the 17th and 18th centuries in chronological order" or "use maps and globes to trace the migration of various groups during specific periods of time."

Instructional Implications

In our examination of standards in seven states, we also looked at their references to specific pedagogy. Although the references varied across the standards, the standards did suggest at least two implications for instruction. First, with respect to content, most of the standards call on students to be able to apply, demonstrate, or use some set of knowledge and skills, rather than just to know isolated facts or be able to perform basic computations or operations. Second, in terms of instructional format, the standards refer to group problem solving and cooperation, to specific projects or demonstrations students are expected to develop, and to specific materials, resources, and technology students are expected to use.

These pedagogical features noted by the committee in its examination of state standards appear to be part of a larger trend across national and state content standards. The review of math and science standards by the Council of Chief State School Officers (Blank and Pechman, 1995) indicated that within the 40 state standards frameworks reviewed, the National Council of Teachers of Mathematics (1989) standards, the AAAS benchmarks (1993), and the National Research Council's science education standards (1996) were represented. A total of 32 of the frameworks provided pedagogical guidance within the standard and 30 of them included pedagogical strategies that were considered as "constructive and active" lessons.

This pedagogical influence reflects recent cognitive research on such questions as how to present and sequence information, how to organize practice, how to motivate students, and how to assess learning. Findings from cognitive research have challenged the traditional view that most knowledge can be transferred more or less intact from teacher to learner. This research proposes that, in order for some kinds of learning to occur, students must play an active role in acquiring and organizing their own knowledge and skills (e.g., Resnick, 1987). This cognitive approach to instruction, called constructivism, asserts that the learner is the most important element in the teaching-learning situation—more important than materials, lessons, teachers, and other external factors.

The influential standards developed by the National Council of Teachers of Mathematics (NCTM) exemplify how many of the new standards have embraced pedagogical principles such as constructivism: "This constructive, active view of the learning process must be reflected in the way much of mathematics is taught" (National Council of Teachers of Mathematics, 1989:10). The NCTM standards call for problem solving to become the basis of instruction. They also recommend increased attention to areas such as teaching students to develop a sense of what numbers signify, to understand the meaning behind mathematical operations, to develop strategies for learning basic facts, and to be able to justify their thinking (p. 20). Examples of areas to receive decreased attention include isolated treatment of paper-and-pencil computations, use of clue words to determine which math operations to use, an emphasis on one right answer and one correct method, and teaching by telling. Similar principles are evident in the national science standards, which reflect a more experiential approach to learning (National Research Council, 1996). It is important to note that the impacts of content standards on actual classroom curriculum and instruction are largely unknown at this time and are likely to be influenced by the extent to which the standards are mandated or voluntary and whether they are linked to assessment.

POST-SCHOOL OUTCOMES, CURRICULUM, AND INSTRUCTION IN SPECIAL EDUCATION

In order to consider the potential impact of participation in standards-based reform on students with disabilities, it is first necessary to understand the kinds of post-school outcomes, curriculum, and instruction that currently characterize special education. This section describes the post-school outcomes traditionally valued in special education for many students with disabilities and their instructional implications. It also provides an overview, drawn from empirical literature, of the characteristics of effective instruction for many students with disabilities.

Student Outcomes and Their Relationship to Curriculum

Historically, many of the outcomes expected of human service programs for people with disabilities were primarily oriented to protection and care. This philosophy resulted in services that often isolated the individual and provided physical care rather than preparation for life in a heterogeneous world. With the civil rights movement of the past two decades, one aspect of which focused on educating students with disabilities in public schools, traditional outcomes were reconceptualized to encompass: (1) employment, useful work, and activity valued by the community; (2) access to further education when desired and appropriate; (3) personal autonomy, independence, and adult status; (4) social interaction, community participation, leisure, and recreation; and (5) participation in the life of the family.

This broader set of outcomes aims to better prepare students with disabilities to become productive and independent adults. The importance of explicitly focusing the education of students with disabilities on the transition to adult life has been well documented (Rusch et al., 1992). The Individuals with Disabilities Education Act (IDEA) recognizes its importance by mandating the provision of transition services.[2]

The National Center on Educational Outcomes (NCEO), in consultation with state directors of special education, teachers, parents, policy groups, and local school administrators, has developed a model for conceptualizing the broad range of educational outcomes relevant to special education and the goal of productive adult status. The model has eight outcome domains: (1) presence and participation, (2) accommodation and adaptation, (3) physical health, (4) responsibility and independence, (5) contribution and citizenship, (6) academic and functional literacy, (7) personal and social adjustment, and (8) satisfaction. A set of indicators has been developed to measure progress toward attainment of the desired outcomes. This model suggests that these outcomes should be applicable to all students, not just those with disabilities (Ysseldyke et al., 1994).

A successful schooling experience will provide the student with the tools and skills necessary to make the transition effectively to the next stage of life. For some, this means going on to college or another educational experience. For others, it means entering the workforce. The NCEO outcomes take into account the skills students need to succeed in each domain.

For students with severe disabilities, the "criterion of ultimate functioning" is often used to guide instructional and curricular planning (Brown et al., 1976). In this approach, each student's long-term outcomes (e.g., degree of independence, employment) are designated through the IEP process; instruction then focuses on building skills that will lead to these outcomes in age-appropriate natural settings. The premise is that effective instruction involves systematic planning to determine the kinds of skills to be taught and the most effective contexts in which to teach and apply them.

Based on the criterion of ultimate functioning, instruction for students with severe disabilities has evolved into an ecological approach, meaning that the student's learning needs and functioning level are considered in conjunction with

---

[2]The statutory meaning of the term *transition services* is "a coordinated set of activities for a student, designed within an outcome-oriented process, which promotes movement from school to post-school activities, including postsecondary education, vocational training, integrated employment (including supported employment), continuing education, adult services, independent living, or community participation" (Individuals with Disabilities Education Act Amendments, 1990, Section [A], 20 U.S.C. 1401 [A]).

the demands of the environment; skills are never taught in isolation from actual performance demands. For elementary-school-age students, curricular priorities most often involve communication, socialization, self-help, motor skills, and functional academics (Fredericks, 1990; Fredericks and Brodsky, 1994; McDonnell et al., 1995; Snell and Brown, 1993). For secondary-school-age students, curricular priorities include employment preparation and placement, personal management, and leisure (McDonnell et al., 1991; Wehman, 1996).

For students with mild disabilities, a combination of academic, vocational, and functional outcomes is often selected with the specific mix of components dependent on individual student goals and needs. Although several researchers have suggested that students with mild disabilities, particularly those identified as having a learning disability, may well be able to achieve beyond their current performance levels in academic content areas (Carnine et al., 1990; Ellis et al., 1990; Zigmond and Miller, 1992), many of these students nevertheless encounter difficulties meeting the general education requirements (see Chapter 3). As students with mild disabilities enter junior and senior high school, they face an array of expectations similar to those of students without disabilities. In many schools, these students are expected to earn high school diplomas and to meet the same coursework requirements as students without disabilities.

Research has identified several important components of effective programming that can help high school students with mild disabilities meet these expectations. For those who intend to move on to postsecondary education, these elements include curricula that use a variety of approaches and instruction that teaches students "how to learn"; a system for coordinating the efforts of teachers, school administrators, parents, and community agencies; a transition component that teaches decision-making, problem-solving, and goal-setting skills; and an evaluation component that enables school personnel to systematically assess and refine the specific educational strategies being used for a student (Schumaker et al., 1986; Deshler et al., 1982, 1984; Tollefson et al., 1983; Levin et al., 1983).

For students whose primary option is to enter the work world immediately after school, the curriculum will focus more on the development and application of functional or compensatory skills. A growing body of research suggests that training in natural environments is an important instructional tool for the skill to be useful and maintained over time in community work settings (McDonnell et al., 1995; Snell and Brown, 1993; Gaylord-Ross and Holvoet, 1985; Horner et al., 1985; McDonnell et al., 1984; Brown et al., 1983; Coon et al., 1981; Hupp and Mervis, 1981).

There also has been considerable research during the past decade about strategies for improving the employment potential of students with disabilities. Research and demonstration programs have shown that many individuals can take their place in the community workforce if provided with comprehensive employment training. Results suggest that these training programs are best initiated while the student is still in school, so that valuable instructional time is not lost.

Research has suggested that students with disabilities who were successful in obtaining and maintaining paid work in the community after they exited high school were those who received ongoing opportunities for direct training in community employment sites throughout their high school careers and obtained a paying job prior to graduation (Hasazi et al., 1985, 1989; Wehman et al., 1985). Research has indicated further that effective employment preparation programs for students with disabilities include: (1) a curriculum that reflects the job opportunities available in the local community, (2) training that takes place in actual job sites, (3) training that is designed to sample the individual's performance across a variety of economically viable alternatives, (4) training that provides opportunities for interaction with people without disabilities in a work setting, and (5) training that culminates in a specific job placement (McDonnell et al., 1992; Wehman, 1996; Hasazi et al., 1989; Hill et al., 1987).

Students with disabilities may find their employability affected by another issue above and beyond the actual skills that they have achieved—namely, whether they have received a high school diploma. States take various approaches to awarding high school diplomas or other school completion credentials to students with disabilities who do not meet traditional criteria. Some students, for example, receive a nonstandard diploma or certificate of attendance (see Chapter 3). This issue of credentialing is likely to assume greater importance in a climate of standards-based reform because some states are linking receipt of a diploma to attainment of state content and performance standards. Some students with disabilities who do not reach state standards, and thus do not meet high school diploma criteria, may find themselves disadvantaged in the job market regardless of the educational outcomes they can demonstrate (Box 4-1).

In sum, special education has long valued educational outcomes that are broader than the academically oriented outcomes exemplified in state content standards developed thus far. The emphasis on post-school outcomes has shaped the curricular and instructional experiences of many students with disabilities. Whether or not states will develop standards in vocational/career areas is an as yet unknown but important consideration in efforts to include students with disabilities in content standards.

Characteristics of Effective Special Education Instruction

Research provides a great deal of information about what constitutes an effective instructional environment for students with disabilities. We discuss three broad characteristics of effective instruction, each supported by research as important for enhancing learning among many students with disabilities: (1) a focus on the individual student as the unit for instructional decision making, (2) intensive instructional delivery, and (3) explicit contextualization of skills-based instruction.

BOX 4-1   Credentialing, the High School Diploma, and Students with Disabilities

The credentialing issue is critical in standards-based reform because credentials are the means for communicating students' high school performance to the public. Since a high school diploma is the minimum requirement for a variety of employment opportunities, some educators are concerned about the impact standards-based reform could have on the high school credentialing process for a number of students, including some with disabilities.

Over the last several decades, as the proportion of high school students receiving a high school diploma has increased, not having a diploma is regarded as damning to one's job prospects. At the same time, *having* a diploma has seemed, for some time now, to be only minimally impressive to employers (Bishop, 1996; Hawkins, 1978; Pedulla and Reidy, 1979). Some argue that there is no substantive relationship between academic content and the awarding of a high school diploma (Bishop, 1989, 1994; Sedlak et al., 1986). They see the move to ratchet up standards required for a diploma as an attempt "to hold schools to standards that the lay public could easily measure and understand" (Sedlak et al.,1986:28). Raising standards in a credible way is thus a response to employer concerns about the devaluing of a diploma, as well as to more general concerns about U.S. international competitiveness.

Some students with disabilities in certain states receive differentiated diplomas, which distinguish students following a rigorous academic track from those following a minimally academic or vocational track. The latter group receives certificates of attendance or other nonacademic diplomas (see Chapter 3). Thus, students with disabilities operate in a credentialing universe much more complex than their general education counterparts. Potential employers may face difficulty in putting an applicant's credential in the appropriate context, given the diversity in the credentialing of students with disabilities. This diversity makes it that much harder for students with disabilities to showcase their achievements and abilities.

A number of issues about credentialing for students with disabilities warrant attention. First, if standards for a high school diploma are increased, more students—including those with disabilities—may not receive diplomas and, more to the point, they will not easily be able to convey to potential employers what they have achieved in high school. Some students, including some with disabilities, who currently receive certificates of attendance face this problem. All students—whether they currently would receive a diploma, certificate of attendance, or no certification whatsoever—deserve to leave high school able to signal credibly to potential employers what they have achieved.* The students who do not attain a diploma may experience hardship, particularly in the short run. In the medium to long run, job requirements will presumably adjust to the new standards, although what form of readily ascertainable certification will replace the high school diploma is unclear.

Second, as one changes the nature of the credentialing process, whether by increasing standards or by requiring minimum competency tests, students must first be adequately prepared to meet the challenges posed by the new credentialing process. In other words, the K-12 curriculum ought to provide students with opportunities to learn the material required for the credential. This concept has proved controversial and subject to litigation (*Debra P.* v. *Turlington* 644 F. 2d 397, 1981), both for students with disabilities and for other disadvantaged groups (see Chapter 5 for further discussion). The issue is further complicated by the laws requiring accommodations for students with disabilities. Phillips (1993) and Vitello (1988) discuss issues relevant to this debate in more detail.

Third, it is important to recognize that employers are constantly looking for ways to lower costs. To the extent that the credentialing system makes it more, rather than less, costly for business to evaluate the capabilities of students with disabilities, the system makes the transition to employment harder. The importance of providing clear and credible evidence of what students have achieved and are capable of should not be underestimated.

---

*Such certification should be flexible enough to signify differential achievement to allow potential employers to distinguish among them. Bishop sees students having the opportunity to signal higher achievement to potential employers as providing an important incentive. Michigan, New York, and Tennessee have honors diplomas to acknowledge those whose achievements sufficiently surpass the basic requirements (Bond et al., 1996).

In considering the three characteristics of effective instruction, it is important to note six assumptions.

• These characteristics apply to the large subset of students whose disabilities involve cognitive (rather than physical or sensory) impairments. We considered only students with cognitive disabilities because they represent the majority of students identified as having a disability. Among individuals with cognitive disabilities, the characteristics apply to the entire range of students, from those with mild to those with severe disabilities.

• These characteristics represent broad principles that, in light of the heterogeneity of the population of students with cognitive disabilities, must be particularized to meet individual student needs.

• These characteristics are placement-neutral; that is, they describe *how* instruction occurs, not *where* instruction takes place.

• Research on these characteristics is limited to how students acquire and use a range of relatively basic or middle-order skills, from functional personal management skills, to the achievement of literacy and numeracy, to the extraction of conceptual themes or "big ideas" (Carnine and Kameenui, 1992). Research has not been conducted to determine the extent to which these characteristics apply when students with cognitive disabilities learn content that requires high levels of abstraction or creativity.

• Although research on positive educational interventions supports the effectiveness of these characteristics and demonstrates that they can be applied in actual school settings, a gap exists between what is known about effective special education instruction and the typical state of practice.

• The characteristics we describe may apply, to varying extents, to students with and without disabilities alike.[3]

Individually Referenced Decision Making

Research shows that, in general education, teachers typically judge the success or failure of an instructional activity primarily by its capacity to maintain classroom flow, orderliness, and cooperation (Clark and Elmore, 1981; Yinger, 1979). At critical junctures, the teacher may determine whether reteaching is necessary for the entire class by assessing learning among a steering group of children who perform near the middle of the class (Clark and Elmore, 1981). Instructional adaptation to address individual learning problems, however, occurs rarely in the regular classroom and in minor ways (Baker and Zigmond, 1990; Kagan and Tippins, 1991; McIntosh et al., 1993; Peterson and Clark, 1978; Zigmond and Baker, 1995).

By contrast, effective practice in special education, as measured by teacher decision making about instructional modifications and student achievement in reading, math, and spelling, centers instructional decision making on the individual student (Fuchs and Fuchs, 1995). Research has specified methods for tracking student progress and for using the resulting database to formulate ambitious learning goals (Fuchs et al., 1989a) and to test alternative hypotheses about which instructional methods produce satisfactory growth rates (Fuchs et al., 1989b; Jones and Krouse, 1988; Stecker, in press; see Fuchs, 1995, for a review). Over time, the special educator empirically tests and develops an instructional

---

[3]Many low-achieving students do well with general classroom instruction that incorporates some elements of these principles. However, for many students with disabilities, the level or intensity of application that is necessary may exceed what can reasonably be provided through general education programming.

program tailored to the individual student. This process is called *individually referenced decision making.*

Individually referenced decision making is perhaps the signature feature of effective special education practice, exemplifying a basic value and representing a core assumption of special educators' professional preparation. "Effective" is defined as statistically significant gains in specific skills. Individually referenced decision making requires teachers to reserve judgment about the efficacy of an instructional method for a student until the method proves effective for that individual and fosters high expectations of learning. It requires teachers to plan and make ongoing, major adjustments and revisions in response to an individual student's learning, and it requires knowledge of multiple ways to adapt curricula, modify instructional methods, and motivate students.

Corroborating evidence documents how individually referenced decision making enhances learning for students with cognitive disabilities. A meta-analysis of a number of studies summarized the efficacy of individually referenced decision making for students with cognitive disabilities (with an effect size of .70 standard deviation units; Fuchs and Fuchs, 1986). More recent studies in reading, spelling, and mathematics corroborate earlier evidence of positive effects (Fuchs et al., 1991a, 1991b, 1992). Stecker (in press), for example, sought to assess whether individually referenced decision making had benefits over and beyond the effects of less individualized methods for regularly revising instruction and routinely measuring student performance. Pairs of students with cognitive disabilities were matched. The performance of one randomly selected student in each pair was measured twice weekly, and the teacher formulated instructional decisions for both students in the pair based on the one student's assessment results. Moreover, half the matched students were also measured, but teachers had no access to their assessment profiles. Results showed that students whose instructional decisions were tailored to their own ongoing assessment results achieved consistently better than the other of their matched pairs, and that measurement alone contributed little to student achievement.

Intensive Instruction

Intensive instruction refers to a broad set of instructional features that includes, but is not limited to, (a) high rates of active responding at appropriate levels, (b) careful matching of instruction with students' skill levels, (c) instructional cues, prompts, and fading to support approximations to correct responding, and (d) detailed, task-focused feedback—all features that may be incorporated into group lessons (see the work of Wolery and colleagues, e.g., Doyle et al., 1990; Lysakowski and Walberg, 1982).

Meta-analyses and narrative syntheses (Cohen et al., 1982; Glass et al., 1982; Wasik and Slavin, 1993) show that intensive instruction can result in impressive learning for students who otherwise would fail to achieve critical benchmarks

(Glass et al., 1981). Torgesen (1996), for example, has studied students with phonological processing deficits, who had been predicted to experience serious problems in learning to read. Children were assigned randomly to four conditions: a conventional general education control group and one of three experimental conditions, which represented a range of methods but shared the feature of one-to-one tutoring that fostered intensive instruction. Preliminary results of this longitudinal study indicate that children in all three intensive instruction treatments had comparable achievement, significantly better than the control group.

Just as for students with mild disabilities, research indicates that one-to-one intensive instruction helps develop the skills of students with more severe cognitive disabilities, particularly in the area of personal management, including dressing, personal hygiene, money management, and sexual behavior (Billingsley et al., 1994). Researchers have demonstrated that teaching these skills in group settings often dilutes the intensity of the instruction and proves unsuccessful in terms of both acquiring and generalizing the skills (e.g., Reid and Favell, 1984; Alberto et al., 1980).

It is important to note that, although one-to-one tutoring may be necessary to achieve instructional intensity and promote learning within certain domains of functioning, such as reading acquisition and personal management, intensive instruction is not synonymous with one-to-one delivery. In fact, meaningful participation by students with cognitive disabilities among normal, age-appropriate peer groups for instructional activities can be critical for promoting social development and communicative competence (Haring and Ryndak, 1994; Nietupski and Hamre-Nietupski, 1987; Snell and Brown, 1993). As noted by Billingsley et al. (1994:89), group-based intensive instruction can "provide for a natural variance in the people with whom the skill is practiced and less opportunity for the learner to become overdependent on a single teacher or person—thus increasing the potential for successful generalization."

Explicit Contextualization of Skills-Based Instruction

Research demonstrates that many students with cognitive disabilities need extensive, structured, and explicit instruction to develop the processes and understandings that other children learn more easily and naturally (Bransford et al., 1995; Brown and Campione, 1990; Harris and Graham, 1995; Kronick, 1990). For example, in order to learn to read, many children with cognitive disabilities require explicit, structured instruction (Stanovich, 1995). Similarly, without explicit instruction, the language development of many children with cognitive disabilities suffers (Warren and Yoder, 1994). Parallel findings occur in other areas (see Harris and Graham, 1995).

As noted above, constructivism is an important philosophical influence in the current education reform movement. Three assumptions of constructivism are particularly relevant to this discussion of effective special education. First,

Constructivism

constructivism assumes that the child is an active, self-regulated learner, and that the appropriate role of the teacher is to guide the construction of knowledge, rather than to provide direct explicit instruction (Tharpe and Gallimore, 1989). Second, constructivism holds that segmenting the curriculum into a hierarchy of discrete skills runs counter to how children learn (Harris and Graham, 1995). Third, in constructivism, success in basic skills is not necessarily a prerequisite to more advanced learning and higher-order thinking (Means and Knapp, 1991). As noted above, these assumptions are reflected in major general education reform initiatives and many content standards. But they contrast with special education practice that has maintained a strong focus on the explicit teaching of basic skills. Indeed, three empirical literatures question the tenability of constructivist principles for many students with disabilities.

First, the assumption that the appropriate role of the teacher is that of guide rather than provider of explicit instruction appears tenuous in light of research showing that many children with cognitive disabilities cannot be viewed as active, self-regulated learners. Studies demonstrate that students with persistent histories of learning failure experience negative feedback that interferes with their motivation, making them more likely to suffer the phenomenon of learned helplessness (Deci and Ryan, 1985, 1986; Garber and Seligman, 1980). These experiences can result in behavioral patterns characterized by challenge avoidance and low persistence, which necessitate more structured, teacher-directed approaches to learning (Dweck and Leggett, 1988).

The second tenet of constructivism that appears somewhat problematic for students with cognitive disabilities is the assumption that cognitive components should not be isolated or fractionated and that the curriculum should not be taught as a series of discrete skills. Research indicates that analyzing and teaching tasks in their component parts is effective and often necessary for many students with cognitive disabilities. The primary problem characterizing children with reading disabilities, for example, is a phonological processing deficit that impedes word learning and word recognition (Adams and Bruck, 1993; Gough and Tunmer, 1986; Perfetti, 1985; Siegel, 1993; Stanovich, 1986; Vellutino and Scanlon, 1987). To overcome this deficit, these students require explicit instruction in recognizing discrete speech-sound segments and recognizing words (Stanovich, 1995). Analogous research suggests the efficacy of related approaches that analyze and teach reading comprehension and written expression by teaching skills as components (Harris and Pressley, 1991).

Third, the assumption that mastery of basic skills is not a prerequisite for advanced learning appears tenuous for many students with cognitive disabilities. For many of them, there does appear to be a hierarchy of learning, whereby students do better if they first learn number concepts and then learn to apply them. When these students fail to acquire early mathematics proficiency, they do not succeed in an academic track (which requires high-order, problem-solving applications of earlier math content) or a basic track (which requires applications to real-world situations (Bryan et al., 1992). The failure to learn to read undoubtedly puts individuals at risk for poor outcomes in the middle and high school curricula, for which reading proficiency is assumed and required.

Despite some questions about the pertinence of constructivist assumptions to programs for some students with cognitive disabilities, constructivist philosophy nevertheless has influenced concepts of effective special education practice in substantial ways. The notion of isolated skills instruction has been replaced with more contextualized presentations, in which strategies for applying skills in generalized contexts are taught explicitly. Research documents the potential value of situating explicit skills instruction within structured, motivating, and authentic contexts to help students learn how to apply knowledge.

For example, Cunningham (1990) experimented with two approaches to help students develop phonemic awareness (i.e., to recognize speech-sound segments and blends). Phonemic awareness was chosen because there is a large body of research demonstrating its importance in helping students learn early word decoding skills (e.g., Adams and Bruck, 1993; Bradley and Bryant, 1985; Stanovich, 1992, 1993; Wagner and Torgesen, 1987). To teach phonemic awareness, the experiment contrasted a conventional "skill-and-drill" approach, whereby students learn skills through drill and practice but not in an explicit context, with a "metalevel" approach, which teaches skills through learning experiences situated within particular contexts. In this latter approach, students were taught to reflect on the usefulness of phonemic awareness and were taught how to integrate the skill with other strategies. They explicitly discussed the goals and purposes of the training, observed teachers modeling the skill in hypothetical reading contexts, and had routine opportunities to apply the skill under the teacher's direction. Cunningham found that first graders in the metalevel phonemic awareness group displayed greater reading comprehension growth than their peers in the skill-and-drill treatment.

Consequently, for many students with cognitive disabilities, data-based arguments support a situated approach to teaching, which blends explicit teaching of skills with contextually rich learning experiences, a position that echoes important principles of constructivism. Nevertheless, it is clear that explicit teaching is fundamental even within this situated teaching approach: the teacher reveals or makes transparent the connections between knowledge acquisition and knowledge application, rather than leaving the student to discover those connections more incidentally.

The focus on situated context and explicit teaching for transfer is illustrated in the criterion of ultimate functioning, which, as noted earlier in this chapter, is a strategy commonly used to establish and teach valued outcomes for students with severe disabilities. Applying explicit, intensive instruction in a contextualized setting results in more meaningful participation and performance in normal, age-based routines for children with severe disabilities (Nietupski and Hamre-Nietupski, 1987; Snell and Brown, 1993) and helps them develop general social and communication skills that enhance their interactions with peers and adults in home, school, and community settings (Forest and Pearpoint, 1992; Gaylord-Ross et al., 1984; Haring and Lovinger, 1989; Haring and Ryndak, 1994).

Together, these three broad characteristics of effective special education instruction—individually referenced decision making, intensive instruction, and explicit contextualization of skills-based instruction—represent a potent set of practices, which have been demonstrated to enhance the learning for students with cognitive disabilities. Research on specific interventions that applied these three characteristics to teach students with cognitive disabilities documented positive effects ranging from .50 to over 1.5 standard deviations (Forness and Kavale, 1996; Swanson, 1996).

We note that these three instructional characteristics represent practices that often differ from those of general education. Model special education instruction focuses on the individual as the unit of analysis, whereas general education relies on the group. Students with cognitive disabilities require intensive instruction, whereas carefully designed nonintensive instruction appears to meet the needs of most students without disabilities. Model special education practice relies on skills-based instruction, making explicit the connections between knowledge acquisition and application; by contrast, some current content standards and curricular reforms have been influenced by a constructivist philosophy, which deemphasizes explicit instruction of discrete skills.

A discussion of effective instruction would be incomplete without mentioning the use of technology, which can produce dramatic educational benefits for many students with disabilities both as an assistive device and as an instructional tool (Box 4-2).

PARTICIPATION OF STUDENTS WITH DISABILITIES IN CONTENT STANDARDS AND CURRICULUM

Increasing the participation of students with disabilities in standards-based reform will mean that they will be taught and held accountable for the new kinds of knowledge and skills reflected in state content standards. It is important to understand the extent to which many students with disabilities are already involved in the general education curriculum and thus will be held to new standards once they are put into place. It is also important to understand the extent to which students with disabilities have or have not been considered in the design of standards-based reforms, particularly content standards.

Participation in the General Education Curriculum

As noted in Chapter 3, nationally representative data are limited regarding how many and to what extent students with disabilities currently participate in the general education curriculum and instruction. Data are mostly confined to vari-

BOX 4-2   The Promise of Technology

Technology is an extremely promising tool for improving the education of students with disabilities and is already an effective component of special education instruction in many classrooms. Advances in technologies that are useful for individuals with disabilities are being made continually. Unfortunately the training of teachers, therapists, and parents to use technology for students with disabilities lags far behind the advances that are being made. Nevertheless, much has been achieved and the future holds greater promise.

Clearly, technology can improve the quality of life for most individuals with disabilities. Historically, two kinds of relevant technologies have been developed: assistive and instructional. Assistive technology refers to mechanical, electrical, or computerized tools for enhancing the routine functioning and communication capabilities of people who have physical or sensory disabilities. Instructional technology refers to the use of computers and other related technologies to deliver and support instruction. It has been used traditionally with students who have milder disabilities (as well as with those without disabilities).

Some of the most successful examples of technology use for students with disabilities have occurred with assistive technology devices. Many of these applications can adapt information so that students with disabilities can understand it and/or so that they can supply it. Assistive technology includes both high-tech and low-tech devices. High-tech assistive technologies include sensory devices for individuals with hearing disabilities, voice output devices for individuals who are unable to speak for themselves, computer screen readers and braille printers for people with visual impairments, and even speech recognition systems and robotic devices for people with severe physical disabilities. Low-tech devices, which can also be extremely useful, include head pointers and key guards for use with standard computer keyboards, adaptive eating utensils, and even Velcro. Not only do these applications directly affect quality of life, but they also increase the individual's access to the environment, expanding the ability to gain maximally from such opportunities as education.

Over the years, the use of assistive devices has produced dramatic benefits for many individuals with disabilities. For example, positioning devices have allowed students with physical disabilities to join classmates at tables, on the floor, or in a standing position. Auditory trainers have allowed students with hearing disabilities to remain in classrooms with their nondisabled peers. Portable Kurtzweil reading devices have allowed individuals with visual impairments to independently access text information from libraries and other sources. In laboratories around the world, engineers and other researchers are looking for ways to make assistive devices faster, more intuitive, and easier to use.

Although much has been done in the field of assistive technology, it is in instructional technology that most of the attention has been directed, especially for students with mild disabilities. Many advances have been made since the computer was first used in school classrooms for delivering simple instructional programs. Computers and related technologies are now used in a number of sophisticated ways for helping students achieve. These applications can help individualize instruction for students with disabilities by adjusting both the presentation mode and the time a student can spend working on any given task. Generally, the use of instructional technologies can be categorized in four ways:

Tutorial. Included under the category of tutorial is drill-and-practice software and other explicit instruction applications. Typically the tutorial application controls the presentation of information and the student responds in some way. Although newer models of technology use have been proposed recently, tutorial applications continue to be a predominant mode of technology use with special needs students.

Exploratory. The exploratory use of technology in special education has evolved more recently with the development of multimedia platforms and software. In an exploratory application, the student is free to roam through the application and search for information. Exploratory applications include electronic versions of encyclopedias, multimedia databases, and the World Wide Web. The exploratory use of technology differs from the tutorial in that the student navigates through the program and controls the learning that goes on.

Communication. Communication technologies are becoming more prevalent in special education settings. Access to the Internet provides students with opportunities to send and receive information, in a variety of forms, literally around the world. Other uses of communication technologies include interactive distance learning and more recently, electronic field trips.

Production. Production applications include the familiar word processor as well as multimedia development tools. With these applications, technology becomes a tool to facilitate the student synthesis and production of information in the form of multimedia presentations. These applications allow the learner to go from a passive recipient of information to an active producer of information.

The use of technology for delivering instruction to students with disabilities dates back to the 1960s, when mainframe computers at Stanford University were used to deliver mathematics instruction over phone lines to deaf students at Gallaudet University. Although much has been learned since that time about how to use technology for instructing students with disabilities, there is still much to learn.

Over the past decade a number of empirical studies have examined

continued

BOX 4-2—Continued

the effects of instructional technology on the learning of special needs students. The results of this research have been equivocal. Some studies have demonstrated that certain technology applications have had a positive effect on student learning in areas such as mathematics (Bottge and Hasselbring, 1993; Hasselbring et al., 1988); writing (Graham and MacArthur, 1988; Morocco and Neuman, 1986); and literacy (Higgins and Boone, 1990; Jones et al., 1987). However, other researchers have reported less positive results (Anderson-Inman, 1990; Higgins and Boone, 1991; van Daal and van der Leij, 1992). These equivocal findings should not be surprising. There is no reason to believe that simply putting technology in front of a student with disabilities should automatically make the student a better learner. Even though technologies have advanced over the past 30 years and have provided us with new and improved ways for delivering instruction, simply improving the delivery system does not guarantee instruction will be improved. To the contrary, improved learning is dependent on the quality of instruction and not on the medium with which it is delivered. Weak or poorly designed instructional programs are not improved simply because they are delivered using a computer or any other form of technology. Clark (1983:445) made this point quite clearly when he stated that instructional technologies are "mere vehicles that deliver instruction but do not influence student achievement any more than the truck that delivers our groceries causes changes in our nutrition." It is simply not enough to use technology for teaching students with special needs. Researchers and developers need to develop powerful instructional programs that can be delivered with technology, and the technology in turn needs to be used in appropriate ways. More research is needed in order to determine the most effective uses of assistive and instructional technologies for students

ables such as the amount of time in regular classrooms and course-taking patterns. Furthermore, data linking participation in the general education curriculum to academic achievement are largely absent due to the lack of representation of students with disabilities in large-scale national studies, such as the National Education Longitudinal Study (NELS) and the National Assessment of Educational Progress (NAEP) (McGrew et al., 1993, 1995).

This lack of data is particularly pronounced at the elementary school level. Analyses conducted for the committee of the *Prospects* study (see Appendix C) provide information on third and fourth grade students. These data suggest that, for this nationally representative sample, students with disabilities were exposed to selected instructional practices (e.g., cooperative learning, mastery learning, whole language instruction) at approximately the same rates in both mathematics and language arts as general education students (see Table 4-1).

TABLE 4-1   Percentage of Fourth Grade Students With and Without Disabilities Whose Teachers Report Using Various Instructional Methods in Reading and Mathematics

	No Disability	All Disabilities	Emotional Disability	Learning Disability	Physical Disability	Speech Disability	Other Disability
1992 Regular Classroom Reading/English/Language Instructional Methods (weighted)							
Madeline Hunter Methods	71.9%	67.7%	58.8%	63.5%	75.1%	75.6%	69.6%
Mastery Learning	41.6	30.5	21.7	25.8	38.2	27.0	39.2
Cooperative Learning	73.5	70.4	52.6	67.5	78.9	74.2	77.7
Phonetic Reading	16.4	19.3	25.8	22.8	7.3	17.9	18.8
Whole Language	63.3	63.3	48.7	67.7	64.3	62.1	68.4
Writing Process Methods	69.1	66.8	57.8	67.6	74.9	66.5	68.0
Individualized Instruction	26.3	30.3	24.7	36.7	35.5	23.2	26.6
Other Classroom Methods	10.4	11.1	18.6	9.2	11.4	5.8	17.5
Total N	2,440,590	274,078	29,207	114,789	38,554	73,968	64,692
1992 Regular Classroom Mathematics Instructional Methods (weighted)							
Madeline Hunter Methods	71.1%	74.6%	63.1%	75.8%	78.0%	79.9%	74.0%
Mastery Learning	48.7	42.9	24.7	42.6	49.8	40.5	45.0
Cooperative Learning	79.2	73.5	59.2	76.0	81.4	80.4	69.8
Individualized Instruction	35.6	41.9	56.6	41.4	43.9	39.6	40.8
Other Classroom Methods	13.2	13.6	14.6	12.0	24.9	12.9	11.8
Total N	2,435,636	270,167	26,794	113,741	37,992	72,874	63,659

NOTE: Data from The *Prospects* Study Classroom Teacher Questionnaire. See Appendix C. Madeline Hunter methods emphasize anticipatory set, input and modeling, checking for understanding and other features; in mastery learning students who do not perform at preestablished levels (e.g., 80 percent correct on quizzes) receive corrective instruction while others receive enrichment; in cooperative learning students often work in small groups and are expected to help each other learn.

Much of the available data regarding secondary school students comes from the National Longitudinal Transition Study (NLTS), a longitudinal study of students with disabilities (see Chapter 3 for a description of the study sample). The available data are briefly reviewed in the next section.

Time in General Education Courses in Secondary School

Data from the NLTS indicate that, across all disabilities, students in secondary school spend an average of 56 percent of their instructional time in general education courses. About 62 percent of students spend half or more of their instructional time in general education; this varies considerably by disability. The vast majority of youth with speech impairments (81 percent of that group), visual impairments (81 percent of that group), learning disabilities (73 percent), other health impairments (67 percent), hearing impairments (67 percent), and emotional disturbances (62 percent) spend at least half of their instructional time in general education courses. Those least likely to spend half or more time in general education include students with multiple disabilities (15 percent of that group) and mental retardation (29 percent of that group).

Students with disabilities received better grades in special education classes than they did in general education classes, but a number of students failed special education courses, too. Across all disability groups, students with emotional disturbances experienced the greatest difficulties in both special and general education courses. Nearly one-third of students with visual impairments and those with speech impairments spent 75 percent or more of their time in high school in general education courses and maintained a B average or better.

An examination of the relationship between performance and time in general education courses showed that, as time in academic general education went up, so did the student's likelihood of failing a course, especially early in secondary school. Students with more time in general education were less likely to be absent in ninth grade but more likely to be absent in twelfth grade. No relationship was found between time in general education and dropping out of school at any grade level (Wagner et al., 1993b:4-23).

Course-Taking in Secondary School

In recent years, educational reform efforts have focused on trying to raise academic standards for all students. In some instances, this has led to policies that increase academic credit requirements for high school graduation. Recent nationally representative data on secondary school course-taking patterns in 1987 and 1992 confirm that academic course-taking has increased (see Table 4-2). During this period the average number of credits earned by public high school graduates over four years increased from 22.8 to 23.8; this rise is almost entirely accounted for by increases in academic courses (from 15.6 to 17.3 credits). High school graduates decreased their average number of vocational credits from 4.4 to 3.8 (National Center for Education Statistics, 1996).

Students with disabilities tended to earn fewer academic credits and more vocational credits than their peers without disabilities at both points in time. However they show a similar increase over time in academic course-taking (from 12.6 to 14.2 credits), whereas vocational course-taking has remained level (See Table 4-2). Data from the NLTS indicate that students with disabilities who completed high school generally met the typical state requirements of 11 or 12 credits in English, social studies, mathematics, and science (Wagner, 1993:S-2).

Most students, with or without disabilities, take at least one vocational course during high school. However, data suggest that students with disabilities earn more credits in vocational education (5.6 versus 3.7). Similarly, students with disabilities are more likely to concentrate in a vocational program—defined as completing three or more courses in a single occupationally specific field—than are other students (National Center for Education Statistics, 1996:Table 3.7).

Data from the NLTS indicate that for many students with disabilities (68 percent) vocational course-taking began in the ninth grade. By twelfth grade, 89 percent of students with disabilities were taking at least one vocational education course (Wagner et al., 1993a:2-4). As students with disabilities progress through high school, there appears to be a general shift away from academic course-taking, toward a heavier concentration of vocational courses. For example, students in upper grades spent significantly less time in academic courses than did those in the lower grades. This trend is paralleled by a significant increase in the amount of time spent in vocational education courses by older students.

TABLE 4-2   Average Number of Credits Earned by Public High School Graduates in the Academic, Vocational, and Personal Use Curricula by Disability Status: 1987 and 1992.

Year of Graduation and Disability Status	Average Credits Earned in			
	Total	Academic	Vocational	Personal Use
1987				
Total	22.8	15.6	4.4	2.7
Has Disability	21.9	12.6	6.0	3.3
No Disability	22.8	15.8	4.4	2.7
1992				
Total	23.8	17.3	3.8	2.7
Has Disability	23.2	14.2	5.6	3.4
No Disability	23.8	17.4	3.7	2.7

NOTE: Average total credits may not sum exactly due to rounding.

SOURCE: 1987 High School Transcript Study, and National Education Longitudinal Study of 1988 as summarized in National Center for Education Statistics, 1996, Table 2.5.

Data from the NLTS suggest that vocational course-taking confers advantages for some youth with disabilities. For example, youth who took a concentration of four or more related classes in vocational education were less likely to drop out of school in either eleventh or twelfth grade (Wagner et al., 1993a:2-9). The authors speculate that "this holding power may have been due to the fact that youth not only experienced a different curriculum but also met with greater success there" (p. 2-9). Data from this study also suggest that eleventh and twelfth grade youth in work experience programs had a lower probability of dropping out.

As the data presented at the beginning of this discussion suggest, efforts to raise standards for all students appear to have already had the effect of increasing academic course-taking among all students, whether or not they have disabilities. Some observers have raised concerns that, as these efforts continue, "increases in credit requirements (may) force some students with disabilities to choose courses with an academic orientation that may not have been the most appropriate or relevant to their postschool goals" (Wagner, 1993). Any discussion of desired outcomes and standards relevant to all students will need to consider these important findings. In addition, data are needed regarding the extent to which elementary schoolchildren with disabilities participate successfully in the regular academic curriculum.

Rationale for Participation in Standards

The potential benefits of content standards on student achievement are largely unknown and empirical evidence in support of content standards is mainly inferential. However, there are a number of arguments to support the idea that students with disabilities will benefit from participation in general education curriculum and the accompanying challenging expectations and more stringent accountability for their achievement. Participation in standards-based curriculum could improve post-school outcomes by increasing opportunities to access a broader curriculum and raising expectations for the performance of students with disabilities. The need to improve outcomes derives in part from data documenting problematic post-school outcomes for students with disabilities (Edgar et al., 1986; Hasazi et al., 1985; Blackorby and Wagner, 1996; see Chapter 3). However, as these studies have demonstrated, post-school outcomes for many special education students are improved if they have access to strong vocational/career programs and other opportunities to develop important functional skills.

Some special educators and advocates are also concerned about what they perceive as low expectations and lack of learning opportunities provided to students with disabilities. Increased participation of these students in general education curriculum frameworks could mean upgraded expectations and opportunities. Research on IEPs has indicated a lack of focus on broad learner goals and an emphasis on discrete skills such as mathematical computation, phonics, and functional skills (Smith, 1990). For example, Shriner et al. (1993) examined the mathematics goals and objectives specified in the IEPs of 76 fourth and eighth grade students from two school districts and compared them to mathematics examination items taken from NAEP and to the mathematics curriculum in each district. Using an established taxonomy, these researchers found significant discrepancies between the IEP goals and both the NAEP items and the district curricula. For example, over 81 percent of the IEP objectives across grades addressed computation, whereas only 12 percent addressed applications or any form of problem solving—in contrast to what is expected in district curricula and NAEP items. The IEPs did not address essential elements of the NCTM standards such as estimation, algebraic equations, decimals, and fractions. This suggests that the special education provided to students with disabilities in the math content area does not reflect the knowledge standards of current mathematics curricula.

These documented problems with IEPs are particularly troublesome because of concerns that IEPs represent the entire curriculum in a specific subject matter for some students with disabilities (Pugach and Warger, 1993; Sands et al., 1995). Innovative and systematic procedures exist for writing and implementing IEPs that can set higher expectations than at present, and that hold promise for improving teaching and learning across the whole curriculum for students with disabilities (Deno, 1985). But in actual practice, most schools are not using these approaches.

Addressing Students with Disabilities in Standards

Students with disabilities have not been specifically referred to in voluntary national content standards (Shriner et al., 1993), although science standards include references to students with specific disabilities, such as those with physical or learning disabilities (National Research Council, 1996). Among the states, consideration of students with disabilities varies (Goertz and Friedman, 1996). Examples of state responsiveness to students with disabilities include assigning special educators to content standard-setting teams, seeking reviews of content standards from representatives of special populations, and identifying accommodations for specific content standards.

Some states, for example Kentucky and Vermont, have developed content standards within broad learner outcomes for students with disabilities and have explicitly considered students with even the most severe cognitive disabilities. Michigan has developed outcomes for seven types of students with disabilities at ages 10, 13, and 16 (Michigan Department of Education, 1995). Maryland is developing a set of alternate outcomes and content and performance standards for students with severe cognitive disabilities who participate in a functional curriculum. These state efforts are designed to provide greater consistency across students' programs in terms of the quality of educational experiences and instructional focus. In several of the states noted above, the standards also are aligned with performance assessments.

A recent survey conducted by the Council of Chief State School Officers (in press) focused on state policies of applying content standards to students with disabilities. All 50 and 6 "extra states" (e.g., District of Columbia and Puerto Rico) were asked whether *any* of their content standards being implemented or developed will apply to students with IEPs. Of the 48 states responding to this survey question, 35 reported that standards will apply to students with disabilities with IEPs; 9 states reported that their content standards will not apply; 4 states qualified this as follows: Iowa allows local school districts to decide whether state standards are applicable for students with IEPs. Maine and Pennsylvania reported that students with IEPs will be "required to accomplish all standards to [the] extent able." Alaska reported that application of standards to students with disabilities is voluntary (Rhim and McLaughlin, 1996).

Of the 35 states responding that their content standards will apply to special education students, 17 reported that *all* standards will apply to students with a mild disability; 17 states added the qualifier that the extent of participation in standards for those with a mild disability is an IEP decision. One state did not differentiate *which* standards would apply to students with mild and severe disabilities.

Of the 35 states responding that any of their standards will apply to students with disabilities, only 30 specified which would apply to students with severe disabilities. Of these 30, 12 reported that all of their content standards will apply to students with severe disabilities, and 18 reported that the decision about which standards will apply to students with a severe disability will depend on the IEP. States were not asked to specify how the content standards would apply or whether modifications or accommodations would be provided or expected.

Potential Impact of Content Standards on Learning

As described in Chapter 2, most studies of the impact of standards on classroom teaching and achievement in general education are still ongoing. Thus the effects of standards on learning have not yet been demonstrated. As a result, information about the specific effects of participation in new content standards on students with disabilities is largely anecdotal or derived from local case studies. Moreover, this information is limited to effects on instruction rather than achievement. Evidence of potential effects of content standards on the instruction provided to students with disabilities appears in a report of a national investigation of the national curriculum of England and Wales conducted by the National Foundation for Educational Research/Bishop Grosseteste College (Christophers et al., 1992). Under the 1988 Education Reform Act of the United Kingdom, all schools are required to provide the national curriculum to each student, regardless of special needs. The purpose of the national curriculum study was to investigate how both mainstream and special educational needs students coped with standard assessment tasks and how special education teachers perceived the national curriculum. The study considered children with a wide range of special needs and used case studies of special schools, special units attached to mainstream schools, and mainstream schools along with questionnaires, interviews, and teachers' logs.

The report indicated that those who work in special education refer to two separate curricula, the national curriculum and the special education curriculum. For many teachers, the implementation of the national curriculum reportedly broadened the whole curriculum for students with disabilities, particularly by increasing the emphasis on science and technology. A contrasting opinion, however, was that the entire curriculum offered to students with disabilities was becoming too broad, which meant that schools could not offer any topics in depth because of the slow rate at which their students learned and the amount of reinforcement and repetition needed. Moreover, the study found variation in the amount of instructional time devoted to the national curriculum. For example, between 90 and 95 percent of instructional time in schools for the visually impaired was spent on the national curriculum; schools for students with emotional and behavior difficulties spent the least amount of time, an average 66 percent of available instructional time. Findings also corroborated the impression that teachers in special education tend to place greater emphasis on social skills, practical life skills, and cultural experiences than on fostering intellectual development of their students through the national curriculum (Wylie et al., 1995:289).

Similar findings are emerging from local cases studies completed in Colorado, Maryland, Nebraska, and Washington, states in which students with disabilities are being included in new general education curricula based on state or voluntary national content standards.[4] Interviews and classroom observations conducted by a team of researchers indicate that both general and special educators are experiencing the effects of new content standards in the form of expanded content as well as new pedagogical demands. General education teachers describe changes in math, science, and reading instruction that have been implemented in their districts during the past decade. In particular, they note an increased emphasis on experiential learning through projects, experiments, and other forms of active engagement. Special and general educators report that these changes have been positive for many students with disabilities because they provide greater flexibility to adjust assignments to meet student needs and still provide more cognitively demanding tasks. Special educators support the focus and breadth of learning goals the curriculum standards provide. However, they often express concern over the amount of time required to assist students with disabilities in the new content areas and the decreased attention to specialized skill development.

---

[4]Five local school districts were selected on the basis of multiple recommendations of the prominence of their reform efforts. The districts are demographically and geographically diverse. Case studies were developed through analyses of interview data, document reviews, and observations conducted during on-site visits (M.W. McLaughlin, unpublished data, 1997).

Educational and Legal Implications

Two important motives for standards-based reform are to inspire all students to perform at high levels and to prevent the self-fulfilling consequences of holding lower expectations for historically low-achieving groups, including many students with disabilities (McLaughlin and Shepard., 1995). But simply declaring that all students ought to meet high standards without providing them access to the knowledge, skills, and resources necessary to reach them victimizes those who fail to meet the standards (McLaughlin and Shepard, 1995).

Several key questions arise with respect to the participation of students with disabilities in standards-based curricula, instruction, and post-school outcomes. What are the legal and ethical responsibilities of educational agencies to ensure that students with disabilities are provided with the necessary opportunities to learn to high standards? What constitutes an appropriate education for students with disabilities in a standards-based educational environment? How can standards-based reform raise expectations specifically for students with disabilities and stimulate schools and districts to address their educational needs? How can the curriculum and instructional methods that work best for students with different disabilities be incorporated into a common standards-based curriculum? In which situations, if any, should standards and outcomes be altered for students with disabilities? How should key decisions be made about participation of these students in standards-based reform? This section examines some of these issues.

Requirements for an Appropriate Education

Efforts to include students with disabilities in standards-based reform need to be considered in relationship to the requirements in federal law to provide them with an appropriate education. As defined by the IDEA, this commitment requires the provision of a free and appropriate public education for students with disabilities (20 U.S.C. 1401[a][18]). In addition, for an education to be deemed appropriate, the package of special education and related services must be defined in an IEP, in conformity with the IDEA's procedural requirements, and must be reasonably calculated to allow the student to receive educational benefits (*Board of Education of Hendrick Hudson Central School District* v. *Rowley*, 458 U.S. 176, 1982). Furthermore, both Section 504 of the Rehabilitation Act of 1973 and the Americans with Disabilities Act require that government services provided to persons with disabilities be equally beneficial or equally effective as services provided to those without disabilities.

The implementation of common content and performance standards for all students directly affects efforts to ensure that students with disabilities receive an appropriate education. Introducing content and performance standards into the curricular goals of an educational system alters the expectations for all students. Although the precise legal requirements are not yet clear, the legal analysis conducted for the committee indicates that, once a state or local school system adopts a standards-based reform initiative for its students, this initiative is presumed to include students with disabilities, who are entitled to the benefit of standards-based reform along with all other students (Ordover et al., 1996:43).

State and federal disability laws are likely to require educational agencies to align the curriculum, instruction, and related services provided to students with disabilities with the general state standards for all students (Ordover et al., 1996). Thus, to meet the IDEA requirement for an appropriate education under a system of standards-based reform, special education and related services for students with disabilities will probably need to include specialized instruction and support services that are aligned with the common standards applicable to all students. When content and performance standards are part of the general curriculum, it can be further argued that the IEP team should address these standards when they make determinations about appropriate education and plan a curriculum and instruction for students with disabilities. In particular, legal analysis of the existing law suggests that IEP teams will need to pay specific attention to content and performance standards when they write or review the sections of the IEP addressing current levels of educational performance, annual goals, short-term objectives, extent of participation in general education programs, and use of objective criteria and evaluations (20 U.S.C. 1401[a][20]).

Adequate Opportunities to Learn

There is also a relationship between the legal requirements for an appropriate education described above and the concept of "opportunity to learn" (OTL), an issue that is relevant to all children, not just students with disabilities. As explained in Chapter 2, the concept of opportunity to learn holds that it is unfair to expect students to attain standards unless they have been provided with instructional practices, conditions, and resources of sufficient quality and quantity to enable them to learn the content in the standards. Political opposition has curbed efforts to develop and implement standards for evaluating opportunities to learn. Nevertheless, a basic question of equity remains as to whether all students, regardless of where they attend school or what their special needs are, will be provided with adequate instructional opportunities to learn the content for which they will be held accountable. As we discuss further in Chapter 5, the issue of opportunity to learn becomes especially important in the testing arena, when high-stakes consequences for individuals and institutions are attached to student performance as gauged by test results. In these instances, existing case law indicates that states and school districts have an obligation to provide students with adequate instructional opportunities to learn the material being tested and must ensure a sufficient relationship between what is tested and what is actually taught.

The three characteristics of effective instruction for students with cognitive disabilities—instruction that is individually referenced, intensive, and contextualized—could be said to define the OTL standards for the majority of students with disabilities. At the current time it is unknown, however, whether the necessary instructional characteristics can be delivered comprehensively enough to allow all students with disabilities to meet common content standards.

This proposition remains largely untested because research on students with disabilities to date has focused primarily on their acquisition of discrete functional skills and fundamental academic skills. The paucity of instructional research related to more complex tasks and knowledge means that it is uncertain how to deliver the promises of higher expectations and a standards-based curriculum to the large number of students with cognitive disabilities.

Resource Implications

Although it seems quite likely that educating all children to meet higher standards will require some additional resources, research sheds little, if any, light on how much this will cost. Although a few studies focus on the costs of specific education interventions (such as some early reading interventions), none looks systematically at what resources are required to bring all students to higher standards, what these resources cost, and where these resources will come from (new dollars or the reallocation of existing dollars). Furthermore there are almost no data about what it may cost to include students with disabilities in standards-based reform, above and beyond the general costs of implementing these reforms. The curricular and instructional issues raised in this chapter do, however, suggest a number of potential areas that will require additional resources.

Among the most important investments will be those required for professional development, inservice preparation, and ongoing technical assistance for teachers. Under standards-based reforms, both general and special education teachers will need to learn new content, new ways of teaching this content to students with a variety of educational needs and learning styles, and new approaches to assessing student learning. As more students with disabilities are included in the general education curricula, general educators must also develop knowledge of how to modify instruction and assessment to better meet the needs of these students. In addition, special education teachers, who are trained quite differently from general education teachers, will require inservice preparation and professional development to increase their understanding of common standards and the teaching and learning principles implied by them. Special educators will also need to learn effective methods for modifying the general curriculum for students with disabilities. In sum, standards-based reform holds considerable expectations for educators, and preparing them to meet these expectations is likely to require significant resources (Box 4-3).

Additional personnel may also be required to implement standards-based reforms effectively. The intensive instruction that will be necessary to help some students with disabilities meet new standards will require even more instructional

BOX 4-3   Implications of Standards-Based Reform for Teacher Education and Professional Development

A report by the National Commission on Teaching and America's Future (1996) concluded after a two-year study that the single most important strategy for achieving higher standards is to recruit, prepare, and support excellent teachers for every school. This report calls for changes in teacher preparation and recruitment, teacher professional development, teacher pay, and school structure. Many researchers concur that the traditional model of professional development, which focuses on improving and expanding teacher skills and classroom techniques, is inadequate to prepare teachers for the ambitious vision of teaching and learning that is driving current reform efforts (see, for example, Little, 1993). Instead of skills training, teachers need opportunities to learn, experiment, consult, and evaluate new practices. And time must be provided for collegial activities and teacher reflection. Promising alternatives to traditional professional development models include teacher collaboratives and other networks, subject matter associations, collaborations between schools and universities, professional development schools, and teachers as researchers (Corcoran, 1995; Little, 1993; National Commission on Teaching and America's Future, 1996; O'Day et al., 1995).

This new paradigm of professional development has been incorporated into national professional teaching standards (National Staff Development Council, 1994, 1995), as well as federal and state policy. For example, Goals 2000 encourages states and local school districts to develop and implement new forms of sustained professional development. Some states, for example Michigan, are revamping professional development around new professional standards and coordinating professional development funding and activities across several state and federal programs. Other states, including California, Maryland, Missouri, and Vermont, have established regional and statewide teacher networks and professional development centers (Goertz and Friedman, 1996).

We know little about the cost of new or current professional development practices. Neither states nor most local school districts have systems in place to account for these expenditures. The costs of implementing new professional development programs will depend on how they are structured and what they include. The components of these programs that need to be costed out include: (1) direct expenditures on formal professional development activities, (2) time for administrators and teachers who supervise the process of improving instruction, (3) costs associated with reduced instructional time if teachers are released from their classrooms, (4) increases in teachers' salaries that will occur as a result of enhanced qualifications, and (5) participants' own investments of uncompensated time and out-of-pocket expenses. Estimates of past ex-

continued

BOX 4-3—Continued

penditures on professional development that included the first four components ranged from $1,000 to $1,700 per teacher in 1980 dollars, or 3.4 to 5.7 percent of district budgets. Other researchers found that teachers contributed 60 cents for every public dollar spent on professional development (Corcoran, 1995).

The National Commission on Teaching and America's Future (1996) has recommended that states allocate 1 percent of state and local funds for "more focused and effective professional development," in addition to providing matching grants to local school districts that increase their investments in professional development (p. 121). This investment would cost $2.75 billion a year.

It is difficult to imagine how students with disabilities will be included in standards-based reform without a significant investment in teacher preparation and teacher development. In fact, federal IDEA regulations require states to ensure that students with disabilities receive special education and related services from personnel who meet the highest possible professional standards. A set of personnel licensure standards, separate from those of regular education, has evolved from this requirement and has resulted in special educators learning distinctive kinds of skills and knowledge in their preparation and professional development programs. Concerns have been raised about whether, as a consequence, special educators have had less time to acquire knowledge related to content standards and core curriculum and instruction. Similar concerns have been raised about whether general classroom teachers are hampered by a lack of knowledge about how to effectively educate and individualize instruction for students with disabilities.

Amid these concerns, teacher licensure for special education and general education teachers has remained on separate tracks (Andrews, 1995). A 1995 survey by the Council of Chief State School Officers (in press) indicates that 22 states require some special education coursework for elementary school teachers, and 21 states have a similar requirement for secondary school teachers, but only 11 states require practical experience with students with disabilities.

Thus, additional professional development will be essential to help both general educators and special educators understand new content standards and their pedagogical implications and to prepare them to accommodate a range of learners. Maryland, Kentucky, Colorado, and other states are undertaking promising new approaches that draw from both categorical and general funding to support joint professional development for general and special educators. In these states, teachers of diverse students come together to develop thematic units and classroom performance assessments based on standards. These activities are supported by redirecting current professional development dollars and, in some cases, adding new dollars.

support, but how much more is unknown. Current special education caseloads averaging 27 pupils per professional educator may need to be revised and more efficient use of special education staff may be necessary to allow implementation of this kind of intensive instruction.

New curricula and pedagogy call for changes in the types of instructional tools used in classrooms, so additional resources are likely to be needed for instructional materials and technology. Teachers are encouraged to supplement, if not replace, textbooks with primary and secondary source materials and literature. The new national standards in mathematics and science call for teachers and students to use manipulatives, hands-on science materials, and calculators. Yet many children do not have access to these materials.[5]

In addition, parents, educators, business, and the public all agree that students need to learn how to use computers in order to succeed in the 21st century. Computer technology has shown particular promise for the education of students with disabilities. Currently, however, too few schools have the infrastructure or the hardware required. In addition, schools will face the ongoing expense of computer maintenance, software purchases, and telephone charges for using the Internet.

Determining How Standards Apply

The complex educational and legal issues surrounding the participation of students with disabilities in standards-based reform suggest that it will be necessary to develop a defensible procedure that can be used to determine the appropriateness of the content standards for each student with a disability. A determination to alter the common standards in any way will need to be made systematically, individually, and deliberately. A defensible decision-making process will need to consider at least three issues:

- Do the common content standards represent skills critical to the individual's success once he or she leaves school?
- Do the common content standards represent critical skills appropriate for the particular age of the student?
- Can the curriculum of the common content standards be fully taught to the student without jeopardizing his or her opportunity to master other critical, functional behaviors?

A negative response to any one of these questions may require alterations of the common standards for that student. The committee's overall recommendations

---

[5]For example, although the price of calculators has dropped significantly over the years, in 1992, 40 percent of the nation's fourth grade students and 28 percent of eighth graders were in classrooms that did not have school-owned calculators available for their use. Two-thirds of the eighth grade students did not use scientific calculators in their schoolwork (National Assessment of Educational Progress, 1993).

for a decision-making process are outlined in Chapter 6, but we discuss several key points regarding this process here.

First, the needs of each student ought to be considered individually, taking into account the nature, type, and level of each child's disability rather than his or her disability label or service delivery arrangement. For many students with sensory or motor impairments or other noncognitive disabilities, for example, the common content standards are likely to be highly appropriate, perhaps requiring accommodations only in instruction and assessment. It will be important, however, to allow educators the flexibility to teach students with disabilities using whichever of several instructional strategies are most effective to pursue the same learning goals. Standards-based reform ought not to preclude an instructional program built on effective approaches for students with disabilities.

For students with severe cognitive impairments, the conditions necessary to enable them to learn to common content standards are currently unknown. In addition, the common content standards may bear little resemblance to the skills and knowledge that most students with severe cognitive disabilities require for successful post-school adjustment. Allocating instructional time to such non-functional learning activities is likely to divert effort from more relevant instruction. Alternate standards in critical domains such as career/vocational and functional life skills may be needed for many students with severe cognitive disabilities. However, in keeping with the goals of standards-based reform, such alternate standards will need to be challenging and set high expectations for these students, and systems must be held accountable for student progress.

Decisions about common content standards and competing instructional goals may also be problematic for some students with milder cognitive disabilities—including students with learning disabilities, behavior disorders, and mild-to-moderate mental retardation, who together constitute the vast majority of students with cognitive disabilities. For many of these students, the state's content standards may be appropriate and related to intended post-school outcomes; for others, they may not. Many of these students may need additional, specially designed instruction beyond what is provided in the general curriculum. For example, some need intensive instruction in reading as well as time in nonacademic courses, such as vocational education. Others may need explicit instruction in behavioral or social areas. As with students with more severe cognitive disabilities, one must consider the potential trade-offs involved in diverting instruction toward achieving the content standards and away from other important employment, social adjustment, and personal management skills, as well as from such basic academic skills as decoding words on the written page.

As a second consideration, the decision to alter standards should be formulated on a domain-by-domain basis for each individual, so that for some students with disabilities, alternate standards will apply only to limited portions of the curriculum. For example, a secondary student with a learning disability might be included in the common standards for the vast majority of his or her program but have alternate standards for English or language arts, if it is determined that the competing priority of learning to read is higher than studying American literature.

As a third consideration, decision makers are advised to give systematic and deliberate consideration to the implications of participation in alternate standards for a subset of the curriculum. For example, if a secondary student misses American literature and a science class while working intensively on learning to read, the system should not hold this individual accountable for meeting content standards if no opportunity to learn has been provided. It will be important to ensure a match between the individual student's curriculum/standards, especially if they have been altered, and the assessments given to evaluate that child's progress. This will be particularly important when there are consequences attached to individual student results, such as the awarding of a high school diploma.

Fourth, as key participants in the IEP process, parents (and the students themselves, as appropriate) need to be active participants in decisions concerning content standards and valued post-school outcomes. IEPs focus only on services directly related to a student's disability and on areas of the curriculum for which there is specifically designed instruction; therefore, IEP goals may not directly relate to all of the content embodied in the common curriculum. If students are expected to achieve common standards, parents will want to know about the relationship between the IEP goals and the content standards.   Parents of children with disabilities will need to participate in decisions about altering standards and to understand the ramifications of these decisions—such as whether their children will be eligible for a standard high school diploma.

For parents to participate meaningfully in these decisions, they will need in-depth knowledge of the various aspects of standards-based reform and the meaning of any decisions to alter content standards. Under standards-based reform, curriculum and instruction may become more abstract and more academic, and children may be taught in ways that are unfamiliar to parents. Thus, building parent understanding may entail a major information dissemination and training effort. Within this effort, particular attention must be paid to the needs of minority and economically disadvantaged parents of students with disabilities, who, as noted in Chapter 3, already face barriers to active participation in planning their child's individualized program.

Implications for the IEP Process

If common standards are altered in one or more domains, they will still need to ensure ambitious expectations, and this will require a revised and more rigorous IEP system. Some well-developed methods do exist for enhancing the IEP as a mechanism for accountability for student learning (e.g., Deno, 1985; Shapiro and Kratochwill, 1988).

Using these methods, the IEP identifies the broad outcomes that the student is expected to perform by the end of the year, along with validated indicators of proficiency for each of those outcomes. Research demonstrates that such alternative frameworks can result in more ambitious goals for students with disabilities (e.g., Fuchs et al., 1989a) as well as stronger student learning (e.g., Fuchs et al., 1991b; Jones and Krouse, 1988; Wesson, 1991). Methods such as these for developing IEPs reorient practitioners toward a stronger focus on student outcomes and high expectations, but they also permit consideration of individual goals.

Nevertheless, technical problems remain in aggregating information across students within an individually oriented outcomes framework for the IEP. Furthermore, the individual performance goals may not align with a state or district assessment. Moreover, reorienting the IEP process to increase expectations and measure meaningful outcomes will require considerable professional development for special educators.

Finally, it should be noted that permitting alterations for some students within standards-based reform may be viewed as a capitulation to present inequalities in performance and could represent a political liability. Political problems notwithstanding, the provision of realistic alternatives for addressing the specific learning requirements of certain students with disabilities, acknowledging their skill requirements for successful post-school adjustments, and creating challenging but personalized standards seems to reflect the spirit of the standards-based reform movement. And such alternatives can be designed in a fair and rigorous manner, so that schools cannot use that system as an excuse to set low performance standards for students with disabilities or deny them access to participation in a challenging curriculum.

CONCLUSIONS

In this chapter we have reviewed evidence regarding what is known about curricular and instructional conditions for students with disabilities; in addition, we examined expectations for content and standards under standards-based reforms. As in other chapters of this report, we have been constrained by the fact that data are not yet available regarding the implementation of curriculum and instructional practice under standards-based reform. Many content standards are still in the developmental phase, and almost no data are available about their effects on classroom practice and student learning, let alone their specific impacts on students with disabilities.

The goals of standards-based reform to raise expectations, improve educational outcomes, and strengthen curriculum content are as important to students with disabilities as they are to children without disabilities. Our analyses have raised several concerns regarding the compatibility of common content standards with the curriculum and instruction required for at least some students with disabilities.

Setting educational goals for a number of students with disabilities has long meant looking beyond academic goals to a broader set of outcomes. An educational focus on these broader outcomes improves the likelihood that children with disabilities will become productive, independent adults. *The focus on a broad set of outcomes has meant that curricula for some students with disabilities, particularly at the secondary school level, include significant nonacademic components.* At the secondary level, many aspects of the curriculum for students with disabilities explicitly focus on the transition to work and other aspects of adult life—a long-recognized need in special education.

In contrast, many of the standards developed thus far by states and national organizations are focused on academic content in core subjects, such as language arts, mathematics, science, and history. Less common are standards addressing vocational and workplace skills and other areas of learning, although some state standards refer to broad learning goals rather than to specific content to be learned. If it continues, this trend toward academic standards will have important implications for some students with disabilities who, as noted above, benefit from a strong focus on the school-to-work transition, vocational education, and functional skills, in addition to purely academic learning. For these students, allocating instructional time to nonfunctional learning activities may detract from more relevant information. In many places, there has not been specific consideration of the needs of all students with disabilities in the development of content standards. *Therefore, questions exist about whether all common content standards are realistic and useful goals for some students with disabilities.* As professionals who work with students with disabilities participate more in the design and development of standards, there may be increased compatibility of standards with the diverse learning needs of students. It is important that broader outcomes and school-to-work transition planning not be neglected in the move toward standards-based reform.

Research has identified three broad characteristics of effective instruction for students with cognitive disabilities (who constitute the majority of students with disabilities): individually referenced decision making that focuses on the individual student's needs, intensive methods of delivering instruction, and explicit contextualization of skills-based instruction Currently, it is not known whether these three characteristics of effective instruction can be delivered comprehensively enough to allow students with cognitive disabilities to meet common content standards.

Some content standards assume a constructivist view of teaching and learning that may not be fully compatible with these characteristics of effective instruction for students with cognitive disabilities. Constructivism emphasizes active, self-regulated learning, higher-order thinking skills, and synthesis of knowledge from various sources and content areas. Many content standards also stress more advanced skills, such as critical thinking and problem solving, over basic skills; at this time, it is unknown whether these broad characteristics of effective instruction work with more abstract and complex skills. Even so, it will be difficult for some students with significant cognitive disabilities to attain these more advanced skills, regardless of instructional methods or the extent of their participation in standards-based reform. Research is needed that examines the interaction between specific special education interventions and the instructional methods called for in many content standards.

Participation of students with disabilities in common content standards raises a number of complex legal and educational issues. As a result, a defensible decision-making process will need to be developed to determine the appropriateness of common content standards and the conditions under which standards should be altered for individual students. A revised IEP system may be needed to ensure accountability for this process.

Although our analyses suggest that some of the specific aspects of standards-based reform may not be very well matched with the characteristics of effective special education for some students with disabilities, this does not mean that these students should be left out of standards-based reform. Rather, it suggests that the details of standards-based reform should be considered with input from people knowledgeable about special education. It is equally important that the nature of participation in standards-based reform for each child with disabilities be considered carefully and systematically.

5

Accountability and Assessment

Public accountability has always been a hallmark of public schooling in the United States, although it takes a variety of forms. For example, in casting its votes for school board and state legislative candidates, the public holds elected officials accountable for educational quality. Policy makers, in turn, hold professional educators accountable when they decide under what conditions schools will be funded, how curriculum and instruction will be regulated, and how high performance will be rewarded and low performance sanctioned. The assumption in all these transactions is that a social contract exists between communities and their schools: the public supports and legitimates the schools and, in exchange, the schools meet the community's expectations for educating its children.

No matter what type of accountability mechanisms are imposed on schools, information about performance lies at the core. Only with public reporting on performance can policy makers and the public make informed decisions, and only with reliable and useful data do educators have the information necessary to improve their work. Data on school performance are varied and include revenue and expenditure reports, descriptions of school curricula, and student attendance records. But assessments of student achievement are the most significant indicator for accountability purposes. In fact, over the past 20 years, student scores on standardized tests have become synonymous with the notion of educational accountability.

The accountability system for general education differs in two major ways from that for special education: it is public, and it typically focuses on aggregate student performance. In contrast, for special education, accountability is centered on the individualized education program (IEP), an essentially private document that structures the educational goals and curriculum of an individual student and then serves as a device for monitoring his or her progress. The accountability mechanisms for general and special education are not inconsistent with one another and, for students with disabilities, the IEP serves as the major vehicle for defining their participation in the common, aggregated accountability system. Nevertheless, if students with disabilities are to participate in standards-based reform, their individualized educational goals must be reconciled with the requirements of large-scale, highly standardized student assessments.

The education standards movement has emphasized assessment as a lever for changing curriculum and instruction, at the same time continuing and even amplifying its accountability purposes. Indeed, assessment has often been the most clearly articulated and well-publicized component of standards-based reform.

The appeal of assessment to policy makers who advocate education reform is understandable. Compared with other aspects of education reform, such as finding ways to implement and fund increased instructional time; improve recruitment, professional development, and retention of the most able teachers; and reduce class size, assessments are relatively inexpensive, can be externally mandated and implemented quickly, and provide visible results that can be reported to the press (Linn, 1995).

The preeminent role of assessment in standards-based reform has also attracted considerable controversy. Some observers have cautioned that a heavy reliance on test-based accountability could produce unintended effects on instruction. These include "teaching to the test" (teachers giving students practice exercises that closely resemble assessment tasks or drilling them on test-taking skills) and narrowing instruction to emphasize only those skills assessed rather than the full range of the curriculum. Indeed, research suggests that raising assessment stakes may produce spurious score gains that are not corroborated by similar increases on other tests and do not reflect actual improvements in classroom achievement (Koretz et al., 1991,1992; Shepard and Dougherty, 1991; Shepard, 1988, 1990).

Analysts have also questioned the potential effects of assessment-based accountability on low-achieving students. Will schools choose to focus their efforts on students closest to meeting acceptable performance levels? What happens to students who fail to meet performance standards? Observers have questioned whether the same assessments can fulfill both their intended roles of measuring performance and inducing instructional change. Researchers have also raised concerns about the technical difficulties of designing and implementing new forms of assessment (Hambleton et al., 1995; Koretz et al., 1996a).

These potential effects do not appear to have dampened enthusiasm for assessment as a lever for reform; the basic purposes and uses of assessment in standards-based reform are proceeding unchanged.

Many students with disabilities, however, are exempted from taking common assessments for a variety of reasons, including confusion about the kinds of testing accommodations that are available or allowable, local concerns about the impact of lower scores on average performance, concerns about the impact of stressful testing on children, and difficulties in administering certain tests to students with severe disabilities. But regardless of the reason, many students with disabilities who are exempted from assessments are not considered full participants in other aspects of the general curriculum. And if the performance of these students does not count for accountability purposes, then there may be less incentive for educational agencies to try to enhance their educational offerings and improve their performance. Eliminating these assessment barriers is therefore an important component of efforts to include more students with disabilities in standards-based reform.

Efforts to increase participation of students with disabilities in assessment programs reflect two distinct goals. One goal is to improve the quality of the educational opportunities afforded students with disabilities. For example, some reformers maintain that holding educators accountable for the assessment scores of students with disabilities will increase their access to the general education curriculum. A second goal is to provide meaningful and useful information about the performance of students with disabilities and about the schools that educate them. Although they recognize that student test scores alone cannot be used to judge the quality of a particular school's program, reform advocates assume that schoolwide trends in assessment scores and the distribution of those scores across student groups, such as those with disabilities, can inform parents and the public generally about how well a school is educating its students. Ideally, an assessment program should achieve both goals.

With efforts to include increasing numbers of students with disabilities in standards-based reform, questions about assessment remain pivotal. For example, are assessments associated with existing standards-based reform programs appropriate for students with disabilities? The answer to this question may well depend on the nature of a student's disability, the nature of the assessment program, whether accommodations (i.e., modified testing conditions) are provided, and whether accountability rests at the student, school district, or state level. If accommodations are provided, what are their effects on the validity of the assessment? Should scores earned when accommodations are provided be so indicated with a special notation in score reports? Many students with disabilities spend part of their school day working on basic skills, reducing their opportunity to learn the content tested by standards-based assessments. Is it fair, then, to hold them to standards of performance comparable to their peers without disabilities?

In the remainder of this chapter, we first provide an overview of accountability systems in standards-based reform. We then consider the role of assessment systems in standards-based reform. The next section describes the current participation of students with disabilities in state assessment programs. The fourth, and longest, section focuses on the necessary conditions for increasing their participation in large-scale assessments, with particular attention to reliability and validity considerations, the design of accommodations, test score reporting, the legal framework, and resource implications. The following section discusses implications of increased participation, and a final section presents the committee's conclusions.

Our focus on the assessment of students with disabilities in the context of standards-based reform has precluded consideration of a number of more general issues concerning assessment of children with disabilities. Examples of key issues that are not addressed include proposed changes in the IQ-achievement discrepancy criterion used to identify students with learning disabilities (see Morison et al., 1996) and other issues related to assessment for program eligibility purposes and preparation of the IEP.

OVERVIEW OF ACCOUNTABILITY SYSTEMS

Accountability systems are intended to provide information to families, elected officials, and the public on the educational performance of students, teachers, schools, and school districts, to assure them that public funds are being used legitimately and productively. In addition, some accountability systems are intended to provide direct or indirect incentives to improve educational outcomes. Assessment results are usually the centerpiece of educational accountability systems. The intended purpose and the design of accountability systems affect the type of assessments that are used, how the assessment data are collected, how they are reported, and the validity standard to which assessment results are held.

The different purposes of accountability systems lead to distinctions that result in quite different assessment system designs. The first critical factor is the *unit* to which accountability is directed. Although some systems are geared to provide state-level accountability, these systems build on data collected about districts, schools, and individuals. Most standards-based reforms rest accountability at the district and school levels. Some systems, such as that of Tennessee, focus on classrooms. In addition, some reform programs seek to provide individual-level accountability by giving parents explicit information about the current status, progress, and relative educational performance of their children. This latter kind of accountability is particularly relevant for students with disabilities.

The second important distinction is the *relevant comparison group* in the accountability system. There are three common alternatives. The most basic system provides information that simply allows comparisons among similar units (districts, schools, teachers, or individuals). A more elaborate system also includes comparisons among subgroups, either at the system level or within units. For example, one may wish to compare performance indicators broken down by gender, income, or racial/ethnic groups. Comparisons could also be made between students with and without disabilities or among types of disabilities.

Finally, the appropriate *time frame* for accountability information is an issue. Variables to be decided include how often single period information is collected, whether multiple years are employed, and whether accountability relies on measures of individual student progress over time.

These distinctions yield considerable variation in assessment and accountability systems across states. For example, Tennessee has implemented a "value-added" assessment system that measures changes in classroom-level achievement over time. The system also has the unique characteristic of holding teachers accountable not only for the year they teach the students tested, but also for three subsequent years of student performance after students leave their classrooms. Most state accountability systems, however, hold schools responsible for student performance only in the grades in which state assessments are administered, with comparisons made among grade cohorts (e.g., fourth graders) in different years, rather than of the same students over time.

According to a recent survey of state assessment programs, nearly every state and many school districts and schools now have some kind of assessment-based accountability framework in place (Bond et al., 1996). In 1994-95, 45 states had active statewide assessment programs. Most of the remaining states were in some stage of developing or revising their assessment programs. Two of the states without active assessments (Colorado and Massachusetts) suspended them while they were being revised. Nebraska is developing its first assessment program. Two states had no plans to implement a statewide assessment program of any kind (Iowa and Wyoming).

The assessments that form the basis of these statewide accountability programs are extremely diverse in the content covered, the grades assessed, testing format, and purpose. In general, students are assessed most often at grades 4, 8, and 11; five subjects (mathematics, language arts, writing, science, and social studies) are likely to be assessed. Most states use their assessments for multiple purposes, with the most common based on school- or program-level data: "improving instruction and curriculum" (n = 44), "program evaluation" (n = 39), and "school performance reporting" (n = 35). Twenty-three states report that they attach consequences at the school level to assessment results; these consequences include funding gains and losses, loss of accreditation status, warnings, and eventual state takeover of schools. Thirty states report that they use individual students' assessment results to determine high school graduation (18 states), grade promotion decisions (5), or awards or recognition (12) (Bond et al., 1996).

ASSESSMENT IN STANDARDS-BASED REFORM

Because standards-based assessments are diverse, it is difficult to generalize about them. Nonetheless, some common themes are discernible.

Dual Purposes—in standards-based reform, large-scale assessment programs usually have two primary, sometimes competing purposes. First, they are expected to provide a primary basis for measuring the success of schools, educators, and students in meeting performance expectations. Second, they are also expected to exert powerful pressure on educators to change instruction and other aspects of educational practice. In this respect, many current standards-based reforms echo the themes of "measurement-driven instruction" (Popham et al., 1985) that shaped state testing programs during the minimum-competency testing movement of the 1970s and the education reform movement of the 1980s (Koretz, 1992). Current assessments differ from those of previous reform movements, however, in their emphasis on higher standards, more complex types of performance, and systemic educational change.

Externally Designed and Operated—the assessments that are most central to the standards-based reform movement are external testing programs—that is, they are designed and operated by authorities above the level of individual schools, often by state education agencies. Internal assessments—those designed by individual teachers and school faculties—also play an important role in many standards-based reforms; indeed, one explicit goal of some standards-based reforms is to encourage changes in internal assessments. External assessments, however, are typically considered the critical instrument for encouraging changes in practice, including changes in teachers' internal assessments.

Use for Individual or Group Accountability—many large-scale external assessments are used for accountability, although the means of doing so vary greatly. Some assessments have high-stakes accountability for individuals, meaning that individual students' results are used to determine whether a student will graduate from high school, be promoted to the next grade, or be eligible for special programs or recognition. An example is the recently announced high school assessments in Maryland, which will be required for graduation. Other assessments impose serious accountability consequences for educators, schools, or districts but not for students. For example, schools that use aggregated student results to show sufficiently improved performance on the Kentucky Instructional Results Information System (KIRIS) assessments receive cash rewards, and, beginning in 1997, schools that fail to show improvement will be subject to sanctions. In yet other instances, the publicity from school-by-school reporting of assessment results is the sole or primary mechanism for exerting pressure. As we discuss later in this chapter, the method used to enforce accountability—in particular, whether consequences are attached to group performances (schools or classrooms) or individual students—has important implications for the participation of students with disabilities.

Infrequently Administered—in many standards-based systems, the external assessments used for accountability are administered infrequently. For example, Maryland's School Performance Assessment Program (MSPAP) is administered in only three grades (third, fifth, and eighth). Kentucky's KIRIS was originally administered in three grades (fourth, eighth, and twelfth); in the last several years, the assessments have been broken into components that are administered in more grades, but a given component, such as writing portfolios, is still administered in only three grades. These assessments are intended to assess a broad range of skills and knowledge that students are expected to have mastered by the grades at which they are administered. In this respect, they differ from course-based examinations, such as the College Board advanced placement tests and the former New York Regents examinations, and they contrast even more sharply with various types of assessments given throughout the school year to assess individual progress.

Reporting by Broad Performance Levels—in keeping with the central focus of standards-based reform, these assessments typically employ standards-based rather than normative reporting. That is, student results are reported in terms of how they compare against predetermined standards of what constitutes adequate and exemplary performance, rather than how they compare with the performance of other students in the nation or other distributions of performance. Moreover, the systems typically employ only a few performance standards. For example, Kentucky bases rewards and sanctions primarily on the percentages of students in each school reaching four performance standards (novice, apprentice, proficient, and distinguished) on the KIRIS assessments; Maryland publishes the percentages of students in schools and districts reaching the satisfactory level. In these systems, gradations in performance within one level—that is, between one standard and the next—are not reported. In Kentucky, for example, variations among students who have reached the apprentice level but not the proficient level are not reported.

Reporting of results in normative terms, such as national percentile ranks, is downplayed, although it is not always abandoned altogether. For example, the Kentucky Education Reform Act required that the results of the proposed assessment that has become KIRIS be linked to the National Assessment of Educational Progress to provide a national standard of comparison, and the most recent version of KIRIS will include some use of commercial tests, the results of which are reported in terms of national norms.

Performance Assessment—the standards-based reform movement has been accompanied by changes in the character of assessments to reflect the changing goals of instruction, as discussed in Chapter 4. In an effort to better measure higher-order skills, writing skills, and the ability to perform complex tasks, large-scale assessments are increasingly including various forms of performance assessment, either in addition to or in lieu of traditional multiple-choice testing. The term *performance assessment* encompasses a wide variety of formats that require students to construct answers rather than choose responses; these include conventional direct assessments of writing, written tasks in other subject areas (such as explaining the solution to a mathematical problem), hands-on tasks (such as science tasks that require the use of laboratory equipment), multidisciplinary tasks, small-group tasks, and portfolios of student work. In some instances, the specific skills or bits of knowledge that would have been assessed by short, specific items in traditional tests are instead embedded in complex tasks that take students a longer time to complete.

CURRENT PARTICIPATION OF STUDENTS WITH DISABILITIES IN ACCOUNTABILITY AND ASSESSMENT SYSTEMS

Although several studies have documented that the participation of students with disabilities in statewide assessments generally has been minimal, it is also extremely variable from one state to another, ranging from 0 percent to 100 percent (Erickson et al., 1995; McGrew et al., 1992; Shriner and Thurlow, 1992). Inconsistent data collection policies make it difficult to compare participation rates from place to place or to calculate a rate that has the same meaning across various locations; in addition, states tend to use methods that inflate the rates (Erickson et al., 1996).[1]

Forty-three states have written guidelines about the participation of students with disabilities in state assessments. Most states rely to some extent on the IEP team to make the decision, but only about half the states with guidelines require that participation decisions be documented in the IEP (Erickson and Thurlow, 1996). A number of other factors also affect (and often complicate) these decisions, including vague guidelines that can be interpreted in a variety of ways, criteria that focus on superficial factors rather than on student educational goals and learning characteristics, and concerns about the potentially negative emotional impact of participation on the student (Ysseldyke et al., 1994). In addition, anecdotal evidence suggests other influences, such as pressures to keep certain students out of accountability frameworks because of fears that these students will pull down scores.

In most states, nonparticipation in the assessment means that students are also excluded from the accountability system (Thurlow et al., 1995b). Indeed, in many states, even some students who participate in a statewide assessment may still be excluded from "counting" in the accountability framework. Sometimes states or school districts simply decide to exclude from aggregated test scores any students who are receiving special education services (see Thurlow et al., 1995b). For example, in one state the scores of students with IEPs who have taken the statewide accountability assessment are flagged and removed when aggregate scores are calculated for reporting back to districts and to the media; the scores of the students with IEPs are totaled separately and given to principals, who then can do with them what they wish (which frequently means discarding them). Unfortunately, these practices, if unmonitored, may lead to higher rates of exclusion of students with disabilities from accountability frameworks, particularly when incentives encourage exclusion (e.g., if high stakes are associated with aggregated test scores without regard to rates of exclusion). In fact, researchers (Allington and McGill-Franzen, 1992) have demonstrated that the exclusion of

---

[1]These authors suggest that participation rates should be calculated by dividing the number of test-takers with IEPs by the total number of students with disabilities at the relevant age or grade level. Interpretations vary about how to define test-takers and how to define the eligible population in the denominator.

students with disabilities from high-stakes assessments in New York has led to increased referrals to special education, in part to remove from accountability decisions students who are perceived to be performing at low levels.

One of the avenues for increasing participation of students with disabilities in assessments is allowing accommodations. Accommodations currently in use fall into four broad categories (Thurlow et al., 1993). Changes in *presentation* include, for example, braille forms for visually impaired students and taped versions for students with reading disabilities. Changes in *response mode* include use of a scribe or amanuensis (an individual who writes answers for the examinee) or computer-assisted responses in assessments that are not otherwise administered by computer. Changes in *timing* include extra time within a given testing session and the division of a session into smaller time blocks. Changes in *setting* include administration in small groups or alone, in a separate room. In addition, some students with disabilities may be administered an assessment in a standard setting with some form of physical accommodation (e.g., a special desk) but with no other alteration.

Within the past five years, increasing numbers of states have written guidelines outlining their policies on the use of accommodations. In 1992, 21 states indicated they had written guidelines on the use of accommodations by students with disabilities in their statewide assessments; by early 1995, 39 states had such written guidelines (Thurlow et al., 1995a).

An analysis of these state accommodations guidelines found a great deal of variation in their format and substance (Thurlow et al., 1995a). Some are one sentence long, and others take up numerous pages. States use diverse terms (e.g., nonstandard administration, mediation, modification, alteration, adaptation, accommodation), sometimes indistinguishably. Some states vary their guidelines depending on the type or purpose of the assessment, and others use the same guidelines for all purposes. States also classify accommodations in different ways: by category of disability, by the specific test being administered, or by whether accommodations are appropriate for score aggregation.

Perhaps most important, states take different approaches regarding which accommodations they allow or prohibit and how they treat the scores of students with disabilities who use accommodations. An accommodation that is explicitly permitted in one state might be excluded in another (Thurlow et al., 1995a). This variation is not surprising, given that little research exists on the impact of specific accommodations on the validity of various elementary and secondary achievement tests (Thurlow et al., 1995d). States also have divergent policies about whether to include the scores of students with disabilities who used accommodations in assessment-based accountability frameworks. Some states exclude these scores because of concerns about their validity (Thurlow et al., 1995a).

Despite the variability of state guidelines on accommodations, some generalizations can be made (Thurlow et al., 1995a). First, the majority of states with guidelines (n = 22) recognize the importance of the IEP and the IEP team in making decisions about accommodations for individual students. Second, many states (n = 14) specifically refer to a link between accommodations used during assessment and those that are used during instruction. Third, relatively few states (n = 4) require written documentation about assessment accommodations beyond what is written in the IEP. Even without such a requirement, however, many state assessment directors still document the use of assessment accommodations. A 1995 survey found that 17 of the 21 states that collect data on individual students with disabilities in their statewide assessment databases also document whether an individual student used an accommodation. Not all of these states, however, can identify exactly which accommodations a student used (Elliott et al., 1996a; Erickson and Thurlow, 1996).

In most states, the net effect of policies on exclusion and accommodation is to keep at least some students with disabilities out of the accountability framework. However, most states are now reviewing the participation of students with disabilities in their assessment and accountability systems and the use of accommodations.[2] (We examine the design of assessment accommodations in the next section of this chapter.)

The large-scale assessments that typify standards-based reform are in many ways unlike those typically used in special education. Although including students with disabilities in these assessments may benefit them, the assessments themselves are not designed to manage the instruction delivered to individual students with disabilities.

Large-scale assessments are not intended to track the progress of individual students. Assessments are infrequent; often they are administered late in the school year, so that teachers do not see results until the following school year. They are not designed to provide longitudinal information about the progress of individual students, and in many cases, they do not place results from different grades on a single scale to allow measurement of growth over time. In fact, some large-scale assessments used in standards-based reform are also not designed to provide high-quality measurement of individual performance; measurement quality for individuals was deliberately sacrificed in the pursuit of other goals, such as broadening the content coverage of the assessment for schools and incorporating more time-consuming tasks.

Moreover, unlike some assessments used to manage special education, the large-scale assessments in standards-based reform focus on high-performance standards that are applied without distinction or differentiation to most students, including low-achieving students and students with disabilities. In contrast, a fundamental tenet of the education of students with disabilities is individualization and differentiation, as reflected in the IEP. The educational goals for each student with disabilities are required to reflect his or her capabilities and needs, as

---

[2]Both the Office of Special Education Programs and the Office of Educational Research and Improvement in the U.S. Department of Education are now supporting research on these issues.

should the instructional plan and assessments. For example, one IEP may call for a sign language interpreter to assist a student in the advanced study of history; another IEP may call for training in basic functional skills, such as telling time. Standards-based reform calls for uniformity in outcomes, allowing educators variations only in the path to those ends.

Many of the new, large-scale assessments deliberately mix the activities and modes of presentation required by individual tasks to mirror real-world work better and to encourage good instruction. A task may require substantial reading and writing as well as mathematical work, group work as well as individual work, or hands-on activities as well as written work. This mixture of modes is a reaction against the deliberately isolated testing of skills and knowledge found in traditional tests. But the instructional programs of many students with disabilities focus on developing very special skills, which are tested most effectively with narrowly focused tasks.

The methods used to report assessment results may limit their utility for tracking the progress of some students with disabilities. New large-scale assessments typically use only a few performance levels, wherein the lowest level is high relative to the average distribution of performance. Consequently, no information is provided about modest gains by the lowest-performing students, including some students with disabilities, and the reporting rubric signals that modest improvements are not important unless they bring students above the performance standard. Ideally, the tests used in special education should track the kinds of modest improvements that a student can reasonably achieve in the periods between measurements.

INCREASING THE PARTICIPATION OF STUDENTS WITH DISABILITIES IN LARGE-SCALE ASSESSMENTS

Including more students with disabilities in large-scale assessments in a way that provides meaningful and useful information will require confronting numerous technical issues. In addition, these assessments must be designed and implemented within the legal framework that defines the educational rights of students with disabilities and with consideration of the resources that new assessments will require for development, training, and administration. We address these technical and political issues in this section.

Assessment Design

Assessment programs associated with standards-based reform should satisfy basic principles of measurement, regardless of whether the assessment is traditional, performance-based, or a combination. Performance assessments, which comprise the bulk of standards-based assessments, are relatively new, and empirical evidence on their quality, although growing, is limited. Nonetheless, measurement experts agree that "performance assessments must be evaluated by the same validity criteria, both evidential and consequential, as are other assessments. Indeed, such basic assessment issues as validity, reliability, comparability, and fairness need to be uniformly addressed for all assessments because they are not just measurement principles, they are social values that have meaning and force outside of measurement wherever evaluative judgment and decisions are made" (Messick, 1994:13, cited in Linn, 1995).

These basic principles hold regardless of whether the students to be assessed receive general education services only or also receive additional services due to economic disadvantage (e.g., Title I) or disability. The importance of complying with basic measurement principles was acknowledged by Congress when it amended the Title I assessment requirements (P.L. 103-382). The amendments require states to develop or adopt for Title I challenging content standards, challenging performance standards that define advanced, proficient, and partially proficient levels of performance, and high-quality yearly assessments in at least reading and math. The law requires that these assessments:

(a) be used only for purposes for which they are reliable and valid;
(b) be consistent with nationally recognized professional and technical standards; and
(c) make reasonable adaptations for students with diverse learning needs.

To date, the evidence suggests that creating performance assessments that are reliable and valid remains a challenging and costly endeavor. Measurement error consistently is greater than that associated with traditional tests (Koretz et al., 1994). The ability to make generalizations from a limited number of performance tasks about students' competence in performing purportedly similar tasks is problematic (Breland et al., 1987; Dunbar et al., 1991; Gao et al., 1994).

By design, many performance assessments associated with standards-based reform require students to integrate a variety of knowledge and skills to produce a product or performance. Thus, for example, performance assessments in the area of mathematics are likely to involve reading and writing in the context of problem solving. In theory, this approach increases the probability that reading or writing disabilities, which are among the most common, will interfere with the assessment of mathematics. A similar situation exists for assessments of other areas, as when demonstrating knowledge of a scientific principle requires writing or relatively complex physical manipulation compared with a traditional multiple-choice item. Thus, creating reliable and valid performance assessments for students in general will be a challenging endeavor, and creating assessments that also are reliable and valid for students with disabilities is likely to be even more difficult. Empirical data are needed to inform the design of performance assessments and their use with students with disabilities.

Reliability

"Reliability" refers to the consistency of performance across instances of measurement—for example, whether results are consistent across raters, times of measurement, and sets of test items.[3]

Reliability takes many forms, and the choice of both a measure of reliability and an acceptable level of reliability depends on how scores will be used. Three factors that influence reliability—the sampling of students, variation among tasks, and excessive difficulty levels—are particularly important in the assessment of students with disabilities.

Sampling of Students

In standards-based reform, assessments are often used to make inferences about groups—for example, changes in the percentage of a school's students who have reached standards. A key aspect of reliability for measures of group performance is sampling error—that is, the variation in results from one group of students to the next.

Sampling error can be a concern for two reasons. First, in some standards-based systems, results are drawn from only a sample of students rather than the entire population in a given grade. For example, state-level reporting of portfolio scores in Vermont is based on random samples of students drawn from each school. Second, even when all students are tested, sampling error is important if inferences are going to be made beyond the performance of those particular students—for example, to compare them to another group. Such inferences are often made in standards-based systems, as when trends over time are used to judge *schools'* progress in meeting educational goals. Thus, for example, each successive group of third graders is compared with the one before to see if progress is being achieved. However, due to sampling error, some of the year-to-year change in a school's scores will reflect differences in the characteristics of the particular groups (or cohorts) of third grade students rather than changes in educational effectiveness within a school: a given year's third graders may be easier or harder to teach than the prior year's.

Sampling error is inversely related to the number of students included in the group's total (or aggregated) score: the fewer students included, the more unstable or unreliable the results. Accordingly, results for small schools (e.g., elementary schools and small rural secondary schools) or for small groups, such as students with disabilities, are likely to be less reliable and more subject to fluctuations due to random characteristics of individual members of the group. Sam-

---

[3]Reliability is an essential element of validity. Unreliability undermines the validity of inferences; if performance on a test varies too much as a function of irrelevant factors (choice of raters, the particular tasks chosen from an item pool, etc.), it provides a weak basis for inferences about performance. High reliability, however, is no guarantee of validity.

pling error will be a particularly serious concern if assessment results are to be reported separately for students with disabilities because of their relatively small numbers. The problem of sampling error is likely to be compounded further when scores need to be reported for students with different types of disabilities—both because their numbers will be even smaller and because, as discussed in Chapter 3, categories of disability are so variable. These issues are discussed further in the section on reporting.

Variation Among Tasks

Another aspect of reliability that may be particularly important in the assessment of students with disabilities is "task variance": differences in performance across tasks in an item pool. Evidence suggests that, particularly when tasks are complex, the relative performance of students at the same level of proficiency in a domain (say, students with roughly equal facility in writing) tends to vary markedly from one task to the next (Dunbar et al., 1991; Shavelson et al., 1993). This variation is a particular concern in the case of some performance assessments, in which tasks are complex and the relatively small number of them makes it difficult to average out the variations among tasks.

A more serious issue is the possibility of student-by-task interactions: differences in the ranking of students from one task to the next, independent of the average difficulty of the tasks. Although empirical evidence is not yet available, it is possible that this problem may be exacerbated for some students with disabilities because the irrelevant attributes of individual tasks may have greater impact on their performance than on the performance of many students without disabilities. For example, in a performance assessment of science, one task may require the student to manipulate objects, making that task especially difficult for students with orthopedic disabilities; other tasks may not require any physical manipulation. The ranking of some students with orthopedic disabilities on the first task is likely to be markedly lower than on other tasks, but this score would not reflect their true understanding of science.

Excessive Task Difficulty

General constraints on the reliability of performance assessments include the relatively few numbers of tasks and scoring categories and the subjective nature of scoring. An additional constraint is at work for students who score particularly high or low. Although traditional test theory assumes that error is constant along the full range of test scores (Green et al., 1984), in fact, measurement precision varies as a function of level of performance for most tests (Thissen, 1990). Most tests provide more precise estimates for average performers and less precise estimates for either low or high performers (Hambleton and Swaminathan, 1985).

A defining feature of assessments associated with standards-based reform is that the performance standards are set at high, "world class" levels (Linn, 1995).

Results from California, Kentucky, and Maryland show that there is a substantial gap between the performance levels specified in the standards and the actual, current levels of performance for general education students. The gap is likely to be even wider for many low-achieving students, such as some students with disabilities and those participating in Title I programs.

The result of this gap will be a decrease in the reliability of information about low-achieving students, including some with disabilities, and a corresponding decrease in the reliability of some scores and performance reports. If assessments are used only to estimate the proportion of students reaching a high performance standard, this additional unreliability will not be a serious concern; the assessment will correctly identify most of the low-performing students as failing to reach the standard. This source of unreliability could be important, however, if assessments are used to provide other information about the performance or progress of low-achieving students, such as changes in their mean scores, changes in the proportion reaching lower performance thresholds, or information about the performance of individual low-performing students.

Consideration of these three factors that influence reliability—sampling of students, variation in performance among tasks, and inappropriate difficulty levels—suggests that in particular cases the reliability of scores obtained by some students with disabilities may be lower than the reliability of results for the general student population. Additional empirical evidence is needed, however, to explore this possibility. When feasible, reliability should be examined empirically for specific groups and for particular test uses. When appropriate reliability studies are not feasible, results for students with disabilities should not be assumed to be as reliable as those for other students.

Furthermore, the relative importance of these reliability considerations are greatly influenced by whether inferences are being made about individuals or about groups. The reliability of test scores for individual students is critical when scores are used to make decisions about instructional placements or receipt of a diploma, but it is often relatively unimportant when scores are aggregated to characterize the performance of large groups. Conversely, the sampling of students is irrelevant when a score is used only to draw inferences about the individual who has taken the test, but it can be a major source of unreliability when scores are aggregated to describe the performance of small groups.

Validity

Two general themes become apparent in considering the validity of assessments of students with disabilities.[4] The first is that the degree of validity for students with disabilities may not be similar to that for other students. For ex-

---

[4]Many in the measurement profession use the term *validity* to refer both to the quality of information yielded by an assessment and to its effects (or *consequential validity*). For example, Messick

ample, the potentially lower reliability noted above could threaten the validity of inferences about students with disabilities.

The second theme tempers the first: there is a severe shortage of empirical research pertaining to the assessments of students with disabilities. A decade and a half ago, a National Research Council panel noted (Sherman and Robinson, 1982:141): "Almost from the promulgation of the Section 504 [of the Rehabilitation Act of 1973] regulations, it has been clear that there exists insufficient information to allow for the demonstrably valid testing of handicapped people, as required by the regulations." Although some research has been conducted since then, the National Research Council's generalization remains more true than not today, particularly for students younger than high school juniors and seniors for whom there is almost no empirical evidence. Both measurement theory and the available research raise concerns about the validity of assessments of students with disabilities. Research tailored more directly to elementary and secondary school students participating in the kinds of assessments used in standards-based reform is urgently needed to evaluate these concerns.

Link Between Use and Validity

Although people often speak of "valid" or "invalid" tests, validity is not an attribute of a test per se. Rather, validity is an attribute of a specific inference or conclusion based on a test. A valid inference is a conclusion well supported by the results of a given assessment; a less valid inference is poorly supported. To say, for example, that a given test is a valid measure of high school algebra means that conclusions about mastery of high school algebra are well supported by scores on that test. Therefore, validity depends on a test's particular uses and the specific inferences it is used to support.

The assessments at the core of standards-based reform have various functions, but, in one way or another, they are most often used to determine whether groups of students have reached acceptable levels of educational achievement, as embodied in explicit performance standards. They are generally not used for many of the traditional purposes governing assessments of students with disabilities. For example, the new assessments are generally not used for making decisions about individual students, including diagnosing disabilities, monitoring short-term progress toward IEP goals, or making placement decisions.[5] Accord-

---

(1989:20) distinguished the "evidentiary" basis of validity (construct validity, relevance, and utility) from the "consequential basis" of validity (value implications and social consequences). For simplicity, however, we use *validity* in this section to refer only to the quality of information yielded by assessments.

[5]However, schools or local districts may decide independently to use the results of these tests to make decisions about individual students. For example, Kentucky's KIRIS assessment is designed only to support inferences about the performance of schools. Nonetheless, some Kentucky educators report that they use KIRIS results in deciding about remedial placements for individual students (Koretz et al., 1996b).

ingly, some of the considerations of validity that are important for these traditional uses are less important in standards-based reform. For example, a central concern that arises when tests are used for individual decision making is the frequency of misclassifications—such as placing a child in the wrong instructional program—stemming from measurement error (Shepard, 1989; Taylor and Russell, 1939). This is not a concern when scores are reported only for groups such as schools and districts.[6] As long as the assessments used in standards-based reform are not used to determine placements, they will not raise this issue.

As explained earlier, some assessments for standards-based reform have consequences for individual students, whereas others are intended to monitor the educational achievement of groups of students at the school, district, or state levels. Assessments aimed at measuring group performance, such as KIRIS and MSPAP, have been designed to optimize measurement at the aggregate level, at the cost of precluding high-quality measurement of individual students.[7]

The unit of accountability (group or individual) has substantial implications for validity. For example, in the case of aggregate measurement, low reliability of scores for individual students may pose little or no threat to the validity of the intended inferences, and inappropriateness of tasks for some students may become much less important. Sampling error, however, which is irrelevant to individual measurement, may become a serious threat to the validity of inferences about groups, particularly in the case of small groups.

The fairness of assessments of students with disabilities is another issue related to validity that warrants consideration. Like other aspects of validity, fairness hinges fundamentally on how scores are used. In particular, assessments that are not fair when individual students are held accountable for scores may be fair when schools or districts are the unit of accountability. Suppose that two hypothetical schools, A and B, have similar populations of students with disabilities. School A has been diligent in searching for the most appropriate and effective instructional approaches for its students with disabilities, but School B has not. In a system that imposed high stakes for individual test scores, the students with disabilities in School B would be unfairly disadvantaged, perhaps to the extent that the assessment would fail to meet ethical and legal scrutiny. However, if scores are used to reward and penalize staff, not students, the low scores of students with disabilities in School B would be fair, in that they would accurately reflect bad practice and would lead to negative consequences for the staff. Temporarily exempting students with disabilities in School B from consequences for their low scores would increase the fairness of the system, whereas exempting their teachers from consequences would decrease its fairness.

---

[6]An analogous concern can arise, however: schools or districts can be misclassified. For example, in Kentucky, a prominent issue is the rate at which schools are misclassified as deserving rewards for improved performance (Hambleton et al., 1995).

[7]Both programs are now moving toward reporting scores for individual students, but schools rather than students will remain the unit of accountability.

Attaching high stakes to test results, as many states plan to do, has several general implications for the validity of these assessments. First, high-stakes tests are typically held to higher standards of quality because the consequences of incorrect test-based decisions are substantial. Validity evidence that would be deemed sufficient in the case of low-stakes assessments will often be judged insufficient in the case of high-stakes assessments. This suggests that the lack of validity evidence for some students with disabilities will be an even more pressing concern when stakes are high.

Second, evidence indicates that, when consequences are imposed for test performance, scores may become inflated (Koretz et al., 1991). High stakes increase incentives to teach to the test, sometimes to the point of deemphasizing important aspects of the domain (e.g., biology, algebra) that should be taught but that the test does not directly measure. The result is that test scores can increase even when performance has not increased across the whole domain.

Performance Comparability

Because the assessments of standards-based reforms are generally used to support the same inferences for all students—that is, whether students have reached performance standards—the comparability of test results for students with and without disabilities is a critical aspect of validity.

Comparability of test scores has many meanings, and the movement toward standards-based reform and performance assessment has made the issue of comparability even more complex. Recent papers suggest the need for caution in inferring comparability, especially for results from different assessments (Haertel and Linn,1996; Linn, 1993; Mislevy, 1992). Two conclusions from this work are particularly important for the present discussion. First, even when the results of different assessments are linked by statistical methods, justifiable inferences about the comparability of performance across assessments may be severely limited. Second, an approach that makes results more comparable for one purpose may actually degrade comparability for another. For example, under many circumstances, linking two assessments in a manner that improves the comparability of estimates for groups distorts estimates for individual students (Mislevy, 1992).

In standards-based reforms, the central issue of comparability could be called "performance comparability": the degree to which similar scores obtained by students with and without disabilities support similar inferences about their current level of achievement with respect to performance standards. Performance comparability is questionable whenever students with disabilities are administered assessments that differ appreciably from those administered to peers without disabilities.

A number of factors may influence comparability. Some students with disabilities will be administered assessments that differ only modestly from those administered to other students, for example, in the provision of slightly more time to complete the assessment; in other instances, the assessments administered to students with disabilities will be considerably altered. Performance comparability is likely to be problematic for students with very low levels of academic performance, such as many students with severe cognitive disabilities. Within a reasonable range, one can have measures that differ in difficulty but measure the same construct. When differences in performance are very large, however, the tests may not be measuring the same underlying construct. Performance comparability is also likely to be affected when disabilities are related to the construct measured. This issue, which potentially affects a substantial percentage of students with disabilities, is revisited below in the discussion of accommodations.

Performance comparability may also be particularly difficult to evaluate and document because of the difficulty of obtaining concurrent indicators of achievement against which to validate a given score. Other performance measures, such as grades or performance on other assessments, are likely to be similarly affected by a student's disability or the accommodations provided. Even when information on later performance would be useful for this purpose, it is likely to be scarce. For example, information about later performance in postsecondary education or employment is generally unavailable for representative groups of students.[8]

Three clear implications emerge from this discussion of score comparability. First, one should be very cautious in assuming that the results of any assessment that differs from the common one in format or testing conditions are comparable in meaning to those of the common assessments. Second, comparability of meaning may hinge on the specific inferences the assessment is used to support; comparability for one purpose may not indicate comparability for another. Third, additional empirical exploration of the comparability of results from modified assessments for standards-based reform is badly needed.

Context Dependence of Performance

The performance of an individual in a given domain tends to vary across contexts, sometimes in idiosyncratic ways. For example, the proficiency of some people in writing or mathematical computation falls off markedly when they are placed under time pressure, whereas other people are less affected. This is one of many reasons why measurement experts caution against drawing broad inferences from a single measure of performance.

It is possible that the performance of some students with disabilities may be particularly affected by contextual differences, which could interfere with the validity of inferences. For example, some students have disabilities that cause them to work somewhat slowly on certain tasks, thereby making their perfor-

---

[8]Kentucky's education reform program, widely considered pathbreaking in both general and special education, is an exception. The transition to later work or schooling is an element of Kentucky's accountability system, and the state is building a system to monitor these outcomes.

mance more susceptible to time pressure than that of many other students. An assessment that is a "power" test for most students (that is, performance is constrained by knowledge and skill but rarely by time limits) may be a "speed" test (where speed of performance limits scores) for many students with disabilities, and the provision of additional time is one of the most frequently offered testing accommodations for students with disabilities. As Bennett (1995) has pointed out, a test that is speeded for students with disabilities but not for other students may measure different attributes for the two groups.[9]

Contextual differences may constrain the justifiable inferences that can be reached about some students with disabilities on the basis of assessments for standards-based reform. The explicit inferences based on these assessments tend to be very broad, along the lines of "35 percent of fourth graders reached the minimally acceptable standard in writing"; these are oversimplifications for students in general education but may be untenable for some students with disabilities. At this time, however, there is little empirical basis for judging when contextual effects are particularly problematic for students with disabilities.

Relationship Between Disabilities and the Constructs Measured

Many approaches to the assessment of individuals with disabilities, particularly assessment accommodations, assume that disabilities are not directly related to the construct tested. Case law indicates that rights to accommodations do not apply when the disability is directly related to the construct tested (see Phillips, 1994). In other words, a student with a reading disability might be allowed help with reading (the accommodation) on a mathematics test, since reading is not in the construct being measured, but would not be allowed help with reading on a reading test, since the disability is directly related to the construct of reading.

However, the groups of students with clearly identifiable disabilities (such as motor impairments) that are largely unrelated to the constructs being tested constitute a small number of the identified population of students with disabilities. Most students with disabilities have cognitive impairments that presumably are related to at least some of the constructs tested.

Relationships between disabilities and assessed constructs have important implications for the validity of inferences based on test scores. For example, if a new assessment includes communication skills as an important part of the do-

---

[9]Contextual variations are a potentially major concern in the case of predictive inferences as well because the later performance of most individuals is likely to vary across contexts; in addition, the performance of some students with disabilities is likely to be more context-dependent. Phillips (1994) offered several illustrations. For example, she noted that the ability of a person with a reading disability to function as a mechanic would be influenced by the availability of other people or appropriate technology to help with tasks heavily dependent on reading. Such examples illustrate that generalizing about the predictive value of test scores for the later performance of students with disabilities may be difficult.

main of mathematics, then, to score well in mathematics, students would need to be able to read and write reasonably well.[10] On such an assessment, it is possible that students with reading disabilities might score worse than their proficiency in other aspects of mathematics would warrant, but providing them with accommodations such as the reading of questions or the scribing of answers is likely to undermine the validity of inferences to the broader, more complex domain of mathematics.

Several factors are likely to complicate efforts to evaluate this problem and to decide, for example, how best to use accommodations to maximize validity. First, as already noted, many performance assessments deliberately mix constructs and modes of response, making it more difficult to segregate the specific skills involved, especially those pertinent to a given disability. Second, the inconsistent classification of students with cognitive and learning disabilities does not provide clear criteria for describing the characteristics of various categories of disability, thus making guidelines for valid accommodations problematic (see Chapter 3).

Assessment Modifications and Accommodations

Tests are often altered in response to individuals' disabilities. For example, a blind individual cannot take a test that is normally presented in printed form unless it is presented orally or in braille. Such alterations are intended to remove irrelevant barriers to performance and allow the individual to demonstrate his or her true capabilities. As increasing percentages of students with disabilities are included in large-scale assessment programs, requests for such accommodations are likely to become more frequent. However, research on alterations of assessments for elementary and secondary school students is extremely sparse and provides only limited guidance for policy makers and educators.

Types of Alterations

Assessments are altered for individuals with disabilities in numerous, diverse ways, and the terminology used to describe these alterations is not always consistent. For purposes of this discussion, we will distinguish among (1) accommodations, (2) modifications, and (3) the substitution of different assessments. The distinction among these three categories is not always clear, and other classifications are also in use. This classification nonetheless helps to clarify the issues that arise in using altered assessments.

We label as *accommodations* changes in assessments intended to maintain or

---

[10]In recent surveys in Maryland and Kentucky, large percentages of teachers strongly agreed that the emphasis on writing in the states' assessments makes it difficult to judge the mathematical competence of some students (Koretz et al., 1996a, 1996b). The surveys, however, did not ask these questions specifically about students with disabilities.

even facilitate the measurement goals of the assessment. Accommodations are generally intended to offset a distortion in scores caused by a disability, so that scores from the accommodated assessment would measure the same attributes as the assessment without accommodations administered to individuals without disabilities. But, like any alteration in standardized administration procedures, accommodations may alter what an assessment measures, even when it appears on its face not to do so.

We use *modification* to refer to alterations of the content of an assessment.[11] Most content modifications are likely to change what a test measures. For example, educators may delete from an assessment specific items, subtests, or tasks that are deemed inappropriate or impractical for a specific examinee, or they may replace such a task with an alternative that would be more reasonable for that individual.

One common type of modification of tests is the administration of easier forms intended for younger children ("out-of-level testing"). Under certain restrictive conditions, out-of-level testing may preserve the measurement functions of an assessment, but it is unlikely to do so in the case of many standards-based assessments.[12] Moreover, testing that is substantially out of level may not produce comparable results (Plake, 1976), and out-of-level testing may be problematic in subjects in which curriculum content differs markedly across grades. Moreover, standards-based assessments are typically not constructed, administered, or reported in ways that would help preserve their measurement functions if administered out of grade. Perhaps most important, they are typically reported in terms of standards that are set within grades and are not linked between grades. Accordingly, in the case of the assessments used in standards-based reform, it is safest to consider out-of-level testing to be a modification that threatens performance comparability, not an accommodation that has the potential to maintain or even enhance it.

Finally, in some instances, students with disabilities may be administered *different assessments* rather than accommodated or modified versions of the same assessments administered to other students. These different tests may or may not be related conceptually to the regular assessments, but they are constructed as distinct assessments. Examples include Kentucky's alternative portfolio assessments and Maryland's Independence Mastery Assessment Program (IMAP) assessment, both of which are administered to a small percentage of students with

---

[11]Such changes have sometimes been called "content accommodations," but it is important to note that they are not accommodations in the sense that we use the term.

[12]For example, if the assessment measures a skill that accumulates over grades (such as reading in the elementary grades), contains an appropriate overlap of material across adjacent grades, and is scaled in appropriate ways, a score obtained by administering an assessment that is modestly out of level to a student with below-average proficiency may support the same inferences as are supported by in-level testing of other students. These restrictive conditions, however, are often violated.

disabilities who meet specific requirements for exemption from the states' regular assessments (Box 5-1).

These latter two kinds of alterations, modified and different assessments, typically will not support the same inferences as the regular assessments administered to students without disabilities. The measurement question raised by these altered assessments is the degree to which they support similar inferences. For example, they may be able to support only a subset of the inferences supported by the regular test, or inferences about some of the same content standards but not the same performance standards, or weaker forms of the same inferences, or, in some cases, they may be unable to support similar inferences at all. Which of these is true depends on the specific inferences at issue and the particular attributes of the modified or different assessments.

Accommodated assessments, in contrast, should have at least the potential for supporting the same inferences as regular assessments. Accommodations are widely viewed as the best means for increasing participation of students with disabilities in assessments. Accordingly, the design and evaluation of accommodated assessments entail a number of difficult conceptual and empirical issues, which are discussed in the following sections.

Logic of Accommodations

Traditionally, standardization (of content, administrative conditions, scoring, and other features) has been used to make the results of assessments comparable in meaning from one test-taker to the next. For some students with disabilities, however, a standard assessment may yield scores that are not comparable in meaning to those obtained by other students because the disability itself biases the score. In many cases, students with disabilities would get a lower score than they should because the disability introduces construct-irrelevant variance, variations in the scores unrelated to the construct purportedly measured. Therefore, "in the case of students with disabilities, some aspects of standardization are breached in the interest of reducing sources of irrelevant difficulty that might otherwise lower scores artificially" (Willingham, 1988a:12).

Accommodations are intended to correct for distortions in a student's true competence caused by a disability unrelated to the construct being measured (Box 5-2). The risk of accommodations is that they may provide the wrong correction. They may provide too weak a correction, leaving the scores of individuals with disabilities lower than they should be, or they may provide an irrelevant correction or an excessive one, distorting or changing scores further and undermining rather than enhancing validity. This risk is explicitly recognized in the guidelines provided by some state education agencies for avoiding these errors, although their guidance is sometimes very general and limited. For example, Maryland's *Requirements and Guidelines for Exemptions, Excuses, and Accommodations for Maryland Statewide Assessment Programs* (Maryland State Department of Edu-

BOX 5-1   Alternate Assessments for
Some Students with Disabilities

Most students with disabilities have mild disabilities and therefore will be able to participate in state assessment programs, although some will require accommodations. A much smaller percentage of students with disabilities require an alternate or different assessment because their curriculum does not match the content and performance standards assessed by the common test. Section 504 of the Rehabilitation Act of 1973 and the Americans with Disabilities Act require states and school districts to provide different assessments to the limited number of students who cannot otherwise participate effectively in the common assessment program. Goals 2000 and Title I also require administration of alternate assessments.

For students with such severe cognitive impairments that they require different assessments to measure different content, an "equally effective" aid, benefit, or service "must . . . afford [disabled] persons equal opportunity to obtain the same result, to gain the same benefit, or reach the same level of achievement" (34 CFR and 104.4[b][2]). The aid, benefit, or service would be the opportunity to participate, albeit by utilizing a different assessment that will provide these particular students "the same result" (Ordover et al., 1996:71-72).

The concept of a state-level alternate assessment for those students who cannot participate in the general assessment system was first proposed and developed by Kentucky. The alternate assessment is designed for those students with the most severe cognitive disabilities—in other words, students for whom traditional paper-and-pencil tests and certain performance events would be inappropriate. In Kentucky, the alternate assessment is a portfolio system in which information is kept on the student's progress toward academic expectations. The information in the portfolio can take many forms, including paper documents, recordings or videotapes, and pictures. Students' portfolios are rated using the same rubric as for the performances of students in the regular assessments—novice, advanced, proficient, and distinguished—and aggregated along with the scores of all other students.

Maryland also has an alternate assessment system for the subset of students with disabilities who are working on different standards from most students. These students are working on standards in four content domains (personal management, community, career/vocational, and recreation/leisure) and four learner domains (communication, decision making, behavior, and academic). The alternate assessment system is called

IMAP (Independence Mastery Assessment Program). Students in the alternate system complete a variety of performance tasks as well as a portfolio of their best work. The nature of the performance tasks and the contents of the portfolios are defined by the IMAP. Maryland's IMAP is still being field tested and its eventual use for accountability is questionable at this time.

Several aspects of the notion of an alternate assessment reflect larger issues that surround the whole concept of increased participation of students with disabilities in assessments associated with standards-based reform. The major issue is defining who will participate in the alternate assessment rather than the common standards-based assessment system. Kentucky's definition limits this group to a relatively small number. This policy is reinforced by state admonitions that the percentage of students participating in the alternate probably should not exceed 2 percent of the student population and that, if it does exceed this percentage, an audit will be performed to make certain that students are not inappropriately being moved into the alternate assessment. During its initial year, only 0.5 percent of students with disabilities were placed in the alternate assessment. In Maryland, the definition of who participates in IMAP is less clear. The state does generally admonish that the percentage of students not participating in the general assessment system should be small; the percentages are published along with test results.

Only six states currently offer students with disabilities alternates to the common assessment (Bond et al., 1996), and no research exists on either the ability of alternate assessments to measure students' educational progress validly or to encourage greater accountability for students with disabilities. We do know, however, that the design of alternate assessments poses all the same technical challenges as the development of valid accommodations for the common assessment. Nevertheless, alternate assessments remain a promising strategy for expanding the participation of students with disabilities in the public accountability system, even for those unable to take the common assessment. However, if accountability is a primary reason for expanding the participation of students with disabilities in state assessments, then it is important that those who take alternate assessments are also accounted for publicly. The scoring rubric may not be the same for an alternate version as for the common assessment, thus making it difficult to report comparable data. Still, the criteria used to assign students to the alternate assessment should be well defined and the number of students taking that test publicly reported.

BOX 5-2   Accommodation as a Corrective Lens

A useful metaphor for understanding accommodations is that of a corrective lens. Even in the absence of disabilities or other complicating factors, tests are imperfect measures of the constructs they are intended to assess. Envision a student's true competence in reading, for example, as a point on a vertical scale. To one side, is an identical scale of that student's observed competence, as reflected by performance on an assessment. Between the two scales is a lens causing some diffraction, so that true competence is represented (over repeated measurements) by an array of points on the observed-competence scale that form a blurry image of the true, unmeasured competence. If the test is well designed, this image will be centered on the true value (i.e., it will be unbiased), and it will not be too blurry (i.e., it will be reliable). Standardization of assessment methods and procedures is a key to obtaining a reasonably good image of the true attribute. Without standardization, some individuals will obtain scores that are inaccurate because of irrelevant factors, such as being given different amounts of time to take the assessment or having their work scored according to different criteria. This could increase the blurriness of the image and bias it.

Accommodations are based on the premise that, for some individuals with disabilities, the logic of standardization is misleading and scores obtained under standard conditions provide a distorted view of the true attribute of interest. The average for a group may be lower than it should be (or biased downward) and the scores for individuals will be biased to various degrees, depending on such factors as the severity of the disability, the coexistence of multiple disabilities, or perhaps less familiarity with assessments. Accommodations are intended to function as a corrective lens that will deflect the distorted array of observed scores back to where they ought to be—that is, back to where they provide a more valid image of the performance of individuals with disabilities.

---

cation, 1995) says that "accommodations *must not invalidate the assessment for which they are granted*" (p. 2, emphasis in the original). However, the only guidance it provides for meeting this standard is a single pair of examples (p. 3):

> Addressing the issue of validity involves an examination of the purpose of the test and the specific skills to be measured. For example, if an objective of the writing test is to measure handwriting ability, that objective would be substantially altered by allowing a student to dictate his/her response. On the other hand, if a writing objective stated that the student was to communicate thoughts or ideas, handwriting might be viewed as only incidental to achieving the objective. In the latter case, allowing the use of a dictated response probably would not appreciably change the measurement of the objective.

Unfortunately, many cases will be far less clear than this, and accommodations may not succeed in increasing validity even when they seem clear and logical on their face.

Designing and Evaluating Accommodations

To design an accommodation that will increase the validity (meaningfulness) of scores for students with disabilities, one must first identify the nature and severity of the distortions the accommodation will offset. These distortions depend on the disability, the characteristics of the assessment, the conditions under which the assessment is administered, and the inferences that scores are used to support.

Research has shown that different disabilities can cause different distortions in scores. Ragosta and Kaplan (1988), for example, surveyed students with disabilities about their experiences taking the Scholastic Aptitude Test (SAT) and the Graduate Record Examination (GRE). Although the poor response rate to the survey makes generalization risky, respondents' answers indicated that different disability groups face different difficulties in taking tests.[13] One blind student explained that items requiring extensive reading were particularly difficult for him, even when given a braille test, because "braille does not permit skimming" (Ragosta and Kaplan, 1988:62). Bennett et al. (1988) showed that time pressure varied for test-takers with disabilities depending on their disability and the accommodations they were offered. They also showed that, in the case of the SAT, unexpected differential item performance (that is, items that were relatively too hard or too easy for examinees, given their overall performance) were generally rare for most students with disabilities but were more common for blind students taking braille examinations.

However, predicting distortions in scores on the basis of disabilities is likely to be more difficult and controversial for elementary and secondary school students with disabilities than for the older students in the aforementioned research studies. One reason is the ambiguity of many classifications. Much of the case law and research pertaining to accommodations has focused on disabilities that are fairly unambiguous in terms of both diagnosis and functional implications, such as visual, hearing, and physical disabilities. In contrast, many of the students currently identified for special education have disabilities—in particular, learning disabilities—that do not have clear or consistently used diagnostic criteria or characteristics, as explained in Chapter 3. The classification of students

---

[13]About a fourth of the SAT examinees with visual impairments, but 11 percent or fewer of students in other disability groups, reported that questions involving graphics were especially difficult for them. Fully 66 percent of students with physical disabilities, in contrast to 24 percent of those with hearing disabilities and 11 percent of students with learning disabilities, reported that no type of test question was particularly difficult for them as a consequence of their disabilities.

with certain disabilities has been inconsistent among school jurisdictions and over time, and the classification of students in school settings is often inconsistent with research or clinically based definitions (Bennett and Ragosta, 1988; Shepard, 1989; Willingham, 1988b; Lyon 1996). The co-occurrence of more than one disability, which is common, clouds classification even further.

Because disability classifications tell us who may have underlying functional characteristics that are linked to potential score distortions, ambiguities or inconsistencies in classifying students with disabilities have serious implications for assessments. To the extent that a disability classification is valid for a particular student, then testing accommodations can be selected that offset any potential score distortions resulting from the student's disability, without compromising assessment data about performance on the domains measured. However, if classification of a disability is incorrect or imprecise, determining whether the accommodations selected are valid will be difficult.

A second source of difficulty, as previously noted, is that many elementary and secondary school students with disabilities have cognitive disabilities that are related to the achievement constructs being measured. The decrease in the reported prevalence of mental retardation (MR) and increase in the reported prevalence of specific learning disabilities (SLD) in recent years underscores this problem. In certain cases, a low score may be accurate for a student with mental retardation but misleadingly low for certain students with specific learning disabilities, and an inability to distinguish between them reliably clouds the interpretation of their test scores.

Efforts to identify the links between disability categories and distortions in test scores are likely to be complicated by the widespread trend in special education policies away from the use of formal taxonomies of disabilities to make decisions about individual children. For example, Maryland's guidelines for accommodations expressly mandate that "accommodations must be based upon individual needs and not upon a category of disability" (Maryland State Department of Education, 1995:2).

The tension between different needs and the uses of taxonomies of disability has been recognized for some time, but the inclusion of students with disabilities in standards-based reforms may make it more prominent. For example, Shepard (1989) noted that, for purposes of placement, it is often more important to ask what characteristics of a given child would make him or her a good candidate for special education treatments than to formally categorize his or her disability. Shepard, noted however, that the taxonomy that is useful for "construct diagnosis" (p. 568) or research purposes is often different from that needed for decisions about placement or practice. The taxonomic information needed to design validity-enhancing accommodations may be more like that needed for research than that needed for educational placement and practice. For decisions about placement and instruction, the critical information for disability classification is whether a particular group of students shares the need for, or ability to profit from, specific educational interventions. For research purposes, however, other bases for classification may be important, such as shared causation of the disability (etiology). For assessment purposes, the key basis for classification is shared distortions in the meaning of unaccommodated test scores and shared responsiveness to specific accommodations. Therefore, it would be profitable for purposes of assessment to group students on the basis of a disability, if doing so made it more feasible to implement specific accommodations that would enhance the validity of their scores, even if that classification had little usefulness for decisions about placement or instruction.

Research Evidence About Accommodations

Research on the validity of scores from accommodated assessments is limited, and little of it is directly applicable to the assessments that are central to standards-based reform. Much of the available evidence pertains to college admissions tests and other postsecondary tests (e.g., Wightman, 1993; Willingham et al., 1988).

Generalizing from the research on college admissions and postsecondary examinations would be risky. The populations are both higher-achieving and generally older than those taking the standards-based assessments, and the tests are different. In addition, given the purposes of college admissions tests, this research focused on predictive evidence of validity, which is less germane than concurrent evidence in the case of standards-based reform. Nonetheless, this research is suggestive, and there are reasons to suspect that it understates the difficulties that may arise when accommodations are offered in standards-based assessments. The groups taking tests like the SAT and GRE are higher-achieving than the student population as a whole and presumably include relatively few of the students who obtain low scores because of disabilities. In addition, until recently, students whose disabilities are directly related to tested constructs constituted a relatively small percentage of those taking college admissions tests and postsecondary exams; students with mental retardation generally do not take them, and until recently, relatively few of the students who took them were reported to have learning disabilities. Thus, most of these studies include relatively few students from the groups for whom the validity of scores is likely to be particularly problematic or especially difficult to ascertain, yet these students constitute well over half of all elementary and secondary school students with disabilities.

During the 1980s, researchers at the Educational Testing Service (ETS) conducted a series of studies of students with disabilities taking the SAT and the GRE, under both normal and accommodated conditions (Willingham et al., 1988). In terms of internal criteria—that is, evidence from the tests themselves—the results of the ETS studies found that reliability, factor structure, and test content appeared similar for students with and without disabilities. There was little evidence of differential item functioning for students with hearing impairments, physical impairments, and learning disabilities.[14]

Predictive evidence for accommodated scores of students with disabilities, however, was weaker than for scores obtained under standard conditions. In general, test performance less accurately predicted subsequent grade point average (GPA) for students with disabilities than for individuals without disabilities.[15] Furthermore, GPA was overpredicted for most groups with disabilities, suggesting that test scores had been overcorrected or inflated somewhat by accommodations.

These findings on the amount of time offered during assessments are particularly important. Certain disabilities and accommodations can slow the pace of examinees and, in such cases, providing additional time may be required to offset this distortion. However, ETS researchers found no evidence that individuals with disabilities taking the SAT *in the aggregate* actually required more time to complete the test. On the contrary, they found that, regardless of whether accommodations were used or which accommodations were used, students with hearing impairments, learning disabilities, physical disabilities, and visual impairments (even those students using a braille form) were *more* likely than other test-takers to complete both the verbal and mathematics sections in the scheduled time (Bennett et al., 1988:89).[16]

Some of these studies also found that the overprediction was strongest for relatively high-scoring students with learning disabilities who were given more time (Braun et al., 1988). They suggest that the extra time offered to some students with disabilities on the SAT may contribute to the overprediction of GPA by overcompensating for disabilities. Another study showed similar results when students with disabilities were given extra time on the Law School Admission Test (LSAT), leading the authors to suggest that "refinements in testing accommodations that adjust the amount of extra time to meet the specific needs of each accommodated test taker might decrease the amount of overprediction" (Wightman, 1993:52).

---

[14]Results for internal criteria varied somewhat by type of disability. Some mathematics items were differentially difficult in braille format for visually disabled students. Test content appeared similar for students without disabilities and those with physical and learning disabilities (despite the reports of some of the latter that verbal items were particularly difficult). Some students with visual impairments, however, had difficulty with some reading and graphical material. Factor structures were basically comparable, except that the mathematical and verbal factors were less strongly related to each other in the case of examinees with disabilities.

[15]When all administrative conditions are pooled, this effect was small, but it was large for some disability-by-accommodation groups. However, the SAT underpredicted GPA for students with hearing impairments entering special college programs for those with hearing disabilities.

[16]In the case of the GRE, however, students with physical disabilities and those with visual impairments taking the standard form were less likely than students without disabilities to complete the quantitative and analytical sections of the test.

It is unclear how these findings apply to elementary and secondary school students with disabilities. The effects may vary, for example, as a function of the type of assessment or the age of students. Nonetheless, these findings suggest that a need for additional time should not be assumed. Clearly, the effects on test scores of providing additional time warrant empirical investigation.

The 1995 field test of the National Assessment of Educational Progress (NAEP) in mathematics and science provided evidence about accommodations more directly relevant to standards-based reform, because NAEP is similar to state standards assessments in terms of the students tested and the focus on measuring achievement. Because of study limitations, however, additional research is needed to confirm the NAEP findings. In order to explore the feasibility of including more students with disabilities in NAEP, the field test introduced two changes in NAEP procedures. First, the study introduced stricter rules governing the exclusion of students with disabilities from NAEP. Second, the study permitted a variety of assessment accommodations, which until then had been unavailable.

The study results showed that it is feasible to assess an appreciable percentage of students with disabilities who had previously been excluded from the assessment. Most of these students (approximately 60 percent) had learning disabilities. All but 13 percent were in general education classrooms for some part of the day. The authors attributed the increased participation rates of students with disabilities more to the provision of accommodations than to the new inclusion criteria (Phillips, 1995). In both grades 4 and 8, approximately 48 percent of the test-takers with disabilities used accommodations for achievement testing.

However, the field trial results for students with disabilities who had been offered accommodations could not be reported on the NAEP scale. The NAEP researchers offered several reasons for this conclusion: "Generally, the assessment was less discriminating for the IEP sample, with about two-thirds of the items having smaller item-total correlations for the IEP group and with [some] items having negative correlations. Also, omit rates were generally higher [for the IEP sample]" (Anderson et al., no date:39). The negative correlations on some items indicate that, as the proficiency of students with disabilities increased, their performance on those items actually decreased; this finding was confirmed by other analyses. In addition, a substantial number of items showed "differential item functioning," indicating a bias either for or against students with disabilities.

The study results, however, are only suggestive in their findings about the effects of accommodations on score comparability. The study was limited by small sample sizes, a problem exacerbated by the matrix-sampled nature of the test, which dramatically reduces the number of students administered any given item. In addition, study results were made more equivocal because of "the multiplicity of student disabilities and corresponding accommodations" (Anderson et al., no date:37). It is possible that, if samples were sufficiently large for specific combinations of disabilities and accommodations, assessment results could be adequately scaled for some groups of students with disabilities. However, most state assessments will be faced with similar heterogeneity and small group sizes. Consequently, standards-based assessments are most likely to generate results for a multiplicity of disabilities and accommodations, with few of the specific combinations frequent enough to support separate scaling of assessment results.

Clearly, more research on the validity of scores from accommodated testing is needed—in particular, research tailored directly to the particular assessments and inferences central to standards-based reform. In the interim, the existing research, although limited and based largely on different populations and types of assessments, suggests the need for caution. The effects of accommodation cannot be assumed and may be quite different from what an a priori logical analysis might suggest.

Promising Approaches in Test Design

Research and development in the field of measurement is continually experimenting with and expanding the modes, formats, and technologies of testing and assessment. In addition to performance assessment, test developers and psychometricians are studying new ways of constructing test items and using computer technologies. Continued development of new forms of test construction may hold promise for the assessment of students with disabilities.

Item response theory (IRT) is one promising development. It is rapidly displacing classical test theory as the basis for modern test construction. IRT models describe "what happens when an examinee meets an item" (Wainer and Mislevy, 1990:66). IRT refers to a broad class of methods for constructing and scaling tests based on the notion that students' performance on a test should reflect one latent trait or ability and that a mathematical model should be able to predict performance on individual test items on the basis of that trait.[17] To use IRT modeling in test construction and scoring, test items are first administered to a large sample of respondents. Based on these data, an IRT model is derived that predicts whether a given item will be answered correctly by a given individual on the basis of estimates of the difficulty of the particular item and the ability level of the individual. A good fitting model yields information about the difficulty of items for individuals of differing levels of ability. Items for which the model does not fit—that is, for which students' estimated ability does not predict performance well on the specific item—are typically discarded. This information is used subsequently to score performance when the test items are given to actual examinees.[18]

---

[17]Most IRT models are predicated on the notion that a test is unidimensional and that scores should therefore reflect a single latent trait. Recently, however, IRT models have been extended to multidimensional domains as well.

[18]For additional information about how IRT modeling is done, a readable introduction is provided by Hambleton and Swaminathan (1985).

Item response theory offers several potential advantages for including students with disabilities in large-scale assessments. First, in many instances, assessments based on item response theory allow for everyone's scores to be placed on a common scale, even though different students have been given different items. Given the wide range of differences in performance levels across all students, including students with disabilities, it is unlikely that the same set of items will be appropriate for everyone. Second, item response theory makes it possible to assess changes in the reliability (precision) of scores as a function of a student's level of ability in what the assessment is measuring. Thus it is possible to identify an assessment that may not be reliable for low-scoring students with disabilities despite the fact that it has adequate reliability for high-scoring students. Third, item response theory provides sophisticated methods for identifying items that are biased for students with disabilities. Its use in this specific context raises a number of theoretical and practical issues, the exploration of which could prove very useful.

Computer-based testing is another area in which research holds great promise (Bennett, 1995). One of the assessment accommodations most often given to students with disabilities is extra time. But as noted earlier, extra time should be provided with caution, as it may undermine the validity of scores. Computer-based "adaptive" assessments allow students with a wide range of skills to be tested at a reasonable level of reliability and in a shorter amount of time by individually adapting the items presented to a test-taker's estimated level of skill, as gauged by his or her performance on an initial set of items. When tests can be administered individually on a computer, and when time pressure is lessened, it becomes possible to "give more time to everyone." Thus, computer-based adaptive tests can be shorter than traditional tests but still comply with measurement principles. The test is changed in a way that reduces the need for accommodated administration, thereby circumventing the problem of changes in the validity of scores due to accommodations. Finally, computer-based tests may allow students with disabilities to participate in simulated hands-on assessments by the addition of adaptive input devices, for example, a light pen mounted on a head strap. Such assessments can replace actual hands-on assessments that often require manual movements that are impossible for some students with disabilities. However, as Baxter and Shavelson (1994) have shown, computerized simulations of hands-on tasks can yield results surprisingly unlike those generated by the original tasks, so this approach will require careful evaluation.

Reporting on the Performance of Students with Disabilities

Because educational accountability depends on public knowledge about school and student performance, scores on assessments must be communicated in ways that provide accessible, valid, and useful information. Systems vary in their reporting mechanisms, depending on their primary units of accountability (state, district, school, classroom, individual student), the frequency of testing and grade levels tested, and the uses of assessment data. The design of reporting mechanisms always involves critical choices because schools and groups of students are typically compared with each other, with themselves over time, or against a set of performance standards. In some cases, these comparisons may also result in rewards and sanctions. Consequently, ensuring fair comparisons becomes a major issue. The public's right to know and to have accountable schools must be balanced against individual student rights and the disparate resources and learning opportunities available to different schools and students.

Creating a fair and responsible reporting mechanism is one of the major challenges associated with expanding the participation of students with disabilities in large-scale assessments and public accountability systems. In this section, we examine two issues that must be considered in reporting on the performance of students with disabilities. One issue pertains to flagging—making a notation on the student's score report that identifies scores as having been obtained with accommodations or under other nonstandard conditions. A second issue relates to disaggregation—the separate reporting of scores for groups such as students with disabilities. In part, the resolution of these issues hinges on the uses to which scores are put, such as whether scores are reported at the aggregate or individual level. However, in many instances, there is no unambiguous resolution of these issues. The research base that might guide decisions is limited and, perhaps more important, an emphasis on different values leads to different conclusions about the best resolution.

Flagging

Flagging is a concern when a nonstandard administration of an assessment— for example, providing accommodations such as extra time or a reader—calls into question the validity of inferences (i.e., the meaning) based on the student's score. Flagging warns the user that the meaning of the score is uncertain. The earlier section on validity and accommodations identified factors that suggest uncertainty about the meaning of scores from accommodated assessments.

However, since flagged scores are typically not accompanied by any descriptive detail about the individual or even the nature of accommodations offered, flagging may not really help users to interpret scores more appropriately. It may confront them with a decision about whether to ignore or discount the score simply because of the possibility that accommodations have created unknown distortions. Moreover, in the case of scores reported for individual students, flagging identifies the individual as having a disability, raising concerns about confidentiality and possible stigma.

In some respects, flagging is less of a problem when scores are reported only at the level of schools or other aggregates. Concerns about confidentiality and unfair labeling are lessened. Moreover, to the extent that the population with disabilities and assessment accommodations is similar across the aggregate units being compared (say, two schools in one year, or a given school's fourth grades in two different years), flagging in theory would have little effect on the validity of inferences. In practice, however, the characteristics of the group with disabilities may be quite different from year to year or from school to school. Moreover, decisions about accommodations and other modifications may be made inconsistently. Thus, even in the case of scores reported only for aggregates, flagging may be needed to preserve the validity of inferences.

When testing technology has sufficiently advanced to ensure that accommodations do not confound the measurement of underlying constructs, then score notations will be unnecessary. Until then, however, flagging should be used only with the understanding that the need to protect the public and policy makers from misleading information must be weighed against the equally important need to protect student confidentiality and prevent discriminatory uses of testing information.

Disaggregation

It is not yet clear what kinds of policies states and districts will adopt about disaggregating results for students with disabilities and other groups with special needs, but they will have to do at least some disaggregation under the Title I program. The new federal Title I legislation requires the results of Title I standards-based assessment to be disaggregated at the state, district, and school levels by race and ethnicity, gender, English proficiency, migrant status, and economic disadvantage and by comparisons of students with and without disabilities.

There are several arguments in favor of disaggregating the scores of students with and without disabilities. The first argument is one of validity: if the scores of some students with disabilities are of uncertain meaning, the validity of comparisons for the whole group would be enhanced by separating those scores. The second is about fairness: schools have varying numbers of students with disabilities from one cohort to another, and, to the extent that some of these students face additional educational burdens, disaggregation would lead to fairer comparisons. The third argument is one of accountability: separately reporting the scores of students with disabilities will increase the pressure on schools to improve the education offered to them. (Note that these same arguments apply for any group of students for whom scores are of uncertain meaning or who could benefit from a separate analysis of their performance, for example, students with limited English proficiency and Title I students.)

Whatever its merits, however, disaggregation confronts serious difficulties pertaining to the reliability of scores. One reason is simply the small number of students involved. The problems of low numbers will be most severe for school-level reporting. An elementary school that has 50 students in a tested grade, for example, is likely to have perhaps 4 to 6 students with disabilities in that grade. The unreliability of disaggregated scores is exacerbated by the ambiguous and variable identification of students as having a disability; a student identified and hence included in the score for students with disabilities in one school or cohort may well not be identified in another. The diversity of these students also augments the problem of reliability; in one cohort of five students with disabilities, there might be one with autism and one with retardation, whereas another cohort might include none with autism or retardation but a highly gifted student with a visual disability. Thus, for example, a change that would appear to indicate improvement or deterioration in the education afforded students with disabilities in fact could represent nothing but differences in the composition of the small groups of students with disabilities.

The enormous diversity among those in the category of students with disabilities is the primary argument in favor of a more detailed disaggregation of scores by type of disability. In theory, detailed disaggregation could alleviate some of the distortions caused by cohort-to-cohort differences in disabilities. Moreover, it could provide more meaningful comparisons. Students whose disability is partial blindness, for example, might be more meaningfully compared with students without disabilities than with students with mental retardation or autism. Detailed disaggregation exacerbates the problem of small numbers, however, particularly for the less common disabilities. For example, the national prevalence rate for identified visual disabilities served under the Individuals with Disabilities Education Act (IDEA) or the state-operated programs of Chapter 1 in the 6-17 age range was 0.05 percent in the 1993-94 school year (U.S. Department of Education, 1995:Table AA16). Thus, in our hypothetical example of an elementary school with 50 students in a tested grade, one can expect a student identified as visually impaired to appear in that grade, on average, once every 40 years. Although detailed disaggregation may improve the meaningfulness of results for larger groups and larger aggregates, it will not provide useful aggregate comparisons for smaller disability groups or smaller aggregates. Detailed disaggregation also would run counter to the current movement within special education to avoid formal classifications and to focus instead on individual students' functional capabilities and needs.

As with flagging, those making decisions about data disaggregation in state reporting systems should weigh the need for valid and useful information equally with consideration of any potentially adverse effects on individuals. Care must be taken so that disaggregated data do not allow identification of results for individual students. The usual approach to this problem is not to report results for any cell in a table with a sample size below a certain number of students (e.g., five).

Legal Framework for Assessing Students with Disabilities[19]

The federal statutes and regulations governing the education of students with disabilities recognize the importance of the validity of tests and assessments. The

---

[19]This section is based on the legal analysis prepared for the committee (Ordover et al., 1996).

regulations implementing both the IDEA and Section 504 of the Rehabilitation Act of 1973 require that tests and other evaluation materials must be validated for the specific purpose for which they are used. Both sets of regulations also require that, when a test is administered to a student with impaired sensory, manual, or speaking skills, the test results accurately reflect the child's aptitude or achievement level or whatever other factors the test purports to measure, rather than reflecting the student's disabilities.

Accommodations for disabilities in testing or assessment are also required by these federal statutes and regulations. Both Section 504 and the Americans with Disabilities Act (ADA) require that individuals with disabilities be protected against discrimination on the basis of disability and be allowed access to equally effective programs and services as received by their peers without disabilities. The ADA regulations require that public entities must make "reasonable modification" in policies, practices, and procedures when "necessary to avoid discrimination on the basis of disability, unless the public entity can demonstrate that making the modifications would fundamentally alter the nature of the service, program, or activity" (28 CFR 35.130[b] [7]). Alternate forms or accommodations in testing are required, but alterations of the content of what is tested are not required by law.

For purposes of analyzing potential legal claims on behalf of students with disabilities, distinctions among the various purposes and uses of assessments become critical. Assessments may, for example, be designed primarily as an accountability mechanism for schools and school systems. They may also be used as an integral part of learning, instruction, and curriculum. Or a particular test or tests may be used as a basis for making high-stakes decisions about individual students, including who is placed in the honors curriculum, who is promoted from grade to grade, who receives a high school diploma or a certificate indicating that a student has mastered a certain set of skills deemed relevant to the workplace. Each use raises its own set of legal issues and has different implications.

As a general rule, the greater the potential harm to students, the greater the protection that must be afforded to them and the more vulnerable the assessment is to legal challenge. One set of federal courts has already addressed the constitutional issues arising when a state links performance on a statewide test to the award of a high school diploma. A federal appellate court held unconstitutional a Florida law requiring students to pass a statewide minimum competency test in order to receive a high school diploma. The court in *Debra P.* v. *Turlington* held that the state's compulsory attendance law and statewide education program granted students a constitutionally protected expectation that they would receive a diploma if they successfully completed high school. Since the state possessed this protected property interest, the court held that the state was barred under the due process clause of the federal Constitution from imposing new criteria, such as the high school graduation test, without adequate advance notice and sufficient educational opportunities to prepare for the test. The court was persuaded that such notice was necessary to afford students an adequate opportunity to prepare for the test, to allow school districts time to develop and implement a remedial program, and to provide an opportunity to correct any deficiencies in the test and set a proper cut score for passing (644 F. 2d 397, 5th Cir. 1981; see also *Brookhart* v. *Illinois State Bd. of Ed.*, 697 F. 2d 179, 7th Cir. 1983). [20]

The court in *Debra P.* further held that, in order for the state's test-based graduation requirements to be deemed constitutional, the high school test used as its basis must be valid. In the view of the court, the state had to prove that the test fairly assessed what was actually taught in school. Under this concept, which the court referred to as "curricular validity," the test items must adequately correspond to the required curriculum in which the students should have been instructed before taking the test, and the test must correspond to the material that was *actually* taught (not just supposed to have been taught) in the state's schools.

As the court in *Debra P.* held: "fundamental fairness requires that the state be put to the test on the issue of whether the students were tested on material they were or were not taught. . . . Just as a teacher in a particular class gives the final exam on what he or she has taught, so should the state give its final exam on what has been taught in its classrooms" (644 F.2d at 406). In reaching this ruling, the court specifically rejected the state's assurance that the content of the test was based on the minimum, state-established performance standards, noting that the state had failed to document such evidence and that no studies had been conducted to ensure that the skills being measured were in fact taught in the classrooms (Pullin, 1994).

The same types of issues addressed by the court in *Debra P.* were also assessed in federal litigation on the impact of a similar test-for-diploma requirement imposed by a local school district in Illinois. The Illinois case, *Brookhart* v. *Illinois State Board of Education* (697 F. 2d 179), specifically assessed the impact on students with disabilities who had been in special education of using a minimum competency test to determine the award of high school diplomas. The court held that students with disabilities could be held to the same graduation standards as other students, but that their "programs of instruction were not developed to meet the goal of passing the [minimum competency test]" (697 F. 2d at 187). The court found that "since plaintiffs and their parents knew of the [test] requirements only one to one-and-a-half years prior to the students' anticipated graduation, the [test] objectives could not have been specifically incorporated into the IEP's over a period of years." The court counseled that the notice or opportunity to learn requirement could be met if the school district could ensure that students with disabilities are sufficiently exposed to most of the material that

---

[20]It is important to note that, although *Debra P.* has shaped legal thinking about students' entitlement to the teaching of the content on which they will be tested, this decision and the one in *Brookhart* apply only within the jurisdictions of the Fifth and Seventh federal Circuit Courts respectively. If the same questions were posed to the U.S. Supreme Court, a different decision might result.

appears on the test. These constitutional principles are consistent with the opportunity-to-learn requirements derived from the IDEA, Section 504, the ADA, and state constitutions.

The expanded participation of students with disabilities in state assessments, coupled with the curriculum and performance standards embodied in standards-based reform, are likely to raise new legal questions and require additional interpretations of existing statutes. Nevertheless, it is clear that several legal principles will continue to govern the involvement of students with disabilities in state assessments. Chief among them are the requirements that reasonable accommodations or alternate testing forms be provided consistent with the content being measured and that, in the case of assessments with individual consequences, students be afforded the opportunity to learn the content tested.

Resource Implications

As states and school districts implement new forms of assessment, they face both development and operations costs. Performance-based assessments need to be developed, field tested, and made available to teachers and schools. While most development costs are incurred in the first few years, item pools need to be replenished and upgraded. The cost of replenishing the pool will be driven in part by the use of, and thus the need to secure, the items. Operational costs are ongoing. Teachers must be trained in how to administer and score new assessment formats, as well as how to integrate performance-based tasks into their daily teaching. Teachers also need to be shown how to make appropriate modifications and adaptations in assessments for students with special needs, including students with disabilities. Unlike standardized tests, which are scored externally and have computer-generated reports, teachers must then be given the time to score and interpret the results of the new assessments.

We know little about the cost of developing and implementing large-scale performance-based assessment systems, and we have no empirical data on the cost of including students with disabilities in these assessments. Estimated costs of performance-based assessment programs range from less than $2 to over $100 per student tested. This variation reflects differences in the subjects tested, how many students are tested, how they are assessed (e.g., mix of multiple-choice, open-ended questions, performance tasks, portfolios), who is involved in the development, administration, and scoring of the test (e.g., paid contractors or volunteer teachers), how much and what kind of training is provided, and the type and source of materials used in the assessment tasks. We do know, however, that compared with machine scoring of traditional tests, scoring costs for performance tasks are much greater. In addition, because of the large number of items on traditional tests, individual test items can be retained over several years. But tasks used for performance assessments must be replaced more frequently, compounding costs associated with item development and equating.

Comfort (1995, as cited in Stecher and Klein, 1997), for example, reported that the science portion of the California Learning Assessment System (CLAS)—half multiple-choice and half hands-on testing—cost the state just $1.67 per student, but much of the time needed to develop, administer, and score the science performance tasks was donated by teachers, and many of the materials used in the assessment were contributed as well. Picus (1995) found that Kentucky spent an average of $46 per student tested for each annual administration between 1991 and 1994, or about $9 per student for each of the five subjects tested. This figure also does not include any teacher or district expenditures (e.g., for training or teacher time for scoring student portfolios).

In contrast, Monk (1995) projects the cost of implementing the New Standards Project assessment system at $118 per tested student; this approach, involving a consortium of states and local districts, incorporates a considerable level of professional development (about 20 percent of operating costs) and a heavy emphasis on cumulative portfolio assessment. Stecher and Klein (1997) estimate that one period of hands-on science assessment for a large student population, administered under standardized conditions, would cost approximately $34 per student, about 60 times the cost of a commercial multiple-choice science test. Although one session of performance assessment is sufficient to generate reliable school or district scores, three to four periods of performance tasks are needed to produce an individual student score as reliable as one period of multiple-choice testing, potentially raising the cost of performance assessment even higher.

Accommodations in assessment and instruction generally entail additional costs. Sometimes these costs are minimal, such as providing a student with a calculator. But often the costs are more significant and involve additional personnel, equipment, and materials; examples include providing a reader or scribe, preparing a braille or large-print editions of an assessment, and providing high-tech equipment.

IMPLICATIONS OF INCREASED PARTICIPATION OF STUDENTS WITH DISABILITIES

As noted earlier, many people have encouraged the participation of students with disabilities in large-scale assessments with the hope that it will increase their participation in the general education curriculum and result in greater accountability for their educational performance. At this time, evidence is scarce about how the participation of students with disabilities in assessments affects their educational opportunities. Research is currently under way in a few states that have taken the lead with policies to increase participation, but it will be some time before those efforts can provide substantial information.

Greater participation of students with disabilities in large-scale assessments could have both positive and negative effects on aggregated test scores. To some degree, the effects will hinge on the extent to which valid scores can be provided for individual students with disabilities—for example, by determining which accommodations can contribute to more accurate measurement. On one hand, if rules pertaining to accommodations (or modifications) are too permissive, they may falsely inflate scores for students who should not get the accommodation. This result could provide an escape valve, lessening the pressure on educators to bring students with disabilities up to the performance standards imposed on the general education population. On the other hand, policies that guide educators toward providing appropriate accommodations in both assessment and instruction could improve the validity of scores for students with disabilities. Linking accommodations in assessment and instruction—for example, by requiring, as Kentucky does, that accommodations be provided in the state's large-scale assessment only if they are also offered in ongoing instruction—may help limit inappropriate accommodation in assessment and encourage appropriate instructional accommodation. Evidence on the effects of these policies, however, is still lacking.

Decisions about participation and accommodations will need to be linked to decisions about reporting and, ultimately, accountability. Keeping track of who is included in the data being reported and under what conditions will be of central importance to ensuring fair comparisons between aggregates. Current decisions about which students with disabilities will participate in assessments are made inconsistently from place to place. This variation makes comparisons between two districts problematic if, for example, one has excluded only 2 percent of its students, and the other has excluded 10 percent. In addition to making results noncomparable from place to place, high rates of exclusion create an incomplete, and possibly inaccurate, view of student performance. For example, a recent study of four states with widely different exclusion rules for the 1994 NAEP reading assessment was conducted by the National Academy of Education (1996). The study found that applying a consistent rule for excluding students with low reading levels increased the number of participating students with disabilities by an average of 4.3 percent in each state; furthermore, when these students were included in the reporting, the mean fourth grade NAEP reading scores were somewhat lower. The size of the decrease varied from state to state (ranging from 1.5 to 3.1 points on the NAEP scale); predictably, the lowest decrease occurred for the state that was already including more students with disabilities. Reporting participation rates of students with disabilities in a consistent and systematic manner is important if comparisons are to be made fairly. Increased participation rates could also contribute to a more accurate description of student performance.

If greater participation of students with disabilities is achieved through the use of highly permissive policies about accommodations, the aggregated results may not be accurate, either. For example, the 1995 NAEP field test results suggested that a combination of stricter rules for exclusion and permissive rules about accommodations apparently led some schools to use accommodations for students who could have participated without them (Phillips, 1995). Although empirical evidence is limited, it has been suggested (as reviewed earlier) that some accommodations may inflate scores for some students. If accommodations are offered to a number of students who do not really need them, their scores may be artificially inflated, offering an overly optimistic view of progress. Parents, teachers, and schools clearly need meaningful information and do not want to become falsely complacent about the progress of students with disabilities. Careful policies about what accommodations can be offered and to whom is important, as is keeping track of who has been tested with what accommodations.

CONCLUSIONS

If students with disabilities are to gain any benefits from standards-based reform, the education system must be held publicly accountable for every student's performance. Although the IEP will remain the primary accountability tool for individual students with disabilities, the quality of their learning should also count in judgments about the overall performance of the education system. Without such public accounting, schools have little incentive to expand the participation of students with disabilities in the common standards. Therefore, regardless of the different ways that students with disabilities may be assessed, they should be accounted for in data about system performance.

The presumption should be that all students will participate in assessments associated with standards-based reform. Assessments not only serve as the primary basis of accountability, but also they are likely to remain the cornerstone and often the most well-developed component of the standards movement. The decision to exclude a student from participation in the common assessment should be made and substantiated on a case-by-case basis, as opposed to providing blanket exclusions on the basis of categories of disability, and should be based on a comparison of the student's curriculum and educational goals with those measured by the assessment program.

Existing data are inadequate to determine participation rates for students with disabilities in extant assessments associated with standards-based reform or to track the assessment accommodations they have received. What few data do exist suggest considerable variability in participation rates among states and among local educational agencies within states. Policies pertaining to assessment accommodations also vary markedly from one state to another, and there is little information indicating the consistency with which local practitioners in a given state apply those guidelines. Variability in participation rates and accommodations threatens the comparability of scores, can distort trends over time as well as comparisons among students, schools, or districts, and therefore undermines the use of scores for accountability.

Significant participation of students with disabilities in standards-based reform requires that their needs and abilities be taken into account in establishing standards, setting performance levels, and selecting appropriate assessments.

Mere participation in existing assessments falls short of providing useful information about the achievement of students with disabilities or for ensuring that schools are held accountable for their progress. Assessments associated with standards-based reform should be designed to be informative about the achievement of all students, including those with low-incidence, severe disabilities whose curriculum requires that they be assessed with an alternate testing instrument. Adhering to sound assessment practices will go a long way toward reaching this goal. In particular, task selection and scoring criteria need to accommodate varying levels of performance. However, it may also prove essential that the development of standards and assessments be informed by knowledge about students with disabilities. Representatives of students with disabilities should be included in the process of establishing standards and assessments.

Assessment accommodations should be used only to offset the impact of disabilities and should be justified on a case-by-case basis. Used appropriately, accommodations should be an effort to improve the validity of scores by removing the distortions or biases caused by disabilities. In some instances, accommodations may also permit inclusion of students who otherwise would not be able to participate in an assessment; for example, braille editions of tests permit the assessment of blind students who would otherwise be excluded. Although accommodations will often raise scores, raising scores per se is not their purpose, and it is inappropriate to use them merely to raise scores. Research on the effects of accommodations, although limited, is sufficient to raise concerns about the potential effects of excessive or poorly targeted accommodations.

The meaningful participation of students with disabilities in large-scale assessments and compliance with the legal rights of individuals with disabilities in some instances require steps that are beyond current knowledge and technology. For example, regulations implementing the IDEA and Section 504 require that tests and other evaluation materials must be validated for the specific purpose for which they are used. Individuals with disabilities are also entitled to "reasonable" accommodations and adaptations that do not fundamentally alter the content being tested. Even in the case of traditional assessments, testing experts do not yet know how to meet these two requirements for many individuals with disabilities, particularly those with cognitive disabilities that are related to measured constructs. Moreover, the nature of assessments associated with standards-based reform is in flux. The validity of new forms of assessment has not yet been adequately determined for students in general, and we have even less evidence available for students with disabilities, particularly when testing accommodations are provided.

A critical need exists for research and development on assessments associated with standards-based reform generally, and on the participation of students with disabilities in particular. The recent development of assessments associated with standards-based reform, combined with the existence of legal rights governing the education of students with disabilities, has required that state education agencies, local education agencies, and local school personnel design and implement assessment procedures that in some cases are beyond the realm of existing, expert knowledge. The sooner the research base can match the demands of policy, the more likely that students with disabilities can participate meaningfully in standards-based assessments.

6

Recommendations

The Committee on Goals 2000 and the Inclusion of Students with Disabilities was established by the Goals 2000 legislation "to conduct a comprehensive study of the inclusion of children with disabilities in school reform activities assisted under Goals 2000: Educate America Act" (Public Law 103-227, sec. 1015). This report has analyzed the issues that must be considered if students with disabilities are to participate in standards-based reforms. To do so, the committee has accepted as given, without necessarily endorsing, the defining elements of the two policy frameworks that delineate our charge.

Standards-based reform is not a single, uniform policy, and it is being implemented in different ways across states and localities. Therefore, for purposes of this report, we assume that two premises define the standards-based approach to educational reform: standards will be high and they will apply to all students. Standards-based reform includes content standards that specify what students should learn, performance standards that set the expectations for what students must know and do to demonstrate proficiency, and assessments that provide the accountability mechanism for monitoring whether these expectations have been met and by whom. In addition, standards-based reforms assume that schools should be held publicly accountable for student performance.

The committee also accepted as given the key elements of current special education policy, which will shape the participation of students with disabilities in standards-based reforms. Under current law and practice, students with disabilities requiring special education are entitled to a free and appropriate education. The appropriate education to which these students are entitled is defined, by professional practice and by state and federal legal provisions, as containing an individual educational program (IEP), designed and provided:

- by an appropriately constituted IEP team consisting of educators and parents;
- according to assessment information;
- in a way that provides educational benefit; and
- in the least restrictive environment.

Special education legal provisions stipulate that, for each student with a disability, the IEP team must make an individually referenced decision about how that student will participate in the general education curriculum and instructional program for the areas of educational need and the identified disability.

The committee was not asked to evaluate the merits of standards-based reform, nor could it do so adequately given the recency of the policy. Thus this report neither endorses standards-based reform nor encourages such efforts. Similarly, the committee was not charged with evaluating current special education law, policy, or practice; the report thus should not be considered an endorsement of that policy framework, either. Instead, the recommendations that follow represent the committee's advice to states and local communities that have already decided to proceed with standards-based reform and want to make those reforms consistent with current special education policies and practices.

In conducting its analyses, the committee faced a number of constraints. First, research evidence is scarce about the relationship between specific educational programs and the achievement of students with disabilities. In addition, due to the recency of standards-based reforms, there are almost no data about the effects of these reforms generally, much less about the impact and effectiveness of various approaches to including students with disabilities in standards-based curriculum, instruction, and assessment.

Second, the policy and political environments of both standards-based reform and special education are in flux. In most states, content standards are in the developmental phase, and assessment design is proceeding at an even slower rate. Some states are rethinking their assessment strategies, others their pedagogical strategies. States are also examining special education policies, including IEP process requirements, eligibility, and funding.

Third, states, districts, and schools vary considerably in how they interpret and implement both standards-based reform and special education. For example, some state content standards recommend specific curricula and instructional methods, whereas others stipulate general kinds of student outcomes, with methods left entirely to local decision makers and classroom teachers. Evidence about special education identification practices indicates that the criteria for defining some milder types of disabilities, particularly learning disabilities, vary widely from place to place and are implemented based on varying local conditions. Thus children who are found eligible for special education services—and attendant legal rights—in one school may not be so identified in another. Conversely, some students now receiving special education services would not be considered in need of them if they attended a different school.

These inconsistencies in special education placements across schools and local communities highlight a dilemma that the committee recognized throughout its deliberations. Although the committee's charge was to consider the participation of students with disabilities in standards-based reform, we recognize that some other students, not identified as having a disability, share the same characteristics and educational needs as some of their peers with disabilities. Although not eligible under the IDEA, these children may be indistinguishable from some who are eligible. Even though students not covered by the IDEA may not have all the same legal entitlements as those with disabilities, failure to consider their unique needs within the context of standards-based reform may have negative consequences for their achievement. The size of this group is unknown and may vary across local communities. Nevertheless, many of the committee's recommendations will also apply to these students. Therefore, we urge attention to the needs of all low-achieving or educationally disadvantaged students.

The committee's recommendations represent a set of guidelines that can be used in formulating a consistent strategy for including students with disabilities in standards-based reform. Throughout its deliberations the committee has sought an approach that is consistent, workable, integrated with the Individuals with Disabilities Education Act (IDEA) framework and, above all, takes into account the individual educational needs of students with disabilities.

RECOMMENDATIONS

In making its recommendations, the committee has been guided by two principles:

- **All students should have access to challenging standards.**
- **Policy makers and educators should be held publicly accountable for every student's performance.**

These assumptions are consistent with the goals of both standards-based reform and special education policy, but they often are not met in practice. All of our recommendations flow from these principles, although some apply to policies and decisions about individual students, and others apply to the education system as a whole. Together they form a possible approach for integrating students with disabilities in standards-based reform.

Recommendation 1. States and localities that decide to implement standards-based reforms should design their common content standards, performance standards, and assessments to maximize participation of students with disabilities.

To ensure that standards-based frameworks take into account the needs of students with disabilities, the committee recommends that special educators, parents, and the public participate in the development of that framework. Broad-based participation can serve as the core of the consensus-building process so necessary to developing common standards. Such participation can ensure that common standards represent a community's statement of what it believes its children should know and be able to do. Broad participation will also help ensure that standards and assessments are developed to be compatible with the needs of students with disabilities. It can also enhance the professional capacity of those charged with implementing the standards. To participate meaningfully in standards-based reform, special educators and parents of students with disabilities will need to acquire deeper understanding of the standards development process.

A common standards-based framework will profit from including members of the special education community in its development. For example, evidence indicates that several key instructional strategies are effective for many students with disabilities. Participation of special education professionals in the development of content standards could help to ensure that the standards do not preclude the use of these principles by requiring a uniform pedagogical approach.

There are many possible avenues for participation of those involved in special education. Students with disabilities should be included in the pilot samples as new assessments are tested and revised. Special education teachers should participate in the development of curricular frameworks; special education administrative personnel should be involved in developing accountability mechanisms for the standards-based system. As professional development strategies are designed for the new reforms, special education teachers should be included. Parents of students with disabilities can participate on development and implementation teams.

Recommendation 2. The presumption should be that each student with a disability will participate in the state or local standards; however, participation for any given student may require alterations to the common standards and assessments. Decisions to make such alterations must have a compelling educational justification and must be made on an individual basis.

In this recommendation, the committee has been guided by the legal requirements of the IDEA and the aims of federal and state standards policies. Both frameworks converge in their expectation that all students with disabilities will participate in standards-based reform.

The presumption should be that a student with a disability is *included in all standards and assessments* unless there is a compelling educational justification for moving him or her away from some aspect of the common standards and assessments. For any deviation from the common content and performance standards, a determination must be made that the alteration is individually appropriate and educationally justified.

At the same time that it affirms the importance of including all students in the standards-based system, the committee recognizes the legal requirement to consider the individual and widely varying needs of students with disabilities and to provide alterations when appropriate. We therefore acknowledge that decisions may be made to alter certain facets of the standards-based reforms for some individual students with disabilities. However, alterations of the common standards should occur only to the extent necessary. So, for example, a student may have limited modifications in only one or two standards. To the maximum extent possible, all students with disabilities should be included in the common assessments and appropriate accommodations offered to allow this participation. But when alterations are made for individual students, the committee recommends that those students' education be guided by challenging standards and valid assessments with public accountability for their educational progress.

Recommendation 3. The committee recommends strengthening the IEP process as the formal mechanism for deciding how individual students with disabilities will participate in standards-based reforms.

A formal mechanism is needed for deciding whether and how to alter the common standards and assessments to meet the educational needs of any given student with a disability. Because the IEP process is legally required and already in place, decisions about a student's participation in the common standards and assessments should be negotiated through that mechanism. Any alterations from the common standards should be documented in the IEP and their link to alternate and challenging standards should be noted for an individual child. However, research has documented shortcomings in the current IEP process. Thus we recommend strengthening the IEP process and the resulting document so that it can play this important role in a standards-based system.

At a number of key decision points, any movement away from the common standards-based system will need to be justified. The IEP team will need to decide about the extent of a child's participation in common content and performance standards, common assessments, and the extent and kind of assessment accommodations, if any, that will be required. Therefore special educators and parents must be knowledgeable about state and local standards-based policies and practices.

The IEP process should be made more systematic and more public in order to strengthen accountability for the educational progress of students with disabilities. We recommend that states and school districts should develop consistent and systematic guidelines for IEP teams to use in making decisions about and justifying a student's movement away from common standards and assessments. These decisions should be monitored to ensure that students with disabilities are not removed unnecessarily from standards-based reform. This need for consistency in the decision-making process is, to some extent, at odds with the individually referenced decision-making process at the heart of the IDEA. However, it is the committee's view that guidelines and standards can be developed to inform the IEP team in its deliberations and to make these procedures more consistent from student to student. Consistency, as well as professional understanding of standards-based practices, will be central to ensuring equity for students with disabilities.

More district and state-level guidance and oversight of the decisions made in the IEP process—for example, regarding the implications of accommodated test scores, the consequences of assessments, and the setting of alternate standards—will allow parents to become more informed as they pursue the best possible outcomes for their children. Furthermore, greater public accountability for IEP decisions may allow parents to continue to participate fully in decision making without having also to act as the primary instrument of accountability and enforcement.

The committee is concerned that this recommendation for greater public accountability and reporting of IEP decisions not add administrative burden. Evidence suggests that the IEP has evolved largely into a procedural compliance document, sometimes at the expense of its usefulness in instructional planning. Merely requiring that decisions about a student's participation in the standards process be documented is not likely to enhance the usefulness of the IEP. Rather, the IEP needs to focus more clearly on the extent to which an individual student's education will be linked to the common standards and on the substantive curriculum and instructional strategies that will be used to achieve those goals.

A more public locus of accountability is needed for the decisions made during that process. Information about IEP decisions should be systematically reported in a way that allows school systems to aggregate information across IEPs. Public reporting of aggregated IEP information—such as degree of participation in standards and assessments or types of accommodations—could inform policy and promote better accountability while still protecting the confidentiality of individual students and parents. The IEP should continue to serve as a vehicle to convene parents and professionals to design individually tailored educational programs for students with disabilities and to document that they are progressing toward challenging goals and outcomes. These purposes are compatible with the goal of better public accountability under a standards-based framework. Some of the procedural detail contained in many current IEPs (such as time lines) should be deemphasized. Monitoring of IEPs should also focus on the substance and appropriateness of students' educational goals and the performance levels of students relative to these goals.

Recommendation 4. States and localities should revise policies that discourage maximum participation of students with disabilities in the common accountability system and provide incentives to encourage widespread participation.

Currently in many places, incentives favor the exclusion of students with disabilities from the accountability system. If rewards are provided solely for higher average achievement scores (without regard to who is included in the aggregate), incentives are created to exclude students who may score low. Instead, incentives need to be designed to encourage the maximum participation of all students, including those with disabilities. For example, financial incentives could be offered for higher participation rates; alternatively, exclusion rates could be publicly reported and programs monitored if they exceed a designated level of exclusion.

Recommendation 5. When content and performance standards or assessments are altered for a student with a disability:
- **the alternate standards should be challenging yet potentially achievable;**
- **they should reflect the full range of knowledge and skills that the student needs to live a full, productive life; and**
- **the school system should inform parents and the student of any consequences of these alterations.**

If states develop content standards primarily in core academic areas, these standards will not take into account the diverse educational needs of some students with disabilities. To include students with disabilities in common content standards, standards-based systems may need to be designed in one of two ways: (1) by developing content standards in outcome domains that go beyond academic skills but are critical for many students with disabilities, such as career/vocational skills and functional life skills, or (2) by individually modifying existing content standards to include these skills and competencies. In either case, it will be difficult to set alternate standards that are appropriately challenging and signal high expectations for students. This is another area in which the IEP team may need more guidance from state and district officials.

We are particularly concerned that alternate standards do not mean low standards. At the same time, challenging alternate standards ought to be achievable given sufficient opportunity and support. Therefore, the issue of how to define alternate standards that are challenging yet also achievable should be the focus of a strong consensus-building process. The committee wrestled with the several possible meanings of this notion. A system could be established so that each content standard allows for multiple levels of proficiency, several of which are considered "high enough." Or a consensus-building process could be used to develop a separate set of alternate standards for students with disabilities who may require a substantially different curriculum. Another possibility is to include a student in the content standards but to allow an individualized performance standard. Another model would produce a purely individually referenced standard that can also be objectively observed, such as evidence of growth over time in a student's mastery of various content domains. How alternate standards are set, how progress on these standards is monitored, and how decisions are made about when to move to alternate standards remain difficult questions that will require considerable professional and community consensus building. In addition, assessments need to be aligned with an individual student's challenging standards. The committee urges that some systematic assessment method, beyond individual judgment, be used to assess progress on alternate standards.

In deciding whether to move a student to alternate content standards and curricula, particularly at the secondary school level, the IEP team will need to consider several important criteria. First, professional practice in special education stresses the importance of considering the skills critical to an individual student's post-school success when designing his or her instructional programs. This objective means that instructional goals should focus on acquiring skills that will allow them to live productive post-school lives (e.g., greater independence, a good job). This important criterion should be used to help define what a challenging alternate standard is for a particular youth.

A second criterion is whether the curriculum tied to the common standards can be fully taught to a given student without jeopardizing his or her opportunity to master other critical skills. Some students spend time in classrooms focused on nonacademic goals; others receive instruction that helps them improve their basic and applied academic skills. Some students with disabilities need specialized instruction—for example, in nonacademic domains or in basic skill areas— for some part of their school day. Because of this, some students with disabilities will find that there are competing priorities for their instructional time as they try to master common content standards and achieve the goals of their individualized program. Some students, their teachers, and parents will have to confront real, everyday time conflicts. For example, should a high school junior with a reading disability spend his time in intensive reading instruction in order to read at higher than a sixth grade level, or should he take an English literature class, in which the goals are to read and interpret classic literature and write interpretive pieces about the classics? Furthermore, if a student "opts out" of common standards in favor of alternates, what implications does that have for the kind of high school diploma he or she receives?

Recommendation 6. Even if the individual needs of some students require alterations of the common standards and assessments, the committee strongly recommends that these students should be counted in a universal, public accountability system.

Accountability systems are intended to provide information for parents, citizens, and public officials about the performance of students, teachers, schools, districts, and states. Under standards-based reforms, these public accountability systems rely heavily on large-scale assessments of student progress toward mastery of the content standards.

Although policy and practice vary tremendously from place to place, large numbers of students with disabilities currently are not included in the assessment and accountability systems for general education, or their results are not reported even when they have taken the tests. This approach leaves no locus of public accountability for the educational progress of many students with disabilities.

To ensure that the opportunity to participate in standards-based reforms is extended to all students with disabilities, states and localities will need to be accountable for their educational progress. The scores of students with disabilities who participate in the common assessments should be included in the public reporting of scores.

As a related problem, most districts and states do not report the number of students who did *not* participate when publicly reporting aggregated test scores. When participation rates differ widely from place to place (as available data indicate they do), the comparability of average test score comparisons is undermined. The percentage of students who do not participate in the common assessment system should be publicly reported as well as the percentages who receive a modified or different version of the test. This practice will help to ensure that *all* students are accounted for and that accountability comparisons and evaluations are made more equitably from place to place.

Aggregation and disaggregation of test data by various characteristics of test takers (e.g., gender, ethnicity, socioeconomic status, disability status) present some complex technical and ethical issues that will need to be considered carefully. States and districts should be responsible for the appropriate reporting of aggregated and disaggregated data, especially when sample sizes are small or privacy rights may be violated. Decisions about disaggregation should ensure, at a minimum, that individual students are not identifiable.

Although the basic principle should be to include all students in the common assessments (and to provide accommodations to enable them to do so), some number of students is likely to need to participate in a different or substantially modified assessment; the size of this group will depend on the nature of the assessment and the content standards being assessed. Obtaining meaningful information about the educational achievement and progress of these students is a difficult issue. One option for including all students with disabilities in the accountability system is to create an alternate assessment for this group of students with disabilities. The design of such assessments presents considerable challenges to current knowledge about measurement and test design. These assessments should not have important consequences attached to them unless it can be demonstrated that they measure the relevant curriculum content validly and that they are sensitive to achievement gains. Furthermore, a broader set of indicators may be needed to monitor the performance and participation of these students.

Participation of a maximum number of students with disabilities in the common assessments raises a host of technical, political, and legal challenges. For example, setting high performance standards can pose particular problems for students whose achievement levels are very low. A single or very high standard masks important information, such as how far below the standards students fall or whether they are making progress toward achieving the standard. This lack of information limits accountability for these students. The performance levels in large-scale assessments should therefore be designed to reflect a broad range of student performances.

Recommendation 7. Assessment accommodations should be provided, but they should be used only to offset the impact of disabilities unrelated to the knowledge and skills being measured. They should be justified on a case-by-case basis, but individual decisions should be guided by a uniform set of criteria.

The provision of accommodations during testing (such as braille versions, a reader, calculators, extended time) will be necessary to ensure the participation of some students with disabilities. The proportion of students requiring accommodation will depend on the purpose, format, and content of the assessment. At the current time, the number of students who will need accommodations is unknown.

Currently, policies on the kinds of testing accommodations offered and to whom vary widely from place to place, which may threaten the validity of the information and the comparability of aggregated scores. Furthermore, since many of these decisions are made by IEP teams with little or no knowledge about testing procedures, the purposes of accommodations, or their effects, implementation of the policies is also inconsistent. State guidelines often admonish educators not to provide accommodations that would undermine the validity of the assessments, but in many cases it is not clear how to make appropriate accommodations or how accommodations affect validity.

Accommodations should be offered during large-scale assessments for only two purposes: (1) to facilitate participation of students with disabilities and (2) to increase the validity of scores. Validity will be increased when an accommodation offsets inaccuracies caused by a disability. Thus, when a disability causes a score to be erroneously low, a successful accommodation will raise it. However, the appropriate goal of an accommodation is to offset the impact of a disability, not to raise scores per se.

To preserve validity, testing accommodations should be designed specifically to offset distortions in scores caused by specific disabilities. In addition, accommodations should be independent of the construct being measured. For example, assistance in reading should not be offered when reading proficiency is the construct (or an important part of the construct) being measured. However, determining which accommodations are independent of constructs is difficult for students with cognitive disabilities, who constitute the majority of students with disabilities. The shortage of research and the absence of a reliable taxonomy of disability contribute to the difficulty of this problem.

States and local districts should strive for increased consistency in the development and implementation of accommodation policies to guide IEP decision making. Furthermore, in order to achieve better public accountability, the number of students accommodated and the types of accommodations used should be monitored and publicly reported to districts and states.

Recommendation 8. States and local districts should provide information to parents of students with disabilities to enable them to make informed

choices about their children's participation in standards-based reform and to understand the consequences of those choices.

Research evidence indicates that parental involvement and expectations contribute to higher achievement for all students, regardless of other background variables. In addition, parents of students with disabilities play unique roles under special education law as primary advocates for their children's rights, key participants in the IEP decision-making process, and monitors of accountability and enforcement. Including all students with disabilities in standards-based reforms is likely to put new pressures on the IEP process, particularly on the role of the parents. For students who will require alterations to common standards or assessments, the IEP decision-making process, which often places the burden of enforcement on parents, is likely to become considerably more complex.

For example, some students with disabilities, upon completing high school, have traditionally received alternative credentials to the standard high school diploma. It is likely that many standards-based reform systems will continue to include one or more type of alternative high school completion credential. Parents need to understand the different diplomas and the implications of decisions to modify standards and curriculum for the type of diploma their child will receive.

Evidence indicates that the IEP process has not worked well for all parents, particularly minority parents and those with limited education. Surmounting the barriers to parental involvement takes on particular importance under standards-based reform, since some parents will have to make important decisions about appropriate IEP goals, the content of instruction, and the use of alternate standards and assessments. Parents of students with disabilities will require information that allows them to make informed choices about their children's education in a meaningful way. They will also need to understand clearly the implications of their choices for a child's future education and post-school outcomes. Special efforts will be required to involve the considerable number of parents who, until now, have not been actively involved in the IEP process.

Recommendation 9. The committee recommends that, before attaching significant stakes to the performance of individual students, those students should be given an opportunity to learn the skills and knowledge expected of them.

All students should be provided an opportunity to learn the skills and knowledge represented in the common content and performance standards. This requirement is particularly critical for the education of students with disabilities.

Most standards-based systems to date are focused on accountability with high consequences only at the school building or system level. Some states, however, are holding individual students accountable by requiring that they pass a test linked to the state standards for high school graduation, and other states are planning to implement a similar policy in the near future. No standards-based framework should be designed to hold an individual student responsible unless it also has a mechanism for ensuring that students have had an adequate opportunity to learn the content being assessed. This will require some mechanism for ensuring that curriculum and classroom instruction actually reflect the content standards.

If a student with a disability is to be held individually accountable for mastery of the common content standards, his or her IEP should reflect the necessary curricular goals, delivered through instructional strategies consistent with his or her educational needs and learning style. This specification of required curriculum and instruction will define the student's opportunity to learn the skills and knowledge tested on the assessment. Ensuring that the actual instruction provided to an individual student conforms to the IEP can be accomplished informally through classroom observation and conversations between a student's teachers and those responsible for monitoring the IEP at the school level.

Ensuring that the school system as a whole is providing adequate opportunities to learn for all students, including those with disabilities, is a considerably more difficult task. Obtaining comparable information that can be aggregated across schools and classrooms largely depends on teachers' self-reports through surveys of the content covered and the instructional strategies used. Yet research has shown that often these data are collected at too general a level to make useful distinctions among the content covered in different classrooms. Furthermore, because teachers do not share common understandings of the instructional strategies associated with standards-based reforms, it is often difficult to determine how consistent teaching in the aggregate is with the state assessment. If assessments with individual consequences continue as state policy strategies, greater effort will need to be expended to ensure that individual students with disabilities have the opportunity to learn what is expected of them. Systemwide accountability will require that better indicators of curriculum and instruction be designed to allow public monitoring of the learning opportunities afforded all students.

Recommendation 10. Given the enormous variability in the educational needs of students, the committee recommends that policy makers monitor the unintended consequences of participation in standards-based reform, including consequences for students with disabilities.

The effects of standards-based reform, both intended and unintended, should be carefully monitored for all students, as well as the distribution of that impact by ethnic, racial, gender, and disability status.

Because graduation credentials have long-term consequences for individual students, the types of diplomas offered is a particularly important issue to monitor. Policy makers should consider and monitor the individual consequences, such as effects on employability and other transitions to post-school life, when standards-based reforms result in some students receiving different kinds of high school completion credentials. Steps should be taken to ensure that any alternative credential is meaningful—for example, that it conveys information about skills and achievements—for students with disabilities (as well as for other students who may receive the credential).

State and local policy makers should develop a means of monitoring both the intended effects of standards-based reforms, such as increases in test scores, and other unanticipated effects, such as changes in dropout or special education referral or identification rates. As part of an ongoing monitoring system, states should invest in developing indicators to measure the performance of standards-based systems. This system should monitor outcomes for all students, although we have highlighted indicators that will be particularly important for students with disabilities. In order to monitor possible unintended effects, this indicator system should consider the following measures in addition to test scores and other typical forms of accountability reporting:

- special education referral and identification rates;
- retention rates;
- types of disability classifications and rates of classification;
- parental participation in the IEP process;
- changes in types of instructional placements of students with disabilities;
- number of students not participating in the common standards and the broad categories of alternate standards under which these students are being educated;
- rates of exclusion from large-scale assessments;
- number and type of testing accommodations offered to students and the basis for them;
- types of high school completion credentials and proportions of students with disabilities receiving each;
- high school graduation and school dropout rates; and
- indicators of opportunity to learn (when there are high-stakes consequences for individual students).

Recommendation 11. The committee recommends that states design standards policies that realistically reflect the time lines and resource levels needed to implement standards-based reforms.

Effective implementation of standards-based reforms requires a system of content standards, performance standards, and assessments that meet complex technical and professional requirements. At the current time, many expectations of policy makers exceed the technical knowledge and capacity of educators. Curriculum standards assume content knowledge and pedagogy quite different from how most teachers were trained. New forms of assessment are undergoing major modifications as they are implemented, and states and school districts have limited experience accommodating students with disabilities in large-scale, standardized assessments.

We recognize that opportunities to implement policies as comprehensive as standards-based reform are rare and that policy makers need to move quickly to take advantage of them. Still, past experience strongly suggests that implementing policies that represent significant departures from past practice before sufficient resources are available or before educators are adequately prepared can significantly lessen the chances of success for even the most promising reform strategies. We therefore make the following suggestions to guide policy choices.

First, policy makers should assume that standards-based reforms will need to be phased in over a number of years. Mid-course corrections should be encouraged on aspects of the reform that are not working as intended. In addition, considerable time will be necessary for expert knowledge, particularly in the technology of testing, to catch up with the expectations and assumptions underlying standards-based reform. We are not suggesting that the implementation of these reforms be delayed until their feasibility and effectiveness is well understood. Rather, we are cautioning policy makers to consider what they and their constituents can reasonably require of teachers and students before these two groups have the necessary tools to do what is expected of them.

Second, considerable uncertainty exists about the resource levels that will be needed to support standards-based reforms. Additional resources are likely to be needed for developing and acquiring instructional materials and technology, designing and validating assessments, and implementing new accountability and governance models. Considerable investments in professional development, ongoing technical assistance, and preservice teacher education are likely to be needed. Furthermore, little is known about the kinds of programs and resource levels that will be required to help all students, including those with disabilities, meet high standards.

Third, teachers will require significant support, both in time and professional development, for standards-based reform to be effective at the classroom level. Standards-based reform aims to alter some fundamental classroom practices. For many teachers, this change will mean teaching new material and using unfamiliar methods of instruction and assessment. In addition, including students with disabilities in standards-based reforms presents particular challenges for both general and special education teachers.

Fourth, standards-based reforms should be coordinated with other related education policies—such as those affecting school-to-work transitions, disadvantaged and language minority students, and teacher training and certification—so that they mutually reinforce rather than contradict one another. Coordination will be particularly important with regard to school finance policy, since decisions about the allocation of resources for standards-based reforms are occurring at the same time as states are altering special education funding and finance formulas.

Recommendation 12. The committee recommends a long-term research agenda to address the substantial gaps in knowledge about the schooling of students with disabilities and the impact of standards-based reforms.

Throughout its deliberations, the committee found itself without the data necessary to consider many questions related to our charge. These significant data gaps are outlined here as recommendations for a long-term research agenda related to the schooling of students with disabilities and the implementation of standards-based reform.

- *The school experiences of students with disabilities.* Most nationally representative education studies have not included students with disabilities, or have done so in unsystematic ways. Large-scale research studies—particularly those funded by the U.S. Department of Education and the National Science Foundation—should include persons with disabilities in their samples, sample them carefully, and document their procedures for accommodating persons with disabilities in the research protocols. Better data are needed on how students with disabilities compare with other students on variables related to their schooling and educational achievement.

- *Resources and costs of standards-based reforms.* Although the committee agreed that implementing standards-based reforms effectively is likely to require additional resources, there are few data to guide in making precise estimates about these potential costs. Data are needed on the costs, including opportunity costs in time lost to other schooling activities, of developing and implementing these reforms, particularly at the local level.

- *Special education resource allocation models.* A number of alternative models for allocating special education resources are being discussed throughout the country. Alternative resource allocation models generate different types of incentives for how to serve students with disabilities. Data are needed on the effects of such alternative incentives and their interaction with standards-based reform.

- *Local decision-making processes.* In order to guide the formation of consistent policies and rules governing the participation of students with disabilities in standards-based reforms, considerably more data are needed on how local decisions are made about students with disabilities. For example, we need to understand better how IEP decisions are made with regard to participation in standards-based reforms—how and why accommodations are made and how standards-based reforms affect decisions about placements. In addition, research is needed to identify the information parents need to participate effectively in the decision-making process.

- *Special education instruction in the standards-based classroom.* The interaction between specific special education interventions and the instructional methods called for in many standards-based systems should be examined. Greater understanding is needed about the effects of these new instructional methods on the achievement of students with disabilities.

- *Potential of computer-based technologies.* Emerging technologies show promise for enhancing the education of students with disabilities both through the provision of assistive and adaptive technologies and as a means to individualize instruction and assessments. More research is needed on the applications and effectiveness of computer-based technologies for students with disabilities.

• *Alternative student credentials.* Research is needed on the effect of different kinds of high school credentials on employment and other post-school outcomes. In addition, research is needed to aid in developing meaningful alternative credentials that can credibly convey the nature of a student's accomplishments and capabilities.

• *Relationship between accommodations and validity.* Research is needed to develop better assessments, to document the effects of various accommodations on test scores, and to develop criteria for deciding what accommodations will preserve the validity and usefulness of test scores.

• *Development of alternate assessments.* The development of reliable and valid alternate assessments for those students who cannot participate in the common assessments will require a greater investment in research. Methods of equating and scaling such alternatives also need investigation.

As with any worthwhile undertaking, implementing these recommendations will require effort and a willingness to change. The logistical and technical challenges are great and rendered more difficult by the need for political and value choices. But the outcome will be worth that effort if acting on these recommendations can begin to build a foundation for blending two very different approaches to improving education for all students with disabilities.

References

CHAPTER 1   INTRODUCTION

Barrett, M., and J. Allen
  1996   *The Standards Primer.* Washington, DC: The Center for Education Reform.
Cuban, L.
  1990   Reforming again, again, and again. *Educational Researcher* 19(1):3-13.
Darling-Hammond, L.
  1990   Instructional policy into practice: The power of the bottom over the top. *Education Evaluation and Policy Analysis* 12(3):339-347.
Elam, S.M., and L.C. Rose
  1995   The 27th Phi Delta Kappa/Gallup Poll of the public's attitudes toward the public schools. *Phi Delta Kappan* 77(1):41-56.
Johnson, J., and J. Immerwahr
  1994   *First Things First: What Americans Expect From the Public Schools.* New York: Public Agenda Foundation.
Kifer, E.
  1993   Opportunities, talents, and participation. Pp. 279-307 in *The IEA Study of Mathematics III: Student Growth and Classroom Processes*, Leigh Burstein, ed. New York: Pergamon Press.
Oakes, J.
  1985   *Keeping Track: How Schools Structure Inequality.* New Haven, CT: Yale University Press.
O'Day, J.A., and M.S. Smith
  1993   Systemic reform and educational opportunity. Pp. 250-312 in *Designing Coherent Education Policy: Improving the System,* Susan Fuhrman, ed. San Francisco, CA: Jossey-Bass.
Porter, A.C., D.A. Archbald, and A.K. Tyree, Jr.
  1991   Reforming the curriculum: Will empowerment policies replace control? Pp. 11-36 in *Politics of Curriculum and Testing,* Susan Fuhrman and Betty Malen, eds. Philadelphia, PA: Falmer Press.

Powell, A.G., E. Farrar, and D.K. Cohen
1985   *The Shopping Mall High School.* Boston, MA: Houghton Mifflin.

CHAPTER 2   THE POLICY FRAMEWORKS

Airasian, P.W., and G.F. Madaus
1983   Linking testing and instruction: Policy issues. *Journal of Educational Measurement* 20(2):103-118.

Aleman, S.R.
1995   *Special Education: Issues in the State Grant Program of the Individuals with Disabilities Education Act.* Washington, DC: Congressional Research Service.

American Association for the Advancement of Science
1989   *Science for All Americans.* New York: Oxford University Press.

Appalachia Educational Laboratory
1995   *The Needs of Kentucky Teachers for Designing Curricula Based on Academic Expectations.* Frankfort, KY: Kentucky Institute for Education Research.

Bateman, B.D.
1994   Who, how, where: Special education issues in perpetuity (Special issue, theory and practice of special education: Taking stock a quarter century after Deno and Dunn). *Journal of Special Education* 27:504-520.

Benveniste, Guy
1986   Implementation strategies: The case of 94-142. Pp. 146-163 in *School Days, Rule Days*, D. Kirp and D. Jensen, eds. Philadelphia, PA: Falmer Press.

Blank, R.K., and E.M. Pechman
1995   *State Curriculum Frameworks in Mathematics and Science: How Are They Changing Across the States?* Washington, DC: Council of Chief State School Officers.

Bond, L.A., D. Braskamp, and E. Roeber
1996   *The Status of State Student Assessment Programs in the United States.* Oak Brook, IL: North Central Regional Educational Laboratory and Council of Chief State School Officers.

Brauen, M., F. O'Reilly and M. Moore
1994   *Issues and Options in Outcomes-Based Accountability for Students with Disabilities.* College Park, MD: Center for Policy Options in Special Education, University of Maryland.

Broadwell, C.A., and J. Walden
1988   Free and appropriate public education after Rowley: An analysis of recent court decisions. *Journal of Law and Education* 17(1):35-51.

Budoff, M., and A. Orenstein
1982   *Due Process in Special Education: On Going to a Hearing.* Cambridge, MA: Ware Press.

Burstein, L., L.M. McDonnell, J. Van Winkle, T. Ormseth, J. Mirocha, and G. Guiton
1995   *Validating National Curriculum Indicators.* Santa Monica, CA: RAND.

Butts, R.F., and L.A. Cremin
1953   *A History of Education in American Culture.* New York: Holt.

California Department of Education
1995   *Every Child a Reader: The Report of the California Reading Task Force.* Sacramento: California Department of Education.

Children's Defense Fund
1974   *Children Out of School in America.* Cambridge, MA: Washington Research Project, Inc.

Clune, W.H., and M.H. Van Pelt
   1985   A political method of evaluating the Education for All Handicapped Children Act of
             1975 and the several gaps of gap analysis. *Law and Contemporary Problems* 48(1):7-
             62.
Cohen, D.K.
   1996   Standards-based school reforms: Policy, practice, and performance. In *Holding Schools
             Accountable: Performance-Based Reform in Education*, H.F. Ladd, ed. Washington,
             DC: Brookings.
Cohen, D.K., and P.L. Peterson
   1990   *Special issue of Educational Evaluation and Policy Analysis* 12(3):233-353.
Coleman, H., P.H. Burch, E.C. Reock, and J.M. Ponessa
   1994   *Linkages in the Delivery and Financing of Special Education Services in New Jersey.*
             New Brunswick, NJ: The Center for Government Services at Rutgers, The State Univer-
             sity.
Edgar, E., P. Levine, and M. Maddox
   1986   Statewide Follow-up Studies of Secondary Special Education Students in Transition.
             Unpublished working paper of the Networking and Evaluation Team, University of
             Washington, Seattle, WA.
Elam, S.M., and L.C. Rose
   1995   The 27th Phi Delta Kappa/Gallup poll of the public's attitudes toward public schools.
             Phi Delta Kappan 77(1):41-56.
Elam, S.M., L.C. Rose, and A.M. Gallup
   1996   The 28th annual Phi Delta Kappa/Gallup poll of the public's attitudes toward public
             schools. *Phi Delta Kappan* 78(1):41-59.
   1992   The 24th annual Gallup poll of the public's attitudes toward public schools. *Phi Delta
             Kappan* 74(1):41-53.
   1991   The 23rd annual Gallup Poll of the public's attitudes toward the public schools. *Phi
             Delta Kappan* 73(1):41-56.
Engel, D.M.
   1991   Law, culture, and children with disabilities: Educational rights and the construction of
             difference. *Duke Law Journal 1991* (1):166-205.
Fredericksen, N.
   1984   The real test bias: Influences of testing of teaching and learning. *American Psychologist*
             39(3):193-202.
Fuchs, D., and L.S. Fuchs
   1994   Inclusive schools movement and the radicalization of special education reform. *Excep-
             tional Children* 60(4):294-309.
Fuchs, D., L.S. Fuchs, and P.J. Fernstrom
   1993   A conservative approach to special education reform: Mainstreaming through trans-
             environmental programming and curriculum-based measurement. *American Education
             Research Journal* 30:140-178.
Fulcher, G.
   1989   *Disabling Policies? A Comparative Approach to Education Policy and Disability.*
             Philadelphia, PA: Falmer Press.
Gallegos, E.
   1989   Beyond Board of Education v. Rowley: Educational benefit for the handicapped? *Ameri-
             can Journal of Education* 97:258-288.
Gamoran, A., and M. Nystrand
   1991   Background and instructional effects on achievement in eighth-grade English and social
             studies. *Journal of Research on Adolescence* 1(3):277-300.

Gamson, W.A.
    1992   *Talking Politics.* New York: Cambridge University Press.
Gandal, M.
    1996   *Making Standards Matter 1996: An Annual Fifty-State Report on Efforts to Raise Academic Standards.* Washington, DC: American Federation of Teachers Educational Issues Department.
Gartner, A., and D.K. Lipsky
    1987   Beyond special education: Toward a quality system for all students. *Harvard Education Review* 57(4):367-390.
Giangreco, M., R. Dennis, S. Edelman, and C. Cloninger
    1994   Dressing your IEPs for the general education climate: Analysis of IEP goals and objectives for students with multiple disabilities. *Remedial and Special Education* 15(3):288-296.
Goertz, M.E., and D. Friedman
    1996   *State Education Reform and Students with Disabilities: A Preliminary Analysis.* New Brunswick, NJ: Rutgers University, Consortium for Policy Research in Education and Center for Policy Research on the Impact of General and Special Education Reform.
Goertz, M.E., R.E. Floden, and J. O'Day
    1995   *Studies of Education Reform: Systemic Reform, Volume I: Findings and Conclusions.* New Brunswick, NJ: Rutgers University, Consortium for Policy Research in Education.
Goldberg, S.S., and P.J. Kuriloff
    1991   Evaluating the fairness of special education hearings. *Exceptional Children* 57(6):546-555.
Haertel, E.
    1989   Student achievement tests as tools of educational policy: Practices and consequences. In *Test Policy and Test Performance: Education, Language and Culture,* B.R. Gifford, ed. Boston: Kluwer Academic Publishers.
Hambleton, R.K., R.M. Jaeger, D. Koretz, R.L. Linn, J. Millman, and S.E. Phillips
    1995   Review of the Measurement Quality of the Kentucky Instructional Results Information System, 1991-1994. An unpublished report prepared for the Office of Educational Accountability, Kentucky General Assembly, June 20, 1995.
Handler, J.F.
    1986   *The Conditions of Discretion: Autonomy, Community, Bureaucracy.* New York: Russell Sage Foundation.
Hardman, M.L., C.J. Drew, and M.W. Egan
    1996   *Human Exceptionality,* 5th edition. Boston: Allyn and Bacon.
Harry, B., N. Allen, and M. McLaughlin
    1995   Communication versus compliance: African-American parents' involvement in special education. *Exceptional Children* 61(4):364-377.
Hasazi, S., L. Gordon, and C. Roe
    1985   Factors associated with the employment status of handicapped youth exiting high school from 1979-1983. *Exceptional Children* 51:455-469.
Hasazi, S.B., A.M. Liggett, and R.A. Schattman
    1994   A qualitative policy study of the least restrictive environment provision of the Individuals with Disabilities Education Act. *Exceptional Children* 60:491-507
Hehir, Thomas, and Thomas Latus, eds.
    1992   *Special Education at the Century's End: Evolution of Theory and Practice Since 1970.* Cambridge, MA: Harvard Educational Review.

Hoffer, T.B., K.A. Rasinski, and W. Moore
   1995   *Social Background Differences in High School Mathematics and Science Coursetaking and Achievement (NCES 95-206).* Washington, DC: National Center for Education Statistics.
Jenkins, J.R., M. Jewell, N. Leicester, L. Jenkins, and N.M. Troutner
   1991   Development of a school building model for educating students with handicaps and at-risk students in general education classrooms. *Journal of Learning Disabilities* 24:311-320.
Johnson, J., and J. Immerwahr
   1994   *First Things First: What Americans Expect From the Public Schools.* New York: Public Agenda Foundation.
Jolley, L.
   1996   Grading the Honig reforms. *California Journal* 27(6):26-31.
Jones, L.V., E.C. Davenport, A. Bryson, T. Bekhuis, and R. Zwick
   1986   Mathematics and science test scores as related to courses taken in high school and other factors. *Journal of Educational Measurement* 23(3):197-208.
Kauffman, J.M., and D.P. Hallahan
   1993   Toward a comprehensive delivery system for special education. Pp. 73-102 in *Integrating General and Special Education,* J.L. Goodlad and T.C. Lovitt, eds. New York: Merrill-MacMillan.
Kauffman, J.M., and J.W. Lloyd
   1995   A sense of place: The importance of placement issues in contemporary special education. Pp. 3-19 in *Issues in Educational Placement: Students with Emotional and Behavioral Disorders,* J.M. Kauffman, J.W. Lloyd, D.P. Hallahan, and T.A. Artuto, eds. Hillsdale, NJ: Lawrence Erlbaum.
Kavale, K.A., D. Fuchs, and T.E. Scruggs
   1994   Setting the record straight on learning disability and low achievement: Implications for policy making. *Learning Disability Research and Practice* 9(2):70-77.
Kirp, D.
   1973   Schools as sorters: The constitutional and policy implications of student classification. *University of Pennsylvania Law Review* 121(4):705-797.
Knapp, M.S., M.S. Stearns, B.J. Turnbull, J.L. David, and S.M. Peterson
   1983   Cumulative effects at the local level. *Education and Urban Society* 15(4):479-499.
Koretz, D., S. Barron, K.J. Mitchell, and B.M. Stecher
   1996b   *Perceived effects of the Kentucky Instructional Results Information System.* Santa Monica, CA: RAND.
Koretz, D., K.J. Mitchell, S. Barron, and S. Keith
   1996a   *Perceived effects of the Maryland School Performance Assessment Program.* Los Angeles: National Center for Research on Evaluation, Standards, and Student Testing, University of California, Los Angeles.
Kuriloff, Peter J.
   1985   Is justice served by due process?: Affecting the outcome of special education hearings in Pennsylvania. *Law and Contemporary Problems* 48(1):89-118.
Lankford, H., and J. Wyckoff
   1996   The allocation of resources to special education and regular instruction. Pp. 221-257 in *Holding Schools Accountable: Performance-based Reform in Education,* H.F. Ladd, ed. Washington, DC: Brookings.
   1995   Where has the money gone? An analysis of the school district spending in New York. *Educational Evaluation and Policy Analysis* 17(2):195-218.

Lazerson, M.
    1983   The origins of special education. In *Special Education Policies: Their History, Implementation, and Finance*, J. Chambers and W. Hartman, eds. Philadelphia, PA: Temple University Press.
Learning Disabilities Association of America
    1993   *Position Paper on Full Inclusion.* Pittsburgh, PA: Learning Disabilities Association of America.
Lewis, A.C.
    1995   An overview of the standards movement. *Phi Delta Kappan* 76(10):744-750.
Linn, R.L.
    1993   Educational assessment: Expanded expectations and challenges. *Educational Evaluation and Policy Analysis* 15(1):1-16.
Lyon, G.R.
    1996   Learning disabilities. *The Future of Children: Special Education for Students with Disabilities* 6(1):54-76. Los Altos, CA: Center for the Future of Children, David and Lucille Packard Foundation.
Mayer, M.
    1975   *The Schools.* New York: Harper.
McCusic, M.
    1991   The use of education clauses in school finance reform litigation. *Harvard Journal on Legislation* 28(2):307-340.
McDonnell, L.M.
    1997   *The Politics of State Testing: Implementing New Student Assessments.* Los Angeles: National Center for Research on Evaluation, Standards, and Student Testing, University of California, Los Angeles.
    1994   *Policymakers' Views of Student Assessment.* Santa Monica, CA: RAND.
McDonnell, L.M., and C. Choisser
    1997   *Testing and Teaching: Local Implementation of New State Assessments.* Los Angeles: National Center for Research on Evaluation, Standards, and Student Testing, University of California, Los Angeles.
McKnight, C.C., F.J. Crosswhite, J.A. Dossey, E. Kifer, J.O. Swafford, K.J. Travers, and T.J. Cooney
    1987   *The Underachieving Curriculum: Assessing U.S. School Mathematics from an International Perspective.* Champaign, IL: Stipes Publishing.
McLaughlin, M.J.
    1987   Learning from experience: Lessons from policy implementation. *Educational Evaluation and Policy Analysis* 9(2):171-178.
McLaughlin, M.J., and S.H. Warren
    1992   Outcomes assessments for students with disabilities: Will it be accountability or continued failure? *Preventing School Failure* 36(4):29-33.
McLaughlin, M.W., and L.A. Shepard with J.A. O'Day
    1995   *Improving Education through Standards-Based Reform. A Report by the National Academy of Education Panel on Standards-Based Reform.* Stanford, CA: National Academy of Education.
Melnick, R.S.
    1994   *Between the Lines: Interpreting Welfare Rights.* Washington, DC: Brookings.
Minow, M.
    1990   *Making All the Difference: Inclusion, Exclusion, and American Law.* Ithaca, NY: Cornell University Press.

Mithaug, D., C. Horiuchi, and P. Fanning
1985   A report on the Colorado state-wide follow-up survey of special education students. *Exceptional Children* 51:397-404.
Moore, M.T., M.E. Goertz, and T.W. Hartle
1983   Interaction of federal and state programs. *Education and Urban Society* 15(4):452-478.
Moore, M.T., E.W. Strang, M. Schwartz, and M. Braddock
1988   *Patterns in Special Education Service Delivery and Cost.* Washington, DC: Decision Resources Corporation.
National Center on Educational Outcomes
1992   Why Outcomes? *Outcomes* 1(2). Minneapolis, MN: University of Minnesota, National Center on Educational Outcomes.
National Council on Education Standards and Testing
1992   *Raising Standards for American Education: A Report to Congress, The Secretary of Education, The National Education Goals Panel, and The American People.* Available from the U.S. Government Printing Office. Washington, DC: U.S. Department of Education.
National Council of Teachers of Mathematics
1989   *Curriculum and Evaluation Standards for School Mathematics.* Reston, VA: National Council of Teachers of Mathematics.
National Education Goals Panel
1996   *Profile of State Assessment Systems and Reported Results.* Washington, DC: National Education Goals Panel.
National Research Council
1996   *National Science Education Standards.* Washington, DC: National Academy Press.
Neal, D., and D.L. Kirp
1985   The allure of legalization reconsidered: The case of special education. *Law and Contemporary Problems* 48(1):63-87.
Nirge, B.
1970   The normalization principle: Implications and comments. *Journal of Mental Retardation* 16:62-70.
Oakes, J.
1985   *Keeping Track: How Schools Structure Inequality.* New Haven, CT: Yale University Press.
Ordover, E.L., K.B. Boundy, and D.C. Pullin
1996   Students with Disabilities and the Implementation of Standards-Based Education Reform: Legal Issues and Implications. Unpublished paper prepared for the Committee on Goals 2000 and the Inclusion of Students with Disabilities, June 1996, Center for Law and Education.
O'Reilly, F.E.
1996   *State Special Education Funding Formulas and the Use of Separate Placements for Students with Disabilities: Exploring Linkages. Policy Paper #7.* Palo Alto, CA: American Institutes for Research, Center for Special Education Finance.
Osborne, A.G., Jr.
1996   *Legal Issues in Special Education.* Needham Heights, MA: Allyn and Bacon.
Parrish, T.B.
1996   Special education finance: Past, present and future. *Journal of Education Finance* 21(4):451-476.
1995   What is fair? Special education and finance equity. *School Business Affairs* 61(8):22-29.

Pugach, M.C., and C.L. Warger
   1993   Curriculum considerations. Pp. 125-148 in *Integrating General and Special Education*,
             J. Goodlad and T. Lovitt, eds. New York: Merrill-Macmillan.
Raizen, S.A., and L.V. Jones, eds.
   1985   *Indicators of Precollege Education in Science and Mathematics: A Preliminary Review.*
             Committee on Indicators of Precollege Science and Mathematics Education, National
             Research Council. Washington, DC: National Academy Press.
Ravitch, D.
   1995   *National Standards in American Education: A Citizen's Guide.* Washington, DC:
             Brookings.
Research Triangle Institute
   1980   *Final Report: A National Survey of Individualized Education Programs (IEPs) for
             Handicapped Children.* Contract No. 300-77-0529. Research Triangle Park, NC: Re-
             search Triangle Institute.
Rothstein, L.F.
   1990   *Special Education Law.* White Plains, NY: Longman.
Rothstein, R., and K.H. Miles
   1995   *Where's the Money Gone? Changes in the Level and Composition of Education Spend-
             ing.* Washington, DC: Economic Policy Institute.
Sands, D.J., L. Adams, and D.M. Stout
   1995   A statewide exploration of the nature and use of curriculum in special education. *Excep-
             tional Children* 62(1):68-83.
Sarason, S., and J. Doris
   1979   *Educational Handicap, Public Policy, and Social History.* New York: The Free Press.
Schnaiberg, L.
   1995a   No easy answers. *Education Week* (May 31):27-32.
   1995b   Rhetoric outstrips reality in assessing special needs students. *Education Week* (May
             17):6-7.
Schneider, A., and H. Ingram
   1993   Social construction of target populations: Implications for politics and policy. *Ameri-
             can Political Science Review* 87(2):334-347.
Shanker, A.
   1994   Where we stand: Inclusion and ideology. *New York Times* 87.
Singer, J.D., and J.A. Butler
   1987   The Education for All Handicapped Children Act: Schools as agents of social reform.
             Harvard Educational Review 57(2):125-152.
Sizer, T.R.
   1992   A test of democracy. *New York Times* (January 30), Section 1:21.
Smith, M.L.
   1996   *Reforming Schools by Reforming Assessment: Consequences of the Arizona Student
             Assessment Program.* Los Angeles: National Center for Research on Evaluation, Stan-
             dards, and Student Testing, University of California, Los Angeles.
Smith, M., and J. O'Day
   1991   Systemic school reform. Pp. 233-268 In *The Politics of Curriculum and Testing*, Susan
             Fuhrman and Betty Malen, eds. Philadelphia, PA: Falmer Press.
Smith, S.W.
   1990   Individualized education programs (IEPs) in special education: From intent to acquies-
             cence. *Exceptional Children* 57(1):6-14.
Smith, S.W., and M.T. Brownell
   1995   Individualized education program: Considering the broad context of reform. *Focus on
             Exceptional Children* 28(1):1-11.

Spillane, J.P., C.L. Thompson, C. Lubienski, L. Jita, and C.B. Reimann
   1995   *The Local Government Policy System Affecting Mathematics and Science Education in Michigan: Lessons From Nine School Districts.* East Lansing: MSSI Policy and Program Review Component, Michigan State University.

Stainback, S., and W. Stainback
   1984   A rationale for the merger of special and regular education. *Exceptional Children* 51(2):102-111.

Stanfield, R.L.
   1995   Tales out of school. *National Journal* 27(33-34):27-32.

Stanford Research Institute
   1982   *Local Implementation of P.L. 94-142: Final Report of a Longitudinal Study.* Menlo Park, CA: Stanford Research Institute.

Strope, J.L., and C.A. Broadwell
   1990   How P.L. 94-142 has fared in the Supreme Court. *West's Education Law Reporter* 58(1):13-28.

Taylor, C.
   1994   Assessment for measurement of standards: The peril and promise of large-scale assessment reform. *American Educational Research Journal* 31(2):231-262.

Toch, T.
   1995   D.C.'s tuition-free zone: The city pays to send some learning-disabled children of well-off parents to private schools. *Washington Post* (April 2):C1-3.

Trudeau, E.
   1971   *Digest of State and Federal Laws. Education of Handicapped Children.* Arlington, VA: Council for Exceptional Children.

Turnbull, A.P., and H.R. Turnbull
   1982   Parent involvement in the education of handicapped children: A critique. *Mental Retardation* 20:115-122.

   in press *Families, Professionals, and Exceptionality: Collaborating for Empowerment,* 3rd Edition. Columbus, OH: Merrill/Prentice-Hall.

Turnbull, H.R., III
   1993   *Free Appropriate Public Education: The Law and Children with Disabilities,* 3rd Edition. Denver, CO: Lone Publishing Company.

Tweedie, J.
   1983   The Politics of Legalization in Special Education Reform. Pp. 48-112 in *Special Education Policies: Their History, Implementation, and Finance*, J.G. Chambers and W.T. Hartman, eds. Philadelphia, PA: Temple University Press.

Tyler, T., J. Casper, and B. Fisher
   1989   Maintaining allegiance toward political authorities: The role of prior attitudes and the use of fair procedures. *American Political Science Review* 33:629-652.

Underwood, J.
   1995   School finance adequacy as vertical equity. *University of Michigan Journal of Law Reform* 28(3):493-519.

Underwood, J.K., and J.F. Meade
   1995   *Legal Aspects of Special Education and Pupil Services.* Needham Heights, MA: Allyn and Bacon.

U.S. Department of Education
   1996a   *Eighteenth Annual Report to Congress on the Implementation of the Individuals with Disabilities Education Act.* Washington, DC: Office of Special Education Programs.
   1996b   *Goals 2000: Increasing Student Achievement Through State and Local Initiatives.* Washington, DC: U.S. Department of Education.
   1996c   *Pursuing Excellence.* Washington, DC: U.S. Department of Education.

Wagner, M., J. Blackorby, R. Cameto, K. Hebbeler, and L. Newman
  1993   *The Transition Experiences of Young People with Disabilities. A Summary of Findings from the National Longitudinal Transition Study of Special Education Students.* Menlo Park, CA: SRI International.
Wang, M.C., M.C. Reynolds, and H.J. Walberg
  1986   Rethinking special education. *Educational Leadership* 44:26-31.
Weatherley, R.A.
  1979   *Reforming Special Education: Policy Implementation From State Level to Street Level.* Cambridge, MA: The MIT Press.
Weatherley, R.A., and M. Lipsky
  1977   Street level bureaucrats and institutional innovation: Implementing special education reform. *Harvard Educational Review* 47(2):171-197.
Weber, M.C.
  1990   The transformation of the Education of the Handicapped Act: A study of the interpretation of radical statutes. *University of California, Davis, Law Review* 24(2):349-436.
Wegner, J.
  1985   Variations on a theme: The concept of equal educational opportunity and programming decisions under The Education for All Handicapped Children Act of 1975. *Journal of Law and Contemporary Problems* 48(1):169-219.
Weintraub, F., A. Abeson, and D. Braddock
  1971   *State Law and Education of Handicapped Children: Issues and Recommendations.* Arlington, VA: Council for Exceptional Children.
Will, M.C.
  1986   Educating children with learning problems: A shared responsibility. *Exceptional Children* 52(5):411-416.
Winnick, B.M.
  1987   Congress, Smith v. Robinson and the myth of attorney representation in special education hearings: Is attorney representation desirable? *Syracuse Law Review* 37(4):1161-1187.
Wise, A.
  1979   *Legislated Learning.* Berkeley, CA: University of California Press.
Wolfensberger, W.
  1970   The principle of normalization and its implications for psychiatric services. *American Journal of Psychiatry* 127:291-297.
Yudof, M.
  1984   Education for the handicapped: Rowley in perspective. *American Journal of Education* 92(2):163-177.
Zettel, J.
  1982   Impelementing the right to a free appropriate public education. Pp. 23-40 in *Special Education in America: Its Legal and Governmental Foundations,* J. Ballard, B. Ramirez and F. Weintraub, eds. Reston, VA: Council for Exceptional Children.
Zirkel, P.A., and S.N. Richardson
  1989   The explosion in education litigation. *West's Education Law Reporter* 53(3):767-791.

CHAPTER 3   THE DIVERSITY OF STUDENTS WITH DISABILITIES

Abt Associates
  1974   *Assessments of Selected Resources for Severely Handicapped Children and Youth. Volume I: A State-Of-The-Art Paper.* Cambridge, MA: Abt Associates.

Aleman, S.R.
 1995 *Special Education: Issues in the State Grant Program of the Individuals with Disabilities Education Act.* Washington, DC: Congressional Research Service.
Algozzine, B., C.V. Morsink, and K.M. Algozzine
 1988 What's happening in self-contained special education classrooms. *Exceptional Children* 55:259-265.
Allington, R.L., and A. McGill-Franzen
 1992 Unintended effects of educational reform in New York. *Educational Policy* 4:397-414.
American Psychiatric Association
 1994 *Diagnostic and Statistical Manual of Mental Disorders,* 4th Edition. Washington, DC: American Psychiatric Association.
Astone, N.M., and S.S. McLanahan
 1991 Family structure, parental practices and high school completion. *American Sociological Review* 56:309-320.
Batshaw, M., and Y. Perret
 1986 *Children With Handicaps: A Medical Primer,* 2nd Edition. Baltimore, MD: Paul H. Brookes.
Bond, L.A., D. Braskamp, and E. Roeber
 1996 *The Status of State Student Assessment Programs in the United States.* Oak Brook, IL: North Central Regional Educational Laboratory and Council of Chief State School Officers.
Boucher, C.R., and S.L. Deno
 1979 Learning disabled and emotionally disturbed: Will the labels affect teacher planning? *Psychology in the Schools* 16:395-402.
Bursuck, W.
 1989 A comparison of students with learning disabilities to low achieving and higher achieving students on three dimensions of special competence. *Journal of Learning Disabilities* 26:125-138.
Campione, J.C., A.L. Brown, and R.A. Ferrara
 1982 Mental retardation and intelligence. Pp. 392-490 in *Handbook of Human Intelligence,* R.J. Sternberg, ed. Cambridge, MA: Cambridge University Press.
Carter, L.F.
 1984 The sustaining effects study of compensatory and elementary education. *Educational Researcher* 13:4-13.
Chaikind, S., L.C. Danielson, and M.L Brauen
 1993 What do we know about the costs of special education? *Journal of Special Education* 26:344-370.
Chambers, J.G., and T.B. Parrish
 1983 *The Development of a Resource Cost Model Funding Base for Education in Illinois.* Springfield: Illinois State Board of Education.
Chinn, P.C., and S. Hughes
 1987 Representation of minority students in special education classes. *Remedial and Special Education* 8(4):41-46.
Christenson, S.L., T. Rounds, and M.J. Franklin
 1992a Home-school collaboration: Effects, issues, and opportunities. Pp. 19-51 in *Home-School Collaboration: Enhancing Children's Academic and Social Competence,* Sandra L. Christenson and Jane Close Conoley, eds. Silver Spring, MD: National Academy of School Psychologists.
Christenson, S.L., T. Rounds, and D. Gomey
 1992b Family-factors and student achievement: An avenue to increase students' success. *School Psychology Quarterly* 7(3):178-206.

Cleaver, A., G. Bear, and J. Juvonen
   1992   Discrepancies between competence and importance in self-perceptions of children in
           integrated classrooms. *Journal of Special Education* 26:125-138.
Coles, G.S.
   1978   The learning disabilities test battery: Empirical and social issues. *Harvard Educational
           Review* 48:313-340.
Destefano, L., and D. Metzer
   1991   High stakes testing and students with handicaps: An analysis of issues and policies. Pp.
           281-302 in *Advances in Program Evaluation* 1A, R.E. Stake, ed. Greenwich, CT: JAI
           Press.
Donahoe, L.M., and N. Zigmond
   1990   Academic grades of ninth-grade urban learning-disabled students and low-achieving
           peers. *Exceptionality* 1:17-27.
Dunn, L.
   1968   Special education for the mildly retarded: Is much of it justifiable? *Exceptional Chil-
           dren* 35:5-22.
Dunn, R.
   1990   Bias over substance: A critical analysis of Kavale and Forness' report on modality-based
           instruction. *Exceptional Children* 56:352-356.
Edgar, E., P. Levine, and M. Maddox
   1986   Statewide Follow-up Studies of Secondary Special Education Students in Transition.
           Working Paper of the Networking and Evaluation Team. University of Washington,
           Seattle.
Epps, S., and G. Tindal
   1987   The effectiveness of differential programming in serving students with mild handicaps.
           Pp. 213-248 in *Handbook of Special Education: Research and Practice I*, M.C. Wang,
           M.C. Reynolds, and H.J. Walberg, eds. Oxford, England: Pergamon Press.
Epps, S., J. Ysseldyke, and M. McGue
   1984   Differentiating LD and non-LD students: "I know one when I see one." *Learning Dis-
           ability Quarterly* 7:89-101.
Fehrmann, P.G., T.Z. Keith, and T.M. Reimers
   1987   Home influence on school learning: Direct and indirect effects of parental involvement
           on high school grades. *Journal of Educational Research* 80(6):330-337.
Finn, J.D.
   1982   Patterns in special education placement as revealed by OCR surveys. Pp. 322-381 in
           Placing Children in Special Education: A Strategy for Equity, K.A. Heller, W.H.
           Holtzman, and S. Messick, eds. Committee on Child Development Research and Public
           Policy, National Research Council. Washington, DC: National Academy Press.
Fuchs, L.S., D. Fuchs, K. Karns, C.L. Hamlett, M. Katzaroff, and S. Dutka
   in press Effects of task-focused goals on low-achieving students with and without learning dis-
           abilities. *American Educational Research Journal.*
Fuchs, L.S., D. Fuchs, C.L. Hamlett, N.B. Phillips, and J. Bentz
   1994   Classwide curriculum-based measurement: Helping general educators meet the chal-
           lenge of student diversity. *Exceptional Children* 60:518-537.
Gajar, A.
   1979   Educable mentally retarded, learning disabled, and emotionally disturbed: Similarities
           and differences. *Exceptional Children* 45:470-472.
Gelb, S., and D.T. Mizokawa
   1986   Special education and social structure: The commonality of exceptionality. *American
           Educational Research Journal* 23(4):543-557.

Goldstein, S., B. Strickland, A.P. Turnbull, and L. Curry
  1980   An observational analysis of the IEP conference. *Exceptional Children* 46(4):278-286..
Goodman, J.F.
  1989   Does retardation mean dumb? Children's perceptions of the nature, cause, and course of mental retardation. *Journal of Special Education* 23:313-329.
Grosenick, J.K., M.P. George, and N.L. George
  1987   A profile of school programs for the behaviorally disordered: Twenty years after Morse, Cutler, and Fink. *Behavior Disorders* 12:159-168.
Grossman, H.J.
  1983   *Classification in Mental Retardation.* Washington, DC: American Association on Mental Deficiency.
Hallahan, D.P., and J.M. Kauffman
  1977   Labels, categories, and behaviors: ED, LED, and EMR reconsidered. *Journal of Special Education* 11:139-149.
Hammill, D.D.
  1990   On defining learning disabilities: An emerging consensus. *Journal of Learning Disabilities* 23:74-84.
Harris and Associates
  1986   *The ICD Survey of Disabled Americans: Bringing Disabled Americans into the Mainstream.* New York: Harris and Associates.
Harry, B.
  1992a   *Cultural Diversity, Families, and the Special Education System: Communication and Empowerment.* New York: Teachers College Press, Columbia University.
  1992b   An ethnographic study of cross-cultural communication with Puerto Rican American families in the special education system. *American Education Research Journal* 29(3):471-494.
  1992c   Making sense of disability: Low-income, Puerto Rican parents' theories of the problem. *Exceptional Children* 59(1):27-40.
Harry, B., N. Allen, and M. McLaughlin
  1995   Communication versus compliance: African-American parents' involvement in special education. *Exceptional Children* 61(4):364-377.
Hasazi, S.B., L.R. Gordon, and C.A. Roe
  1985   Factors associated with the employment status of handicapped youth exiting high school from 1979-1983. *Exceptional Children* 51:455-469.
Haynes, M.C., and J.R. Jenkins
  1986   Reading instruction in special education resource rooms. *American Educational Research Journal* 23:161-190.
Hebbeler, K.
  1993   *Traversing the Mainstream: Regular Education and Students with Disabilities in Secondary School. A Special Topic Report from the National Longitudinal Study of Special Education Students.* Menlo Park, CA: SRI International.
Heller, K.A., W.H. Holtzman, and S. Messick, eds.
  1982   *Placing Children in Special Education: A Strategy for Equity.* Committee on Child Development Research and Public Policy, National Research Council. Washington, DC: National Academy Press.
Hersh, R.H., and H.M. Walker
  1983   Great expectations: Making schools effective for all children. *Policy Studies Review* 2:47-188.
Hobbs, N.
  1975   *The Futures of Children.* San Francisco: Jossey-Bass.

Hoff, M.K., K.S. Fenton, R.K. Yoshia, and M.J. Kaufman
1978   Notice and consent: The school's duty to inform parents. *Journal of School Psychology* 16(3):265-273.
Javitz, H.S., and M. Wagner
1993   *Report on Sample Design and Limitations, Wave 2 (1990). A Report from the National Longitudinal Transition Study of Special Education Students.* Menlo Park, CA: SRI International.
1990   *Report on Sample Design and Limitations, Wave 1 (1987). A Report from the National Longitudinal Transition Study of Special Education Students.* Menlo Park, CA: SRI International.
Jenkins, J.R., and A. Heinen
1989   Students' preferences for service delivery: Pull-out, in-class, or integrated models. *Exceptional Children* 55:516-523.
Jenkins, J.R., C.G. Pious, and D.L. Peterson
1988   Categorical programs for remedial and handicapped students. *Exceptional Children* 55:147-158.
Justen, J.
1976   Who are the severely handicapped? A problem in definition. *AAESPH Review* 1(5):1-11.
Kauffman, J.M., D. Cullinan, and M.H. Epstein
1987   Characteristics of students placed in special programs for the seriously emotionally disturbed. *Behavior Disorders* 12:175-184.
Kavale, K.
1990   The effectiveness of special education. Pp. 868-898 in *The Handbook of School Psychology,* 2nd Edition, T.B. Gutkin and C.R. Reynolds, eds. New York: Wiley
1980   Learning disability and cultural-economic disadvantage: The case for a relationship. *Learning Disability Quarterly* 3:97-112.
Kavale, K.A., D. Fuchs, and T.E. Scruggs
1994   Setting the record straight on learning disability and low achievement: Implications for policy making. *Learning Disability Research and Practice* 9(2):70-77.
Kavale, K.A., and G.V. Glass
1982   The efficacy of special education interventions and practices: A compendium of meta-analysis findings. *Focus on Exceptional Children* 15(4):1-14.
Keogh, B.K.
1990   Narrowing the gap between policy and practice. *Exceptional Children* 57:186-190.
Keogh, B.K., and D.L. MacMillan
1996   Exceptionality. In *Handbook of Educational Psychology,* D. Berliner and R. Calfee, eds. Washington, DC: American Psychological Association.
Lee, S.
1993   Family structure effects on student outcomes. Pp. 43-75 in *Parents, Their Children, and Schools,* B. Schneider and J.S. Coleman, eds. Boulder, CO: Westview Press.
Lewit, E.M., and L.S. Baker
1996   Child indicators: Children in special education. *The Future of Children: Special Education for Students with Disabilities* 6(1):139-151. Los Altos, CA: Center for the Future of Children, David and Lucille Packard Foundation.
Leyser, Y.
1985   Parent involvement in school: A survey of parents of handicapped children. *Contemporary Education* 57(1):38-43.

Lindle, J.C.
1992   *School Leadership and Educational Reform: Parent Involvement in the Education for Handicapped Children Act Occasional Papers: School Leadership and Education Reform,* OP#4. Urbana, IL: National Center for School Leadership.

Luckasson, R., D.L. Coulter, E.A. Polloway, S. Reiss, R.L. Schalock, M.E. Snell, D.M. Spitalnik, and J.A. Stark.
1992   *Mental Retardation: Definition, Classification, and Systems of Support,* 9th Edition. Washington, DC: American Association on Mental Retardation.

Lyon, G.R.
1996   Learning disabilities. *The Future of Children: Special Education for Students with Disabilities* 6(1):54-76. Los Altos, CA: Center for the Future of Children, David and Lucille Packard Foundation.

MacMillan, D.L.
1988   Issues in mild mental retardation. *Education and Training of the Mentally Retarded* 23:273-284.

MacMillan, D., R. Jones, and G. Aloia
1974   The mentally retarded label: A theoretical analysis and review of research. *American Journal of Mental Deficiency* 79:241-261.

MacMillan, D., C.E. Meyers, and G. Morrison
1980   System-identification of mildly mentally retarded children: Implications for interpreting and conducting research. *American Journal of Mental Deficiency* 85:108-115.

MacMillan, D., and D.J. Reschly
in press Issues in definition and classification. In *Handbook of Mental Deficiency: Psychological Theory and Research,* 3rd Edition, W.E. MacLean, ed. Hillsdale, NJ: Lawrence Erlbaum.

MacMillan, D.L., and J.G. Hendrick
1993   Evolution and legacies. In *Integrating General and Special Education*, J.I. Goodlad and T.C. Lovitt, eds. Columbus, OH: Charles C. Merrill.

MacMillan, D.L., K.F. Widaman, I.H. Balow, S. Borthwick-Duffy, I.G. Hendrick, and R. Hemsley
1992   Special education students exiting the educational system. *Journal of Special Education* 26(1):20-36.

Madigan, T.J.
1994   Parent Involvement and Student Achievement. Unpublished paper presented at the annual meeting of the American Educational Research Association, New Orleans.

McGrew, K.S., B. Algozzine, J.E. Ysseldyke, M.L. Thurlow, and A.N. Spiegel
1995   The identification of individuals with disabilities in national databases: Creating a failure to communicate. *Journal of Special Education* 28(4):472-487.

McGrew, K.S., M.L. Thurlow, and A.N. Spiegel
1993   An investigation of the exclusion of students with disabilities in national data collection programs. *Educational Evaluation and Policy Analysis* 15(3):339-352.

McKinney, J.D., and A.M. Horcutt
1982   Public school involvement of parents of learning disabled children and average achievers. *Exceptional Education Quarterly* 3:64-73.

McLaughlin, M.W., L.A. Shepard with J.A. O'Day
1995   *Improving Education Through Standards-Based Reform.* A report by the National Academy of Education Panel on Standards-Based Reform. Stanford, CA: The National Academy of Education.

Mehan, H.
1995   The Institutional Uses of IQ tests. Unpublished paper presented at a workshop of the Board on Testing and Assessment, La Jolla, CA, January 21, 1995. University of California, San Diego.

Mehan, H., A. Hertweck, and J.L. Meihls
   1986   *Handicapping the Handicapped: Decision Making in Students' Educational Careers.*
          Stanford, CA: Stanford University Press.
Mercer, C.D., P. King-Sears, and A.R. Mercer
   1990   Learning disabilities definitions and criteria used by state education departments. *Learning Disability Quarterly* 13:141-152.
Mercer, J.
   1979   *System of Multicultural Pluralistic Assessment Technical Manual.* San Antonio, TX: Psychological Corporation.
   1973   *Labeling the Mentally Retarded.* Berkeley, CA: University of California Press.
Merrill, K.W.
   1990   Differentiating low achieving students and students with learning disabilities: An examination of performances on the Woodcock-Johnson Psycho-Educational Battery. *Journal of Special Education* 24:296-305.
Milne, A.M., D.E. Myers, A.S. Rosenthal, and A. Ginsburg
   1986   Single parents, working mothers, and the educational achievement of school children. *Sociology of Education* 59:25-39.
Mithaug, D., C. Horiuchi, and P. Fanning
   1985   A report on the Colorado state-wide follow-up survey of special education students. *Exceptional Children* 51:397-404.
Moore, M.T., M.E. Goertz, and T.W. Hartle
   1988   *Patterns in Special Education Service Delivery and Cost.* Washington, DC: Decision Resources Corporation.
Morison, P., S.H. White, and M.J. Feuer, eds.
   1996   *The Use of IQ Tests in Special Education Decision Making and Planning.* Board on Testing and Assessment, National Research Council. Washington, DC: National Academy Press.
Muller, C.
   1995   Maternal employment, parental involvement, and mathematics achievement among adolescents. *Journal of Marriage and the Family* 57:85-100.
Muller, C., and D. Kerbow
   1993   Parental involvement in home, school and the community. Pp. 13-42 in *Parents, Their Children, and Schools*, B. Schneider and J. Coleman, eds. Boulder, CO: Westview Press.
National Association of School Psychologists
   1986   Rights without labels. Reprinted in *School Psychology Review*, 1989 18(4). Washington, DC: National Association of School Psychologists.
National Council on Disability
   1995   *Improving the Implementation of the Individuals with Disabilities Education Act: Making Schools Work for All of America's Children.* Washington, DC: National Council on Disability.
   1989   *The Education of Students with Disabilities: Where Do We Stand?* Washington, DC: National Council on Disability.
National Institute on Disability and Rehabilitation Research
   1996   *Disabilities Among Children.* Disabilities Statistics Abstract, No. 15. Washington, DC: U.S. Department of Education.
Neisser, U., G. Boodoo, T.J. Bouchard, A.W. Boykin, N. Brody, S.J. Ceci, D.F. Halpern, J.C. Loehlin, R. Perloff, R.J. Sternberg, and S. Urbina
   1996   Intelligence: Knowns and unknowns. *American Psychologist* 51(2):77-101.
Neisworth, J., and J. Greer
   1975   Functional similarities of learning disability and mild retardation. *Exceptional Children* 42:17-21.

Patrick, J., and D. Reschly
  1982   Relationship of state educational criteria and demographic variables to school-system prevalence of mental retardation. *American Journal of Mental Deficiency* 86:351-360.
Phillips, S.E.
  1996   Legal defensibility of standards: Issues and policy perspectives. *Educational Measurement: Issues and Practice* 15(2):5-13.
Polifka, J.C.
  1981   Compliance with Public Law 94-142 and consumer satisfaction. *Exceptional Children* 48(3):250-253.
Reschly, D.J.
  1996   Identification and assessment of students with disabilities. *The Future of Children: Special Education for Students with Disabilities* 6(1):40-53. Los Altos, CA: Center for the Future of Children, David and Lucille Packard Foundation.
  1992   Mental retardation: Conceptual foundations, definitional criteria, and diagnostic operations. Pp. 23-67 in *Developmental Disorders: Diagnostic Criteria and Clinical Assessment*, S.R. Hooper, G.W. Hynd, and R.E. Mattison, eds. Hillsdale, NJ: Lawrence Erlbaum Associates.
  1988   Minority mild mental retardation over-representation: Legal issues, research findings, and reform trends. Pp. 23-41 in *Handbook of Special Education: Research and Practice II*, M.C. Wang, M.C. Reynolds, and H.J. Walberg, eds. Oxford, England: Pergamon Press.
  1987a   Learning characteristics of mildly handicapped students: Implications for classification, placement, and programming. Pp. 35-38 in *Handbook of Special Education: Research and Practice I*, M.C. Wang, M.C. Reynolds, and H.J. Walberg, eds. Oxford, England: Pergamon Press.
  1987b   Assessing educational handicaps. Pp. 155-187 in *The Handbook of Forensic Psychology*, A. Hess and I. Weiner, eds. New York: Wiley.
Reschly, D.J., and M.S. Wilson
  1990   Cognitive processing vs. traditional intelligence: Diagnostic utility, intervention implications, and treatment validity. *School Psychology Review* 19:443-458.
Roit, M.L., and W. Pfohl
  1984   The readability of P.L. 94-142 parent materials: Are parents truly informed? *Exceptional Children* 50(6):496-505.
Sawyer, R.J., M.J. McLaughlin, and M. Winglee
  1994   Is integration of students with disabilities happening? An analysis of national data trends over time. *Remedial and Special Education* 15(4):204-215.
Scanlon, C.A., J. Arick, and N. Phelps
  1981   Participation in the development of the IEP: Parent perspective. *Exceptional Children* 47(5):373-374.
Shaywitz, S.E., M. Escobar, B.A. Shaywitz, J.M. Fletcher, and R. Makuch
  1992   Evidence that dyslexia represents the lower tail of a normal distribution of reading ability. *New England Journal of Medicine* 326(3):145-150.
Shepard, L.A.
  1983   The role of measurement in educational policy: Lessons from the identification of learning disabilities. *Educational Measurement: Issues and Practices* 2:4-8.
Shinn, M.R., J.E. Ysseldyke, S.L. Deno, and G.A. Tindal
  1986   A comparison of differences between students labeled learning disabled and low achieving on measures of classroom performance. *Journal of Learning Disabilities* 19:545-552.

Shinn, M.R., G.A. Tindal, and S. Stein
    1988   Curriculum-based measurement and the identification of mildly handicapped students: A research review. *Professional School Psychology* 3(1):69-85.

Silverstein, J., J. Springer, and N. Russo
    1992   Involving parents in the special education process. Pp. 383-407 in *Home-School Collaboration: Enhancing Children's Academic and Social Competence*, Sandra L. Christenson and Jane Close Conoley, eds. Silver Spring, MD: National Association of School Psychologists.

Singer, J.S., J.S. Palfrey, J.A. Butler, and D.K. Walker
    1989   Variation in special education classification across school districts: How does where you live affect what you are labeled? *American Educational Research Journal* 26(2):261-281.

Smith, C.R., F.H. Wood, and J. Grimes
    1988   Issues in the identification and placement of behaviorally disordered students. Pp. 95-123 in *The Handbook of Special Education: Research and Practice II*, M.C. Wang, M.C. Reynolds, and H.J. Walberg, eds. Oxford, England: Pergamon Press.

Smith, S.W.
    1990   Individualized education programs (IEPs) in special education: From intent to acquiescence. *Exceptional Children* 57(1):6-14.

Sui-Chu, E.H., and J. Willms
    1996   Effects of parental involvement in eighth-grade achievement. *Sociology of Education* 69:126-141.

Tateyama-Sniezek, K.M.
    1990   Cooperative learning: Does it improve the academic achievement of students with handicaps? *Exceptional Children* 56:426-427.

Thurlow, M.L., J.E. Ysseldyke, and C.L. Anderson
    1995   *High School Graduation Requirements: What's Happening for Students with Disabilities?* Synthesis Report 20. Minneapolis: National Center on Educational Outcomes, University of Minnesota.

Tur-Kaspa, H., and T. Bryan
    1994   Social information-processing skills of students with learning disabilities. *Learning Disabilities Research and Practice* 9:12-23.

Turnbull, A.P., and H.R. Turnbull
    1982   Parent involvement in the education of handicapped children: A critique. *Mental Retardation* 20:115-122.
    in press   *Families, Professionals, and Exceptionality: Collaborating for Empowerment*, 3rd Edition. Columbus, OH: Merrill/Prentice-Hall.

U.S. Bureau of the Census
    1988   Marital Status and Living Arrangements: March 1987. Washington, DC: U.S. Department of Commerce, CPR P-20, no. 423.

U.S. Department of Education
    1996   *Eighteenth Annual Report to Congress on the Implementation of the Individuals with Disabilities Education Act.* Washington, DC: Office of Special Education Programs.
    1995   *Seventeenth Annual Report to Congress on the Implementation of the Individuals with Disabilities Education Act.* Washington, DC: Office of Special Education Programs.
    1994   *Sixteenth Annual Report to Congress on the Implementation of the Individuals with Disabilities Education Act.* Washington, DC: Office of Special Education Programs.
    1993   *Fifteenth Annual Report to Congress on the Implementation of the Individuals with Disabilities Education Act.* Washington, DC: Office of Special Education Programs.
    1992   *Fourteenth Annual Report to Congress on the Implementation of the Individuals with Disabilities Education Act.* Washington, DC: Office of Special Education Programs.

1988   *Youth Indicators 1988*. Washington, DC: U.S. Department of Education.

Vaughn, S., C.S. Bos, J.E. Harrell, and B.A. Lasky
1988   Parent participation in the initial placement/IEP conference ten years after mandated involvement. *Journal of Learning Disabilities* 21:82-87.

Wagner, M., ed.
1993   *The Secondary School Programs of Students with Disabilities. A Report from the National Longitudinal Study of Special Education Students.* Menlo Park, CA: SRI International.

Wagner, M.M., and J. Blackorby
1996   Transitions from high school to work or college: How special education students fare. *The Future of Children: Special Education for Students with Disabilities* 6(1):103-120. Los Altos, CA: Center for the Future of Children, David and Lucille Packard Foundation.

Wagner, M., J. Blackorby, R. Cameto, K. Hebbeler, and L. Newman
1993a   *The Transition Experiences of Young People with Disabilities. A Summary of Findings from the National Longitudinal Transition Study of Special Education Students.* Menlo Park, CA: SRI International.

Wagner, M., J. Blackorby., R. Cameto, and L. Newman
1993b   *What Makes a Difference? Influences on Postschool Outcomes of Youth with Disabilities. The Third Comprehensive Report from the National Longitudinal Transition Study of Special Education Students.* Menlo Park, CA: SRI International.

Wagner, M., J. Blackorby, and K. Hebbeler
1993c   *Beyond the Report Card: The Multiple Dimensions of Secondary School Performance of Students with Disabilities. A Report from the National Longitudinal Transition Study of Special Education Students.* Menlo Park, CA: SRI International.

Wagner, M., R. D'Amico, C. Marder, L. Newman, and J. Blackorby
1992   *What Happens Next? Trends in Postschool Outcomes of Youth With Disabilities. The Second Comprehensive Report from the National Longitudinal Transition Study of Special Education Students.* Menlo Park, CA: SRI International.

Wagner, M., R. Newman, R. D'Amico, E.D. Jay, P. Butler-Nalin, C. Marder, and R. Cox, eds.
1991   *Youth With Disabilities: How Are They Doing? The First Comprehensive Report From the National Longitudinal Transition Study of Special Education Students.* Menlo Park, CA: SRI International.

Walker, D.K., J.D. Singer, J.S. Palfrey, M. Orza, M. Wenger, and J.A. Butler
1988   Who leaves and who stays in special education: A 2 year follow-up study. *Exceptional Children* 54(5):393-402.

Weddig, R.
1984   Parental interpretation of psychoeducational reports. *Psychology in the Schools* 21:477-481.

Wenger, B.L., S. Kaye, and M. LaPlante
1996   Disabilities among children. *Disabilities Statistics Abstract No. 15* Washington, DC: U.S. Department of Education, National Institute on Disability and Rehabilitation Research.

Westat, Inc., and University of Maryland at College Park
1994   *Issues and Options in Outcomes-Based Accountability for Students with Disabilities.* College Park, MD: University of Maryland.

World Health Organization
1994   *International Classification of Diseases,* 10th Revision, ICD-10. Geneva: World Health Organization.

Ysseldyke, J., and B. Algozzine
    1980   Technical adequacy of tests used by professionals in simulated decision making. *Psychology-in-the-Schools* 17(2):202-209.

Ysseldyke, J.E., B. Algozzine, and J. Mitchell
    1982b   Special education team decision making: An analysis of current practice. *Personnel and Guidance Journal* 60(5):308-313.

Ysseldyke, J., B. Algozzine, M. Shinn, and M. McGue
    1982a   Similarities and differences between low achievers and students classified learning disabled. *Journal of Special Education* 16:73-85.

Ysseldyke, J.E., M. Thurlow, J. Graden, C. Wesson, B. Algozzine, and S. Deno
    1983   Generalizations from five years of research on assessment and decision making. *Exceptional Education Quarterly* 4(1):75-93. Minneapolis: University of Minnesota Institute.

CHAPTER 4   CONTENT STANDARDS, CURRICULUM, AND INSTRUCTION

Adams, M.J., and M. Bruck
    1993   Word recognition: The interface of educational policies and scientific research. *Reading and Writing: An Interdisciplinary Journal* 5:113-139.

Alberto, P., N. Jobes, A. Sizemore, and D. Doran
    1980   A comparison of individual and group instruction across response tasks. *Journal of the Association for the Severely Handicapped* 5:285-293.

American Association for the Advancement of Science
    1993   *Benchmarks for Science Literacy.* New York: Oxford University Press.

Anderson-Inman, L.
    1990   Enabling students with learning disabilities. *The Computing Teacher* 18(4):26-29.

Andrews, T.E., ed.
    1995   *The NASDTEC Manual 1994-1995: Manual on Certification and Preparation of Educational Personnel in the United States.* Dubuque, Iowa: Kendall/Hunt Publishing Company.

Baker, J.M., and N. Zigmond
    1990   Are regular education classes equipped to accommodate students with learning disabilities? *Exceptional Children* 56:525-526.

Billingsley, F.F., K.A. Liberty, and O.R. White
    1994   The technology of instruction. Pp. 81-116 in *Curricular and Instructional Approaches for Persons with Severe Disabilities*, E.C. Cipani and F. Spooner, eds. Boston, MA: Allyn and Bacon.

Bishop, John H.
    1996   Signaling the competencies of high school students to employers. Pp. 79-124 in *Linking School and Work*, Lauren B. Resnick and John G. Wirt, eds. San Francisco, CA: Jossey-Bass.
    1994   *The Economic Consequences of Schooling and Learning.* Washington, DC: Economic Policy Institute.
    1989   The productivity consequences of what is learned in high school. *Journal of Curriculum Studies* 22(2):101-126.

Blackorby, J., and M. Wagner
    1996   Longitudinal postschool outcomes of youth with disabilities: Findings from the National Longitudinal Transition Study. *Exceptional Children* 57:6-14.

Blank, R.K., and E.M. Pechman
    1995   *State Curriculum Frameworks in Mathematics and Science: How Are They Changing Across the States?* Washington, DC: Council of Chief State School Officers.

Bond, L.A., D. Braskamp, and E. Roeber
   1996   *The Status Report of the Assessment Programs in the United States.* Oak Brook, IL: North Central Regional Educational Laboratory and Council of Chief State School Officers.

Bottge, B.A., and T.S. Hasselbring
   1993   A comparison of two approaches for teaching complex, authentic mathematics problems to adolescents with learning difficulties. *Exceptional Children* 59(6):556-566.

Bradley, L., and P.E. Bryant
   1985   *Rhyme and Reason in Reading and Spelling.* Ann Arbor, MI: University of Michigan Press.

Bransford, J., S.R. Goldman, and T.S. Hasselbring (chairs)
   1995   Marrying Constructivist and Skill-Based Models: Should We and Could Technology Help? Symposium presented at the annual meeting of the American Educational Research Association, San Francisco.

Bransford, J.D., and N.J. Vye
   1989   A perspective on cognitive research and its implications for instruction. Pp. 173-205 in *Toward the Thinking Curriculum: Current Cognitive Research*, L. Resnick and L.E. Klopfer, eds. Alexandria, VA: Association for Supervision and Curriculum Development.

Brown, A.L., and J.C. Campione
   1990   Interactive learning environments and the teaching of science and mathematics. Pp. 111-139 in *Toward a Scientific Practice of Science Education*, M. Gardner, J. Greens, F. Reif, A. Schoenfeld, A. di Sessa, and E. Stage, eds. Hillsdale, NJ: Erlbaum

Brown, L., J. Nietupski, and S. Hamre-Nietupski
   1976   The criterion of ultimate functioning and public school services for severely handicapped students. Pp. 2-15 in *Hey, Don't Forget About Me!*, M.A. Thomas, ed. Reston, VA: Council for Exceptional Children.

Brown, L., J. Nisbet, A. Ford, M. Sweet, B. Shiraga, J. York, and R. Loomis
   1983   The critical need for non-school instruction in educational programs for severely handicapped students. *Journal of the Association for the Severely Handicapped* 8(3):71-77.

Bryan, T., M. Bay, N. Lopez-Reyna, and M. Donahue
   1992   Characteristics of students with learning disabilities: A summary of the extant database and its implications for educational programs. Pp. 143-176 in *Perspectives on the Integration of Atypical Learners in Regular Education Settings*, J. Lloyd, A. Repp, and N. Singh, eds. DeKalb, IL: Sycamore.

The Business Roundtable
   1996   *A Business Leader's Guide to Setting Academic Standards.* Washington, DC: The Business Roundtable.

Carnine, D., and E.J. Kameenui
   1992   *Higher Order Thinking: Designing Curriculum for Mainstreamed Students.* Austin, TX: Pro-Ed.

Carnine, D., J. Silbert, and E.J. Kameenui
   1990   *Direct Instruction Reading,* 2nd Edition. Columbus, OH: Merrill Publishing.

Chaikind, S., L.C. Danielson, and M.L. Brauen
   1993   What do we know about the costs of special education? *Journal of Special Education* 26:344-370.

Christophers, U., M. Sainsbury, C. Whetton, J. Ashby, S. Fletcher-Campbell, and S. Hopkins
   1992   *National Curriculum Assessment at Key Stage 1 in the Core Subjects 1992 Evaluation— Children with Statements of Special Education Needs.* Lincoln, England: Bishop Grosseteste College, National Foundation for Education Research.

Clark, C.M., and J.L. Elmore
  1981   *Transforming Curriculum in Mathematics, Science, and Writing: A Case Study of Teacher Yearly Planning.* Research Report No. 99, ERIC Document Reproduction Service No. ED 205 500. East Lansing: Michigan State University, Institute for Research on Teaching.
Clark, R.
  1983   Reconsidering research on learning from media. *Review of Educational Research* 53:445-459.
Cohen, D.
  1995   What standards for national standards. *Phi Delta Kappan* 76(10):751-757.
Cohen, P., J.A. Kulik, and C. Kulik
  1982   Education outcomes of tutoring: A meta-analysis of findings. *American Educational Research Journal* 19:237-248.
Colorado Department of Education
  1995   *Colorado Model Content Standards for Reading and Writing.* Denver: Colorado Department of Education.
  1994   *Higher Expectations, Better Results: Establishing Standards for Colorado Students.* Denver: Colorado Department of Education.
Coon, M.E., T. Vogelsberg, and W. Williams
  1981   Effects of classroom public transportation instruction on generalization to the natural environment. *Journal of the Association for the Severely Handicapped* 6(2):46-53.
Corcoran, T.C.
  1995   *Transforming Professional Development for Teachers: A Guide for State Policymakers.* Washington, DC: National Governors Association.
Council for Basic Education
  1996   *Judging Standards in Education Reform.* Washington, DC: Council for Basic Education.
Council of Chief State School Officers
  1995   *State Curriculum Frameworks in Mathematics and Science: How Are They Changing Across The States?* Washington, DC: Council of Chief State School Officers.
  in press *Key State Education Policies on K-12 Education: Content Standards, Graduation, Teacher Licensure, Time and Attendance.* Washington, DC: Council of Chief State School Officers, State Education Assessment Center.
Council of the Great City Schools
  1996   *Becoming the Best Standards and Assessment Development in the Great City Schools.* Washington, DC: Council of the Great City Schools.
Cunningham, A.E.
  1990   Explicit versus implicit instruction in phonemic awareness. *Journal of Experimental Child Psychology* 50:521-538.
Deci, E.L., and R.M. Ryan
  1986   An analysis of learned helplessness: Continuous changes in performance, strategy, and achievement cognition after failure. *Journal of Personality and Social Psychology* 36:451-462.
  1985   *Intrinsic Motivation and Self-Determination in Human Behavior.* New York: Plenum.
Deno, S.L.
  1985   Curriculum-based measurement: The emerging alternative. *Exceptional Children* 52:219-232.
Deshler, D.D., J.B. Shumaker, G.R. Alley, M.M. Warner, and F.L. Clark
  1982   Learning disabilities in adolescent and young adult populations. *Focus on Exceptional Children* 15:1-12.

Deshler, D.D., J.B. Shumaker, B.K. Lenz, and E.S. Ellis
    1984   Academic and cognitive interventions for LD adolescents: Part II. *Journal of Learning Disabilities* 17(3):170-187.

Doyle, P.H., D.L. Gast, M. Wolery, M.J. Ault, and J.A. Farmer
    1990   Use of constant time delay in small group instruction: A study of observational and incidental learning. *Journal of Special Education* 23:369-385.

Dweck, C.S., and E. Leggett
    1988   A social-cognitive approach to motivation and personality. *Psychological Review* 95:256-273.

Edgar, E., P. Levine, and M. Maddox
    1986   Statewide Follow-up Studies of Secondary Special Education Students in Transition. Unpublished working paper of the Networking and Evaluation Team. CDMRC, University of Washington, Seattle.

Ellis, E.S., D.D. Deshler, J.B. Shumaker, B.K. Lenz, and F. Clark
    1990   An instructional model for teaching learning strategies. *Focus on Exceptional Children* 23:1-24.

Elmore, R.E., and S.H. Fuhrman, eds.
    1994   *The Governance of Curriculum: 1994 Yearbook of the Association for Supervision and Curriculum Development.* Alexandria, VA: Association for Supervision and Curriculum Development.

Forest, M., and J. Pearpoint
    1992   Families, friends and circles. Pp. 65-86 in *Natural Supports in School, at Work, and in the Community for People with Severe Disabilities*, J. Nisbet, ed. Baltimore, MD: Brookes.

Forness, S.R., and K.A. Kavale
    1996   Can 700 Studies Be Wrong? Mega-analyses of Special Education Meta-analyses. Unpublished paper presented at the annual meeting of the Council for Exceptional Children, Orlando, FL, April 1996.

Fredericks, B.
    1990   Education for the child with Down syndrome. Pp. 170-212 in *Parent's Guide to Down Syndrome*, S. Pueschel, ed. Baltimore, MD: Brookes.

Fredericks, B., and M. Brodsky
    1994   Assessment for a functional curriculum. Pp. 31-49 in *Curricular and Instructional Approaches for Persons with Severe Disabilities*, E.C. Cipani and F. Spooner, eds. Boston, MA: Allyn and Bacon.

Fuchs, D., and L.S. Fuchs
    1995   What's "special" about special education? *Phi Delta Kappan* 76(7):522-530.

Fuchs, L.S.
    1995   Incorporating Curriculum-Based Measurement into the Eligibility Decisionmaking Process: A Focus on Treatment Validity and Student Growth. Unpublished paper presented at the Workshop on IQ Testing and Education Decision Making, Board on Testing and Assessment, National Research Council, May 11, 1995, Washington, DC.

Fuchs, L.S., and D. Fuchs
    1986   Effects of systematic formative evaluation on student achievement: A meta-analysis. *Exceptional Children* 53:199-208.

Fuchs, L.S., D. Fuchs, and C.L. Hamlett
    1989a   Effects of alternative goal structures within curriculum-based measurement. *Exceptional Children* 55:429-438.
    1989b   Effects of instrumental use of curriculum-based measurement to enhance instructional programs. *Remedial and Special Education* 10(2):43-52.

Fuchs, L.S., D. Fuchs, C.L. Hamlett, and C. Ferguson
1992   Effects of expert system consultation within curriculum-based measurement using a reading maze task. *Exceptional Children* 58:436-450.
Fuchs, L.S., D. Fuchs, C.L. Hamlett, and P.M. Stecker
1991b   Effects of curriculum-based measurement and consultation on teacher planning and student achievement in mathematics operations. *American Educational Research Journal* 28:617-641.
Fuchs, L.S., D. Fuchs, C.L. Hamlett, and R.M. Allinder
1991a   Effects of expert system advice within curriculum-based measurement on teacher planning and student achievement in spelling. *School Psychology Review* 20:49-60.
Fuchs, L.S., D. Fuchs, C.L. Hamlett, N. Phillips, K. Karns, and S. Dutka
in press Enhancing student's helping behavior during peer-mediated instruction with conceptual mathematics explanations. *Elementary School Journal*.
Gandal, M.
1996   *Making Standards Matter 1996: An Annual Fifty-State Report on Efforts to Raise Academic Standards.* Washington, DC: American Federation of Teachers Education Issues Department.
Garber, J., and M.E.P. Seligman, eds.
1980   *Human Helplessness.* New York: Academic Press.
Gaylord-Ross, R., and D. Browder
1991   Functional assessment: Dynamic and domain properties. Pp. 45-66 in *Critical Issues in the Lives of People with Severe Disabilities*, L.H. Meyer, C.A. Peck, and L. Brown, eds. Baltimore, MD: Brookes.
Gaylord-Ross, R., T.G. Haring, C. Breen, and V. Pitts-Conway
1984   The training and generalization of social interaction skills with autistic youth. *Journal of Applied Behavior Analysis* 17:229-247.
Gaylord-Ross, R.J., and J.F. Holvoet
1985   *Strategies for Educating Students with Severe Handicaps.* Boston, MA: Little, Brown.
Glass, G., L. Cahen, M.L. Smith, and N. Filby
1982   *School Class Size.* Beverly Hills, CA: Sage.
Glass, G.V., B. McGaw, and M.L. Smith
1981   *Meta-analysis in Social Research.* Beverly Hills, CA: Sage.
Goertz, M.E., and D.H. Friedman
1996   *State Education Reform and Students with Disabilities: A Preliminary Analysis. Year 1 Technical Report, Center for Policy Research in the Impact of General and Special Education Reform.* Alexandria, VA: National Association of State Boards of Education.
Gough, P.B., and W.E. Tunmer
1986   Decoding, reading, and reading disability. *Remedial and Special Education* 7(1):6-10.
Graham, S., and C. MacArthur
1988   Improving learning disabled students' skills at revising essays produced on a word processor: Self-instructional strategy training. *Journal of Special Education* 22:133-152.
Hardman, M.L., C.J. Drew, and M.W. Egan
1996   *Human Exceptionality,* 5th edition. Boston, MA: Allyn and Bacon.
Haring, T.G., and D. Ryndak
1994   Strategies and instructional procedures to promote social interactions and relationships. Pp. 289-321 in *Curricular and Instructional Approaches for Persons with Severe Disabilities*, E.C. Cipani and F. Spooner, eds. Boston: Allyn and Bacon.

Haring, T., and L. Lovinger
  1989   Promoting social interaction through teaching generalized play initiation responses to
            pre-school children with autism. *Journal of the Association for Persons with Severe
            Handicaps* 14:58-67.
Harris Education Research Center
  1991   *Assessment of American Education: The View of Employers, Higher Educators, the
            Public, Recent Students, and Their Parents.* New York: Lou Harris and Associates.
Harris, K.R., and M. Pressley
  1991   The nature of cognitive strategy instruction: Interactive strategy instruction. *Excep-
            tional Children* 57:392-404.
Harris, K.R., and S. Graham
  1995   Constructivism: Principles, paradigms, and integration. *Journal of Special Education*
            28:233-247.
Hasazi, S., L. Gordon, and C. Roe
  1985   Factors associated with the employment status of handicapped youth exiting high school
            from 1970-1983. *Exceptional Children* 51:455-469.
Hasazi, S.B., R.E. Johnson, J. Hasazi, L.R. Gordon, and M. Hull
  1989   A statewide follow-up survey of high school exiters: A comparison of former students
            with and without handicaps. *Journal of Special Education* 23:243-255.
Hasselbring, T., L. Goin, and J.D. Bransford
  1988   Developing math automaticity in learning handicapped children: The role of computer-
            ized drill and practice. *Focus on Exceptional Children* 20(6):1-7.
Hawkins, M.
  1978   A new look at the high school diploma. *National Association of Secondary School
            Principals Bulletin* 62:45-50.
Heller, K.A., W. H. Holtzman, and S. Messick, eds.
  1982   *Placing Children in Special Education: A Strategy for Equity.* Committee on Child
            Development Research and Public Policy, National Research Council. Washington,
            DC: National Academy Press.
Higgins, K., and R. Boone
  1991   A supplement to an elementary school basal reader program. *Journal of Special Educa-
            tion Technology* 11(1):1-15.
  1990   Hypertext: A new vehicle for computer use in reading instruction. *Intervention in School
            and Clinic* 26(1):26-31.
Hill, M.L., P.H. Wehman, P.D. Banks, and H.M.D. Metzler
  1987   Employment outcomes of people with moderate and severe disabilities provided sup-
            ported competitive employment after eight years. Pp. 144-164 in *Competitive Employ-
            ment for Persons with Mental Retardation: From Research Practice*, P. Wehman, J.
            Kregal, M.S. Shafer, and M.L. Hill, eds. Richmond, VA: Rehabilitation Research and
            Training Center, Virginia Commonwealth University.
Horner, R.H., D.N. Jones, and J.A. Williams
  1985   A functional approach to teaching generalized street cross. *Journal of the Association
            for Persons with Severe Handicaps* 10(2):71-78.
Hupp, S.C., and C.B. Mervis
  1981   Development of generalized concepts by severely handicapped students. *Journal of the
            Association for the Severely Handicapped* 6(1):14-21.
Jones, E.D., and J.P. Krouse
  1988   The effectiveness of data-based instruction by student teachers in classrooms for pupils
            with mild handicaps. *Teacher Education and Special Education* 11(1):9-19.

Jones, K.M., J. K. Torgesen, and M.A. Sexton
   1987   Using computer guided practice to increase decoding fluency in learning disabled chil-
           dren: A study using Hint and Hunt I program. *Journal of Learning Disabilities*
           20(2):122-127.

Kagan, D.M., and D.J. Tippins
   1991   Helping student teachers attend to student cues. *Elementary School Journal* 91:343-356.

Kentucky Department of Education
   1994   *Kentucky's Learning Goals and Academic Expectations: What Kentucky High School
           Graduates Must Know and Be Able To Do As They Exit Public School.* Frankfort, KY:
           Kentucky Department of Education.

Kronick, D.
   1990   Holism and empiricism as complementary paradigms. *Journal of Learning Disabilities*
           21:425-428.

Levin, E.K., N. Zigmond, and J.W. Birch
   1983   A Follow-up Study of 52 Learning Disabled Adolescents. Paper presented at the annual
           meeting of the American Educational Research Association, Montreal, April 1983.

Little, J.W.
   1993   Teachers' professional development and education reform. *Educational Evaluation and
           Policy Analysis* 15(2):129-151.

Lysakowski, R.S., and H.J. Walberg
   1982   Instructional effects of cues, participation, and corrective feedback: A quantitative syn-
           thesis. *American Educational Research Journal* 19:559-578.

McDonnell, J., B. Ferguson, and C. Mathot-Bucker
   1992   Transition from school to work for students with severe disabilities: The Utah Commu-
           nity Employment Placement Project. Pp. 33-50 in *Transition from School to Adult Life*,
           F. Rusch, L. Destefano, J. Chadsey-Rusch, L.A. Phelps, and E. Syzmanski, eds. Pacific
           Grove, CA: Brookes Cole.

McDonnell, J., M. Hardman, A. McDonnell, and R. Kiefer-O'Donnell
   1995   *Introduction to Persons with Severe Disabilities.* Boston, MA: Allyn and Bacon.

McDonnell, J.J., R.H. Horner, and J.A. Williams
   1984   Comparison of three strategies for teaching generalized grocery purchasing to high school
           students with severe handicaps. *Journal of the Association for Persons with Severe
           Handicaps* 9(2):123-133.

McDonnell, J., B. Wilcox, and M. Hardman
   1991   *Secondary Programs for Students with Developmental Disabilities.* Boston, MA: Allyn
           and Bacon.

McDonnell, L.M.
   1995   Opportunity to learn as a research concept and policy instrument. *Educational Evalua-
           tion and Policy Analysis* 17:305-322.

McGrew, K.S., M.L. Thurlow, and A.N. Spiegel
   1993   An investigation of the exclusion of students with disabilities in national data collection
           programs. *Educational Evaluation and Policy Analysis* 15(3):339-352.

McGrew, K., M. Vanderwood, M.L. Thurlow, and J. Ysseldyke
   1995   *Why We Can't Say Much About the Status of Students with Disability During Educa-
           tional Reform.* Synthesis Report 21. Minneapolis: National Center on Educational
           Outcomes, University of Minnesota.

McIntosh, R., S. Vaughn, J.S. Schumm, D. Haager, and O. Lee
   1993   Observations of students with learning disabilities in general education classrooms.
           Exceptional Children 60:249-261.

McLaughlin, M.W., and L.A. Shepard with J.A. O'Day
   1995   *Improving Education Through Standards-Based Reform: A Report of the National Academy of Education Panel on Standards-Based Reform.* Stanford, CA: The National Academy of Education.
Means, B., and M.S. Knapp
   1991   Cognitive approaches to teaching advanced skills to educationally disadvantaged students. *Phi Delta Kappan* 23:5-8,10.
Means, B., J. Blando, K. Olson, T. Middleton, C. Morocco, A. Remz, and J. Zorfass
   1993   *Using Technology To Support Education Reform.* Washington, DC: U.S. Department of Education.
Mercer, C.D., L. Jordan, and S.P. Miller
   1995   Implications of constructivism for teaching math to students with moderate to mild disabilities. *Journal of Special Education* 28:290-306.
Michigan Department of Education
   1995   *Model Content Standards for Curriculum.* Lansing: Michigan Department of Education.
Morocco, C.C., and S.B. Neuman
   1986   Word processors and the acquisition of writing strategies. *Journal of Learning Disabilities* 19:243-247.
National Assessment of Educational Progress
   1993   *Data Compendium for the NAEP 1992 Mathematics Assessment of the Nation and the States.* Washington, DC: U.S. Department of Education, National Center for Education Statistics.
National Center for Education Statistics
   1996   *Trends in Participation in Secondary Vocational Education: 1982-1992.* Washington, DC: U.S. Department of Education.
National Commission on Teaching and America's Future
   1996   *What Matters Most: Teaching for America's Future.* New York: Carnegie Corporation of New York and Rockefeller Foundation.
National Council of Teachers of Mathematics
   1989   *Curriculum and Evaluation Standards for School Mathematics.* Reston, VA: National Council of Teachers of Mathematics.
National Research Council
   1996   *National Science Education Standards.* Washington, DC: National Academy Press.
National Science Teachers
   1992   *Scope, Sequence, and Coordination of Secondary School Science, Volume 1. The Content Core, a Guide for Curriculum Designers.* Washington, DC: National Science Teachers.
National Staff Development Council
   1995   *Standards for Staff Development: Elementary School Edition.* Oxford, OH: National Staff Development Council.
   1994   *National Staff Development Council's Standards for Staff Development: Middle Level Edition.* Oxford, OH: National Staff Development Council.
Nietupski, J., and S. Hamre-Nietupski
   1987   An ecological approach to curriculum development. In *Innovative Program Design for Individuals with Dual Sensory Impairments,* L. Goertz, D. Guess, and K. Stremel-Campbell, eds. Baltimore, MD: Brookes.
O'Day, J., M.E. Goertz, and R.E. Floden
   1995   Building capacity for education reform. *CPRE Policy Briefs (RBI-18).* New Brunswick, NJ: Consortium for Policy Research in Education, Rutgers University.

O'Day, J.A., and M.S. Smith
    1993   Systemic reform and educational opportunity. Pp. 250-313 in *Designing Coherent Education Policy*, S.H. Fuhrman, ed. San Francisco: Jossey-Bass.
Ordover, E.L., K.B. Boundy, and D.C. Pullin
    1996   Students with Disabilities and the Implementation of Standards-Based Education Reform: Legal Issues and Implications. Unpublished paper prepared for Committee on Goals 2000 and the Inclusion of Students with Disabilities, June 1996. Center for Law and Education.
Oregon Department of Education
    1996   *Draft Common Curriculum Goals and Content Standards.* Salem: Oregon Department of Education.
Pea, R.D., and E. Soloway
    1987   *Mechanisms for Facilitating a Vital and Dynamic Education System: Fundamental Roles for Education Science and Technology.* Final report for the Office of Technology Assessment. Available through the U.S. Department of Commerce, National Technical Information Service, Springfield, VA (no. PB88-194 634/AS).
Pedulla, J., and E. Reidy
    1979   The rise of the minimal competency testing movement. In *Minimal Competency Testing*, P. Airasian, G. Madaus, and J. Pedulla, eds. Englewood Cliffs, NJ: Educational Technology Publications.
Perfetti, C.A.
    1985   *Reading Ability.* New York: Oxford University Press.
Peterson, P.L., and C.M. Clark
    1978   Teachers' reports of their cognitive processes during teaching. *American Educational Research Journal* 15:220-236.
Phillips, S.E.
    1993   *Legal Implications of High-Stakes Assessment: What States Should Know.* Oak Brook, IL: North Central Regional Educational Laboratory and Council of Chief State School Officers.
Pressley, M., K.R. Harris, and M.B. Marks
    1992   But good strategy instructors are constructivists! *Educational Psychology Review* 4:3-31.
Pugach, M.C., and C.L. Warger
    1993   Curriculum considerations. Pp. 125-148 in *Integrating General and Special Education*, J.L. Goodlad and T.C. Lovitt, eds. New York: Merrill-Macmillan.
Reid, D.H., and J.E. Favell
    1984   Group instruction with persons who have severe disabilities: A critical review. *Journal of the Association for Persons with Severe Handicaps* 9:167-177.
Resnick, L.
    1987   *Education and Learning to Think.* Committee on Mathematics, Science, and Technology Education, National Research Council. Washington, DC: National Academy Press.
Rhim, L.M., and M.J. McLaughlin
    1996   *State Level Policies and Practices: Where Are Students with Disabilities?* Alexandria, VA: Center for Policy Research on the Impact for General and Special Education Reform.
Rusch, F.R., L. Destefano, J. Chadsey-Rusch, L.A. Phelps, and E. Syzmanski
    1992   *Transition from School to Adult Life.* DeKalb, IL: Sycamore Publishing.
Sands, D.J., L. Adams, and D.M. Stout
    1995   A statewide exploration of the nature and use of curriculum in special education. *Exceptional Children* 62:1.

Schneider, A., and H. Ingram
   1990   Behavioral assumptions of policy tools. *Journal of Politics* 52:510-529.
Schumaker, J.B., D.D. Deshler, and E.S. Ellis
   1986   Intervention issues related to the education of LD adolescents. In *Learning Disabilities: Some New Perspectives*, J.K. Torgesen, and B.Y.L. Wong, eds. New York: Academic Press.
Secretary's Commission on Achieving Necessary Skills
   1991   *What Work Requires of Schools: A SCANS Report for America 2000.* Washington, DC: U.S. Department of Labor.
Sedlak, M.W., C.W. Wheeler, D. Pullin, and P.A. Cusick
   1986   *Selling Students Short: Classroom Bargains and Academic Reform in the American High School.* New York: Teachers College, Columbia University.
Shanahan, T., and R. Barr
   1995   Reading recovery: An independent evaluation of the effects of an early instructional intervention for at-risk learners. *Reading Research Quarterly* 30:958-996.
Shapiro, E.S., and T.R. Kratochwill, eds.
   1988   *Behavioral Assessment in Schools: Conceptual Foundations and Practical Applications.* New York: Guilford.
Shriner, J.G., D. Kimm, M.L. Thurlow, and J.E. Ysseldyke
   1993   *IEPs and Standards: What They Say for Students with Disabilities.* Tech. Rep. 5. Minneapolis: National Center on Educational Outcomes, University of Minnesota.
Siegel, L.S.
   1993   Alice in IQ land and why IQ is still irrelevant to learning disabilities. Pp. 71-84 in *Reading Disabilities: Diagnosis and Component Processes*, M. Joshi and C.K. Leong, eds. Dordrecht, The Netherlands: Kluwer Academic.
Smith, S.W.
   1990   Individualized education plans (IEPs) in special education: From intent to acquiescence. *Exceptional Children* 57(1):6-14.
Snell, M., and F. Brown
   1993   Instructional planning and implementation. Pp. 99-151 in *Instruction of Students with Severe Disabilities*, M.E. Snell, ed. New York: Merrill Publishing.
Stanovich, K.E.
   1995   Constructivism in reading education. *Journal of Special Education* 28:259-274.
   1993   Problems in the differential diagnosis of reading disabilities. Pp. 3-60 in *Reading Disabilities: Diagnosis and Component Processes*, R.M. Joshi, and C.K. Leong, eds. Dordrecht, The Netherlands: Kluwer Academic.
   1992   Speculations on the causes and consequences of individual differences in early reading acquisition. Pp. 307-342 in *Reading Acquisition*, P. Gough, L. Ehri, and R. Treiman, eds. Hillsdale, NJ: Erlbaum.
   1986   Toward an interactive-compensatory model of individual differences in the development of reading fluency. *Reading Research Quarterly* 16:32-71.
Stecker, P.M.
   in press   Effects of instructional interventions in mathematics with and without curriculum-based measurement. *Learning Disability Quarterly*.
Swanson, H.L.
   1996   Assessing and Synthesizing Interventions for Students with Mild to Moderate Disabilities in Regular and Special Education Classrooms. Unpublished paper presented at the Pacific Coast Research Conference, La Jolla, CA, February 1996.
Taylor, C.
   1994   Assessment for measurement and standards: The peril and promise of large-scale assessment reform. *American Educational Research Journal* 31(2):231-262.

Tharpe, R.G., and R. Gallimore
  1989   *Rousing Minds to Life: Teaching, Learning, and Schooling in Social Context.* New York: Cambridge University Press.
Thurlow, M.L., J.E. Ysseldyke, and C.L. Anderson
  1995   *High School Graduation Requirements: What's Happening for Students with Disabilities?* Synthesis Report 20. Minneapolis: National Center on Educational Outcomes, University of Minnesota.
Tollefson, N., D. Tracy, E. Johnson, and J. Chatman
  1983   *Teaching Learning Disabled Students Goal Implementation Skills.* Research Report No. 69. Lawrence: University of Kansas Institute for Research in Learning Disabilities.
Torgesen, J.K.
  1996   The Prevention and Remediation of Reading Disabilities. Unpublished paper presented in the John F. Kennedy Center Distinguished Lecture Series, Vanderbilt University, Nashville, TN, January 1996.
Underwood, Julie K.
  1995   School finance adequacy as vertical equity. *University of Michigan Journal of Law Reform* 28(3):493-519.
U.S. Department of Labor
  1987   *Workforce 2000: Work and Workers for the 21st Century.* Washington, DC and Indianapolis, IN: U.S. Department of Labor and Hudson Institute.
van Daal, V.H.P., and A. van der Leij,
  1992   Computer-based reading and spelling practice for children with learning disabilities. *Journal of Learning Disabilities* 25(3):186-195.
Vellutino, F., and D. Scanlon
  1987   Phonological coding, phonological awareness, and reading ability: Evidence from a longitudinal and experimental study. *Merrill-Palmer Quarterly* 33:321-363.
Vitello, S.J.
  1988   Handicapped students and competency testing. *Remedial and Special Education* 9(5):22-27.
Wagner, M., ed.
  1993   *The Secondary School Programs of Students with Disabilities. A Report From The National Longitudinal Study of Special Education Students.* Menlo Park, CA: SRI International.
Wagner, M., J. Blackorby, R. Cameto, K. Hebbeler, and L. Newman
  1993a   *The Transition Experiences of Young People with Disabilities. A Summary of Findings from the National Longitudinal Transition Study of Special Education Students.* Menlo Park, CA: SRI International.
Wagner, M., J. Blackorby, and K. Hebbeler
  1993b   *Beyond the Report Card: The Multiple Dimensions of Secondary School Performance of Students with Disabilities. A Report from the National Longitudinal Study of Special Education Students.* Menlo Park, CA: SRI International.
Wagner, M., R. Newman, R. D'Amico, E.D. Jay, P. Butler-Nalin, C. Marder, and R. Cox, eds.
  1991   *Youth with Disabilities: How Are They Doing? The First Comprehensive Report From the National Longitudinal Transition Study of Special Education Students.* Menlo Park, CA: SRI International.
Wagner, R.K, and J.K. Torgesen
  1987   The nature of phonological processing and its causal role in the acquisition of reading skills. *Psychological Bulletin* 101:192-212.
Warren, S.F., and P.J. Yoder
  1994   Communication and language intervention: Why a constructivist approach is insufficient. *Journal of Special Education* 28:248-258.

Wasik, B.A., and R.E. Slavin
1993   Preventing early reading failure with one-to-one tutoring: A review of five programs. *Reading Research Quarterly* 28:179-200.

Wehman, P.
1996   *Life Beyond the Classroom,* 2nd Edition. Baltimore, MD: Paul H. Brookes.

Wehman, P., J. Kregal, and J. Seyfarth
1985   Transition from school to work for individuals with severe disabilities: A follow-up study. Pp. 247-264 in *Competitive Employment for Persons with Mental Retardation: From Research to Practice*, P. Wehman and J.W. Hills, eds. Richmond, VA: Rehabilitation Research and Training Center, School of Education, Virginia Commonwealth University.

Wesson, C.L.
1991   Curriculum-based measurement and two models of follow-up consultation. *Exceptional Children* 57:246-257.

Wylie, E.C., H.G. Morrison, and J. Healy
1995   The progression of pupils with special educational needs: A comparison of standards. *Oxford Review of Education* 21(3):283-297.

Yinger, R.J.
1979   Routines in teacher planning. *Theory Into Practice* 18:163-169.

Ysseldyke, J.E., M. Vanderwood, and B. Reschly
1994   *Availability of Data on School Completion Outcomes and Indicators.* Technical Report 8. Minneapolis: National Center on Educational Outcomes, University of Minnesota.

Zigmond, N., and J.M. Baker, eds.
1995   Case studies of full inclusion for students with learning disabilities. *Journal of Special Education* 29:109-250.

Zigmond, N., and S. Miller
1992   Improving high school programs. Pp. 17-31 *in Transition from School to Adult Life*, F.R. Rusch, L. Destefano, J. Chadsey-Rusch, L.A. Phelps, and E. Syzmanski, eds. DeKalb, IL: Sycamore Publishing.

CHAPTER 5   ACCOUNTABILITY AND ASSESSMENT

Allington, R.L., and A. McGill-Franzen
1992   Unintended effects of educational reform in New York. *Educational Policy* 4:397-414

Anderson, N.E., F.F. Jenkins, and K.E. Miller
no date   NAEP Inclusion Criteria and Testing Accommodations: Findings from the NEP 1995 Field Test in Mathematics. Educational Testing Service Research Memorandum, Princeton, NJ.

Baxter, G.P., and R.J. Shavelson
1994   Performance assessment. *International Journal of Education Research* 21(3):233-350.

Bennett, R.E.
1995   *Computer-based Testing for Examinees with Disabilities: On the Road to Generalized Accommodation.* Princeton, NJ: Educational Testing Service.

Bennett, R.E., D.A. Rock, B.A. Kaplan, and T. Jirele
1988   Psychometric characteristics. Pp. 83-97 in *Testing Handicapped People*, W.W. Willingham, M. Ragosta, R.E. Bennett, H. Braun, D.A. Rock, and D.E. Powers, eds. Boston, MA: Allyn and Bacon.

Bennett, R.E., and M. Ragosta
1988   Handicapped people. Pp. 17-36 in *Testing Handicapped People*, W.W. Willingham, M. Ragosta, R.E. Bennett, H. Braun, D.A. Rock, and D.E. Powers, eds. Boston, MA: Allyn and Bacon.

Bond, L.A., D. Braskamp, and E.D. Roeber
  1996   *The Status of State Student Assessment Programs in the United States.* Oak Brook, IL: North Central Regional Educational Laboratory and Council of Chief State School Officers.

Braun, H., M. Ragosta, and B. Kaplan
  1988   Predictive validity. Pg. 109-132 in *Testing Handicapped People*, W.W. Willingham, M. Ragosta, R.E. Bennett, H. Braun, D.A. Rock, and D.E. Powers, eds. Boston, MA: Allyn and Bacon.

Breland, H.M., R. Camp, R.J. Jones, M.M. Morris, and D.A. Rock
  1987   *Assessing Writing Skill.* Research Monograph No. 11. New York: College Entrance Examination Board.

Comfort, K.B.
  1995   The Cost of Performance Assessment in Science: The California Perspective. Unpublished paper presented as part of the symposium, The Cost of Performance Assessment Science, at the annual meeting of the National Council on Measurement in Education, San Francisco.

Council of Chief State School Officers
  1995   *State Education Accountability Reports and Indicator Reports: Status of Reports Across the States 1995.* Washington, DC: Council of Chief State School Officers.

Dunbar, S., D. Koretz, and H.D. Hoover
  1991   Quality control in the development and use of performance assessment. *Applied Measurement in Education* 4(4):289-303.

Educational Testing Service
  1992   ETS conference examines the technology of computer-based testing for people with disabilities. *ETS Developments*: 6-7.

Elliott, J., M. Thurlow, and J. Ysseldyke
  1996b   *Assessment Guidelines that Maximize the Participation of Students with Disabilities in Accountability Systems: Characteristics and Considerations.* Synthesis Report 25. Minneapolis: University of Minnesota, National Center on Educational Outcomes.

Elliott, J.L., R.N. Erickson, and M.L. Thurlow
  1996a   State-level Accountability for the Performance of Students with Disabilities: Five Years of Change? Paper presented at the annual meeting of the American Educational Research Association, New York City, April.

Erickson, R.N., and M.L. Thurlow
  1996   *State Special Education Outcomes 1995.* Minneapolis: University of Minnesota, National Center on Educational Outcomes.

Erickson, R.N., M.L. Thurlow, and J.E. Ysseldyke
  1996   *Neglected Numerators, Drifting Denominators, and Fractured Fractions: Determining the Participation Rates for Students with Disabilities in Statewide Assessment Programs.* Minneapolis: University of Minnesota, National Center on Educational Outcomes.

Erickson, R.N., M.L. Thurlow, and K. Thor
  1995   *1994 State Special Education Outcomes.* Minneapolis: University of Minnesota, National Center on Educational Outcomes.

Gao, X., R.J. Shavelson, and G.P. Baxter
  1994   Generalizability of large-scale performance assessments in science: Promises and problems. *Applied Measurement in Education* 7:323-342.

Green, B.F., R.D. Bock, L.G. Humphreys, R.L. Linn, and M.D. Reckase
  1984   *Evaluation Plan for the Computerized Adaptive Vocational Aptitude Battery.* San Diego, CA: Manpower and Personnel Laboratory.

Haertel, E.H., and R.L. Linn
   1996   Comparability. Pp. 59-78 in *Technical Issues in Large-Scale Performance Assessment*, G.W. Phillips, ed. Washington, DC: National Center for Education Statistics.
Hambleton, R.K., and H. Swaminathan
   1985   *Item Response Theory: Principles and Applications*. Hingham, MA: Kluwer Boston, Inc.
Hambleton, R.K., R.M. Jaeger, D. Koretz, R.L. Linn, J. Millman, and S.E. Phillips
   1995   *Review of the Measurement Quality of the Kentucky Instructional Results Information System, 1991-1994*. Frankfort: Office of Education Accountability, Kentucky General Assembly, June.
Koretz, D.
   1996   Assessing Students with Disabilities in Large Scale Assessments. Unpublished paper presented at the annual conference of the Center for Research on Evaluation, Standards, and Student Assessment, Los Angeles, September 1996.
   1992   State and national assessment. In *Encyclopedia of Educational Research*, M.C. Alkin, ed. Sixth Edition. Washington, DC: American Educational Research Association.
Koretz, D., S. Barron, K. Mitchell, and B. Stecher
   1996b   *The Perceived Effects of the Kentucky Instructional Results Information System*. Santa Monica, CA: RAND.
Koretz, D.M., R.L. Linn, S.B. Dunbar, and L.A. Shepard
   1991   The effects of high stakes testing: Preliminary evidence about generalization across conventional tests. In The Effects of High Stakes Testing, R.L. Linn, chair, symposium presented at the annual meetings of the American Educational Research Association and the National Council on Measurement in Education, Chicago, April.
Koretz, D., G. Madaus, E. Haertel, and A. Beaton
   1992   National Educational Standards and Testing: A Response to the Recommendations of the National Council on Education Standards and Testing. Testimony before the U.S. House of Representatives, Education and Labor Committee, Washington, DC, RAND.
Koretz, D., K, Mitchell, S. Barron, and S. Keith
   1996a   *The Perceived Effects of the Maryland School Performance Assessment Program*. Los Angeles: National Center for Research on Evaluation, Standards, and Student Testing, University of California, Los Angeles.
Koretz, D., B. Stecher, S. Klein, and D. McCaffrey
   1994   The Vermont portfolio assessment program: Findings and implications. *Educational Measurement: Issues and Practice* 13(3):5-16.
Linn, R.L.
   1995   *Assessment-based Reform: Challenges to Educational Measurement*. Princeton, NJ: William H. Angoff Memorial Lecture Series, Educational Testing Service.
   1993   Linking results of distinct assessments. *Applied Measurement in Education* 6(1):83-102.
Lyon, G.R.
   1996   Learning disabilities. Pp. 54-76 in *The Future of Children: Special Education for Students with Disabilities* 6(1). Los Altos, CA: Center for the Future of Children, David and Lucille Packard Foundation.
Maryland State Department of Education
   1995   *Requirements and Guidelines for Exemptions, Excuses, and Accommodations for Maryland Statewide Assessment Programs*. Baltimore: Maryland State Department of Education.
McGrew, K.S., M.L. Thurlow, J.G. Shriner, and A.N. Spiegel
   1992   *Inclusion of Students with Disabilities in National and State Data Collection Programs*. Minneapolis: University of Minnesota, National Center on Educational Outcomes.

McGrew K.S., M.L. Thurlow, and A. Spiegel
   1993   An investigation of the exclusion of students with disabilities in national data collection
             programs. *Educational Evaluation and Policy Analysis* 15(3):339-352.
Messick, S.
   1994   The interplay of evidence and consequences in the validation of performance assess-
             ments. *Educational Researcher* 23:13-23.
   1989   Validity. Pp. 13-102 in *Educational Measuremen,* 3rd Edition, R.L. Linn, ed. New
             York: American Council on Education and Macmillan Publishing Company.
Mislevy, R.J.
   1992   *Linking Educational Assessments: Concepts, Issues, Methods, and Prospects.* Princeton,
             NJ: Educational Testing Service.
Monk, D.H.
   1995   The costs of pupil performance assessment: A summary report. *Journal of Education
             Finance* 20(4):363-371.
Morison, P., S.H. White, and M.J. Feuer., eds.
   1996   *The Use of IQ Tests in Special Education Decision Making and Planning.* Board on
             Testing and Assessment, National Research Council. Washington, DC: National Acad-
             emy Press.
National Academy of Education
   1996   *Quality and Utility: The 1994 Trial State Assessment in Reading. The Fourth Report of
             the National Academy of Education Panel on the Evaluation of the NAEP Trial State
             Assessment.* Stanford, CA: Stanford University, National Academy of Education.
   1993   *The Trial State Assessment: Prospects and Realities.* Stanford, CA: Stanford Univer-
             sity, National Academy of Education.
Ordover, E.L., K.B. Boundy, and D.C. Pullin
   1996   Students with Disabilities and the Implementation of Standards-based Education Re-
             form: Legal Issues and Implications. Unpublished paper prepared for Committee on
             Goals 2000 and the Inclusion of Students with Disabilities, June 1996. Center for Law
             and Education.
Phillips, G.
   1995   Unpublished memo to Jeanne Griffith and Roy Truby, dated August 1, 1995, summariz-
             ing preliminary results of the 1995 field test.
Phillips, S.E.
   1994   High-stakes testing accommodations: Validity versus disabled rights. *Applied Mea-
             surement in Education* 7(2):93-120.
Picus, L.O.
   1995   *Estimating the Costs of Student Assessment in North Carolina and Kentucky: A State-
             level Analysis.* Los Angeles: National Center for Research on Evaluation, Standards,
             and Student Testing, University of California, Los Angeles.
Plake, B.
   1976   The Comparability of Equal Raw Scores for Children at Different Grade Levels: An
             Issue in "Out-of-Level" Testing. Unpublished doctoral dissertation, University of Iowa.
Popham, W.J., K.L. Cruse, S.C. Rankin, P.D. Sandifer, and P.L. Williams
   1985   Measurement-driven instruction: It's on the road. *Phi Delta Kappan* 66(9)(May):628-
             634.
Pullin, Diana
   1994   Learning to work. *Harvard Educational Review* 64(1):31-54.
Ragosta, M., and B. Kaplan
   1988   Views of disabled students. Pp. 57-70 in *Testing Handicapped People*, W.W.
             Willingham, M. Ragosta, R.E. Bennett, H. Braun, D.A. Rock and D.E. Powers, eds.
             Boston, MA: Allyn and Bacon.

Shavelson, R.J., G.P. Baxter, and J. Pine
    1992   Performance assessments: Political rhetoric and measurement reality. *Educational Researcher* 21(4):22-27.
Shavelson, R.J., G.P. Baxter, and X. Gao
    1993   Sampling variability of performance assessments. *Journal of Educational Measurement* 30(3):215-232.
Shepard, L.A.
    1990   Inflated test score gains: Is the problem of old norms or teaching the test? *Educational Measurement: Issues and Practice* 9(3):15-22.
    1989   Identification of mild handicaps. Pp. 545-572 in *Educational Measurement,* 3rd Edition, R.L. Linn, ed. New York: American Council on Education and Macmillan Publishing Co.
    1988   *The Harm of Measurement-Driven Instruction.* Paper presented at the annual meeting of the American Educational Research Association, Washington, DC, April. New York: American Council on Education and Macmillan.
Shepard, L.A., and K.C. Dougherty
    1991   Effects of high-stakes testing on instruction. Unpublished paper for The Effects of High Stakes Testing symposium presented at the annual meetings of the American Educational Research Association and the National Council on Measurement in Education, Chicago, April.
Sherman, S.W., and N.M. Robinson, eds.
    1982   *Ability Testing of Handicapped People: Dilemma for Government, Science, and the Public.* Panel on Testing of Handicapped People, Committee on Ability Testing, National Research Council. Washington, DC: National Academy Press.
Shriner, J.G., and M.L. Thurlow
    1992   *State Special Education Outcomes 1991.* Minneapolis: University of Minnesota, National Center on Educational Outcomes.
Stecher, B.M., and S.P. Klein
    1997   The cost of science performance assessments in large-scale testing programs. *Educational Evaluation and Policy Analysis* 19(1):1-14.
Taylor, H.C., and J.T. Russell
    1939   The relationship of validity coefficients to the practical effectiveness of test in selection: Discussion and tables. *Journal of Applied Psychology* 23:565-578.
Thissen, D.
    1990   Reliability and measurement precision. Pp. 161-186 in *Computerized Adaptive Testing: A Primer*, H. Wainer, ed. Mawah, NJ: Erlbaum.
Thurlow, M.L.
    1994   *National and State Perspectives on Performance Assessment and Students with Disabilities.* Reston, VA: Council for Exceptional Children.
Thurlow, M.L., D.L. Scott, and J.E. Ysseldyke
    1995a   *A Compilation of States' Guidelines for Accommodations in Assessments for Students with Disabilities* Synthesis Report 18. Minneapolis: National Center on Educational Outcomes, University of Minnesota.
    1995b   *A Compilation of States' Guidelines for Including Students with Disabilities in Assessments.* Synthesis Report 17. Minneapolis: National Center on Educational Outcomes, University of Minnesota.
Thurlow, M.L., J.E. Ysseldyke, and C.L. Anderson
    1995c   *High School Graduation Requirements: What's Happening for Students with Disabilities?* Minneapolis: National Center on Educational Outcomes, University of Minnesota.

Thurlow, M.L., J.E. Ysseldyke, and D.L. Scott
   1996   *Students with Disabilities in State Accountability Reports.* Minneapolis: National Center on Educational Outcomes, University of Minnesota.
Thurlow, M.L., J.E. Ysseldyke, and B. Silverstein
   1995d   Testing accommodations for students with disabilities. *Remedial and Special Education* 16(5):260-270.
   1993   *Testing Accommodations for Students with Disabilities: A Review of the Literature.* Synthesis Report 4. Minneapolis: National Center on Educational Outcomes, University of Minnesota.
U.S. Department of Education
   1995   *Seventeenth Annual Report to Congress on the Implementation of the Individuals with Disabilities Education Act.* Washington, DC: Office of Special Education Programs.
Wainer, H., and R.J. Mislevy
   1990   Item response theory, item calibration and proficiency estimation. Pp. 65-102 in *Computerized Adaptive Testing: A Primer*, H. Wainer, ed. Mawah, NJ: Erlbaum.
Wightman, L.F.
   1993   *Test Takers with Disabilities: A Summary of Data from Special Administrations of the LSAT.* Research Report 93-03. Newton, PA: Law School Admission Council.
Willingham, W.W.
   1988a   Introduction. Pp. 1-16 in *Testing Handicapped People*, W.W. Willingham, M. Ragosta, R.E. Bennett, H. Braun, D.A. Rock, and D.E. Powers, eds. Boston, MA: Allyn and Bacon.
   1988b   Discussion and conclusions. Pp. 143-185 in *Testing Handicapped People*, W.W. Willingham, M. Ragosta, R.E. Bennett, H. Braun, D.A. Rock, and D.E. Powers, eds. Boston, MA: Allyn and Bacon.
Willingham, W.W., M. Ragosta, R.E. Bennett, H. Braun, D.A. Rock, and D.E. Powers, eds.
   1988   *Testing Handicapped People.* Boston, MA: Allyn and Bacon.
Ysseldyke, J., R. Erickson, B. Gabrys, J. Haigh, S. Trimble, and B. Gong
   1996   *A Comparison of State Assessment Systems in Maryland and Kentucky With a Focus on Participation of Students with Disabilities State Assessment Series, MD/KY Report 1.* Minneapolis: National Center on Educational Outcomes, University of Minnesota.
Ysseldyke, J.E., M.L. Thurlow, K.S. McGrew, and J.G. Shriner
   1994   *Recommendations for Making Decisions About the Participation of Students with Disabilities in Statewide Assessment Programs* Synthesis Report 15. Minneapolis: National Center on Educational Outcomes, University of Minnesota.

APPENDICES

APPENDIX
A

Glossary

accommodation: A change in some aspect of a child's educational program. A testing accommodation is a change in the way that a test is administered or responded to by the person tested. Testing accommodations are intended to offset or "correct" for distortions in scores caused by a disability. Examples of testing accommodations include braille and large-print versions of the test for students with visual disabilities, scribes for students who are not physically capable of writing, smaller or separate testing settings for students whose disabilities cause them to be easily distracted, and additional testing time.

accountability: The concept of holding schools, administrators, teachers, and/or students responsible for students' academic performance. Accountability mechanisms vary across states and local districts in the types of school and student data that are used and in whether rewards or sanctions are attached to performance. But most forms of accountability include student standardized test scores as a key element and report the information publicly.

ADA: Americans with Disabilities Act of 1992, a federal antidiscrimination law protecting individuals with disabilities.

alternate assessment: In standards-based reform, an assessment that is substituted for the common large-scale assessment for some students with disabilities; alternate assessments are intended to evaluate students' work and performance on different standards or content. Alternate assessments require more than an accommodation and result in a different test form and/or procedure.

alignment: In standards-based reform, the concept of connecting educational goals, curriculum, instruction, and assessment so that all are consistent and working toward the same purposes.

assessment: Process of collecting data to make decisions about students;

measuring what students know and can do. Testing is the most common form of assessment.

cognitive disability: Disabilities that affect students' learning and thinking process.

competitive employment: Employment in which the work of an individual with a disability is performed in an integrated setting and is not subsidized by public funds.

constructivism or constructivist learning: An approach to teaching and learning that asserts that learners "construct" their own understanding by integrating new information with their own experiences and prior knowledge. Constructivist instruction often seeks to provide students with active learning projects, cognitively demanding projects, group interaction, and opportunities to synthesize knowledge from various sources and content areas.

content standards: As defined by the Goals 2000: Educate America Act of 1994, content standards are "broad descriptions of the knowledge and skills students should acquire in a particular subject area" (P.L. 103-227, Sec. 3[4]).

disability: As defined in the federal regulations for the Individuals with Disabilities Education Act, "'children with disabilities' means those children evaluated in accordance with 300.530-300.534 as having mental retardation, hearing impairments including deafness, speech or language impairments, visual impairments including blindness, serious emotional disturbance, orthopedic impairments, autism, traumatic brain injury, other health impairments, specific learning disabilities, deaf-blindness, or multiple disabilities." See Box 3-1 for federal definitions of each of these categories.

disaggregation: Separating and analyzing group data, such as student test scores, into smaller units based on such characteristics as race, ethnicity, gender, and disability.

Education for All Handicapped Children Act of 1975:   Public Law 94-142, the first compulsory federal special education law; mandates a free, appropriate public education for all students with disabilities between the ages of 3 and 21. In 1990 the name was changed to the Individuals with Disabilities Education Act (IDEA).

eligibility: Eligibility for special education services under the Individuals with Disabilities Education Act rests on two criteria: (1) the student meets the definition of one of the 13 disabilities (see "disability" above) and (2) the student requires special education or related services in order to receive an appropriate education.

free appropriate public education: As defined in the Individuals with Disabilities Education Act, special education and related services that (1) have been provided at public expense, under public supervision and direction, and without charge, (2) meet the standards of the state educational agency, (3) include an appropriate preschool, elementary, or secondary school education in the state involved, and (4) are provided in conformity with the individualized education program (IEP).

general education: Instruction and educational services regularly provided to all students in a school system.

Goals 2000: Educate America Act: P.L. 103-227, enacted by Congress in 1994. This law provides a list of ambitious goals intended to improve education for all students and authorizes federal grants to states and school districts to set high standards and carry out reforms tied to standards.

high-stakes test: Assessments that carry serious consequences for students or for educators. Their outcomes determine such important things as promotion to the next grade, graduation, or college admission, and often include teacher or school "report cards."

IEP team: The following participants meet to develop an individualized education program (IEP) for a child: (1) a representative of the public agency, other than the child's teacher, who is qualified to provide or supervise the provision of special education, (2) the child's teacher, (3) one or both of the child's parents, (4) the child, if appropriate, and (5) other individuals at the discretion of the parent or agency.

Improving America's Schools Act of 1994 (IASA): P.L. 103-382 amended the major federal elementary and secondary school aid programs, including the Title I program for disadvantaged children, to promote high standards for learning for all children.

individualized education program (IEP): A written document required by law to be developed for each child with a disability. The IEP includes (1) a statement of the student's present level of educational performance, (2) a statement of annual goals and short-term objectives for achieving those goals, (3) a statement of services to be provided and the extent of the student's participation in the general education program, (4) the start date and expected duration of services, (5) evaluation procedures and criteria for monitoring progress, and (6) a statement of the transition services needed for students beginning before or at age 16.

Individuals with Disabilities Education Act (IDEA): The primary federal law that provides funding and criteria for the education of children with disabilities. Legislation enacted in 1990 reauthorized and changed the name of the Education for All Handicapped Children Act to the IDEA.

large-scale assessment: Standardized tests and other forms of assessment designed to be administered to large numbers of individuals and to provide information about performance on a standardized scale.

least restrictive environment (LRE):   As defined in the Individuals with Disabilities Education Act (IDEA) regulations (300.550), each public agency shall ensure: "(1) that to the maximum extent appropriate, children with disabilities . . . are educated with children who are nondisabled; and (2) that special classes, separate schooling or other removal of children with disabilities from the regular educational environment occurs only when the nature or severity of the disability is such that education in regular classes with the use of supplementary aids and services cannot be achieved satisfactorily."

local educational agency (LEA):   A public board of education or other public authority legally constituted within a state for administrative control or direction of, or to perform a service function for, public elementary and secondary schools in a city, county, township, school district, or other political subdivision of a state.

National Longitudinal Transition Study of Special Education Students (NLTS):   A study funded by the Office of Special Education Programs of "a sample of handicapped students, encompassing the full range of handicapping conditions, examining their educational progress while in special education and their occupational, educational, and independent living status after graduating from secondary school or otherwise leaving special education" (PL 98-199, Sec. 618).   The study sample consists of more that 8,000 students who were receiving special education during the 1985-86 school year and were between the ages of 15 and 21.

Office of Special Education Programs (OSEP):   The division of the U.S. Department of Education responsible for administering educational programs for children with disabilities.

opportunity to learn: The concept of determining the programs, staff, and other resources sufficient to enable students to meet challenging content and performance standards.

performance standards: As defined in the Goals 2000: Educate America Act of 1994, performance standards are "concrete examples and explicit definitions of what students have to know and be able to do to demonstrate that such students are proficient in the skills and knowledge framed by the content standards" (P.L. 103-227, Sec 3[9]).

post-school outcomes: Goals and achievements expected after high school graduation.   Outcomes include employment, education, independent living, and community participation.

reliability: In testing, reliability refers to the consistency of performance across different instances of measurement—for example, whether results are consistent across raters, times of measurement, or sets of test items.

Section 504:   Section 504 of the Rehabilitation Act of 1973, a federal law that prohibits discrimination in educational and other contexts against individuals with disabilities.

severe disability: Disability requiring extensive continued assistance in more than one major life activity.

special education: As defined in the Individuals with Disabilities Education Act regulations (300.17), special education means specially designed instruction, at no cost, to meet the unique needs of a child with a disability, including: (1) instruction conducted in the classroom, in the home, in hospitals, in institutions, and in other settings and (2) instruction in physical education.

standardized test: Tests that are administered and scored under conditions uniform to all students. Standardization is necessary to make test scores comparable across individuals.

standards-based reform: An approach to education reform that sets standards of performance in designated subject areas as a means of strengthening the content of school curricula, increasing the motivation and effort of students, teachers, and school systems, and thereby improving student achievement. The reform assumes high standards for all students.

state educational agency (SEA):   The agency primarily responsible for the state supervision of public elementary and secondary schools.

systemic reform: An approach to reform that attempts to make fundamental and interrelated changes in an entire educational system (school, district, or state) rather than changes that address only a specific group of students, a particular instructional area, or a single aspect of the curriculum.

Title I of the Elementary and Secondary Education Act: A major federal program, first enacted in 1965, that provides funds to school districts to improve learning opportunities of educationally disadvantaged children residing in low-income areas. Title I was amended in 1994 by the Improving America's Schools Act (see above) to encourage states to set high educational standards for disadvantaged children.

validity: Refers to whether or not a test measures what it is supposed to measure and whether appropriate inferences can be drawn from test results. Validity is judged from many types of evidence.

APPENDIX
B

Workshop Summary: Students with Disabilities and Standards-Based Reform

To help understand the perspectives of those representing students with disabilities as well as those of the policy makers and educators implementing standards-based reform, the committee held a one-day workshop on October 27, 1995. Eleven representatives from groups based in Washington, D.C., made brief presentations organized around three questions posed by the committee in its letter of invitation:

• What does the group you represent see as the two or three major, unresolved issues related to standards-based reform and students with disabilities?

• Under what conditions would standards and assessments, as they are currently being defined nationally and in the states, be most likely to benefit students with disabilities?

• What will be required to include students with disabilities fully in standards, assessment, and accountability systems? What are the incentives and disincentives to do so?

The presenters then participated in an informal discussion with the committee and answered members' additional questions. This appendix summarizes the presentations.

The first group of presenters represented organizations that work on behalf of people with disabilities. Christopher Button, the director of governmental activities for the United Cerebral Palsy Association (UCPA), was the first presenter. Button argued that children with disabilities deserve access to school, which means access to the general curriculum and the accountability system. She views the low standards that accompany the labeling and stereotyping of children with disabilities as a major hindrance to their learning. Inclusion is the answer to this problem. She pointed out that Kentucky has been successful in this area because it has included the overwhelming majority of its students in the state assessment. Agreeing that family involvement is critical to student success, Button noted that currently families participate through the individualized education program (IEP) process, although the nature of their involvement varies considerably. She was uncertain about what mechanisms could be used under standards-based reform to involve parents. UCPA sees technology as providing some of the answers to individualizing curriculum and assessments for students with disabilities. Although children with disabilities should be part of the general curriculum, Button thought that the standards would have to be operationalized individually for some children.

The second presenter was Eileen Ahearn, a senior policy analyst for the National Association of State Directors of Special Education (NASDE). Ahearn also emphasized the participation of children with disabilities in standards and assessments. She commented on the problem of the lack of consistency from school to school in how disabilities are defined and children with disabilities are treated. In her view, greater access to assessments is an effective way of bringing accountability to special education programs. It would emphasize the measuring of learning outcomes rather than only monitoring inputs, such as the number of teachers with appropriate certification. Ahearn argued that: "there needs to be accountability, student by student, for individual student outcomes. . . . Schools really are responsible for the achievement of every student who is there. It is important that schools be required to accommodate—and to modify in order to accommodate—the needs of every individual student."

She also stressed the need for research on the effects of including children with disabilities in the general education program. She admitted that the integration of the IEP-based system with a standards system would be tricky because students with disabilities are often viewed as part of a different curriculum—one conceived of as a "drill and practice program" or in some way separate from the general curriculum. She believes that the IEP should be retained, but that it should be based on the system standards. If adjustments need to be made, they could be made in such areas as the length of time over which students are expected to meet the standards or through accommodations in testing. Ahearn sees including children with disabilities in the standards reforms as helping to change the attitude that schools are not responsible for students with disabilities in the same way they are for other students. She acknowledged, however, that it will be difficult to create incentives that encourage this attitude change. Similarly, she acknowledged that currently there were no solutions to how a standards system might accommodate students who meet performance standards at a slower pace than expected.

The third presenter, Nancy Safer, is the interim executive director of the Council for Exceptional Children (CEC). Safer sees students with disabilities as a good test case for standards: if standards-based reform cannot work for them and for other at-risk students, it probably should not be implemented. "So one of the things we have to talk about is what are the implications of [a] standards-based assessment that does not work for 25 to 33 percent of our students." Solving the problem of standards for students with disabilities has implications for a much broader range of students.

She is concerned about creating accommodations for standardized tests; for instance, do accommodations automatically mean that the tests are no longer standardized? However, she suggested that if standards were more generalized they would necessarily include more students. "If your standards were organized around big ideas or big concepts, then you have some choices as to how refined within those concepts you organize [the] particular . . . content that you are trying to assess." However, too often, the standards are defined narrowly from a disciplinary perspective, rather than broadly, on the basis of the skills and knowledge people need in life. Safer agreed that, if assessments were viewed as report cards for the schools, there would be an incentive to exclude children with disabilities from the assessments.

The fourth presenter, Joseph Ballard, is the director of CEC's department of public policy. Ballard is mainly concerned with questions of how federal, state, and local programs will interact. Like other presenters, he also thinks that standards-based reform will be an effective way of including children with disabilities in the general curriculum. In his view, adjustments to standards and assessments for children with disabilities should be made within the context of the IEP. CEC advocates that the standards curriculum and assessments be specifically referenced in students' IEPs.

The final presenter in the first group was Speed Davis, the executive assistant to the chair of the National Council on Disability. Davis argued that the participation of children with disabilities in standards-based reform would help all students. "If it is done right, if it is done well, if it is done with the right attitude, inclusionary education not only works well for children with disabilities but it works for the entire school and the entire school system." He believes that the biggest barriers are societal attitudes about people with disabilities and funding mechanisms that encourage the segregation of children with disabilities.

The group discussion that followed these presentations ranged from support for participation to family involvement. Button said, "The IEP too often, because it is not tied to the general curriculum, results in a watered-down curriculum because of the automatic assumptions that general educators and special educators too often have about the children, particularly children with severe disabilities, as not being able to do the general curriculum." She maintained that the participation of children with disabilities in standards-based reform could help solve this problem, and that giving these students more time to achieve some of the standards would be a useful accommodation.

The participants agreed that the definition of participation depends on the definition of the general curriculum. Safer is concerned that, if states devise alternative content for children with disabilities, they could effectively exclude them from the standards. Rather, she advocates "representing as much as possible very discrete levels relative to acquisition of particular concepts, so that everyone fits within [them] rather than trying to come up with really different content." Ahearn added that "the broad standards, if they are well chosen and comprehensive and yet at the right level . . . should apply to everyone. It is when you move to the specification that you get the differentiation . . . into an entirely separate curriculum for a very small percentage of students."

Safer is concerned about the comparability of assessments that have been adjusted for children with disabilities. She believes the key to accommodations is to ensure that knowledge is accurately measured without interference from the way it was expressed. Ahearn acknowledged the technical problems in adjusting assessments.

The participants agreed that the way assessment results are reported will affect many things, including how people feel about the participation of children with disabilities. The suggestion was made that schools be judged on how well they do in improving the performance of students with disabilities as well as a range of other students. The presenters also agreed that families need to be involved but were uncertain about the best mechanism to facilitate this participation, particularly since parental involvement in such decisions as whether a student should be included in a state assessment was not part of the concept of family involvement when the IEP process was first designed.

The second group of presenters represented organizations of education policy makers and practitioners with an interest in standards and the participation of students with disabilities. The first presenter in this group was John Barth, a senior education associate at the National Education Goals Panel. Barth noted that there are now unofficial standards that are lower for children with disabilities. He believes that including children with disabilities in explicit, official standards would help solve the problem. In his view, "IEPs have become wonderful process documents, but have ceased to be educational documents." However, he said that, if standards were fully implemented, educators would have to acknowledge that all students learn in different ways and at different paces. "If we are genuinely committed to our standards and in raising every child to that level of performance, then we are going to have to treat almost every child with an IEP." He acknowledged that this might be impractical in the long term because of a lack of resources.

Barth drew on the New Standards project, a consortium of states and local districts, to argue that standards include five different components: (1) content standards, (2) performance standards, (3) scoring rubrics defining what performance is good enough to demonstrate mastery of the standards, (4) benchmark examples of student work, and (5) feedback on those benchmarks. In his view, children with disabilities should be included in the first two components of standards, but the final three components should be treated more flexibly. He believes that the standards debate is still focused on the first component of standards and needs to get beyond it and the second component before accommodations for children with disabilities can be discussed. "It seems to me it is inherently unfair not to have high expectations for all students."

Barth also believes that the participation of children with disabilities in standards-based reform would help hold educators responsible for these students' learning and performance. "I am fearful that if we allow the exclusion of certain categories of children from the assessment process that we will destroy the feedback loop for them and, secondly, we will allow school systems and schools, who are going to be held politically accountable for their performance, to push those students who threaten to lower their scores out of the test loop, off to the side, and conceivably ignore them."

The second presenter was John MacDonald, the director of the state leadership center for the Council of Chief State School Officers. MacDonald argued that the Individuals with Disabilities Education Act (IDEA) is not connected to national reform legislation. In his view, the IDEA's policy framework keeps students with disabilities separate from state and local development of standards-based reform in classrooms. Students with disabilities are still viewed primarily as a special population. . . . What will be required is one standard for all children, not the dual standard afforded by the current legislation and imposed on the states and local districts by IDEA and the U.S. Department of Education.

MacDonald sees the current incentive system as favoring the exclusion of children with disabilities, but agreed that their participation in standards would help hold educators accountable for special education. He thinks that Goals 2000 is a useful backup for what states wanted to do already. "I liken Goals 2000 to a federal block grant to states and local districts to leverage what they want to do, what [they] are doing anyway." In contrast, he noted the growing perception that, because special education has been underfunded by the federal government, it represents a threat to the fiscal stability of the general education program in states and localities. In his view, to the extent that local education budgets have to compensate for declining federal and state revenues, communities will see the inclusion of students with disabilities in standards as another burden, and "it is my belief that you are going to really hear a huge outcry."

The third presenter was Shirley Schwartz, representing the Council of Great City Schools. Schwartz also favors including children with disabilities in standards-based reform. One of her organization's concerns is the overrepresentation of minority, poor, and limited-English-proficient students in special education. She is also concerned about adding more disability categories to the IDEA because member districts report that certain student behaviors lead to socially constructed categories of disability. Consequently, additional categories will place urban students at risk for that type of identification. In addition, the council has found that the IEP process often does not work because "it focuses on procedural compliance and provides no measure of student progress." She feels that including standards in the IEP would help keep special education programs accountable. The council views multiple assessment measures and more authentic assessments as a "potent tool for equity."

Although Schwartz believes that overall participation is necessary, there may still be students with disabilities who need to be in nonacademic programs. "We see the need to develop some different goals and different standards focused on such things as independent living and self-determination." She emphasized the need for networking, professional development, and the flow of information across districts so that educators could learn from each other.

The fourth presenter in this group was Patricia Sullivan, the director of education legislation for the Committee on Human Resources at the National Governors Association. Sullivan said that governors are frustrated with the IDEA for two reasons: it is an unfunded mandate, and there is no flexibility at either the state or the local level. However, the governors support the participation of students with disabilities in standards-based reform. "There was very much a willingness to do that, particularly in exchange for some sort of flexibility, whatever that may be, and it is often undefined, just the perception of trying to get some ability to have some influence over how this program works at the state and local levels." Sullivan noted that, beginning with their education summit in Charlottesville in 1989, the governors have supported the concept of high standards for all students. "There was a coming together around that word very deliberately, but probably not an understanding of how far we had to go to do that and what it would take for all students to be able to achieve the highest standards."

Jeff Schneider, a senior policy analyst at the National Center for Innovation in the National Education Association (NEA), was the next presenter. The NEA also supports the participation of children with disabilities in standards-based reforms, but only when it is done well. That means four things. First, teachers should be adequately trained to deal with students with disabilities. Second, there is effective advocacy by parents of students with disabilities and by organizations working on behalf of children with disabilities. Third, adequate resources are available to ensure that money spent on children with disabilities does not worsen conditions for other students. Fourth, national health insurance is needed to make certain that children with disabilities have adequate health care. Schneider sees three issues raised by Goals 2000: whether the notion of all students meeting higher standards means children with disabilities; who decides about modifications in the standards; and on what basis those modifications are made. He agreed that there would be strong incentives for schools to exclude children with disabilities. He also suggested that it may be necessary to have the same guidelines on criteria for excluding students with disabilities from standards and assessment across states so that state-by-state comparisons will be accurate.

Barbara Huff, the executive director of the Federation of Families for Children's Mental Health, was the final presenter. Huff spoke about children with mental health or emotional problems. In her view, discussing standards is premature for this population because the immediate task is to keep these children in school. "Until people get committed to keeping our kids in school, [standards are] . . . the last on the list of priorities right now, with some of the things we are facing." She feels this population is intellectually capable of being part of the standards and assessments, but that it needs more support in the day-to-day learning process. She also believes that social and emotional development should be assessed as well as content standards. Unlike other populations that might be overclassified as having disabilities, Huff indicated that schools are less likely to identify students with emotional disorders as disabled. "There is also a lack of early identification and systematic intervention."

She emphasized the need to train school personnel adequately to handle emotional and behavioral problems. "In other words, steps will have to be taken to ensure that our children are academically challenged. Steps will have to be taken to ensure that our children attend school. Steps will have to be taken to ensure that our children are not discarded and that there is a zero reject principle: Schools cannot give up on our kids." Huff argued that the community also needs to be part of the support system for children with emotional and behavioral problems. "I do not believe that it is totally the schools' responsibility for the supports and services that begin to accommodate kids in schools."

Huff added, "I think it is going to take more than standards-based assessment to reverse the devastating trends and practices that currently result in poor outcomes for children with serious emotional disturbances. However, standards that are formulated with system change in mind can provide the impetus to help schools begin to address the issue in a comprehensive fashion."

In the general discussion that followed the formal presentations, the group discussed definitions of standards, accommodations, jurisdictional questions, and teacher training. In discussing standards, Schwartz said children with disabilities are included in the development of standards and assessments but she still sees an ongoing disconnect between IEPs and high, general standards. Barth added, "My read on all of the national standards documents is they all got it wrong. They are all too detailed and too explicit for a set of national standards, which should have been a simple articulation of what the nation thinks kids need to know in each of these various areas. Then the states would add more detail to that process." Schwartz agreed, saying that she thought local districts need to adjust state standards to local needs. MacDonald thinks that the IDEA is too top-down, restricting local decision making. He sees this arrangement as prolonging the debate on standards.

In response to the discussion about accommodating students with disabilities within a standards framework, committee member Daniel Koretz said, "I am frankly . . . puzzled [about] what a standard would look like that accommodates students without differentiating among them." The presenters were also puzzled. Schwartz added: "I think the point is not to lower expectations." Barth reiterated that the commonality among all students would be on the level of the content and the performance components of the standards and that the adjustments would be made on the other three components. MacDonald added that "the essence of instruction is reaching each youngster. That requires differentiation." Barth thinks it might be helpful to look at standards in terms of progress from a baseline. He also commented that adjustments should be made, not by lowering the standards, but by giving an individual child more time and more resources.

Barth emphasized the need for teacher training. He said that there is insufficient federal financial assistance for the professional development of special education teachers because the large majority of it goes to general education teachers. Schneider agreed on the importance of teacher training, adding that schools also need to be reformed from the beginning levels on. "What we are kind of shooting for with kids is that all kids will have a small 'IEP,' because every child should have an individualized education, and the only way to do that is to have the decision-making patterns in the school allow that to happen." He also feels that, because of high turnover in principals and superintendents, the emphasis for change needs to be placed on teachers. The key is to ensure that decisions are based on what is best for students rather than for any other group.

The group agreed that standards and the participation of children with disabilities would have important political consequences. MacDonald said, "I think the states are very, very wary of setting any kind of standards that they feel cannot be met or are going to end up having the state look less adequate in terms of what it is providing." Sullivan added that there are problems with political accountability because short-term or one-term governors will not be around to see standards fully implemented. Barth is concerned that using assessment results too much for accountability purposes will ignore the feedback for students. He believes that the primary function of standards and assessments should be tracking student progress rather than school progress. Sullivan thinks that implementation decisions will and should be made at the local rather than the state or federal levels. MacDonald agreed: "I think the faster we free up the system to be able to allow the locals to do this kind of stuff, the better off we are going to be."

Using the *Prospects* Data to Report on the Achievement of Students with Disabilities

INTRODUCTION

In 1988, Congress mandated a "national longitudinal study of eligible children" to assess the effect of Chapter 1 (now renamed Title I) on students' academic achievement and other measures of school success. This study, titled *Prospects: The Congressionally Mandated Study of Educational Opportunity and Growth,* was designed to evaluate the short- and long-term consequences of Chapter 1 program participation by following large national samples of public school-children in three grade cohorts, as well as their parents, teachers, and principals. Baseline data were collected in spring 1991 for third and seventh grade students and in fall 1991 for first grade students.

There were three stages of sampling for Prospects: (1) selection of a sample of school districts, (2) selection of a sample of schools within sampled districts, and (3) subsampling of students, but only in very large schools. Within most sampled schools, all students enrolled in all classrooms containing the target sample grades were included in the sample. Thus, the Prospects study includes all enrolled students within designated grades with no exclusions on the basis of disability, lack of English proficiency, or any other reason. Thus, Prospects was designed to include approximately 7 to 10 percent more students compared with other national studies. If a student with a disability was excused from participating in some activities on which data were gathered, (e.g., achievement testing, self-administered questionnaire), every attempt was made to complete the remainder of the data collection protocol for that student.

A rich collection of information was gathered, including responses to a district Chapter 1 coordinator questionnaire, a school and program questionnaire (completed by principal or other staff member), a classroom teacher questionnaire, a student questionnaire, the Comprehensive Test of Basic Skills, a parent questionnaire, as well as student record information and a student profile (ratings completed by the teacher).

The study was designed as a six-year longitudinal study for evaluating Chapter 1. However, funding for the study was terminated before it was completed. In these analyses, we therefore use only the first two years of the study, 1991 and 1992, and use only the data for the third grade cohort. The design was national in scope and focused on cohorts in grades 1, 3, and 7, with oversampling of low-income districts and schools. The sample include 337 schools, with 10,333 students in the third grade cohort. For a detailed description of the study, see U.S. Department of Education (1993). In this appendix we refer to the program as Chapter 1.

SIMPLE POINT ESTIMATES OF ACHIEVEMENT

By far the most common method of assessing and reporting achievement based on standardized tests is to report single, point estimates or *cohort* scores, perhaps broken down by group categories. The most common statistics are either to report median or mean scores, by selected grades. Because the reported scores are usually based on a national probability distribution, individual student scores are measured relative to the national population of students in a given grade. Institutional scores (by district or school) are aggregates of individual scores and allow for the same comparisons—ignoring within-institution variation.

Examples of third and fourth grade Comprehensive Test of Basic Skills reading and math scores, from the Prospects Study, appear in Table C-1.[1] Normal curve equivalents (NCEs) are used as the basic metric.[2] The table provides means and standard deviations for the total population of students tested and relevant subpopulations. The third set of columns—change scores—is an individual change score based only on students taking both the third and fourth grade tests.

The information conveyed is certainly relevant. The total population, which is a sample of students in schools with high concentrations of Chapter 1 students, is below the national mean of 50 on each test, as expected. And between the third and fourth grades, students decline relative to the national norms—more in math

---

[1] The scores reported in this appendix are unweighted total reading and total math for the third grade sample, although we focus on the fourth grade follow-up for most of the analysis. The fourth grade tests, administered in 1992, included 90 reading test items (40 vocabulary, 50 comprehension) and 94 math items (44 computation, 50 concepts and applications). The subtest reliabilites are between .89 and .94 for the total population.

[2] Normal curve equivalents are used because national percentile rankings are not interval-level data. One of the problems with this transformation is that the very lowest and highest ends of the distribution are compressed. This tends to inflate very low-end scores and deflate very high-end scores. The lower end inflation may affect this population, which has quite a few test scores below the 10th national percentile.

TABLE C-1   Third and Fourth Grade Prospects Achievement Test Data, 1991-1992

	Third Grade		Fourth Grade		Change Scores	
	Reading	Math	Reading	Math	Reading	Math
Total Population						
Mean	46.8	47.7	45.4	45.4	−1.1	−2.7
Standard Deviation	20.6	20.2	20.5	22.0	12.8	14.6
N	13,431	13,167	10,584	10,584	7,906	7,692
Free Lunch						
Mean	41.0	43.0	39.0	39.9	−1.6	−3.1
Standard Deviation	19.0	18.9	18.1	20.1	12.5	14.3
N	4,752	4,696	4,304	4,282	3,109	3,064
Non-Free Lunch						
Mean	55.1	54.9	53.8	53.1	−0.9	−2.1
Standard Deviation	19.2	19.2	19.7	21.4	12.8	14.3
N	5,890	5,744	4,817	4,674	3,891	3,757
Females						
Mean	48.6	48.4	47.5	46.4	−0.8	−2.3
Standard Deviation	19.6	19.4	20.0	21.1	12.2	13.6
N	6,683	6,562	5,223	5,125	4,001	3,897
Males						
Mean	45.2	47.1	43.6	44.7	−1.5	−3.0
Standard Deviation	21.5	20.9	20.8	22.8	13.3	15.0
N	6,625	6,489	5,204	5,101	3,903	3,793
African American						
Mean	37.3	38.3	36.0	35.6	−1.7	−3.0
Standard Deviation	18.3	18.4	17.3	19.1	12.9	14.4
N	2,824	2,801	1,984	1,976	1,524	1,507
Asian American						
Mean	47.4	55.5	48.8	59.2	1.6	1.2
Standard Deviation	19.6	20.0	19.1	21.7	11.4	13.8
N	604	596	469	461	376	369
Hispanic American						
Mean	37.4	41.2	36.2	38.3	1.2	−3.9
Standard Deviation	19.0	19.1	18.0	19.5	12.7	14.0
N	2,125	2,078	1,920	1,889	1,398	1,366
Other American						
Mean	46.2	47.0	43.9	45.3	−2.2	−2.1
Standard Deviation	19.1	19.1	19.0	20.8	11.4	13.2
N	283	278	195	191	150	142
White American						
Mean	53.4	52.8	52.1	50.8	−1.2	−2.7
Standard Deviation	19.5	19.3	19.8	21.5	12.9	14.5
N	6,605	6,423	5,132	4,992	4,027	3,880
Disabled						
Mean	41.7	42.7	40.2	39.9	−1.2	−2.9
Standard Deviation	22.6	21.4	20.4	22.4	12.4	14.7
N	1,152	1,124	821	796	582	562

TABLE C-1   *Continued*

	Third Grade		Fourth Grade		Change Scores	
	Reading	Math	Reading	Math	Reading	Math
Emotional Disability						
Mean	36.3	35.2	33.5	31.5	−1.6	−3.4
Standard Deviation	21.0	21.7	18.5	22.9	12.6	17.0
N	95	98	85	81	56	52
Learning Disability						
Mean	27.1	30.3	29.6	29.3	−0.5	−2.3
Standard Deviation	18.6	17.5	15.8	17.1	12.1	12.2
N	286	278	217	209	133	127
Physical Disability						
Mean	44.7	45.7	43.3	43.5	−1.2	−2.4
Standard Deviation	21.4	21.1	19.1	20.5	12.7	15.2
N	203	189	130	126	100	98
Speech Disability						
Mean	41.1	43.5	41.5	42.7	0.1	−1.2
Standard Deviation	21.2	20.3	20.6	22.9	12.2	15.6
N	307	303	234	225	168	164
Other Health Disability						
Mean	48.6	48.5	45.5	44.4	−1.6	−4.3
Standard Deviation	22.2	20.9	20.6	22.8	12.8	14.6
N	399	388	266	258	195	189

(−2.7 NCEs) than reading (−1.1 NCEs). The group differences are also relevant and often quite stark. For example, at this age, girls do better than boys on all tests, and drop behind the national population over the year less than boys do. Asian American students score lower than whites on reading but somewhat higher on math; however, Asian students improve more than the national population, or any racial group, on both reading and math. The differences between African and Hispanic Americans and whites and Asians is considerable in both grades on both tests—at times approaching a full standard deviation.

The variance within groups also provides useful information. First, as is typical of large sample test data, the variances around the mean are not very different between groups. For example, the largest differences in variances by race for the four tests over the two grades are 17.3 (African American, fourth grade, reading) to 21.5 (white, fourth grade, math) and all but 3 of the 20 variances are between 18 and 20. However—and critical—these variances within groups may be very misleading for assessing both achievement levels and educational progress. And because the variances are misrepresented by such simple reporting, so are the differences in the means between groups. This can be simply illustrated by using relatively simple and then more complex multivariate estimates of group differences.

MULTIVARIATE ESTIMATES OF ACHIEVEMENT

A range of more complex estimation models can be used to provide a more accurate and richer picture of educational achievement than is obtained by reporting simple, mean point estimates of achievement. The problem is that these estimates require increasingly complex statistical procedures and more elaborate and costly data. In Tables C-2a, C-2b, C-3a, and C-3b data complexity increases in the columns marked Model I to Model III (for Table C-2a and C-3a) and Model IV to VI (for Table C-2b and C-3b). The first level of complexity (Models I and IV) requires multivariate estimates. These variables include: (1) a student income measure—qualifying for free lunch or not, (2) student gender, (3) student race, and (4) student disability status.

Models II and V add variables on family status. These variables—family income, parent education, parent employment, and marital status—were acquired in the *Prospects* study through parent surveys. Models III and VI add behavioral and attitude data for individual families—data obtained from parent surveys. For purposes of these analyses, the variables include a measure of parent academic educational expectations for their child, an index of satisfaction with the school their child attends, number of school contacts, and three questions on parental involvement (at home, through participation in school organizations, and through attendance at school events).

Finally, Tables C-2a and C-2b are distinguished from C-3a and C-3b by modeling fourth grade student achievement with (C-3a and C-3b) and without controlling for prior achievement (third grade achievement test scores). Tables C-3a and C-3b include prior test scores as independent variables. These models allow change-score, achievement progress assessments.

Cohort, Point-Estimate Models

Increasingly more complex and more accurate estimations of point or cohort scores (when reporting by grade), are depicted in Tables C-2a and C-2b. Table C-4 provides descriptive statistics for variables used in Tables C-2 and C-3. The differences between Tables C-2a and C-2b (and later Tables C-3a and C-3b) are in the modeling of students with disabilities. In Table C-2a, a general indicator variable for being disabled or not is included; in Table C-2b, indicator variables are included for each of 5 types of disability.[3]

In Model I, for both reading and math, all the variables are indicator variables and the coefficients can be interpreted as differences in means between the relevant categories. Thus, the coefficient for free lunch eligibility for reading means that students whose family income qualifies for government-provided free lunch (1.35 times the poverty line), on average, and *controlling for other gender*

---

[3]The reference group, when individual disability groups are represented by indicator variables, are all students without the relevant disability, including students with other types of disabilities.

and racial differences, scored –9.88 normal curve equivalent points less than students who did not qualify for the subsidy. Similarly, girls scored 3.85 points more than boys, African Americans –11.26 less than whites, Asian American 1.78 points less than whites, etc. The size of these differences can be compared with the standard deviations for the fourth grade tests for these groups reported in Table C-4.

There are several important differences between the results derived from these models and the simple descriptive group differences as reported in Table C-1. First, if one computes the crude differences in means in Table C-1 for any category (free-lunch vs. non-free-lunch; African American vs. white), in each case the indicator variables in Table C-2a represent *smaller differences.* The reason is that several of the independent variables are correlated, and thus failure to control for that correlation produces artificially higher estimates of group differences. Specifically, by simply reporting racial group means, we fail to account for the considerable diversity in group populations—in this simple model, the differences in income and gender of students within racial groups.[4]

Models II and III add precision and explanatory information, but also reduce sample sizes. In this national sample, the reduction in sample sizes results from the failure of sample families to complete surveys. In addition, reduction in sample sizes may affect the accuracy of the estimates of subpopulations, such as students with a given disability. Despite these problems, the added information provides insights into factors affecting achievement, and potentially useful data for specifying realistic expectations for schools and districts. For example, the effect of parent education is obvious and, as we shall see, impervious to the inclusion of almost every variable we can include. Regardless of race, income, employment, or marital status and despite attitudes and direct parent support of education, having a parent who has more education is a significant predictor of higher student achievement.

The same is true of educational expectations held by parents for their children. As measured by a question querying how many years of education they expect their child to complete, "expectations" are a very significant and strong predictor of higher test scores. This result also carries over into more complex models.

These results tell us something not only about the puzzle of education, but also about how to assess educational systems and specify institutional expectations. They also illustrate the variances within groups of students and the policy implications of excluding such control variables from assessments.

Finally, Models I through III provide useful insights into how students with disabilities could be included in systemic reform assessment systems. Model I

---

[4]A fully specified model, such as used in analysis of variance, would also include interactive terms between gender, race, and income. In addition, school-level variables could be included. This would require more complex statistical methods and assumptions.

TABLE C-2a Fourth Grade Cohort Regression Models, 1992: Disability Indicator Variable

	Reading Models			Math Models		
	Model I	Model II	Model III	Model I	Model II	Model III
Prior Tests						
Prior Reading	—	—	—	—	—	—
Prior Math	—	—	—	—	—	—
District SES						
Free Lunch (1 = Yes)	-9.88***	-4.78***	-2.81***	-9.00***	-3.72***	-1.27
Gender (1 = Female)	3.85***	4.69***	3.44***	1.48***	2.00***	0.35
African American	-11.26***	-9.52***	-8.34***	-10.36***	-8.65***	-7.28***
Asian American	-1.78	-3.69***	-6.57***	9.31***	6.88***	4.36***
Hispanic American	-11.87***	-9.80***	-9.74***	-8.69***	-7.49***	-7.09***
Other American	-5.21***	-5.76***	-4.07*	-2.34	-3.11	-2.02
Disabled (1 = Yes)	-6.90***	-6.44***	-3.19***	-6.97***	-6.55***	-3.62***
Family SES						
Income	—	0.87***	0.61***	—	0.91***	0.63***
Respondent Education	—	2.24***	0.90***	—	2.15***	0.86***
Respondent Employment	—	-0.54*	0.04	—	-0.17	0.61
Respondent Marital Status	—	0.80	0.02	—	1.12*	0.13
Family Attitudes/Behavior						
Expectations	—	—	3.39***	—	—	3.54***
School Dissatisfaction	—	—	-0.14***	—	—	-0.19***
Parental Involvement—Home	—	—	0.49***	—	—	0.62***
Parental Involvement—Attendance	—	—	0.20	—	—	0.09
Parental Involvement—Organizations	—	—	0.66***	—	—	1.04***
School Contacts	—	—	-0.60***	—	—	-0.58***
Constants	54.48***	39.02***	19.66***	54.12***	37.63***	14.65***
R^2	.20	.23	.28	.15	.18	.25
SE	18.12	17.89	16.84	20.07	19.90	18.65
F	305.54	187.00	90.28	205.78	133.05	73.43
(df)	(8,393, 7)	(6,681, 11)	(3,807, 17)	(8,234, 7)	(6,545, 11)	(3,741, 17)

*** probability that B = 0 < .001
** probability that B = 0 < .01
* probability that B = 0 < .05

TABLE C-2b   Fourth Grade Cohort Regression Models, 1992: Categories of Disability

	Reading Models			Math Models		
	Model IV	Model V	Model VI	Model IV	Model V	Model VI
Prior Tests						
Prior Reading	—	—	—	—	—	—
Prior Math	—	—	—	—	—	—
District SES						
Free Lunch (1 = Yes)	-9.93***	-4.76***	-2.95***	-9.05***	-3.69***	-1.34
Gender (1 = Female)	3.72***	4.58***	3.41***	1.38**	1.92***	0.40
African American	-11.25***	-9.51***	-8.49***	-10.34***	-8.62***	-7.36***
Asian American	-1.81	-3.65***	-6.38***	9.12***	6.86***	4.42**
Hispanic American	-11.78***	-9.72***	-9.57***	-8.63***	-7.42***	-6.92***
Other American	-4.80**	-5.40**	-4.12*	-2.18	-2.84	-2.28
Disabled						
Emotional	-9.82***	-8.93***	-5.00	-11.34***	-10.05***	-6.98
Learning	-16.81***	-17.44***	-17.49***	-16.44***	-16.78***	-16.12***
Physical	-2.56	-1.80	-2.44	-1.00	-0.53	-4.80
Speech	-2.99*	-2.36	1.30	-2.36	-1.32	2.45
Other	-0.54	-0.54	1.49	-1.92	-2.34	-0.54
Family SES						
Income		0.89***	0.64***		0.94***	0.66***
Respondent Education		2.22***	0.90***		2.15***	0.88***
Respondent Employment		-0.52*	0		-0.18	0.54
Respondent Marital Status		0.68	-0.21		1.24	0.03
Family Attitudes/Behavior						
Expectations			3.33***			3.49***
School Dissatisfaction			-0.15***			-0.20***
Parental Involvement—Home			0.48***			0.60***
Parental Involvement—Attendance			0.26			0.16
Parental Involvement—Organization			0.59***			0.97***
School Contacts			-0.57***			-0.57***
Constants	54.53***	38.97***	20.42***	54.17***	37.55***	15.18***
R^2	.21	.24	.29	.16	.19	.26
SE	18.02	17.75	16.70	19.99	19.81	18.56
F	202.84	143.58	76.13	136.55	101.61	61.27
(df)	(8,264, 11)	(6,583, 15)	(3,741, 21)	(8,106, 11)	(6,448, 15)	(3,676, 21)

*** probability that B = 0 < .001
** probability that B = 0 < .01
* probability that B = 0 < .05

TABLE C-3a Fourth Grade Value-Added Regression Models, 1991-1992: Disability Indicator Variable

	Reading Models			Math Models		
	Model I	Model II	Model III	Model I	Model II	Model III
Prior Tests						
Prior Reading	0.62 ***	0.61 ***	0.61 ***	0.21 ***	0.20 ***	0.17 ***
Prior Math	0.21 ***	0.21 ***	0.19 ***	0.65 ***	0.66 ***	0.66 ***
District SES						
Free Lunch (1 = Yes)	-2.49 ***	-1.66 ***	-0.24	-1.52 ***	-0.50	1.06
Gender (1 = Female)	1.81 ***	2.06 ***	1.75 ***	0.36	0.41	-0.42
African American	-2.25 ***	-1.84 ***	-1.54 *	-1.16 *	-0.79	-0.62
Asian American	0.55	-0.14	-1.04	6.61 ***	5.55 ***	4.76 ***
Hispanic American	-2.53 ***	-2.39 ***	-2.91 ***	-1.46 **	-1.42 *	-1.59 *
Other American	-1.53	-2.29	-1.77	1.26	0.51	0.43
Disabled (1 = Yes)	-0.86	-0.88	0.57	-1.17	-1.35	-0.42
Family SES						
Income	—	0	0.17	—	0	0.21
Respondent Education	—	0.81 ***	0.42 *	—	0.91 ***	0.54 ***
Respondent Employment	—	-0.30	-0.24	—	-0.25	-0.19
Respondent Marital Status	—	0.25	-0.27	—	0.62	-0.12
Family Attitudes/Behavior						
Expectations	—	—	0.73 ***	—	—	0.76 ***
School Dissatisfaction	—	—	-0.06 *	—	—	-0.07 **
Parental Involvement—Home	—	—	0.08	—	—	0.17 **
Parental Involvement—Attendance	—	—	0.11	—	—	-0.06
Parental Involvement—Organizations	—	—	0.19	—	—	0.44 ***
School Contacts	—	—	-0.44 ***	—	—	-0.47 ***
Constants	8.24 ***	5.58 ***	5.32 *	5.47 ***	2.35 *	0.82
R^2	.67	.68	.67	.61	.62	.63
SE	11.55	11.58	11.29	13.45	13.39	12.87
F	1,438.60	814.63	325.23	1,109.74	643.35	268.69
(df)	(6,323, 9)	(5,067, 13)	(2,967, 19)	(6,320, 9)	(5,062, 13)	(2,967, 19)

*** probability that B = 0 < .001
** probability that B = 0 < .01
* probability that B = 0 < .05

TABLE C-3b Fourth Grade Value-Added Regression Models, 1991-1992: Categories of Disability

	Reading Models			Math Models		
	Model IV	Model V	Model VI	Model IV	Model V	Model VI
Prior Tests						
Prior Reading	0.62***	0.61***	0.61***	0.21***	0.20***	0.16***
Prior Math	0.21***	0.21***	0.19***	0.65***	0.66***	0.66***
District SES						
Free Lunch (1 = Yes)	-2.54***	-1.73***	-0.37	-1.54***	-0.54	0.98
Gender (1 = Female)	1.71***	1.99***	1.68***	0.30	0.38	-0.36
African American	-2.26***	-1.84***	-1.68*	-1.16*	-0.77	-0.70
Asian American	0.68	0	-0.91	6.55***	5.54***	4.67***
Hispanic American	-2.43***	-2.30***	-2.79***	-1.43**	-1.38*	-1.54*
Other American	-1.26	-2.02	-1.61	1.30	0.60	0.32
Disabled						
Emotional	-2.57	-3.56	-1.98	-2.58	-4.23	-4.51
Learning	-3.20**	-3.27*	-4.09*	-1.59	-1.97	-3.54
Physical	-0.02	0	0.46	0.41	0.86	-0.68
Speech	0.53	1.00	3.01*	0.57	0.86	2.77
Other	0.34	0.12	2.13	-2.19*	-2.48*	-0.95
Family SES						
Income	—	0	0.15	—	0.01	0.22
Respondent Education	—	0.82***	0.43**	—	0.94***	0.56***
Respondent Employment	—	-0.28	-0.26	—	-0.26	-0.22
Respondent Marital Status	—	0.21	-0.37	—	0.59	-0.19
Family Attitudes/Behavior						
Expectations	—	—	0.77***	—	—	0.78***
School Dissatisfaction	—	—	-0.06*	—	—	-0.07*
Parental Involvement—Home	—	—	0.07	—	—	0.16**
Parental Involvement—Attendance	—	—	0.12	—	—	-0.02
Parental Involvement—Organization	—	—	0.17	—	—	0.44**
School Contacts	—	—	-0.43***	—	—	-0.48***
Constants	8.34***	5.67***	5.83*	5.50***	2.38*	1.10
R²	.67	.68	.68	.61	.62	.63
SE	11.53	11.56	11.25	13.46	13.41	12.88
F	985.78	616.76	266.77	755.12	483.25	218.50
(df)	(6,217, 13)	(4,988, 17)	(2,913, 23)	(6,214, 13)	(4,983, 17)	(2,913, 23)

*** probability that B = 0 < .001
** probability that B = 0 < .01
* probability that B = 0 < .05

TABLE C-4   Fourth Grade Cohort and Value-Added Regressions:
Variable Definitions and Statistics

	Mean	Standard Deviation	Range	(N)
Reading NCE (1992)	45.42	20.48	98.00	10,584
Math NCE (1992)	45.41	21.96	98.00	10,388
Free Lunch (1 = Yes)	0.47	0.50	1.00	9,221
Gender (1 = Female)	0.50	0.50	1.00	10,542
African American	0.20	0.40	1.00	9,810
Asian American	0.05	0.21	1.00	9,810
Hispanic American	0.20	0.40	1.00	9,810
Other American	0.02	0.14	1.00	9,810
Disabled (1 = Yes)	0.08	0.27	1.00	10,543
Emotional	0.01	0.09	1.00	9,791
Learning	0.02	0.15	1.00	9,925
Physical	0.01	0.12	1.00	9,837
Speech	0.02	0.15	1.00	9,945
Other	0.03	0.16	1.00	9,977
Income	6.71	2.72	9.00	8,696
Respondent Education	3.31	1.77	7.00	8,364
Respondent Employment	2.15	0.91	2.00	9,178
Respondent Marital Status	0.68	0.47	1.00	9,387
Expectations	5.12	1.70	6.00	7,697
School Dissatisfaction	39.77	9.35	62.00	6,501
Parental Involvement—Home	24.04	4.78	36.00	7,015
Parental Involvement—Attendance	12.26	2.72	16.00	6,998
Parental Involvement—Organization	8.65	2.19	14.00	7,520
School Contacts	11.64	2.46	18.00	8,763

contains a simple indicator variable for disability. The result, controlling for income, gender, and race, is a very significant –6.90 normal curve equivalents in reading and –6.97 in math. As expected, students with disabilities do less well. However, when we control for more variables, the differential scores are partly dissipated. Controlling for family socioeconomic status has only a modest result, but controlling for expectations, satisfaction with the school, and parental involvement has a major effect in predicting reduced differential scores for students with disabilities. Although not suggesting a causal explanation, it is clear that, as before, within-group variance is considerable and must be taken into account in assessment systems.

The differences in results between Tables C-2a and C-2b highlight this fact. In Table C-2b a series of indicator variables are used to represent different types of disabilities. The effects are quite startling. Essentially, when suitable controls are employed, only emotionally disturbed and learning disabled students have cohort test scores significantly below the rest of the population.[5] Learning disabled student scores are close to a standard deviation below the rest of the population; emotionally disturbed students are less far behind.

The effects of including control variables seem to differ for students with emotional disturbances and learning disabilities. The differences in estimated test scores for students with emotional disturbances are smaller than the expected differences computed for fourth graders in Table C-1. And, as more variables are added to explain the variance, the effect of an emotional disability declines to the point that it may not be significant when we include family attitude and behavior effects. In contrast, for both reading and math, the effects of a learning disability are not reduced very much by inclusion of any control variables. The differences in means for fourth graders computed from Table C-1 are very close to the sizes of the effects for students with learning disabilities in Table C-2b, and the size and significance of the coefficient does not change much as more variables are added.

Value-Added Models

Value-added achievement models are based on the assumption that to adequately measure educational progress and the varying contribution of educational institutions, one must control for prior student achievement. Various measures of change can then be constructed and, controlling for relevant student, family, and institutional differences, reasonable expectations based on student progress can be established.

Tables C-3a and C-3b present results of such models for the *Prospects* study. The tables duplicate those presented in the cohort models depicted in Tables C-2a and C-2b with the addition of third grade reading and math test scores as measures of prior achievement. As expected, the prior tests are very good predictors of fourth grade tests. And the coefficients are quite stable across models. All are significant at the .001 level; the primary tests have coefficients between .61 and .66; and the secondary tests are approximately .2.

What is more interesting are the changes in the coefficients for the remaining independent variables. The most obvious differences are that the coefficients for all independent variables are much smaller. This is to be expected because we are now essentially estimating the variance in changes in achievement, not simply the variance between scores. And changes are smaller numbers.[6] What is more relevant is the statistical significance of the coefficients.

---

[5]"Physical disabilities" include categories for physical, hearing, speech, orthopedic, and deafness disabilities. The other categories were coded as they appear in the tables. Mental retardation was excluded from the analysis because only 5 students with mental retardation were given standardized tests.

[6]The reader can verify the differences by taking the means of fourth grade scores in Table C-4 and subtracting from them the appropriate Bs times the third grade scores for both reading and math. That is the equivalent of what we are estimating once prior achievement has been controlled.

We leave it to the reader to explore the totality of differences emerging from a comparison of Tables C-2 and C-3. We note several interesting observations. Gender differences in math scores are significant in Tables C-2a and C-2b for Models I and II, but none of the value-added differences in Tables C-3a and C-3b are significant, and the Model VI coefficients have a negative sign. This may indicate that the absolute advantage of girls in math in the early years is not matched by greater progress. Similarly, Asian American reading scores are below white scores as indicated in Tables C-2a and C-2b, but those differences disappear once prior achievement is controlled. This means that, in terms of progress on reading, Asian Americans and whites do approximately the same.

Variables that remain significant with value-added measures include: (1) some racial effects—extraordinarily positive for Asian Americans on math, negative for African and Hispanic Americans on reading and at times on math; (2) parent's education, which remains positively related to increased learning; and (3) parental expectations—there is a positive effect of higher parental educational expectations. The only parental involvement measure that seems to matter is the scale measuring the frequency of school contacts—the effect is to depress fourth grade test scores.

The implications of value-added models for students with disabilities are quite striking. If all students with disabilities are considered together, Table C-3a indicates that there is no reason to expect statistically significant differences between the populations with and without disabilities. In fact, controlling for the full range of variables (Table C-3a, Model VI), the coefficients vary closely around zero.

Different disabilities suggest different value-added results. The only consistent significant effect is for reading scores for students with learning disabilities. As reported above, cohort score estimates for students with learning disabilities were consistently close to a standard deviation behind students without learning disabilities—regardless of which model was estimated. It also appears that, between the third and fourth grades, students with learning disabilities fall further behind, and surprisingly, the effect seems to increase in size as more control variables are included in the equation. The only other effects that approach conventional levels of significance are a positive effect for students with speech impairments on the full reading model (Model VI), and small negative effects on math for those with "other" disabilities or health problems.

CONCLUSIONS

If further analysis confirms these results, they suggest several conclusions. First, different types of disabilities need to be treated separately. Second, the conclusions differ when one models cohort and value-added achievement measures. Third, students with learning disabilities need to be studied further and perhaps treated quite differently in assessment systems. Results of these analyses suggest that students with learning disabilities may show persistently poor test scores and poor progress despite variation in a host of exogenous factors, which in other populations are related to achievement success.

Despite differences in opinion about what students should know and what is a valid form for testing that knowledge, policy makers undertaking standards-based reforms still need to compare student achievement over time, across populations, and between organizations. This requires internal and test-retest reliability for the instruments as well as the conversion of scores into a known probability distribution so that unbiased trend and intergroup comparisons can be made.[7] Value-added models, which control for prior achievement, offer promise as a valid method for reporting achievement scores and should be considered by policy makers.

REFERENCE

U.S. Department of Education
   1993   *Prospects: The Congressionally Mandated Study of Educational Growth and Opportunity: The Interim Report.* July. Washington, DC: U.S. Department of Education.

---

[7]Although many probability distributions could produce desired comparisons, normal or Student's T distributions are by far the most commonly assumed ones. They allow the use of numerous, common statistical techniques for analyzing results. This explains the requirement under Chapter 1 funding that tests be administered that can be converted into normal curve equivalents.

Biographical Sketches

LORRAINE M. McDONNELL *(Cochair)* is professor of political science and education at the University of California, Santa Barbara. Previously she was a senior political scientist at the RAND Corporation in Santa Monica, California. Her research interests include the design and implementation of educational reform initiatives, the role of teacher unions, and the development and use of educational accountability systems. In her most recent research, McDonnell is examining the design and implementation of new forms of student assessment in three states. That study, being conducted over four years, is tracing the political origins of new state assessments and monitoring their impact in a sample of schools and classrooms. She has a Ph.D. in political science from Stanford University.

MARGARET J. McLAUGHLIN *(Cochair)* is the associate director of the Institute for the Study of Exceptional Children and Youth at the University of Maryland at College Park, where she directs several national projects related to school reform and special education. Currently she also codirects the National Center for Disability Policy and directs the Center for Urban Special Education, a school/university partnership between the Baltimore city public schools and the University of Maryland. Previously she directed the National Center for Policy Options in Special Education, which investigated critical issues and policy implications related to school restructuring and students with disabilities. Her recent research publications examine the extent to which students with disabilities and special education programs interact with school reform initiatives, such as assessments and new governance structures. She has a Ph.D. in special education from the University of Virginia.

ANSLEY BACON is director of the Westchester Institute for Human Development at the Westchester County Medical Center in Valhalla, NY. She is also director of the Developmental Disabilities Program in the Graduate School of Health Science and associate professor of clinical psychiatry at the New York Medical College. Previously she was assistant professor of psychology at the University of Southern Mississippi, director of the Mississippi University Affiliated Program of the University of Southern Mississippi and the University of Mississippi, and director of the Psychology Department at Hudspeth Retardation Center in Jackson, MS. She is a member of the American Association of Mental Retardation, the American Psychological Association, the Association for Persons with Severe Handicaps, and the Association for the Advancement of Children's Health. Her publications are concerned with pathways to employment for adults with developmental disabilities. She has a Ph.D. in educational psychology from West Virginia University.

STEPHEN N. ELLIOTT is professor of educational psychology and a senior research fellow in the Wisconsin Center for Education Research at the University of Wisconsin, Madison. His research focuses on the assessment of children's academic and social behavior and the use of behavioral consultation to deliver psychoeducational services to students with disabilities. He currently codirects federal grant projects on the use of large-scale performance assessments with students with disabilities and on the effectiveness of school and home-based consultation services for aggressive children. He is the past editor of *School Psychology Review* and coauthor of the *Social Skills Rating System*. He has an M.A. from Michigan State University and a Ph.D. from Arizona State University.

LYNN S. FUCHS is professor of special education and co-director of the John F. Kennedy Center's Institute on Education and Learning at Peabody College of Vanderbilt University. Her research focuses on teachers' use of assessment information in instructional planning, computer applications that enhance the connection between assessment and instructional effectiveness, and methods for helping general educators address the needs of diverse learners. She has over 180 publications in these areas, serves on the editorial boards of eight journals in general and special education, and is the coeditor of *The Journal of Special Education*. She has a Ph.D. in educational psychology from the University of Minnesota.

MARGARET E. GOERTZ is professor in the Graduate School of Education at the University of Pennsylvania and co-director of the Consortium for Policy Research in Education. Previously, she was executive director of the Education Policy Research Division of the Educational Testing Service in Princeton, NJ. A past president of the American Education Finance Association, Goertz's research focuses on issues of education finance, state education reform policies, and state and federal programs for special needs students. Her current research activities include studies of standards-based reform in education and the allocation of school-level resources. Goertz has M.P.A. and Ph.D. degrees in social science from the Maxwell School of Syracuse University.

MICHAEL L. HARDMAN is associate dean for research in the Graduate School of Education and professor of special education at the University of Utah. As a researcher, he has published textbooks and journal articles and directed national demonstration projects in the areas of severe disabilities, inclusive education, transition from school to adult life, and training future leaders in special education. He is active in professional organizations and has served on national boards and committees for the Council for Exceptional Children and the Association for Persons with Severe Handicaps. He is currently the chief education advisor to the Joseph P. Kennedy, Jr., Foundation and past president of the Higher Education Consortium for Special Education. He has a Ph.D. in educational administration with an emphasis on special education policy.

TED S. HASSELBRING is professor of special education, co-director of the Learning Technology Center, and scientist in the John F. Kennedy Center at Peabody College of Vanderbilt University. He is an active member of the Council for Exceptional Children and is past president of its technology and media division. His research is directed at the use of technology for enhancing learning for students with mild disabilities and those who are at risk of school failure. He is also interested in the use of technology for improving undergraduate and graduate teacher education. He has a B.S., M.A.T., and Ed.D. (the latter in special education) from Indiana University.

DANIEL M. KORETZ is a senior social scientist with the RAND Institute on Education and Training in Washington, DC. Much of his research focuses on educational assessment, particularly as a tool of education policy. In response to current initiatives to include students with special needs in education reform, he recently began a five-year series of studies of the assessment of students with disabilities. He began his career as a public school teacher of students with severe emotional disturbance. He has a Ph.D. in developmental psychology from Cornell University.

PATRICIA MORISON (*Study Director*) is a senior program officer for the Board on Testing and Assessment of the National Research Council. Previously she was at the Congressional Office of Technology Assessment, where she served as a senior analyst for reports on educational testing, adult literacy, and teachers' use of technology in the classroom. Her research interests include competence and stress resistance in children, children at educational risk, motivation and learning, and the consequences and public understanding of tests and their uses. Morison has an Ed.M. from the Harvard Graduate School of Education and a Ph.D. in child clinical psychology from the University of Minnesota.

ARIE L. NETTLES is assistant professor and assistant research scientist of education in the School of Education and psychologist in the Department of Pediatric Hematology and Oncology at the University of Michigan. She is pursuing two lines of research that include the study of academic achievement and the impact of sickle cell disease on children, sponsored in part by the W.K. Kellogg Foundation; and the equity issues in educational testing and assessment, sponsored in part by the Ford Foundation. She has a B.S. in social science education and an M.S. in education administration from the University of Tennessee and a Ph.D. in psychology specializing in both clinical and school psychology from Vanderbilt University.

IAN E. NOVOS recently joined KPMG Peat Marwick's Economic Consulting Services group in New York City. He has been a faculty member at the University of Southern California and the Georgia Institute of Technology. His research has most recently focused on the nexus between labor markets and the structure and organization of firms. Novos received bachelor of commerce and bachelor of science degrees from the University of Witwatersrand in Johannesburg, South Africa, an M.P.P. from the Kennedy School of Government at Harvard University, and M.A. and Ph.D. degrees (the latter in economics) from the University of Pennsylvania. Since 1992, he has been board president of the Western Law Center for Disability Rights, a leading provider of legal services to the community of people with disabilities in Southern California.

DIANA C. PULLIN is professor in the School of Education at Boston College and has both a law degree and a doctoral degree in education from the University of Iowa. As a practicing attorney, she has represented school districts, teachers unions, parents, students, and educators in a broad range of matters concerning education law, civil rights, and employment. She is most known for her representation of a statewide class of students in Florida who successfully challenged the state's requirement that students pass a minimum competency test in order to receive a high school diploma (*Debra v. Turlington*). She has also been involved in a number of cases addressing the provision of special education services to handicapped students; has served as consultant to and trainer of other attorneys in the area of special education law, written a manual for advocates in this area; and served as an impartial due process hearing officer in special education disputes. As an academic, she has served as a member of the tenured faculties of the School of Education at Boston College and the College of Education at Michigan State University. From 1987-1994, she served as Dean of Education at Boston College. She is the author of many articles, book chapters, and one book in the areas of education law, public policy, law and testing, and education reform.

DANIEL J. RESCHLY is distinguished professor and director of the School Psychology Program at Iowa State University, where he holds a joint appointment in the Departments of Psychology and Professional Studies in Education. He has an M.A. from the University of Iowa and a Ph.D. from the University of Oregon. He has served as a school psychologist in Iowa, Oregon, and Arizona, and was an assistant professor for four years at the University of Arizona. Reschly has published widely on the topics of school psychology professional practices, adaptive behavior, behavioral consultation, mild mental retardation, and legal issues. He has been active in state and national leadership roles, including president of the National Association of School Psychologists, chair of its Graduate Program Approval, and editor of *School Psychology Review*. He has received three distinguished service awards from the National Association of School Psychologists, the Stroud Award, and appointment as a fellow of the American Psychological Association.

MARTHA THURLOW is associate director of the National Center on Educational Outcomes at the University of Minnesota. She has conducted research involving special education for the past 25 years in a variety of areas, including assessment and decision making, learning disabilities, early childhood education, dropout prevention, effective classroom instruction, and integration of students with disabilities into general education settings. She has published extensively on the academic engagement and learning opportunity of elementary students, including those with disabilities. Her current research emphasis is on the implications of contemporary U.S. policy and practice for students with disabilities, including national and statewide assessment policies and practices, standards-setting efforts, and graduation requirements. She currently is a co-editor of *Exceptional Children*, the research journal of the Council for Exceptional Children. She has a B.A., M.A., and Ph.D. (the latter in educational pyschology) from the University of Minnesota.

EDWARD LEE VARGAS is the superintendent of the Santa Fe Public School District, in Santa Fe, NM. He formerly served as the assistant superintendent for California's eighth largest and most diverse school system, the Santa Ana Unified School District. He is a nationally recognized educational leader in reform and restructuring, particularly for categorically funded programs such as Chapter 1, Bilingual Education and Special Education. His experience involves both special and general education, including work as a classroom teacher, school psychologist, and special education director, as well as various central office positions in large urban districts in several states, initiating school improvement efforts for grades K-12. As a recipient of numerous awards for his leadership from various organizations, including the American Association of School Administrators and the California State Department of Education, he has been a featured speaker at various state, national, and international conferences on leadership, school restructuring and special education reform. He has a Ph.D. in educational leadership and policy studies from the University of Washington.

RICHARD K. WAGNER is a professor of psychology at Florida State University. His major area of research interest is the acquisition of complex cognitive knowledge and skills, which he has pursued in two domains. In the domain of reading, his research has focused on the role of reading-related phonological processing abilities in normal and abnormal development of reading skills, and in the prediction, prevention, and remediation of dyslexia. In the domain of human intelligence, his research has focused on the role of practical knowledge and intelligence in intellectual performance manifested outside the classroom setting. Before embarking on a research career, he completed a year of internship and two years of experience as a school psychologist. He has an M.A. in school psychology from the University of Akron and a Ph.D. in cognitive psychology from Yale University.

JOHN F. WITTE is professor of political science at the University of Wisconsin, Madison. Previously, in addition to holding faculty positions at the University of Wisconsin, he was associate director of the Robert M. La Follette Institute of Public Affairs and executive director of the Study Commission on the Quality of Education in the Metropolitan Milwaukee Public Schools. His publications concern workers' participation in American corporations and choice and control in American education. He has a B.A. from the University of Wisconsin and M.A. and Ph.D. degrees, both in political science, from Yale University.

Index